SEVEN SEAS ENT

THE EXO
REINCARNATION GAMES
VOL. 1

MW00649252

story by **KEISO**   art by **ZUNTA**

TRANSLATION
Kat Skarbinec

ADAPTATION
Maneesh Maganti

LETTERING
Carl Vanstiphout

COVER DESIGN
Hanase Qi

PROOFREADER
Kurestin Armada

EDITOR
Kristiina Korpus

COPY EDITOR
Dawn Davis

PREPRESS TECHNICIAN
Rhiannon Rasmussen-Silverstein

PRODUCTION ASSOCIATE
Christa Miesner

PRODUCTION MANAGER
Lissa Pattillo

MANAGING EDITOR
Julie Davis

ASSOCIATE PUBLISHER
Adam Arnold

PUBLISHER
Jason DeAngelis

Cyo Sekai Tensei Eguzo Drive – Gekito ! Isekai Zen Nihon Taikai Hen Vol. 1
© Keiso 2020 © zunta 2020
Originally published in Japan in 2020 by MAG Garden Corporation, TOKYO.
English translation rights arranged through TOHAN CORPORATION, Tokyo.

Seven Seas press and purchase enquiries can be sent to Marketing Manager Lianne Sentar at press@gomanga.com. Information regarding the distribution and purchase of digital editions is available from Digital Manager CK Russell at digital@gomanga.com.

ISBN: 978-1-64827-679-8
Printed in Canada
First Printing: November 2021
10 9 8 7 6 5 4 3 2 1

////// READING DIRECTIONS //////

This book reads from *right to left,* Japanese style. If this is your first time reading manga, you start reading from the top right panel on each page and take it from there. If you get lost, just follow the numbered diagram here. It may seem backwards at first, but you'll get the hang of it! Have fun!!

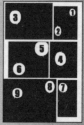

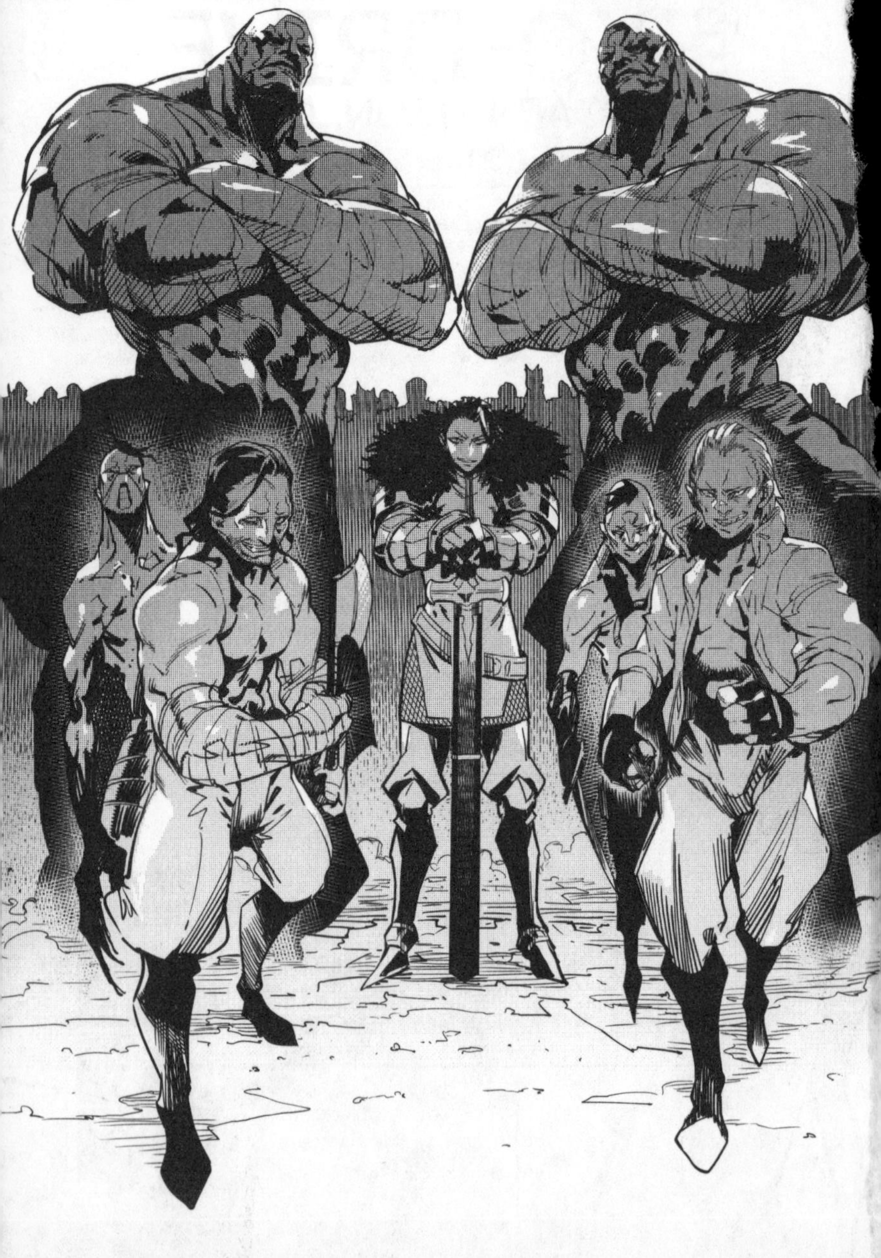

THE EXO-DRIVE REINCARNATION GAMES

ALL-JAPAN ISEKAI BATTLE TOURNAMENT!

STORY: KEISO

ART: ZUNTA

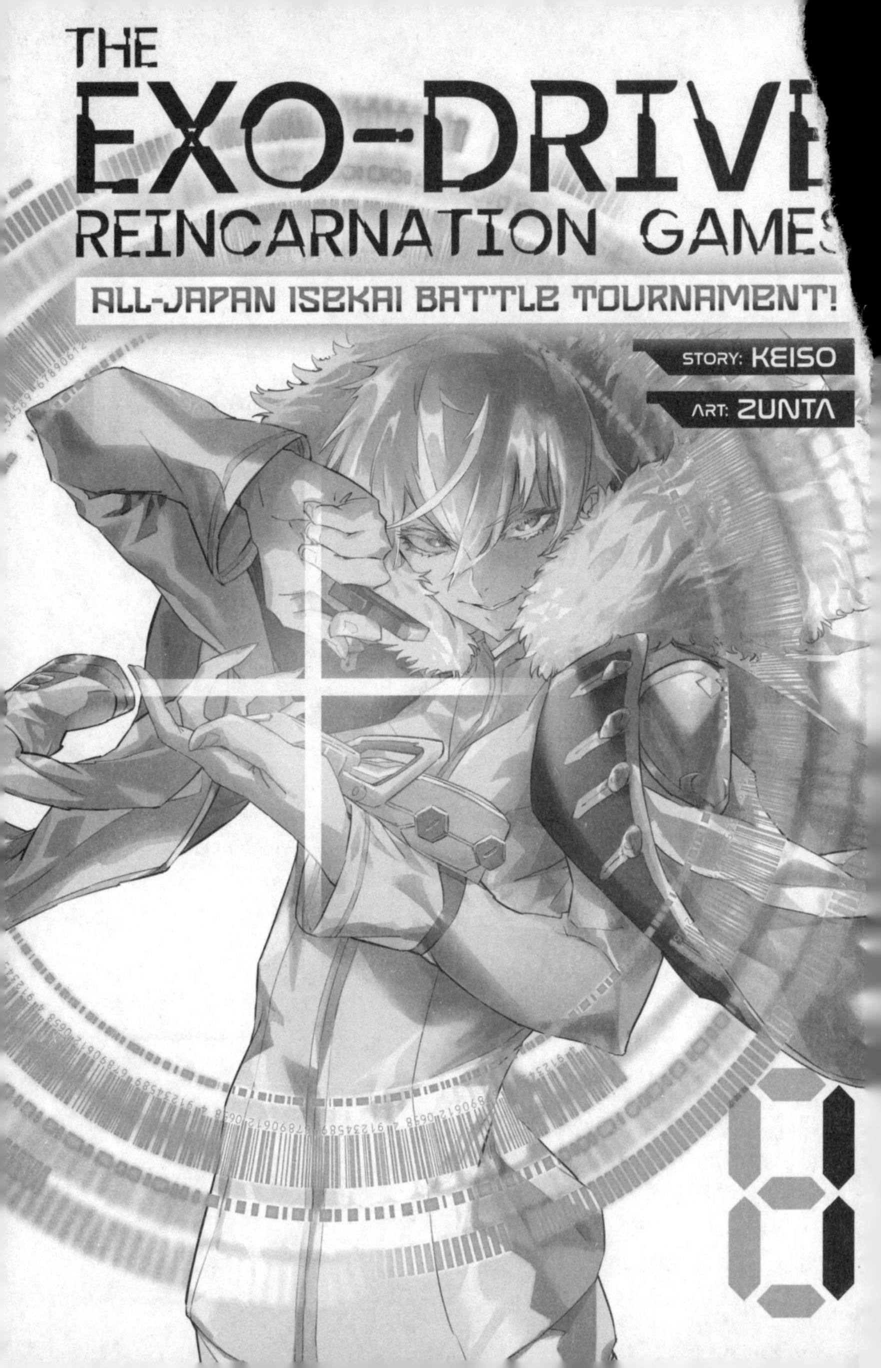

CONTENTS

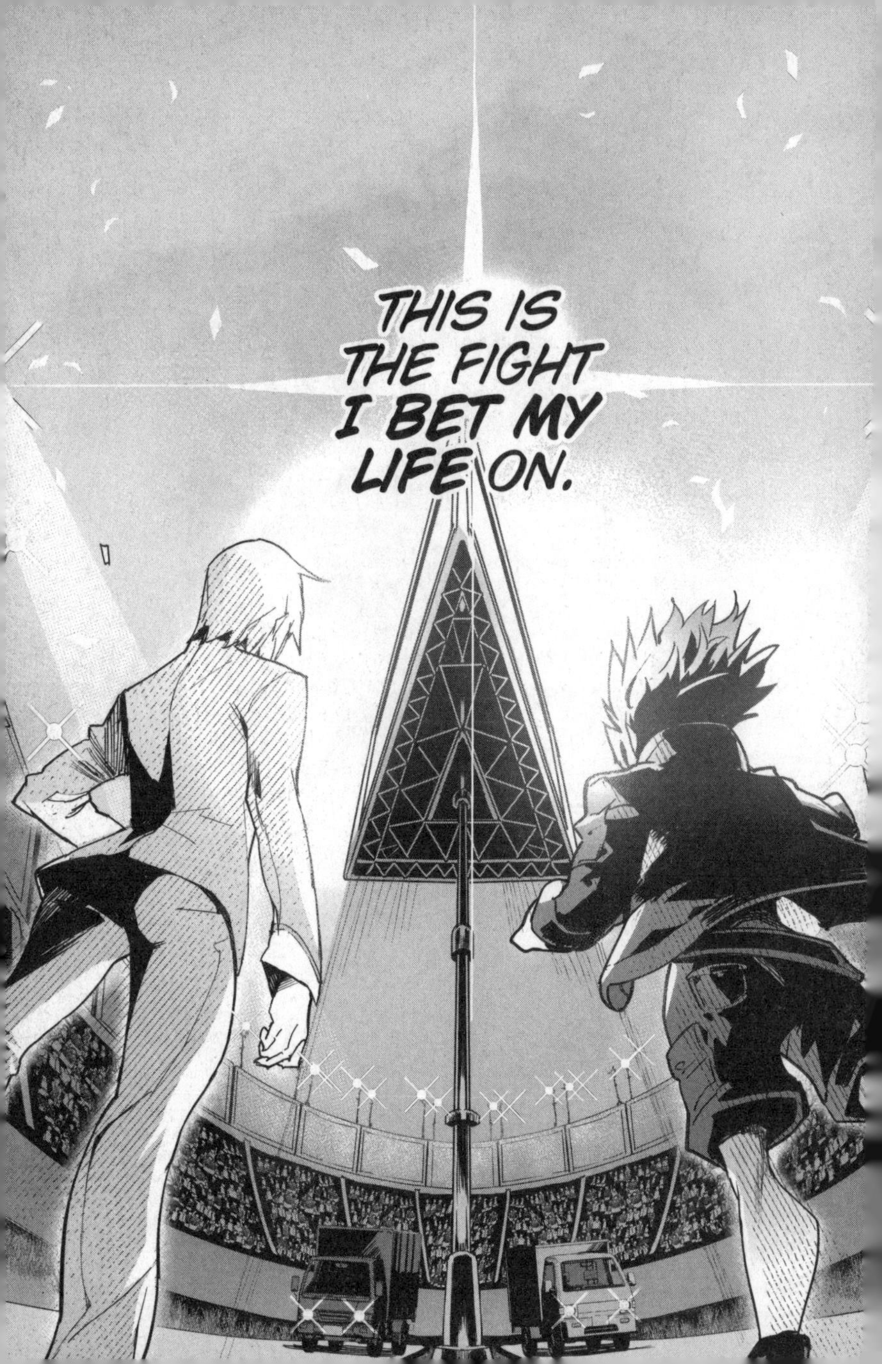
THIS IS THE FIGHT I BET MY LIFE ON.

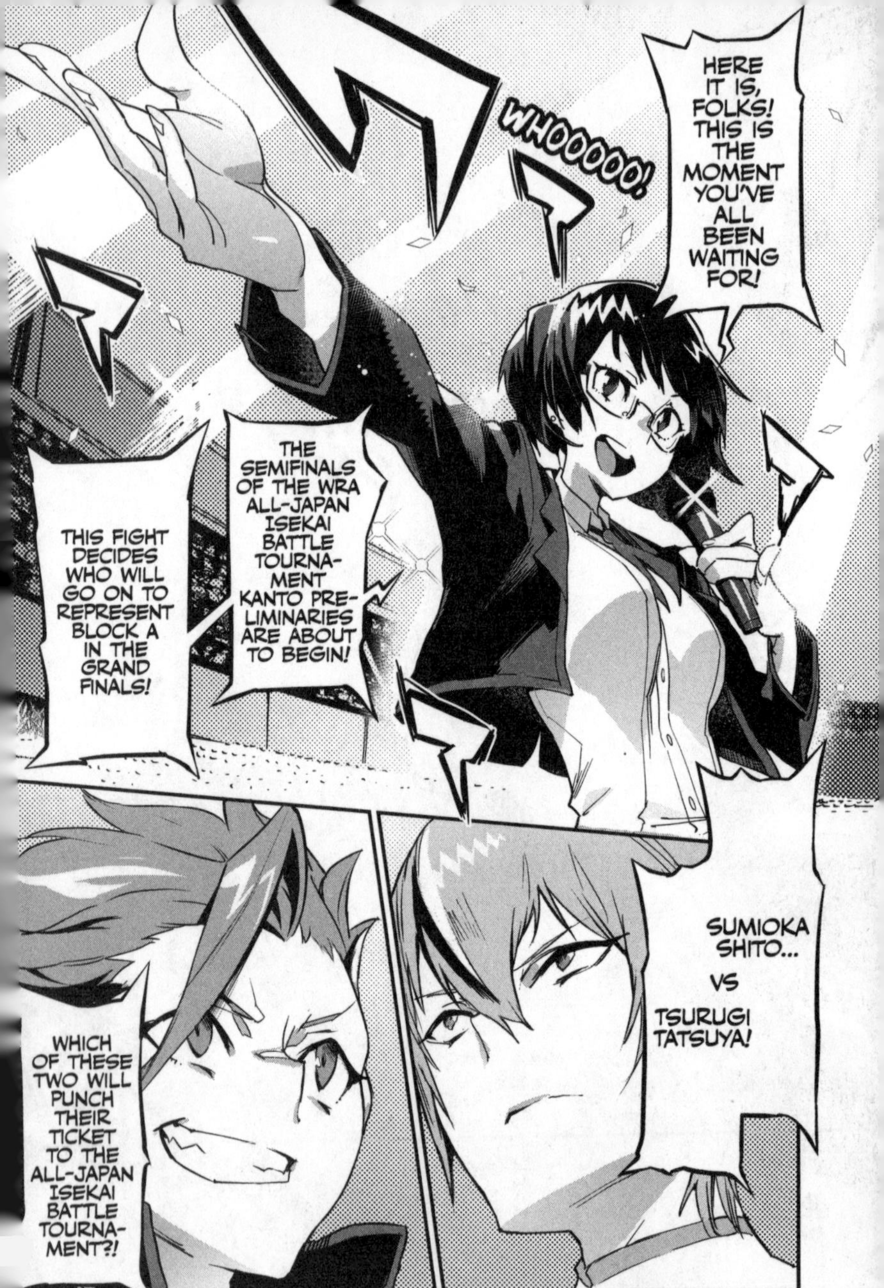
HERE IT IS, FOLKS! THIS IS THE MOMENT YOU'VE ALL BEEN WAITING FOR!
WHOOOOOO!
THE SEMIFINALS OF THE WRA ALL-JAPAN ISEKAI BATTLE TOURNAMENT KANTO PRELIMINARIES ARE ABOUT TO BEGIN!
THIS FIGHT DECIDES WHO WILL GO ON TO REPRESENT BLOCK A IN THE GRAND FINALS!
SUMIOKA SHITO...
VS
TSURUGI TATSUYA!
WHICH OF THESE TWO WILL PUNCH THEIR TICKET TO THE ALL-JAPAN ISEKAI BATTLE TOURNAMENT?!

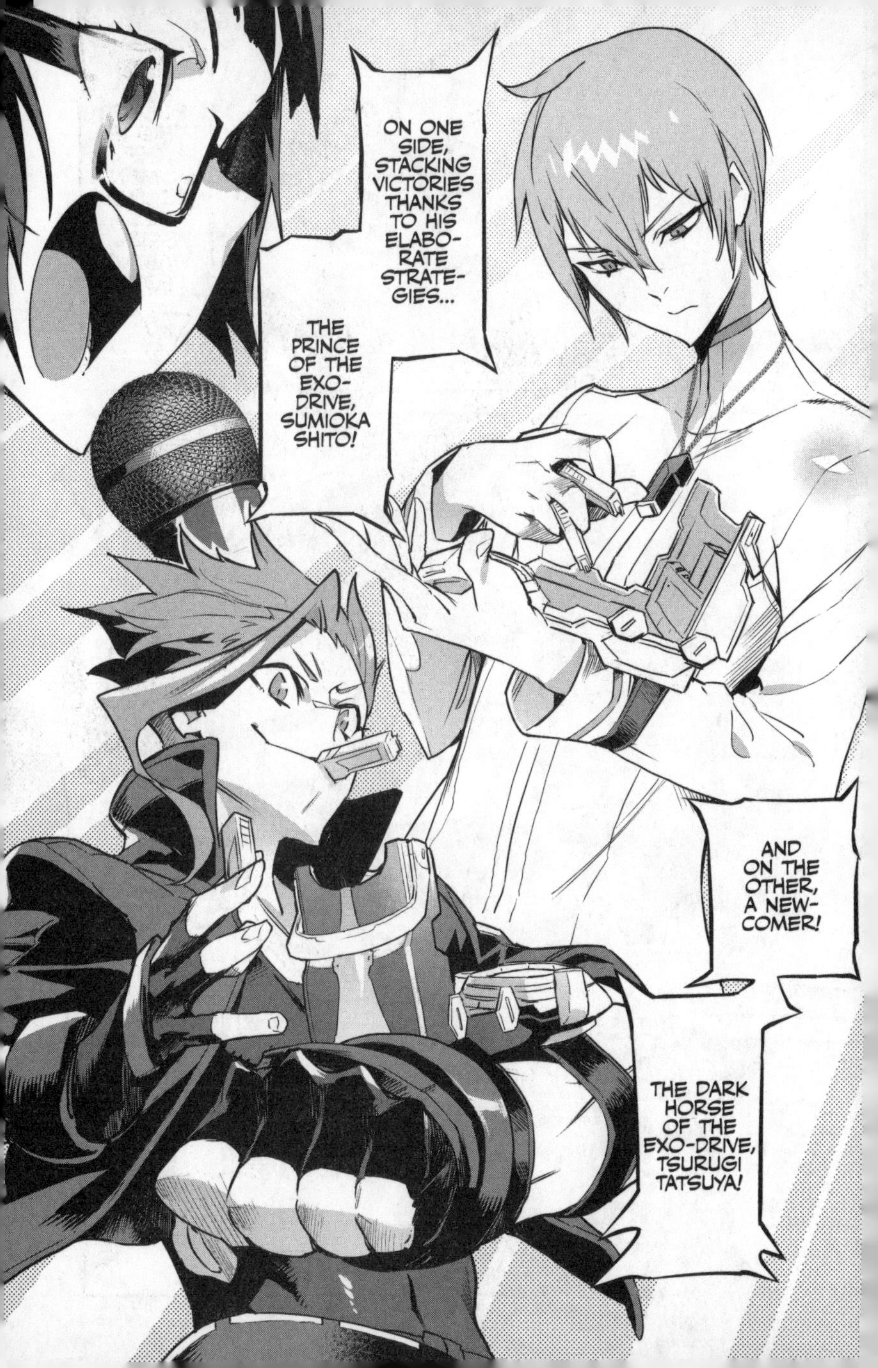
ON ONE SIDE, STACKING VICTORIES THANKS TO HIS ELABO-RATE STRATE-GIES...
THE PRINCE OF THE EXO-DRIVE, SUMIOKA SHITO!
AND ON THE OTHER, A NEW-COMER!
THE DARK HORSE OF THE EXO-DRIVE, TSURUGI TATSUYA!

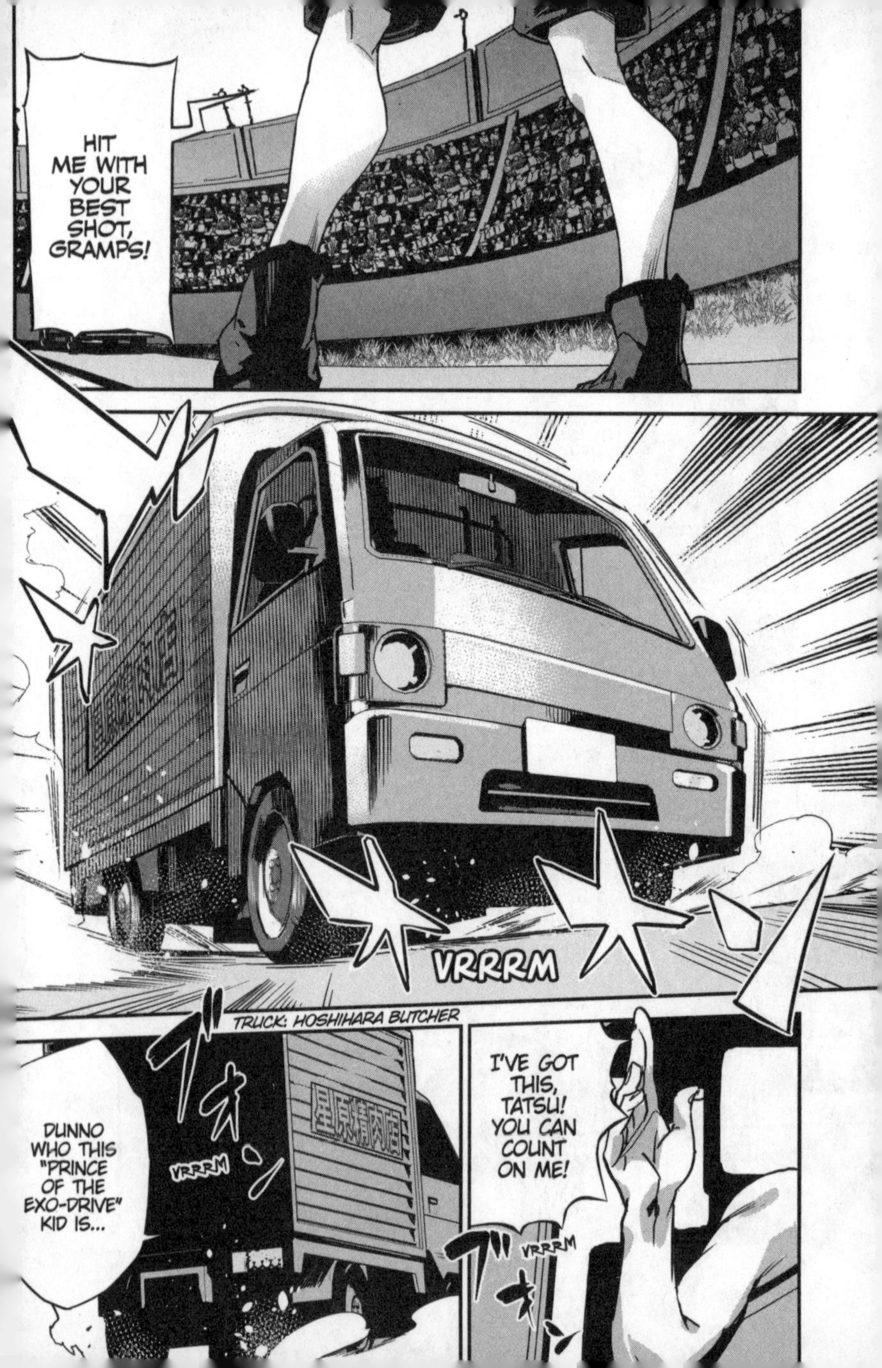
HIT ME WITH YOUR BEST SHOT, GRAMPS!
VRRRM
TRUCK: HOSHIHARA BUTCHER
I'VE GOT THIS, TATSU! YOU CAN COUNT ON ME!
VRRRM
DUNNO WHO THIS "PRINCE OF THE EXO-DRIVE" KID IS...
VRRRM
星原精肉店

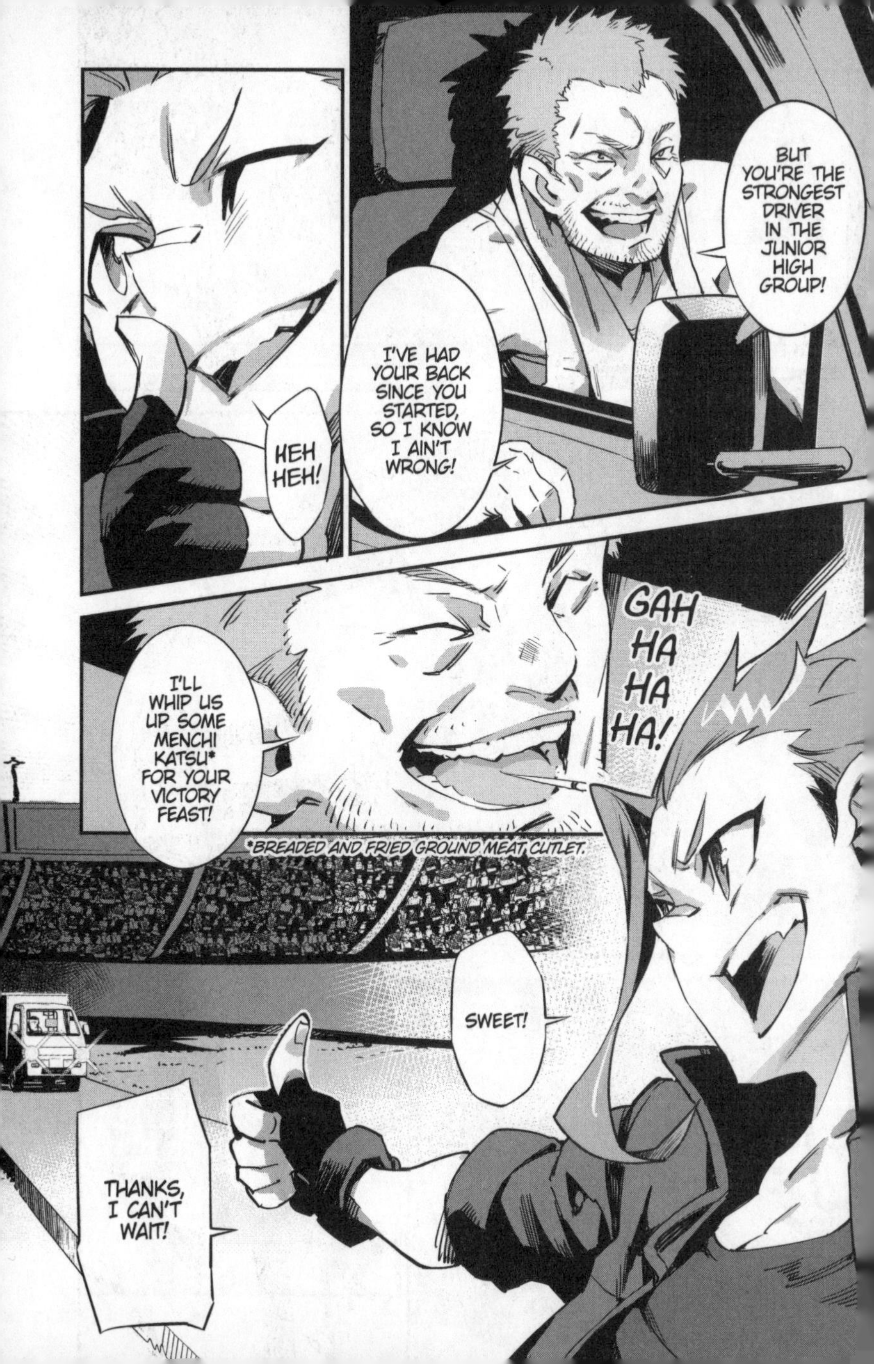
BUT YOU'RE THE STRONGEST DRIVER IN THE JUNIOR HIGH GROUP!
I'VE HAD YOUR BACK SINCE YOU STARTED, SO I KNOW I AIN'T WRONG!
HEH HEH!
GAH HA HA HA!
I'LL WHIP US UP SOME MENCHI KATSU* FOR YOUR VICTORY FEAST!
*BREADED AND FRIED GROUND MEAT CUTLET.
SWEET!
THANKS, I CAN'T WAIT!

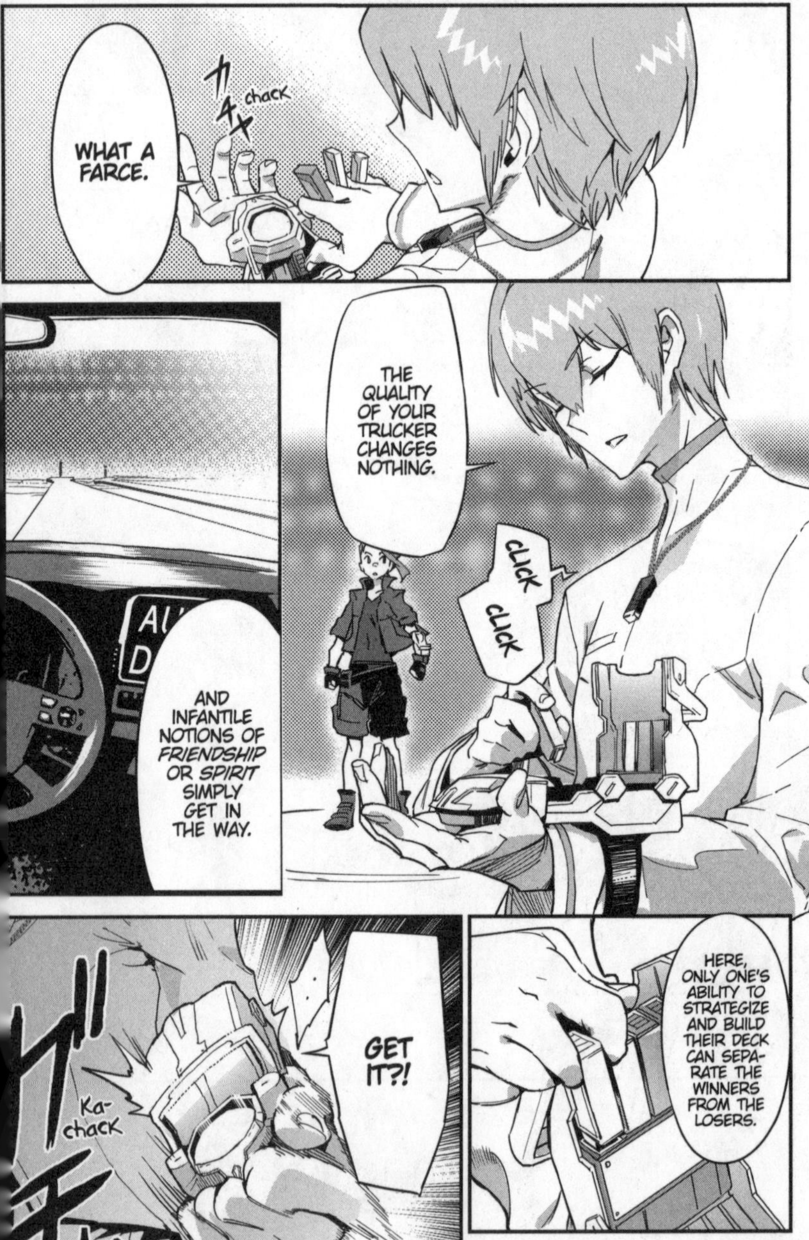
chack
WHAT A FARCE.
THE QUALITY OF YOUR TRUCKER CHANGES NOTHING.
CLICK CLICK
AND INFANTILE NOTIONS OF *FRIENDSHIP* OR *SPIRIT* SIMPLY GET IN THE WAY.
HERE, ONLY ONE'S ABILITY TO STRATEGIZE AND BUILD THEIR DECK CAN SEPA-RATE THE WINNERS FROM THE LOSERS.
GET IT?!
Ka-chack

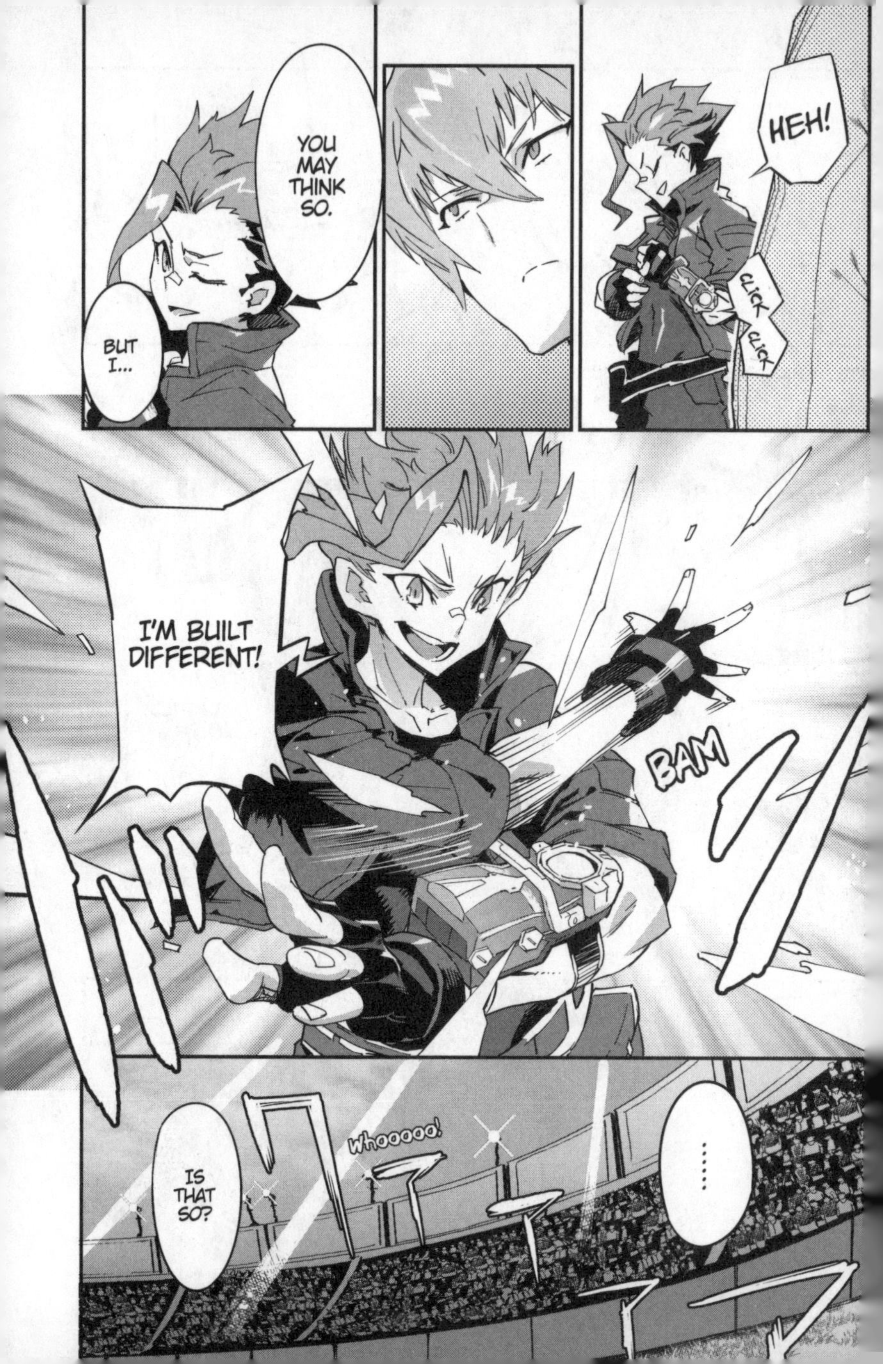
HEH!
CLICK
CLICK
YOU MAY THINK SO.
BUT I...
I'M BUILT DIFFERENT!
BAM
......
Whoooooo!
IS THAT SO?

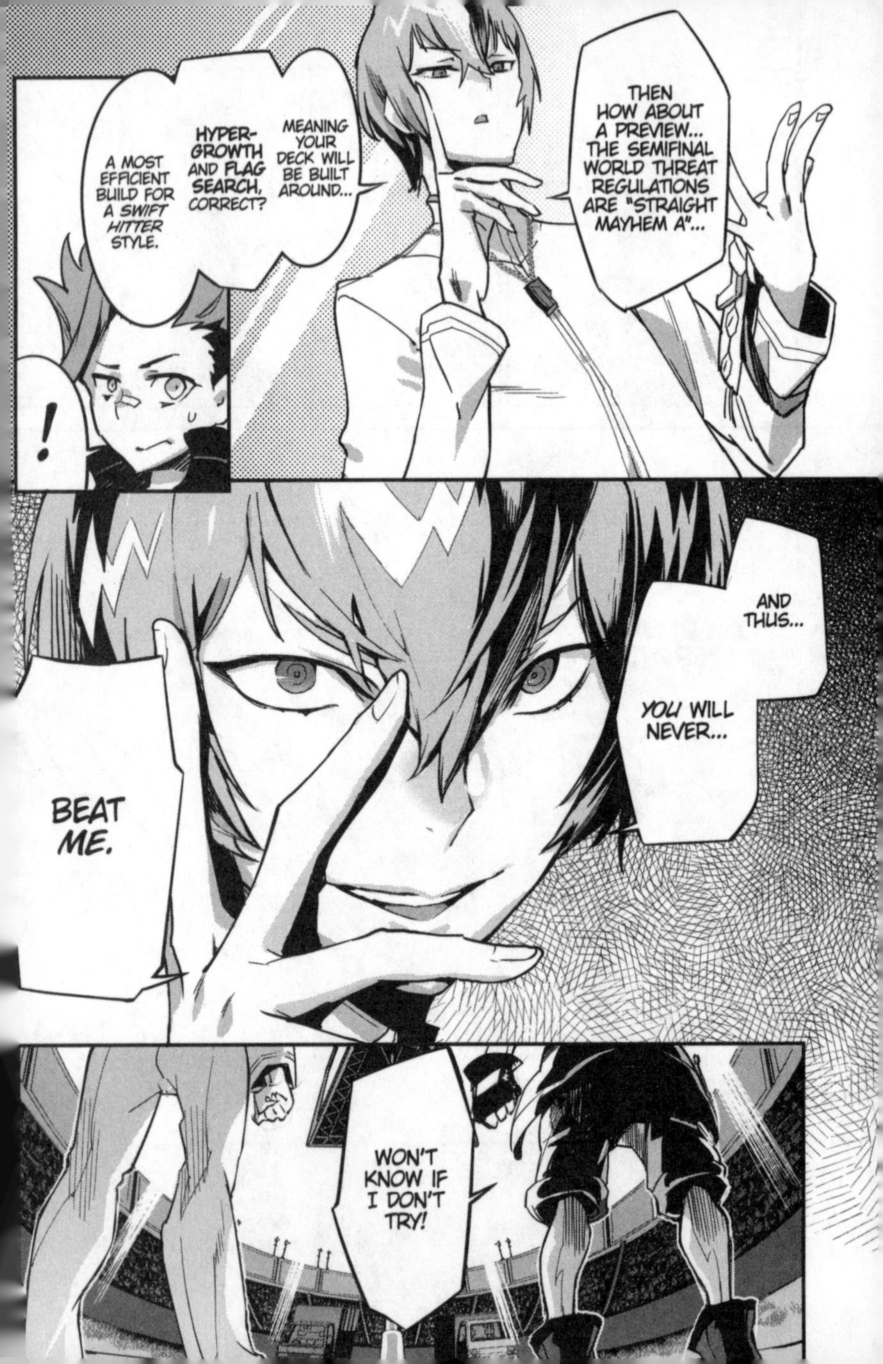
THEN HOW ABOUT A PREVIEW... THE SEMIFINAL WORLD THREAT REGULATIONS ARE "STRAIGHT MAYHEM A"...
MEANING YOUR DECK WILL BE BUILT AROUND...
HYPER-GROWTH AND FLAG SEARCH, CORRECT?
A MOST EFFICIENT BUILD FOR A *SWIFT HITTER* STYLE.
!
AND THUS...
YOU WILL NEVER...
BEAT ME.
WON'T KNOW IF I DON'T TRY!

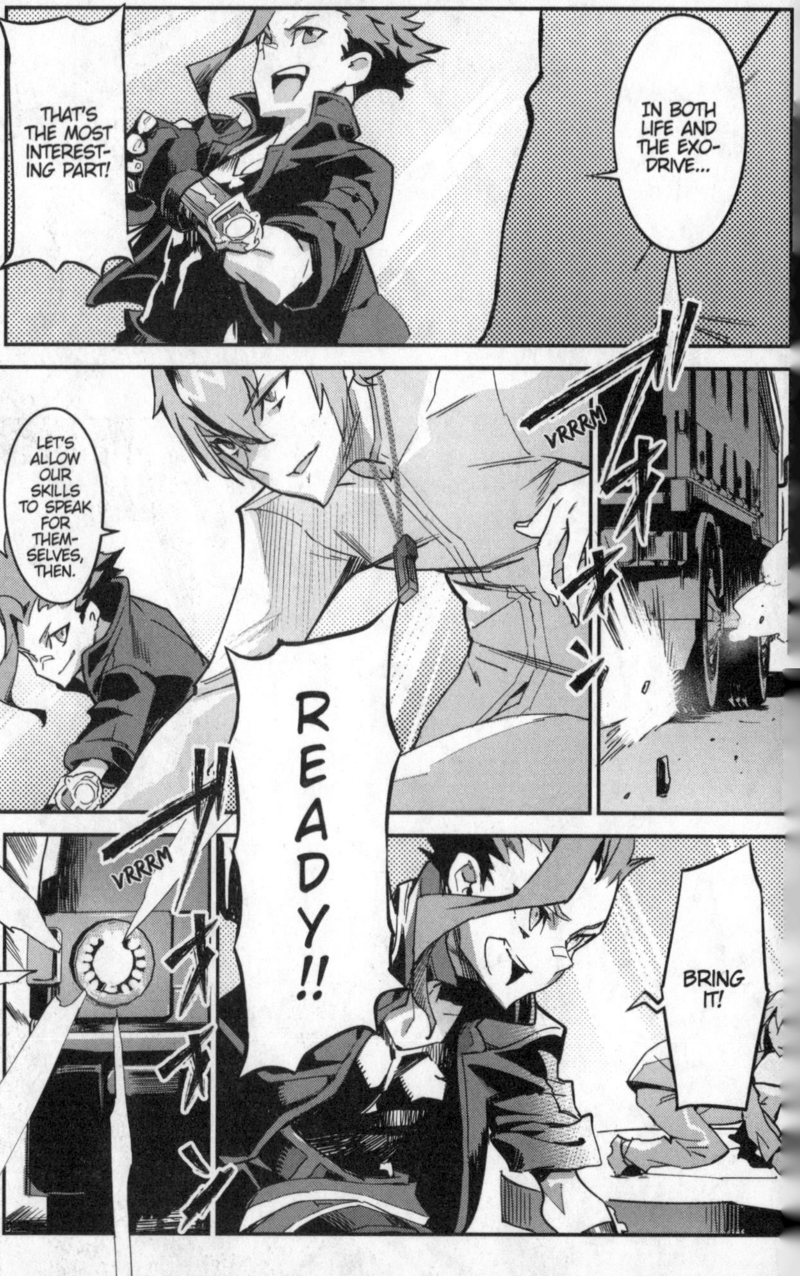

IN BOTH LIFE AND THE EXO-DRIVE...
THAT'S THE MOST INTERESTING PART!
VRRRM
LET'S ALLOW OUR SKILLS TO SPEAK FOR THEMSELVES, THEN.
READY!!
BRING IT!
VRRRM

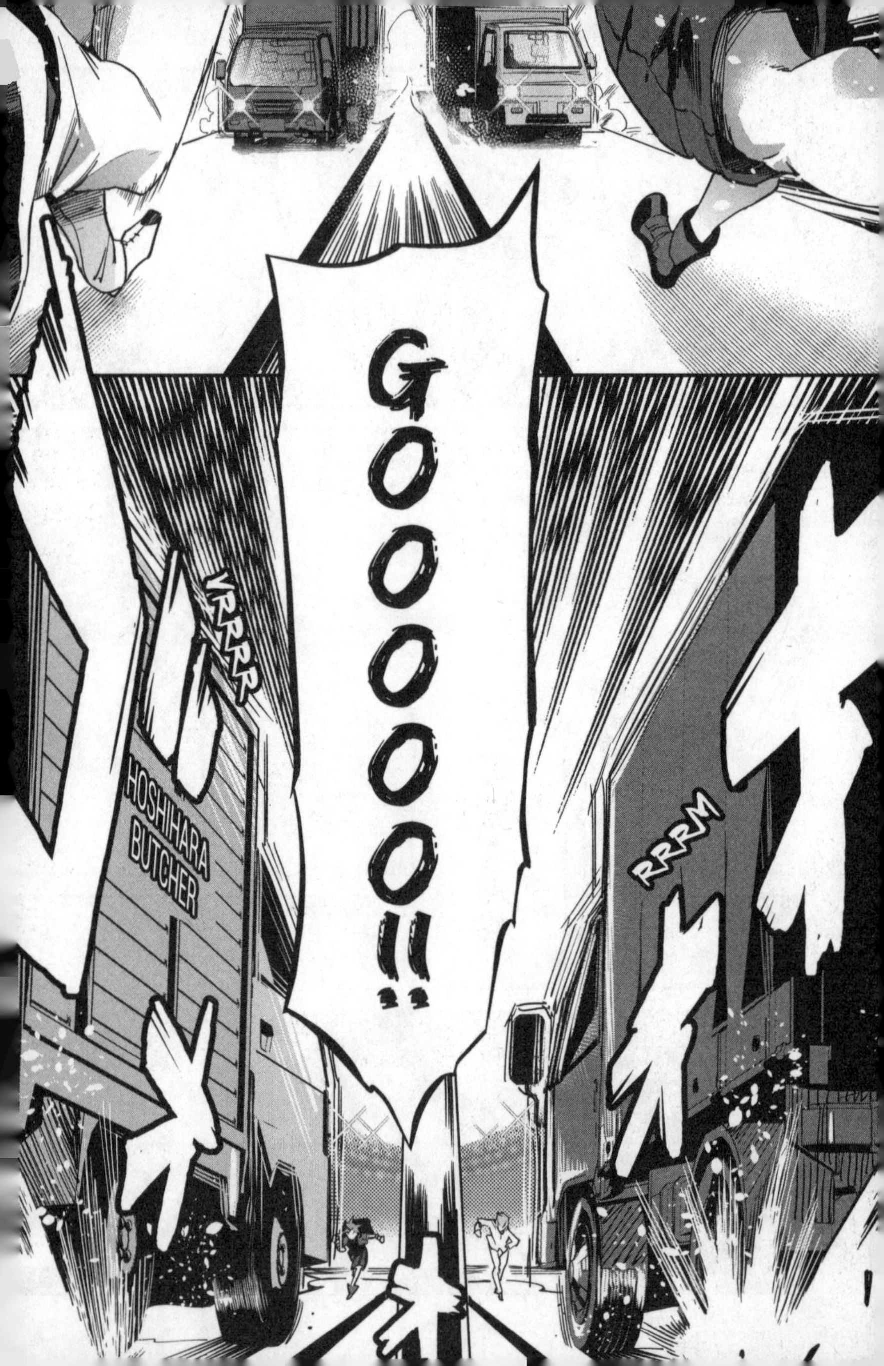
GOOOOOO!!
RRRM
VRRRR
HOSHIHARA BUTCHER

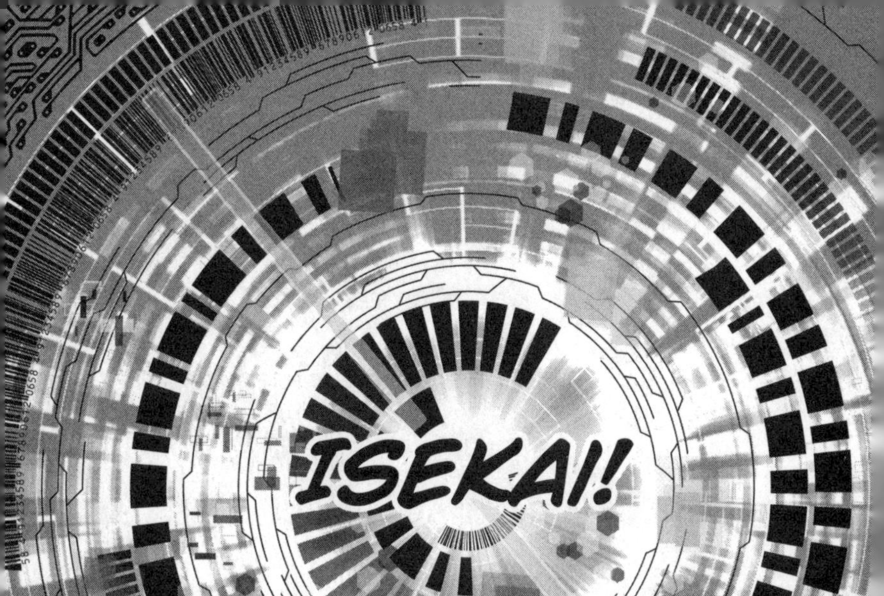
ISEKAI!

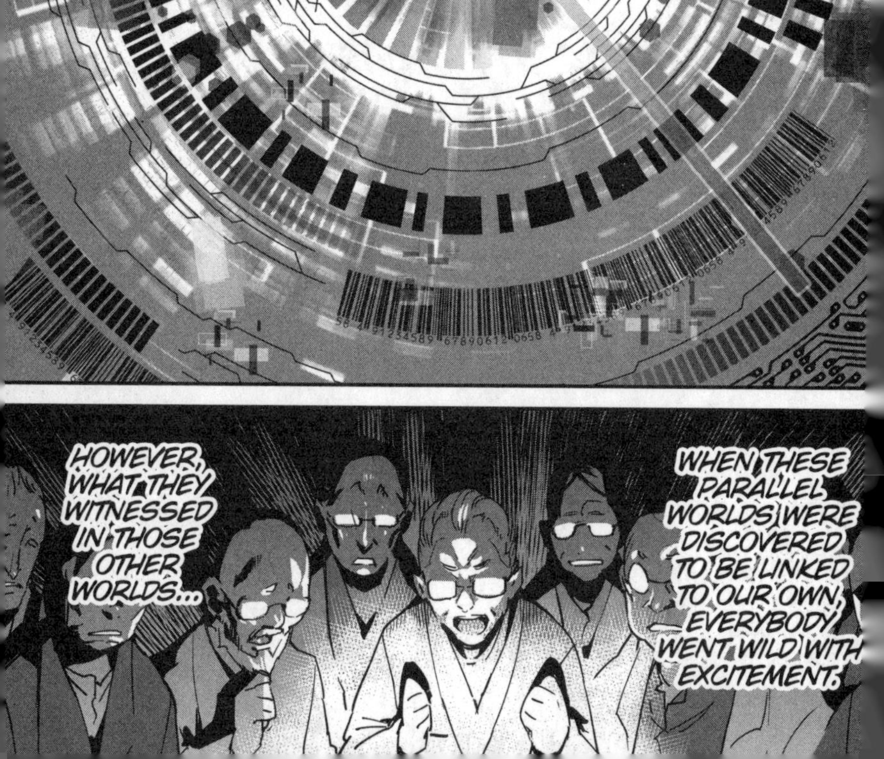
WHEN THESE PARALLEL WORLDS WERE DISCOVERED TO BE LINKED TO OUR OWN, EVERYBODY WENT WILD WITH EXCITEMENT.
HOWEVER, WHAT THEY WITNESSED IN THOSE OTHER WORLDS...

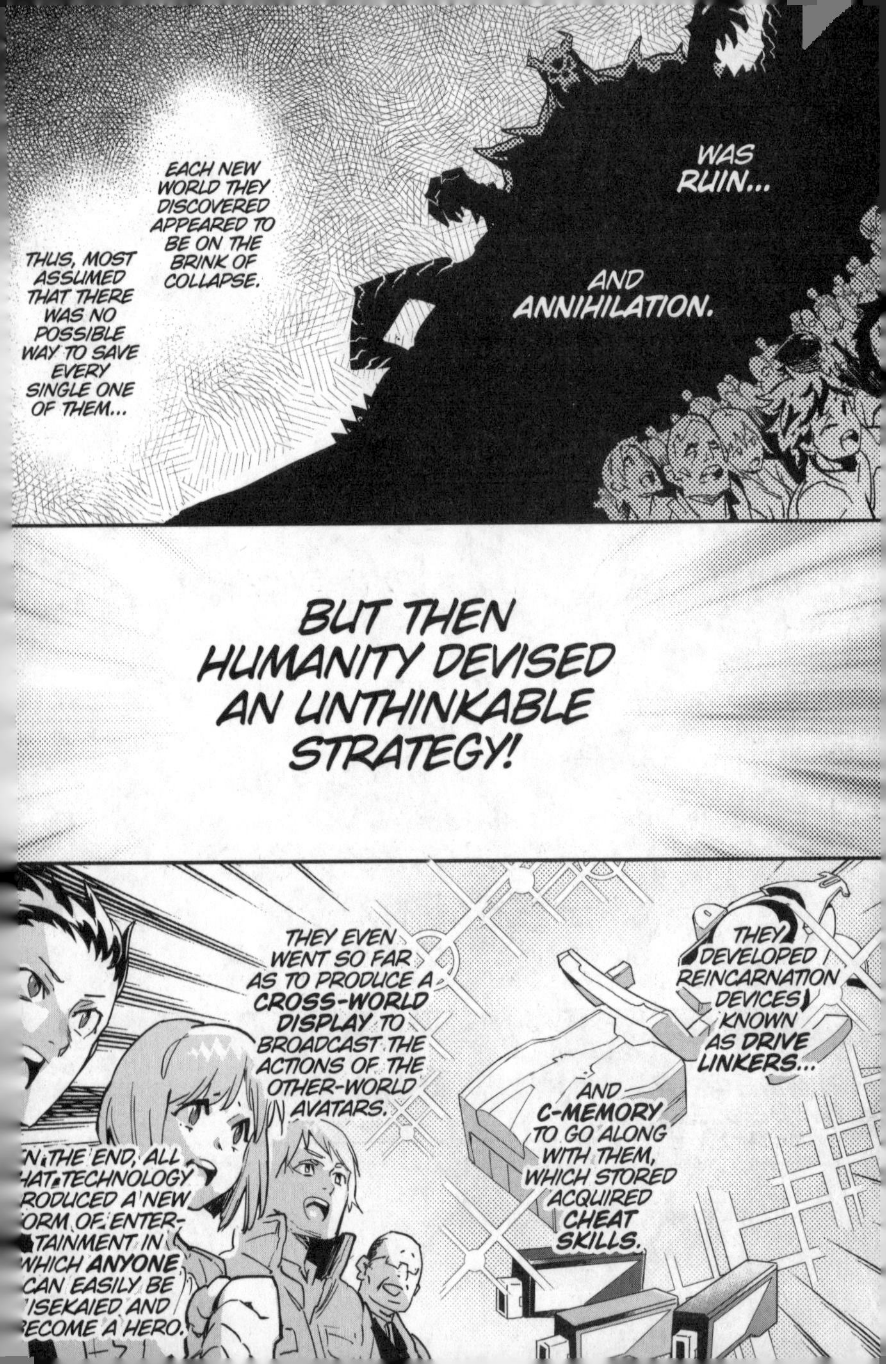
WAS RUIN...
AND ANNIHILATION.
EACH NEW WORLD THEY DISCOVERED APPEARED TO BE ON THE BRINK OF COLLAPSE.
THUS, MOST ASSUMED THAT THERE WAS NO POSSIBLE WAY TO SAVE EVERY SINGLE ONE OF THEM...
BUT THEN HUMANITY DEVISED AN UNTHINKABLE STRATEGY!
THEY DEVELOPED REINCARNATION DEVICES KNOWN AS DRIVE LINKERS...
AND C-MEMORY TO GO ALONG WITH THEM, WHICH STORED ACQUIRED CHEAT SKILLS.
THEY EVEN WENT SO FAR AS TO PRODUCE A CROSS-WORLD DISPLAY TO BROADCAST THE ACTIONS OF THE OTHER-WORLD AVATARS.
N THE END, ALL HAT TECHNOLOGY RODUCED A NEW ORM OF ENTER-TAINMENT IN HICH ANYONE CAN EASILY BE ISEKAIED AND ECOME A HERO.

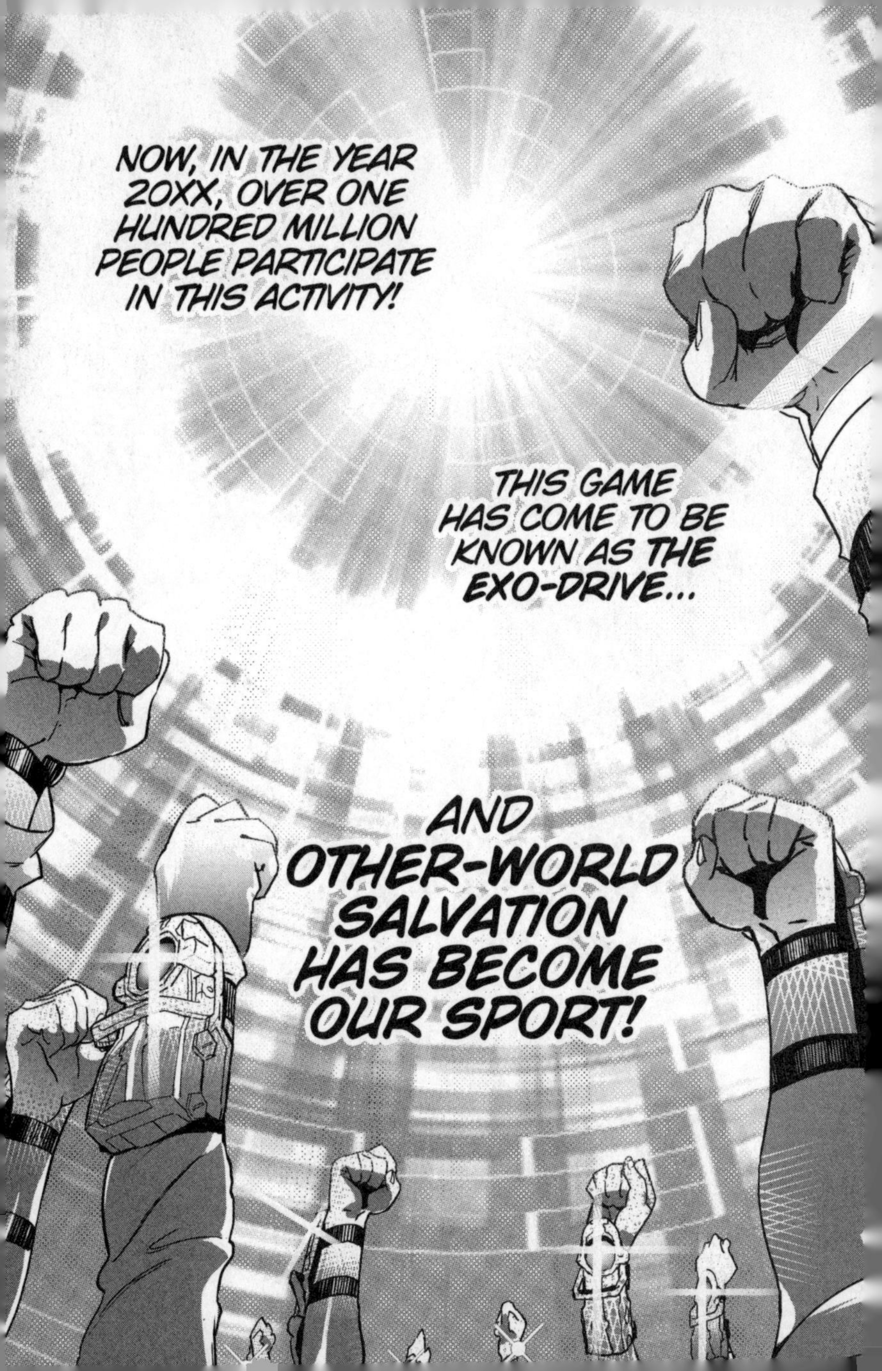
NOW, IN THE YEAR 20XX, OVER ONE HUNDRED MILLION PEOPLE PARTICIPATE IN THIS ACTIVITY!
THIS GAME HAS COME TO BE KNOWN AS THE EXO-DRIVE...
AND OTHER-WORLD SALVATION HAS BECOME OUR SPORT!

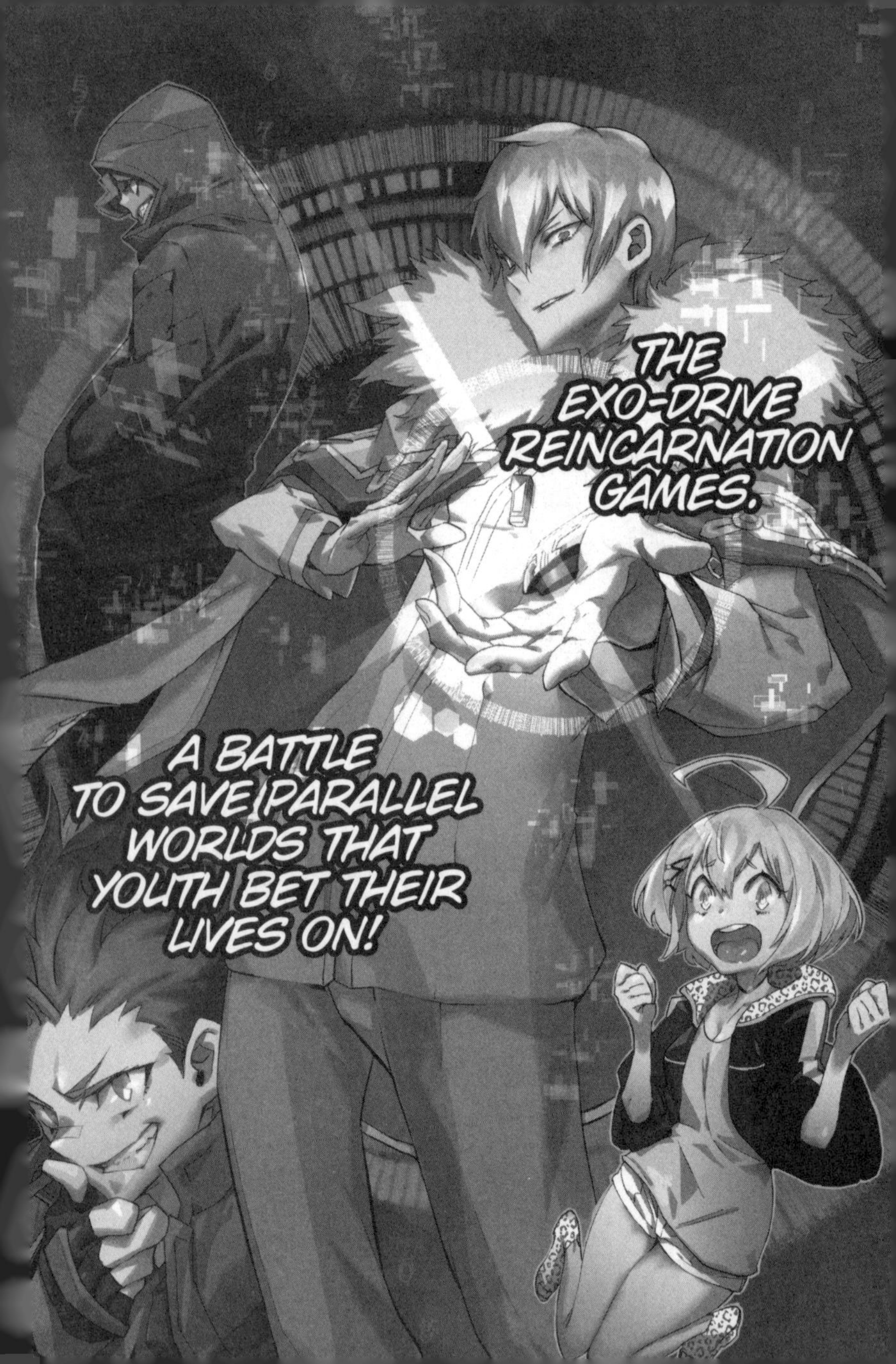
THE EXO-DRIVE REINCARNATION GAMES.
A BATTLE TO SAVE PARALLEL WORLDS THAT YOUTH BET THEIR LIVES ON!

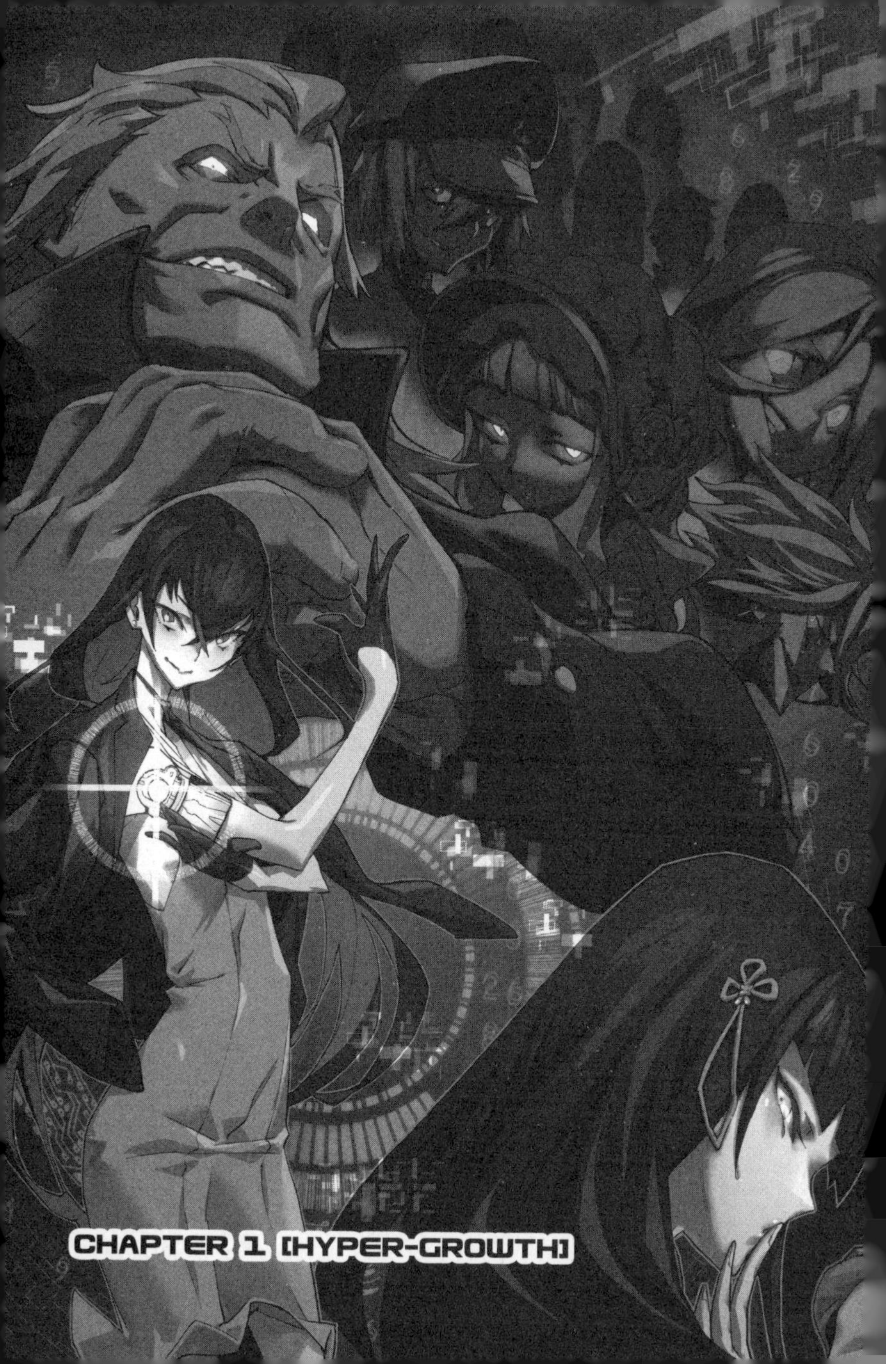
CHAPTER 1 [HYPER-GROWTH]

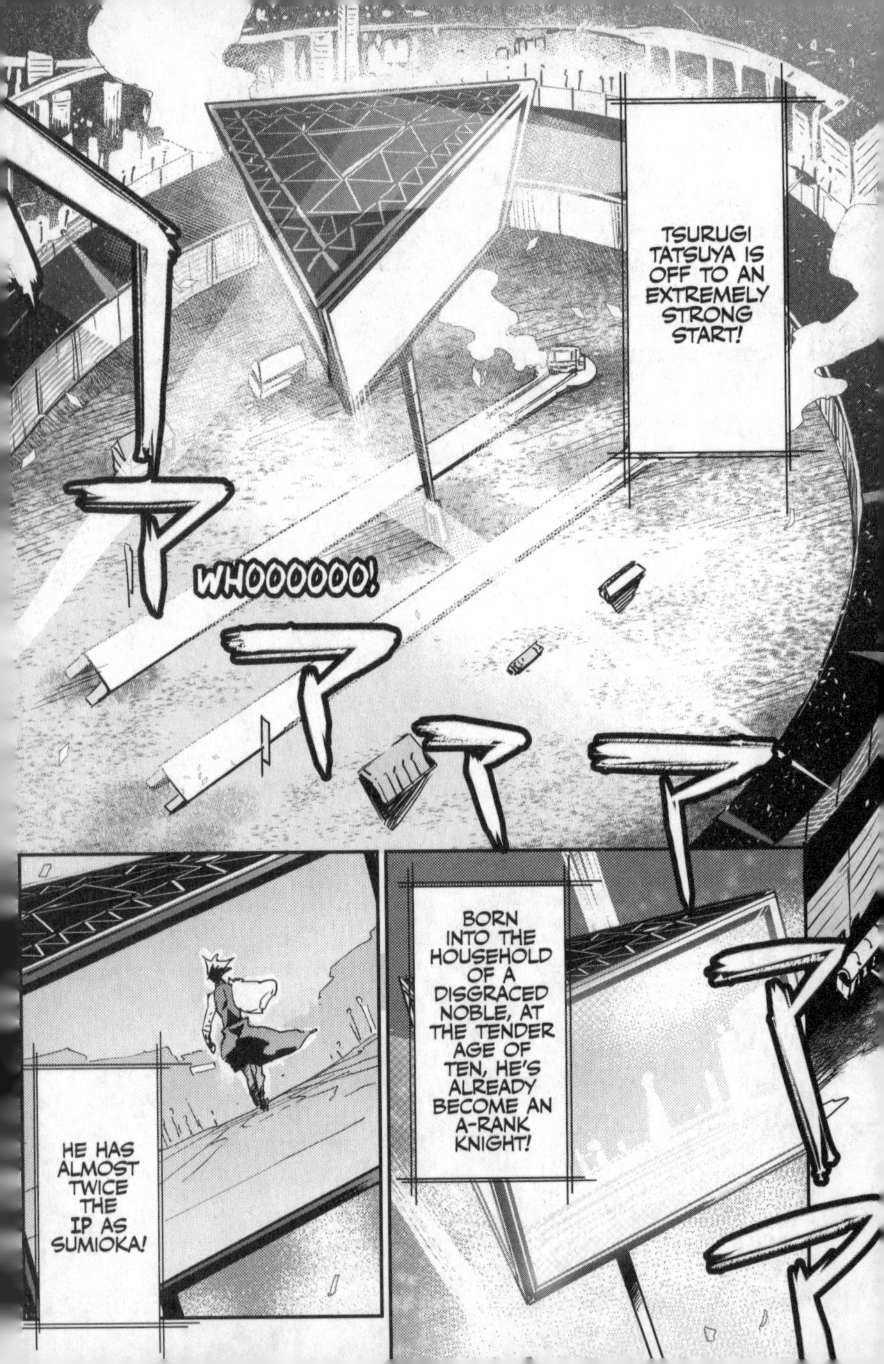
TSURUGI TATSUYA IS OFF TO AN EXTREMELY STRONG START!
WHOOOOOO!
BORN INTO THE HOUSEHOLD OF A DISGRACED NOBLE, AT THE TENDER AGE OF TEN, HE'S ALREADY BECOME AN A-RANK KNIGHT!
HE HAS ALMOST TWICE THE IP AS SUMIOKA!

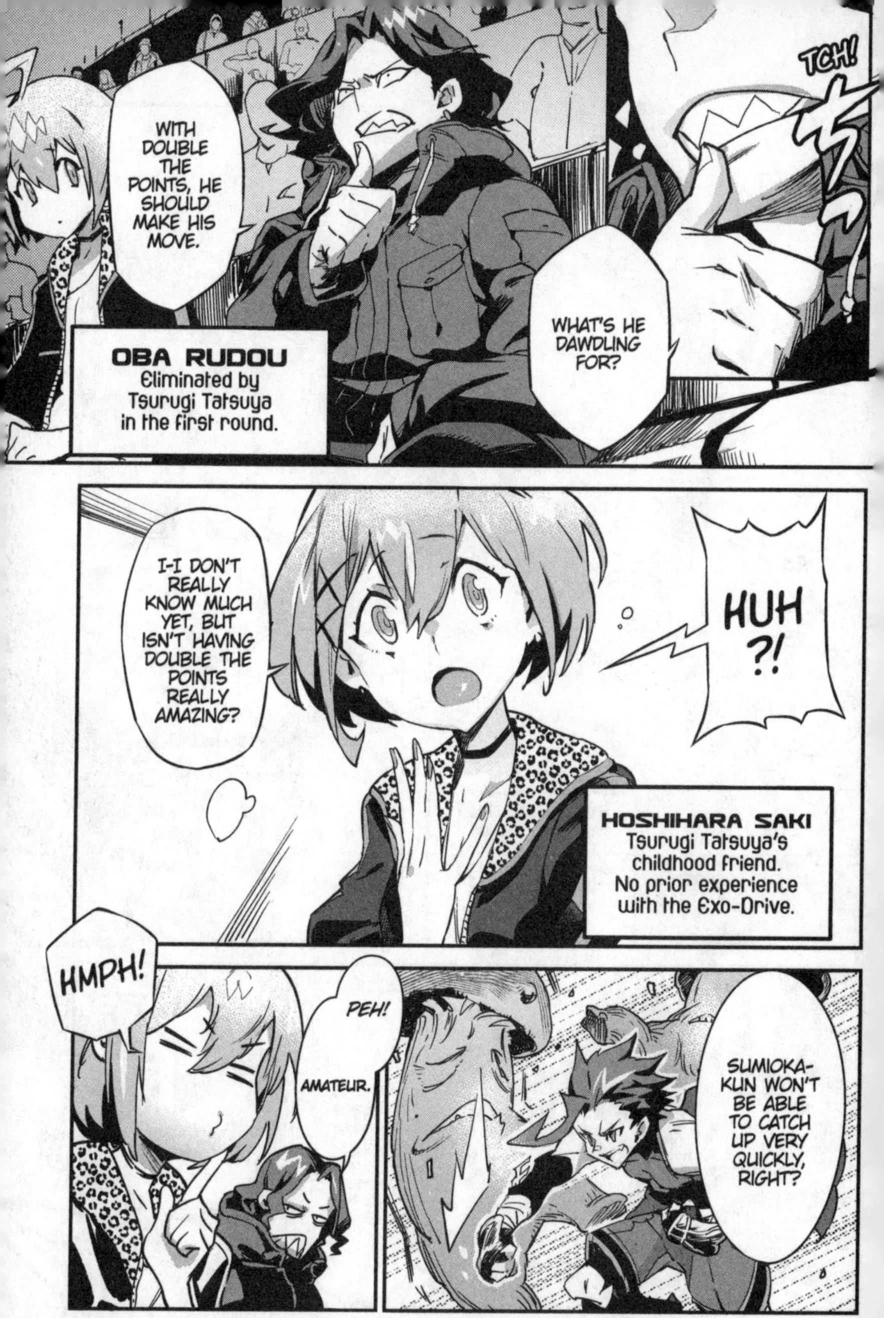
TCH!
WHAT'S HE DAWDLING FOR?
WITH DOUBLE THE POINTS, HE SHOULD MAKE HIS MOVE.
OBA RUDOU
Eliminated by Tsurugi Tatsuya in the first round.
HUH?!
I-I DON'T REALLY KNOW MUCH YET, BUT ISN'T HAVING DOUBLE THE POINTS REALLY AMAZING?
HOSHIHARA SAKI
Tsurugi Tatsuya's childhood friend. No prior experience with the Exo-Drive.
SUMIOKA-KUN WON'T BE ABLE TO CATCH UP VERY QUICKLY, RIGHT?
PEH!
AMATEUR.
HMPH!

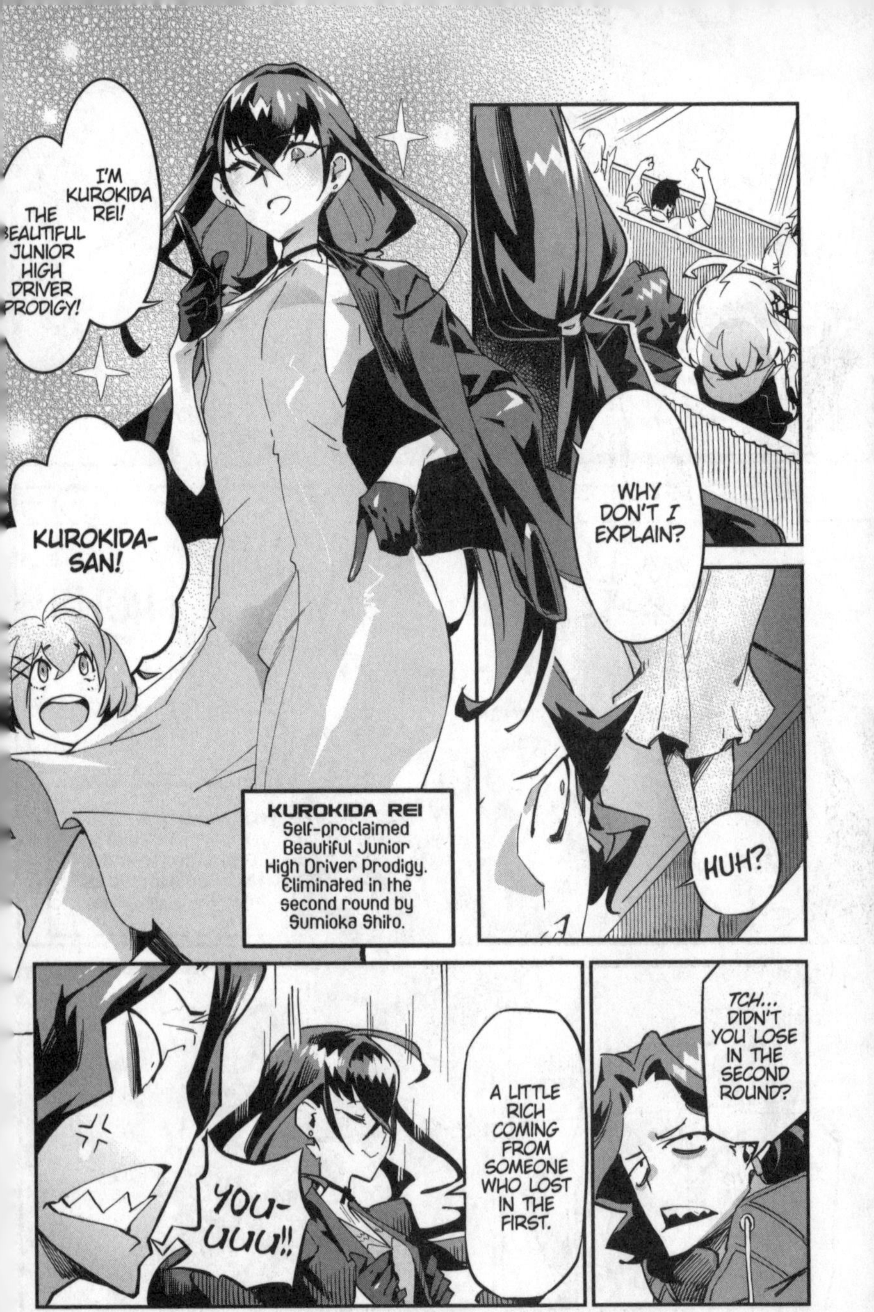
WHY DON'T I EXPLAIN?
HUH?
I'M KUROKIDA REI! THE BEAUTIFUL JUNIOR HIGH DRIVER PRODIGY!
KUROKIDA-SAN!
KUROKIDA REI Self-proclaimed Beautiful Junior High Driver Prodigy. Eliminated in the second round by Sumioka Shito.
TCH... DIDN'T YOU LOSE IN THE SECOND ROUND?
A LITTLE RICH COMING FROM SOMEONE WHO LOST IN THE FIRST.
YOU-UUU!!

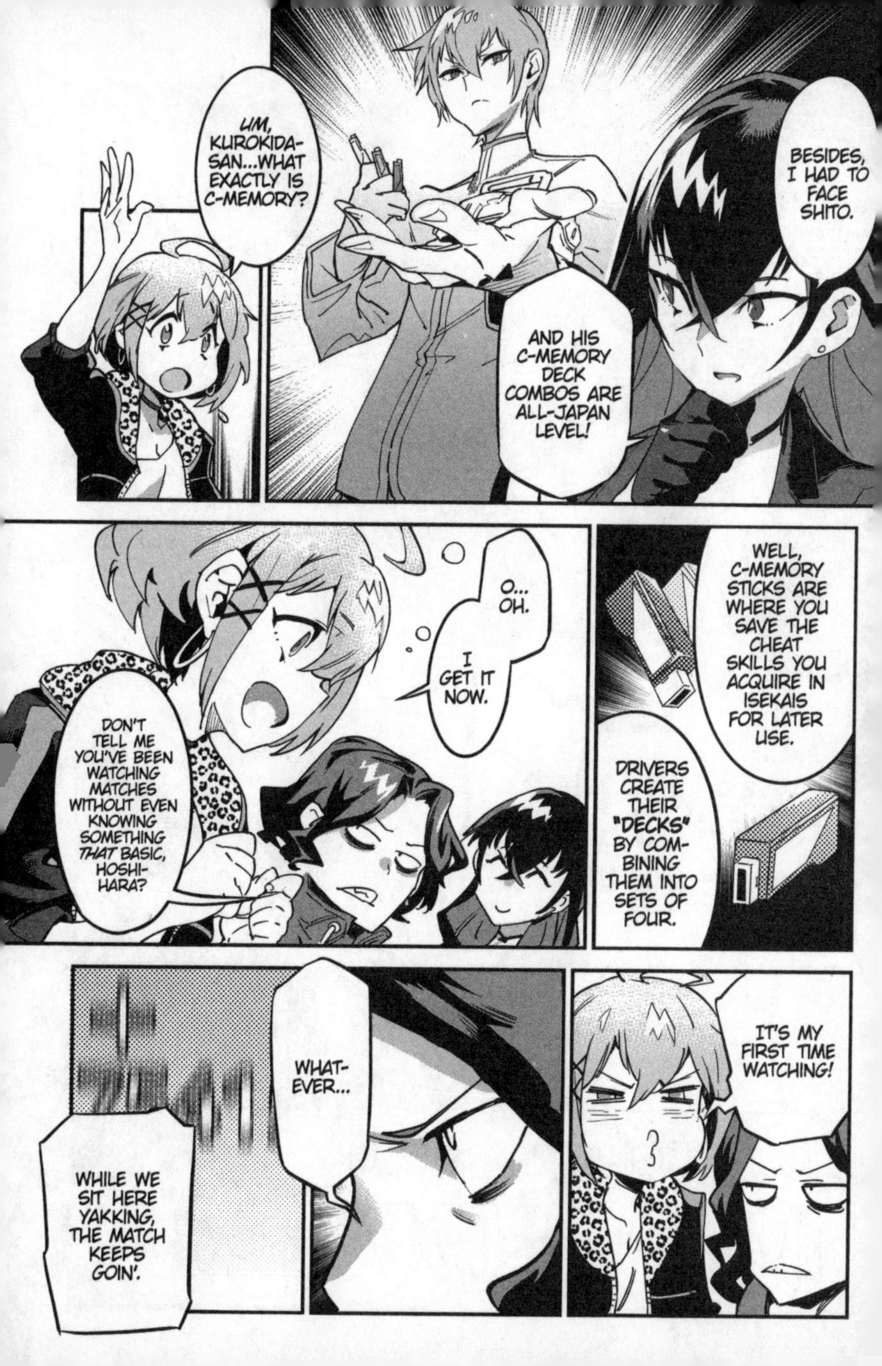
BESIDES, I HAD TO FACE SHITO.
AND HIS C-MEMORY DECK COMBOS ARE ALL-JAPAN LEVEL!
UM, KUROKIDA-SAN...WHAT EXACTLY IS C-MEMORY?
WELL, C-MEMORY STICKS ARE WHERE YOU SAVE THE CHEAT SKILLS YOU ACQUIRE IN ISEKAIS FOR LATER USE.
DRIVERS CREATE THEIR **"DECKS"** BY COMBINING THEM INTO SETS OF FOUR.
O... OH.
I GET IT NOW.
DON'T TELL ME YOU'VE BEEN WATCHING MATCHES WITHOUT EVEN KNOWING SOMETHING *THAT* BASIC, HOSHIHARA?
IT'S MY FIRST TIME WATCHING!
WHAT-EVER...
WHILE WE SIT HERE YAKKING, THE MATCH KEEPS GOIN'.

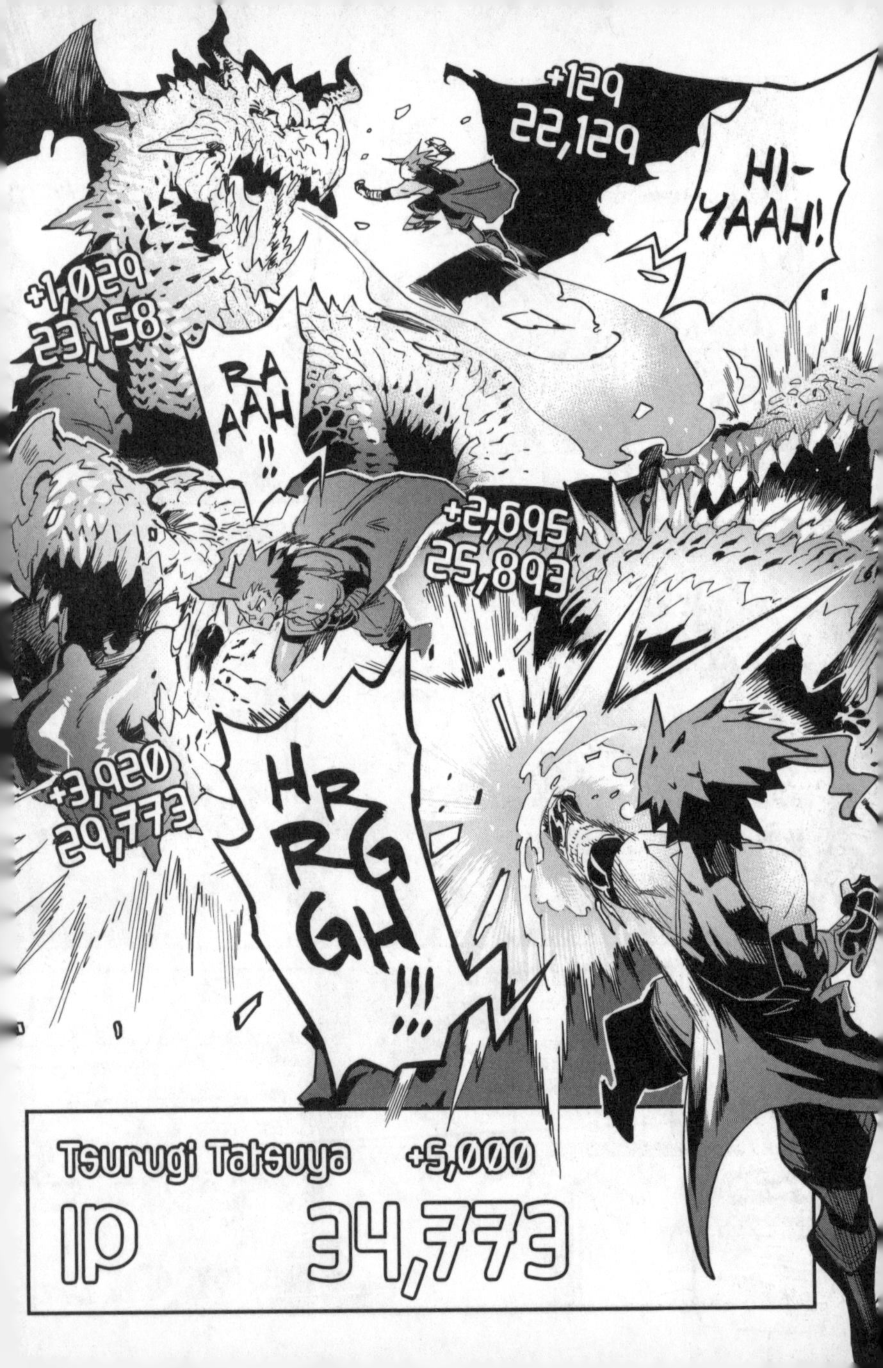
HI-YAAH!
+129
22,129
+1,029
23,158
+2,695
25,893
RAAAH!!
HRRGGH!!!
+3,920
29,773
Tsurugi Tatsuya +5,000
lp 34,773

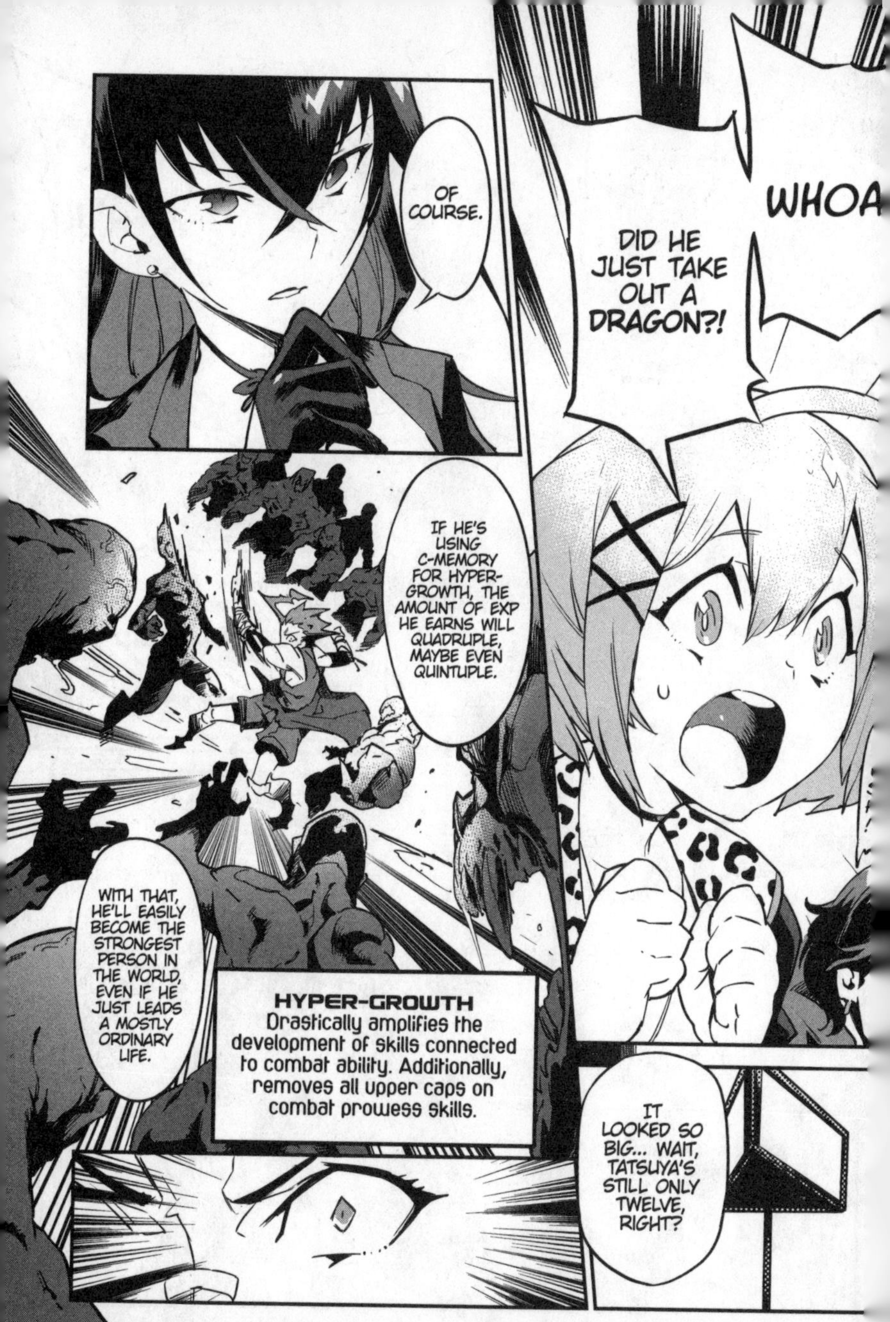
WHOA
DID HE JUST TAKE OUT A DRAGON?!
OF COURSE.
IF HE'S USING C-MEMORY FOR HYPER-GROWTH, THE AMOUNT OF EXP HE EARNS WILL QUADRUPLE, MAYBE EVEN QUINTUPLE.
WITH THAT, HE'LL EASILY BECOME THE STRONGEST PERSON IN THE WORLD, EVEN IF HE JUST LEADS A MOSTLY ORDINARY LIFE.
HYPER-GROWTH
Drastically amplifies the development of skills connected to combat ability. Additionally, removes all upper caps on combat prowess skills.
IT LOOKED SO BIG... WAIT, TATSUYA'S STILL ONLY TWELVE, RIGHT?

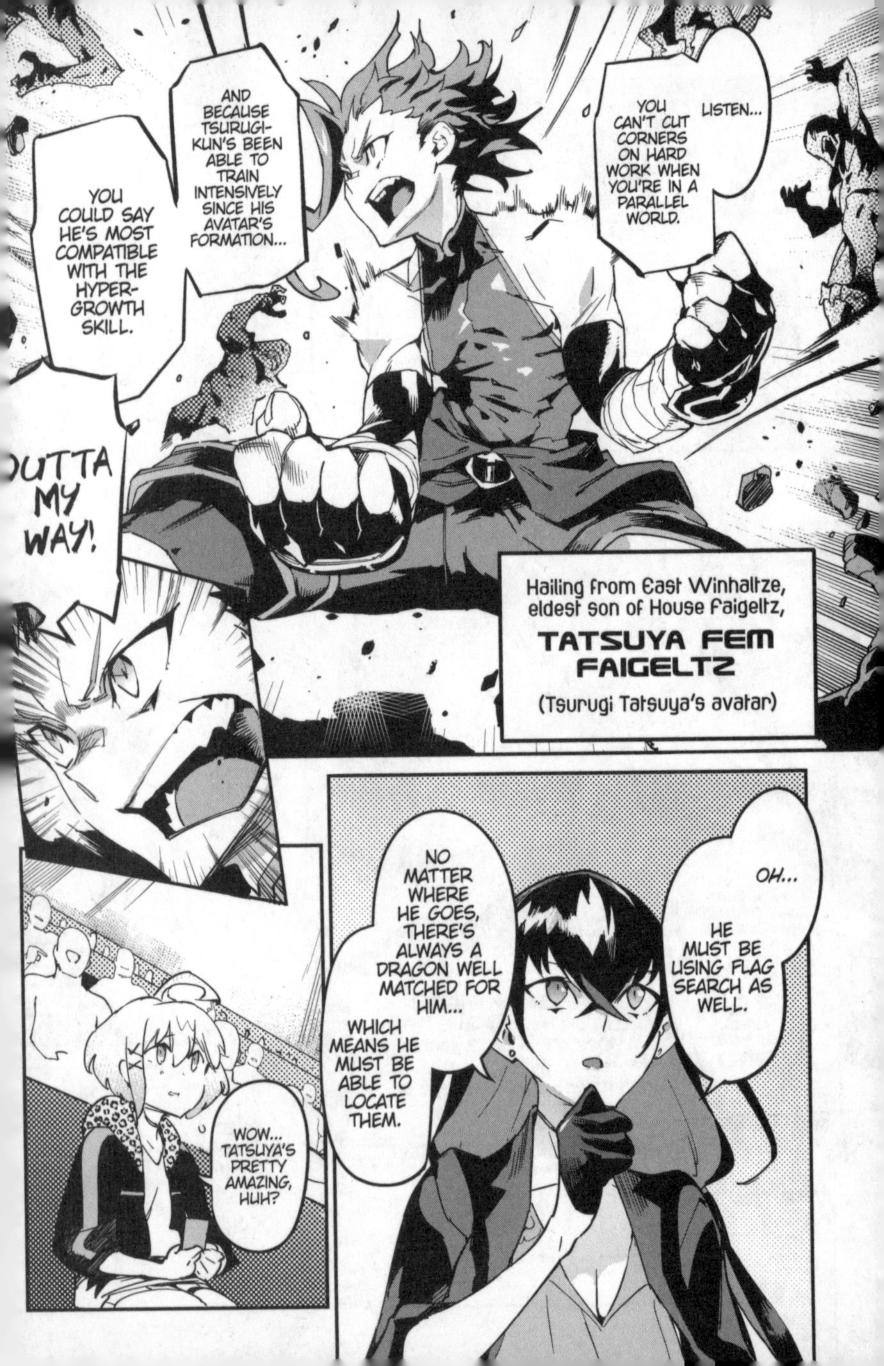
LISTEN...
YOU CAN'T CUT CORNERS ON HARD WORK WHEN YOU'RE IN A PARALLEL WORLD.
AND BECAUSE TSURUGI-KUN'S BEEN ABLE TO TRAIN INTENSIVELY SINCE HIS AVATAR'S FORMATION...
YOU COULD SAY HE'S MOST COMPATIBLE WITH THE HYPER-GROWTH SKILL.
OUTTA MY WAY!
Hailing from East Winhaltze, eldest son of House Faigeltz,
TATSUYA FEM FAIGELTZ
(Tsurugi Tatsuya's avatar)
OH...
HE MUST BE USING FLAG SEARCH AS WELL.
NO MATTER WHERE HE GOES, THERE'S ALWAYS A DRAGON WELL MATCHED FOR HIM...
WHICH MEANS HE MUST BE ABLE TO LOCATE THEM.
WOW... TATSUYA'S PRETTY AMAZING, HUH?

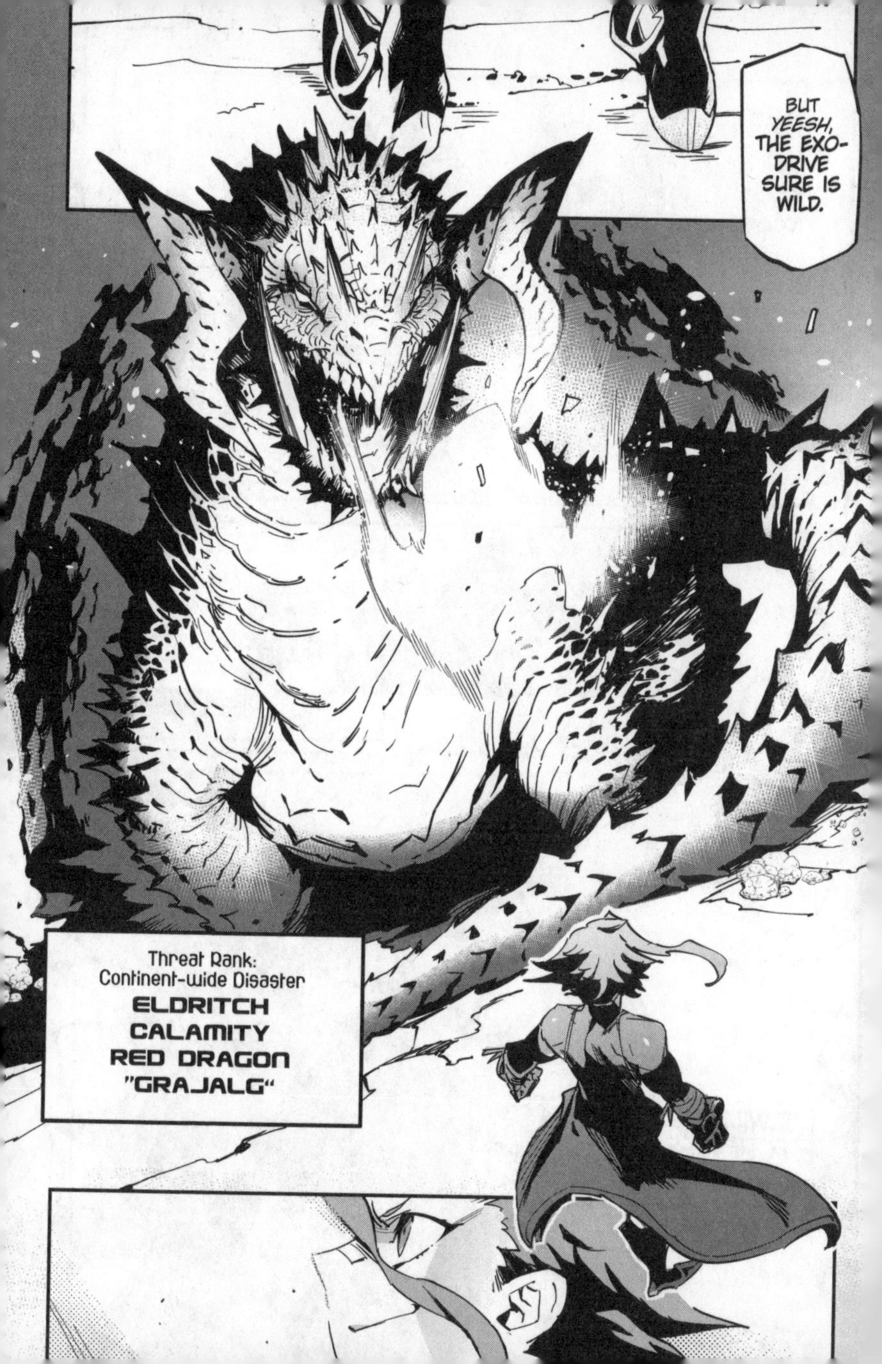
BUT YEESH, THE EXO-DRIVE SURE IS WILD.
Threat Rank: Continent-wide Disaster
ELDRITCH CALAMITY RED DRAGON "GRAJALG"

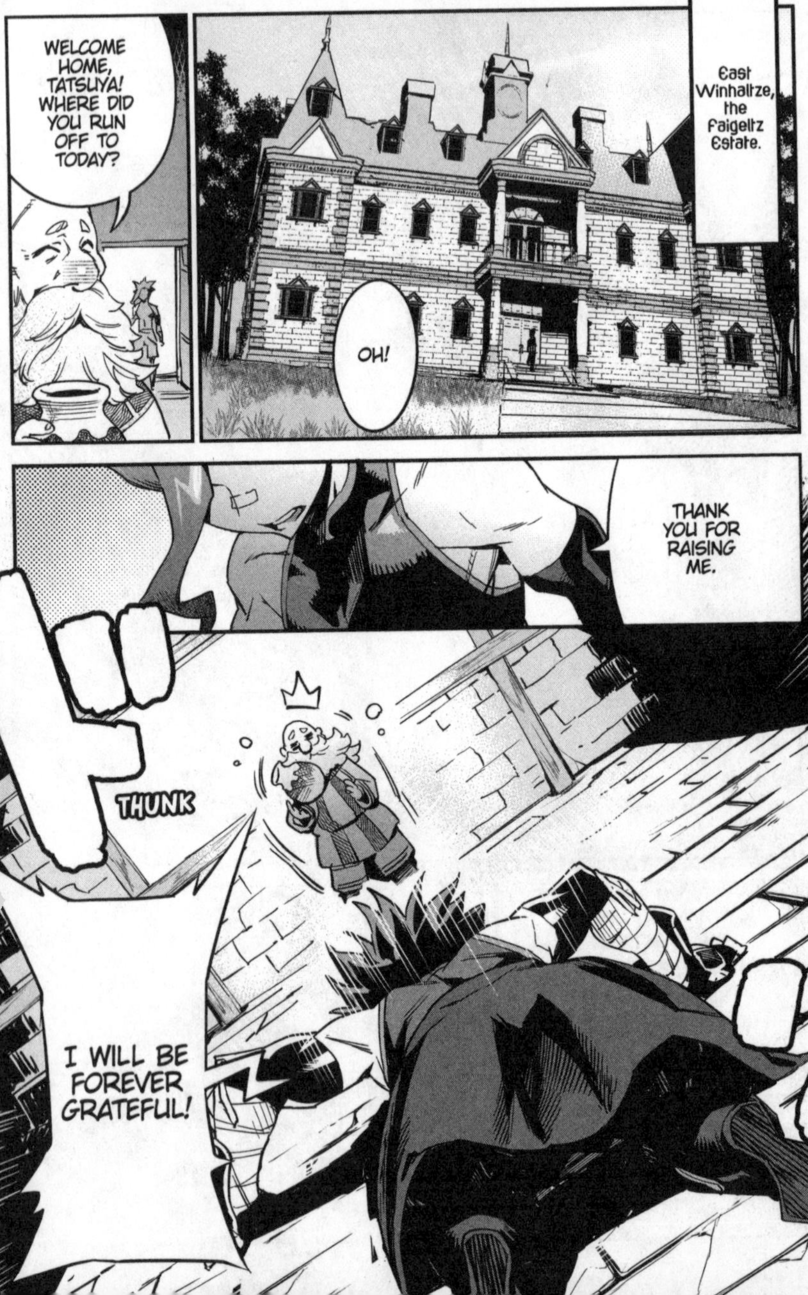
East Winhaltze, the Faigeltz Estate.
OH!
WELCOME HOME, TATSUYA! WHERE DID YOU RUN OFF TO TODAY?
THANK YOU FOR RAISING ME.
THUNK
I WILL BE FOREVER GRATEFUL!

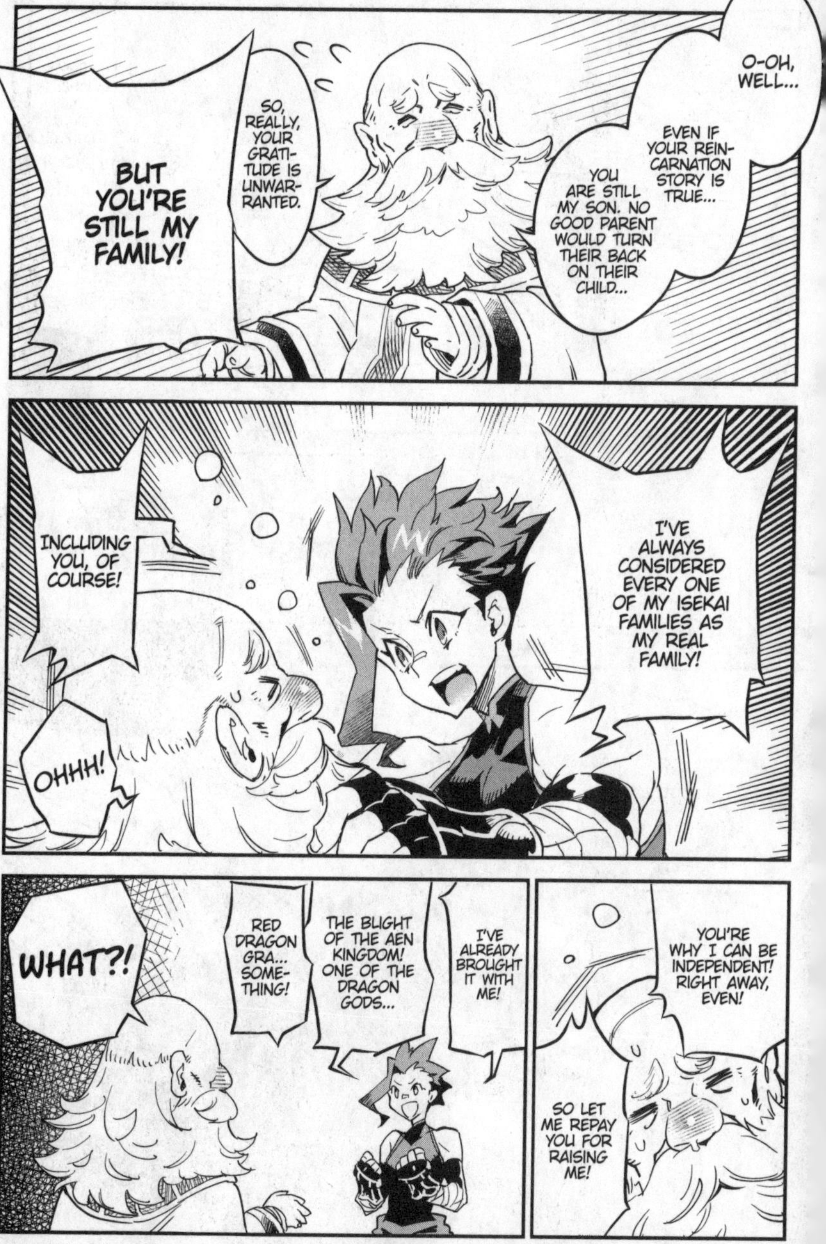
O-OH, WELL...
EVEN IF YOUR REIN-CARNATION STORY IS TRUE...
YOU ARE STILL MY SON. NO GOOD PARENT WOULD TURN THEIR BACK ON THEIR CHILD...
SO, REALLY, YOUR GRATI-TUDE IS UNWAR-RANTED.
BUT YOU'RE STILL MY FAMILY!
I'VE ALWAYS CONSIDERED EVERY ONE OF MY ISEKAI FAMILIES AS MY REAL FAMILY!
INCLUDING YOU, OF COURSE!
OHHH!
YOU'RE WHY I CAN BE INDEPENDENT! RIGHT AWAY, EVEN!
SO LET ME REPAY YOU FOR RAISING ME!
I'VE ALREADY BROUGHT IT WITH ME!
THE BLIGHT OF THE AEN KINGDOM! ONE OF THE DRAGON GODS...
RED DRAGON GRA... SOME-THING!
WHAT?!

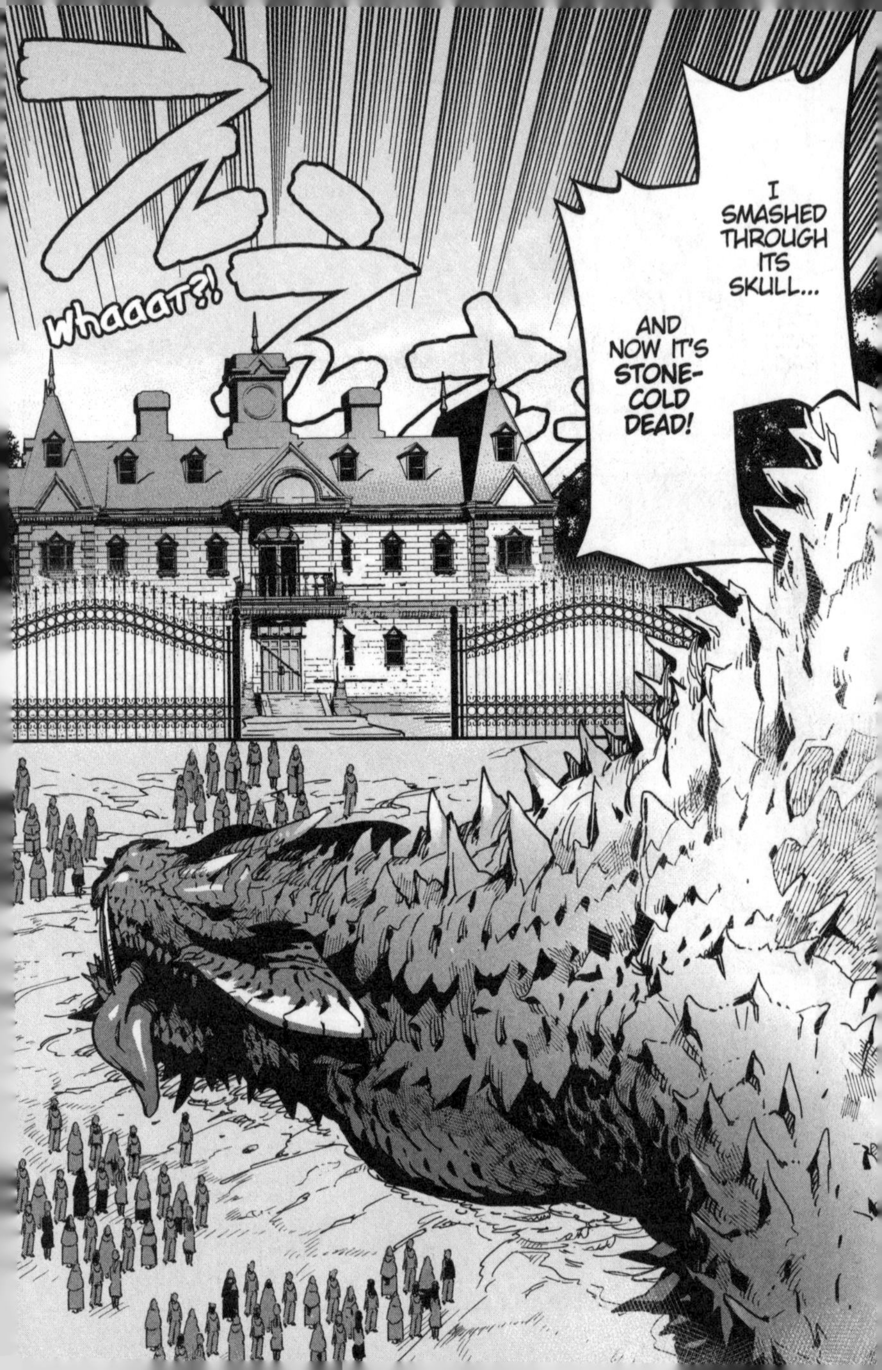
I SMASHED THROUGH ITS SKULL...
AND NOW IT'S STONE-COLD DEAD!
WHAAAT?!

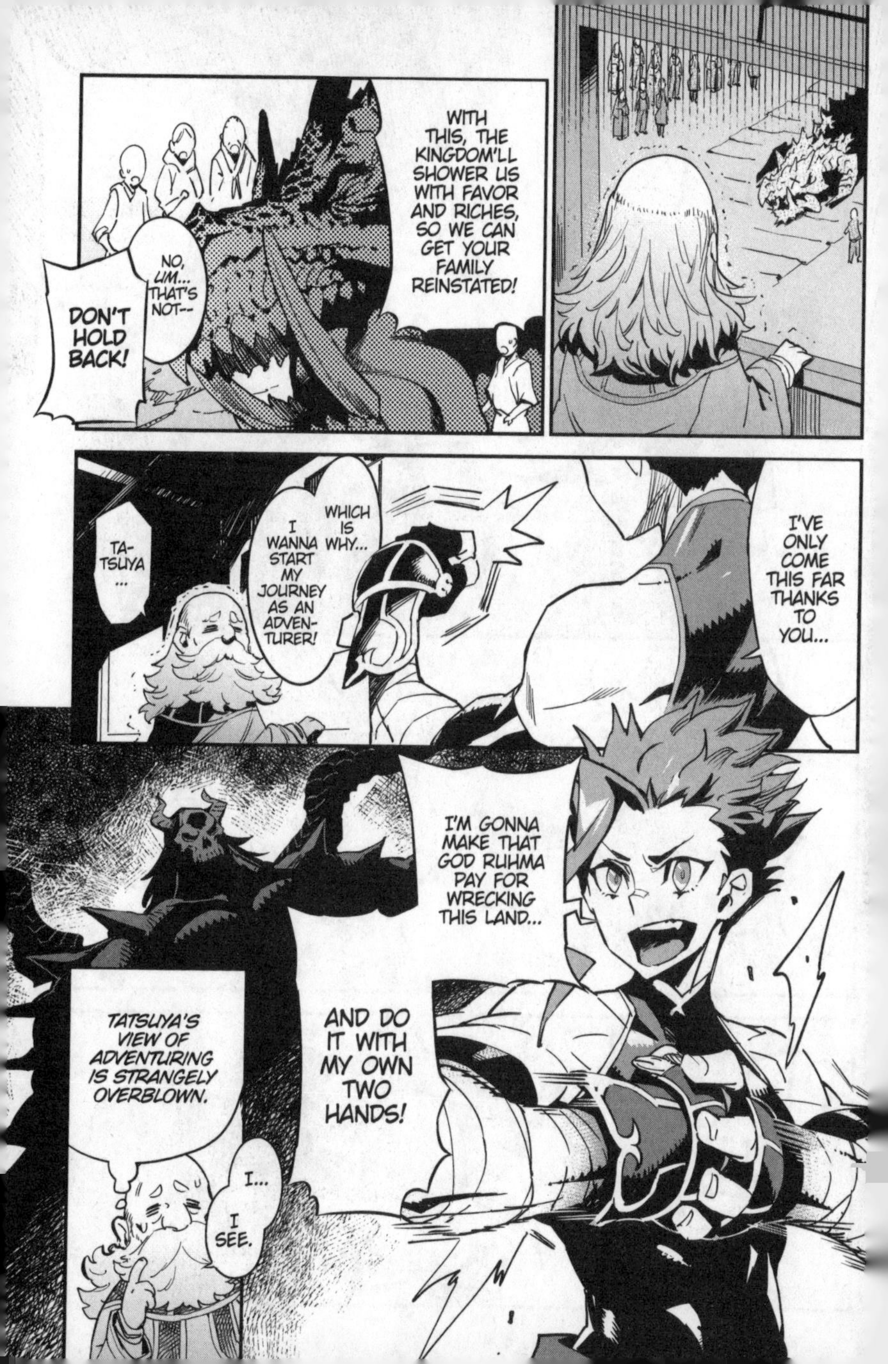
WITH THIS, THE KINGDOM'LL SHOWER US WITH FAVOR AND RICHES, SO WE CAN GET YOUR FAMILY REINSTATED!
NO, UM... THAT'S NOT--
DON'T HOLD BACK!
I'VE ONLY COME THIS FAR THANKS TO YOU...
WHICH IS WHY... I WANNA START MY JOURNEY AS AN ADVENTURER!
TA-TSUYA ...
I'M GONNA MAKE THAT GOD RUHMA PAY FOR WRECKING THIS LAND...
AND DO IT WITH MY OWN TWO HANDS!
TATSUYA'S VIEW OF ADVENTURING IS STRANGELY OVERBLOWN.
I... I SEE.

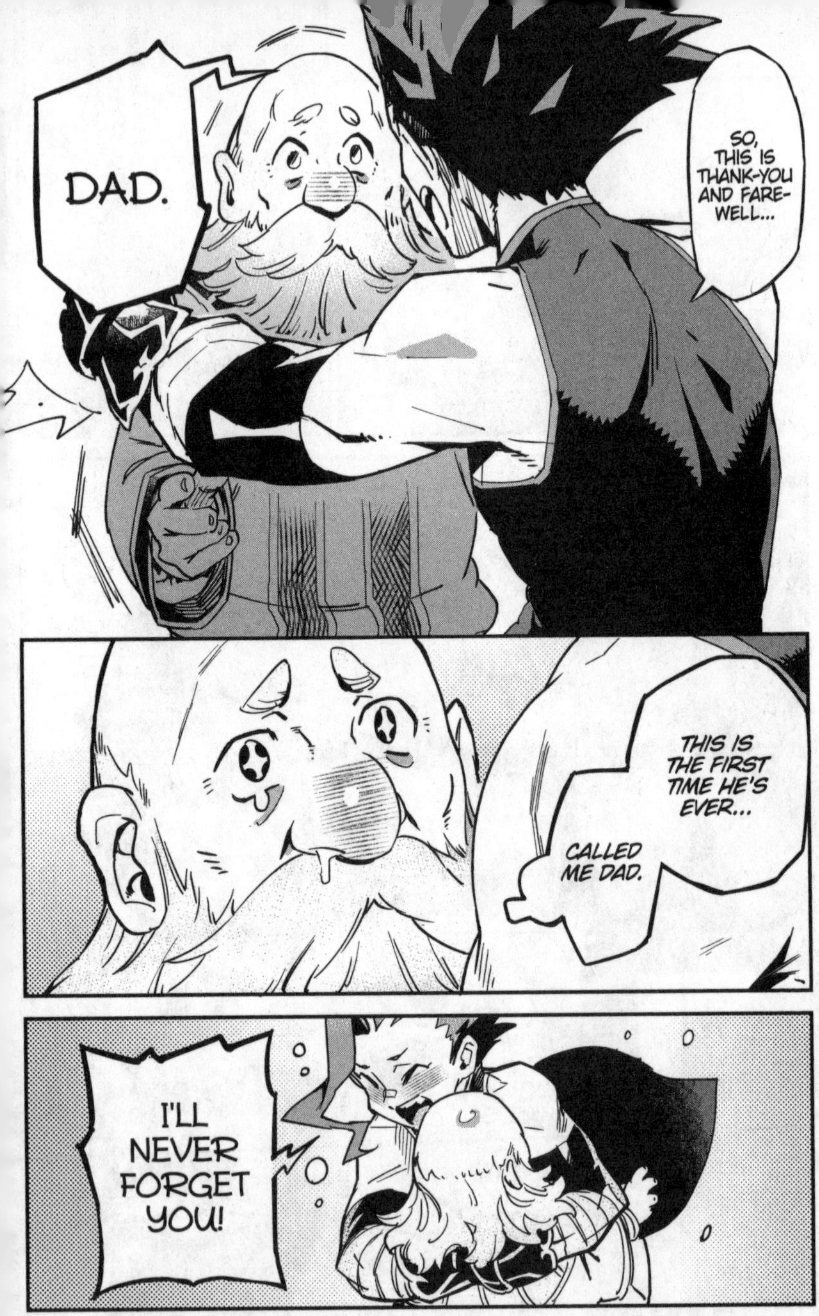
SO, THIS IS THANK-YOU AND FARE-WELL...
DAD.
THIS IS THE FIRST TIME HE'S EVER...
CALLED ME DAD.
I'LL NEVER FORGET YOU!

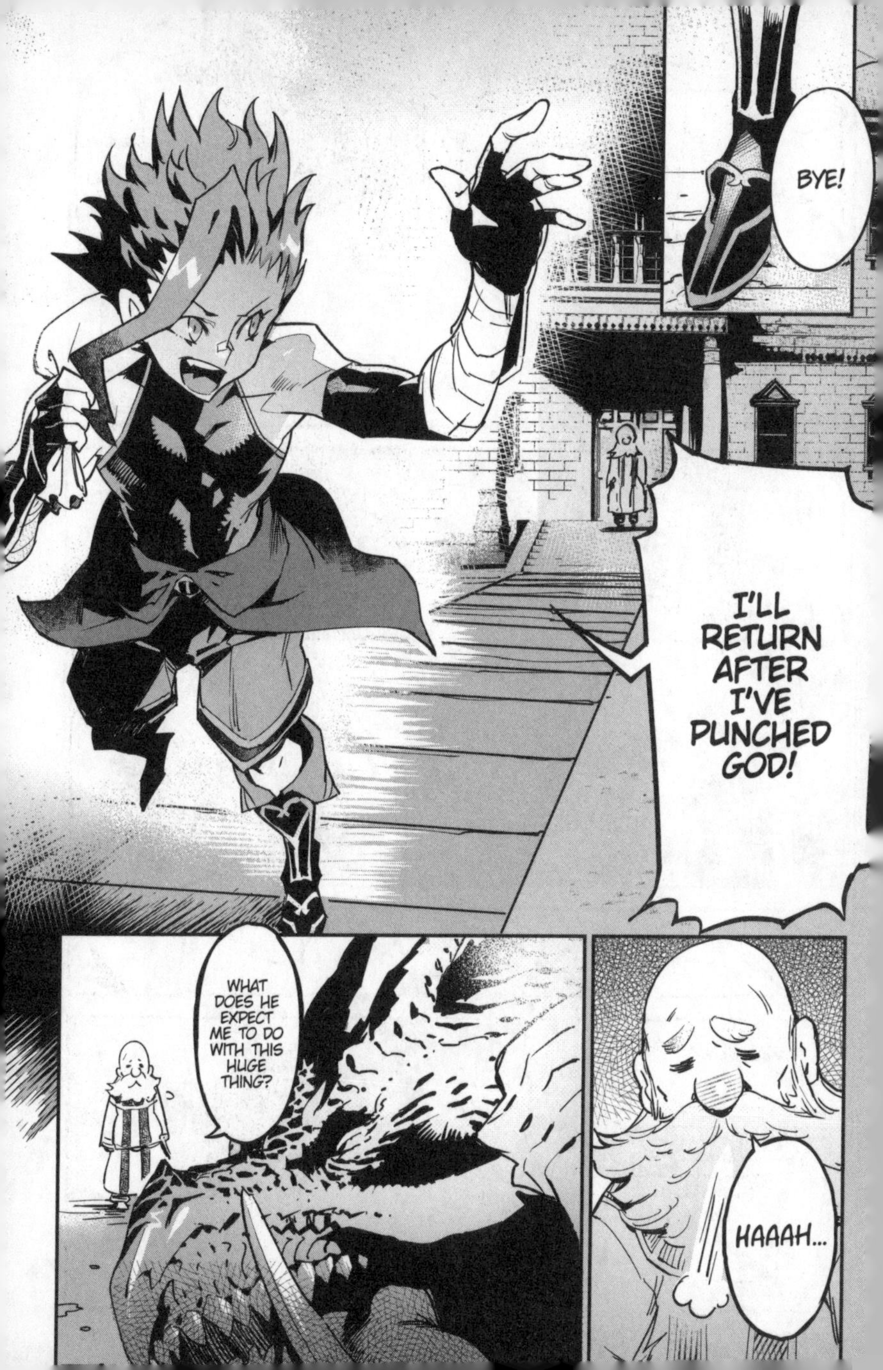
BYE!
I'LL RETURN AFTER I'VE PUNCHED GOD!
HAAAH...
WHAT DOES HE EXPECT ME TO DO WITH THIS HUGE THING?

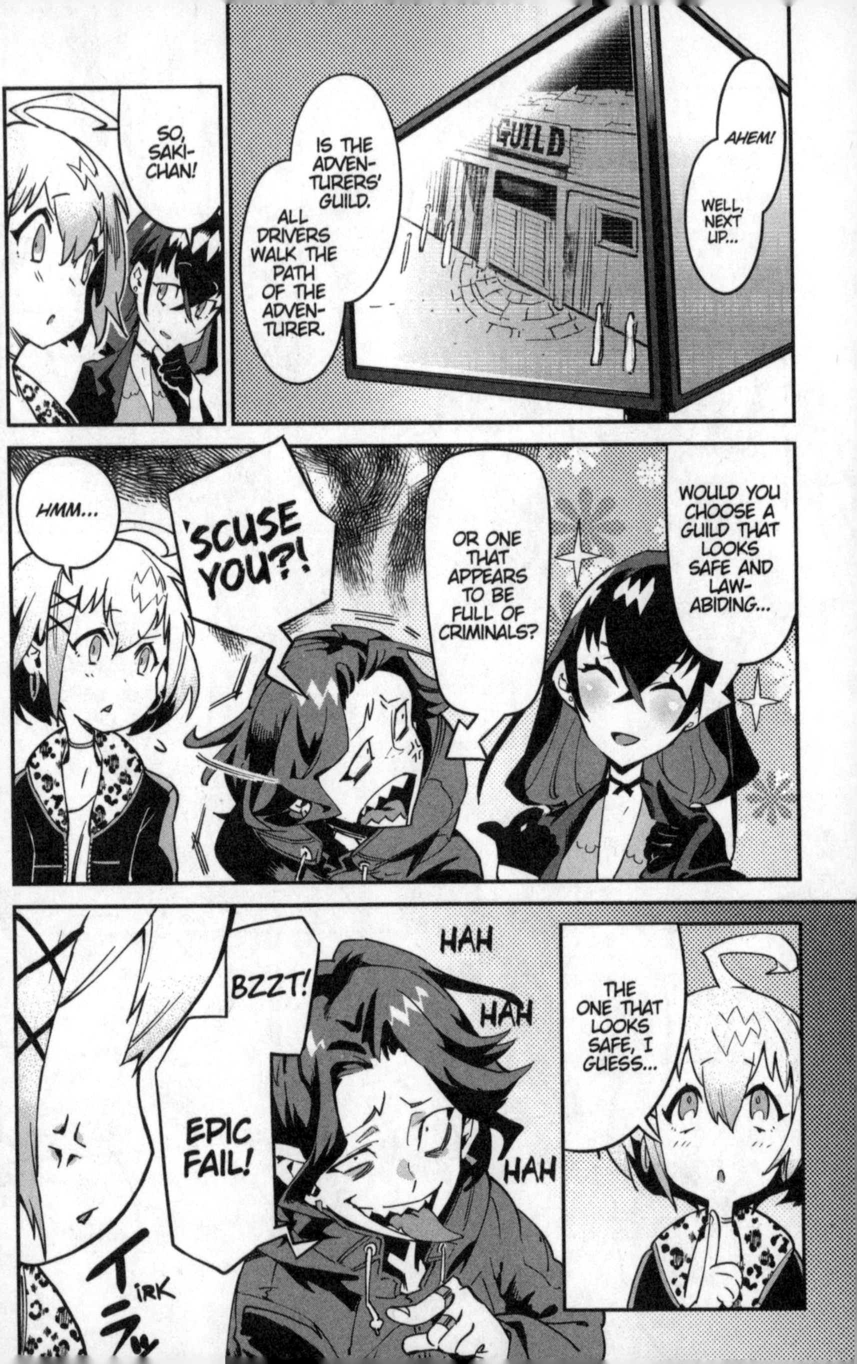
AHEM!
WELL, NEXT UP...
IS THE ADVENTURERS' GUILD.
ALL DRIVERS WALK THE PATH OF THE ADVENTURER.
SO, SAKI-CHAN!
WOULD YOU CHOOSE A GUILD THAT LOOKS SAFE AND LAW-ABIDING...
OR ONE THAT APPEARS TO BE FULL OF CRIMINALS?
'SCUSE YOU?!
HMM...
THE ONE THAT LOOKS SAFE, I GUESS...
HAH
HAH
HAH
BZZT!
EPIC FAIL!
IRK

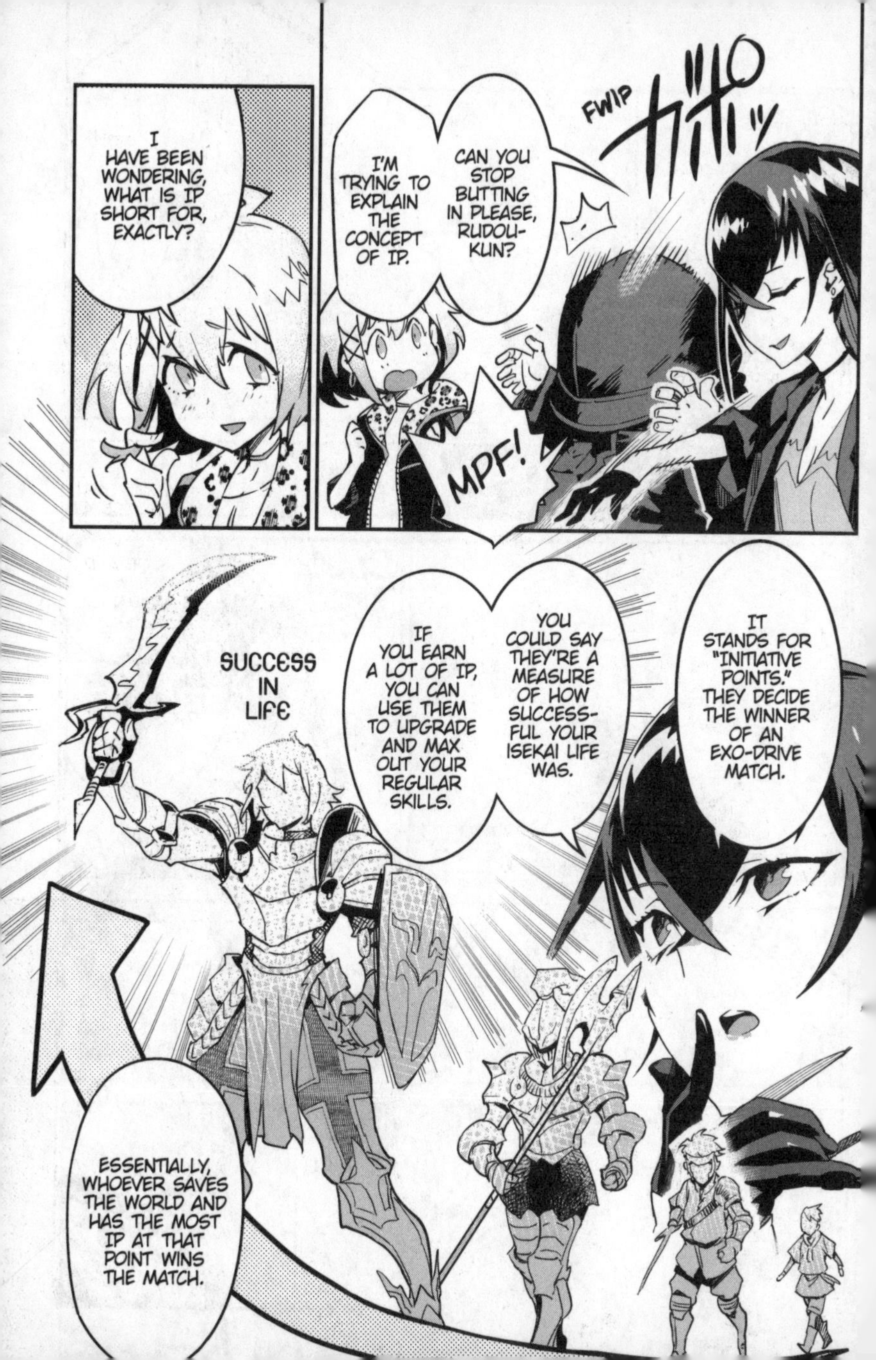
ガポッ
FWIP
CAN YOU STOP BUTTING IN PLEASE, RUDOU-KUN?
I'M TRYING TO EXPLAIN THE CONCEPT OF IP.
MPF!
I HAVE BEEN WONDERING, WHAT IS IP SHORT FOR, EXACTLY?
IT STANDS FOR "INITIATIVE POINTS." THEY DECIDE THE WINNER OF AN EXO-DRIVE MATCH.
YOU COULD SAY THEY'RE A MEASURE OF HOW SUCCESSFUL YOUR ISEKAI LIFE WAS.
IF YOU EARN A LOT OF IP, YOU CAN USE THEM TO UPGRADE AND MAX OUT YOUR REGULAR SKILLS.
SUCCESS IN LIFE
ESSENTIALLY, WHOEVER SAVES THE WORLD AND HAS THE MOST IP AT THAT POINT WINS THE MATCH.

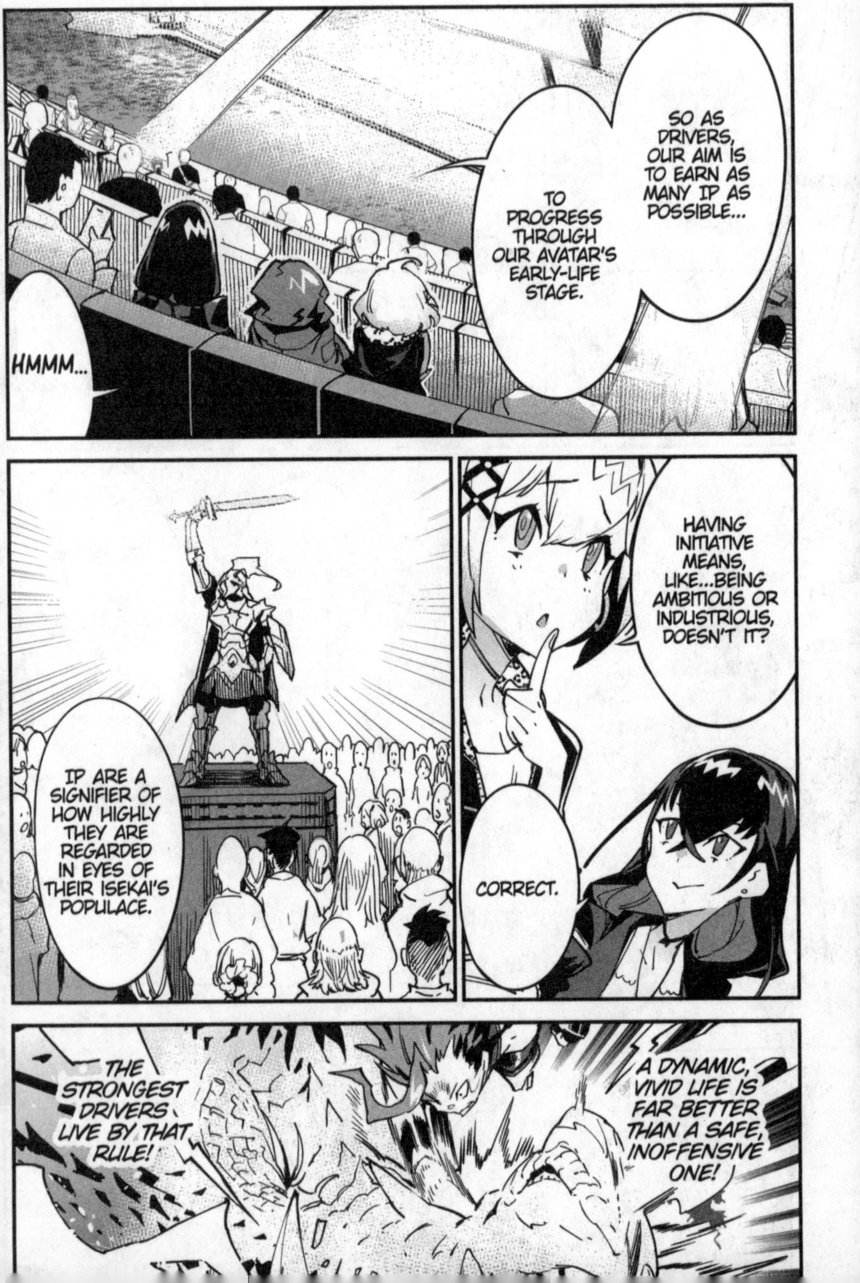
SO AS DRIVERS, OUR AIM IS TO EARN AS MANY IP AS POSSIBLE...
TO PROGRESS THROUGH OUR AVATAR'S EARLY-LIFE STAGE.
HMMM...
HAVING INITIATIVE MEANS, LIKE...BEING AMBITIOUS OR INDUSTRIOUS, DOESN'T IT?
CORRECT.
IP ARE A SIGNIFIER OF HOW HIGHLY THEY ARE REGARDED IN EYES OF THEIR ISEKAI'S POPULACE.
A DYNAMIC, VIVID LIFE IS FAR BETTER THAN A SAFE, INOFFENSIVE ONE!
THE STRONGEST DRIVERS LIVE BY THAT RULE!

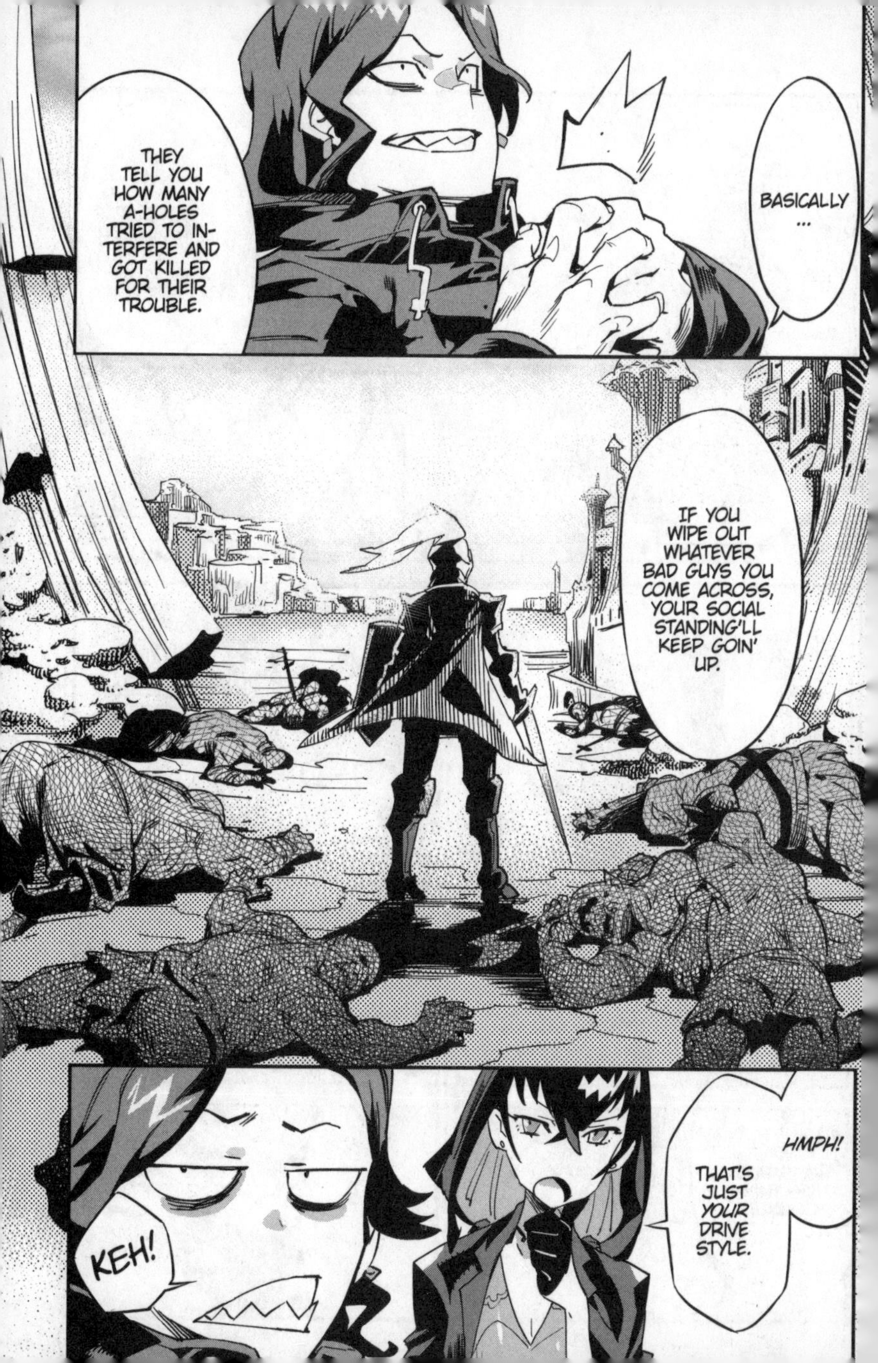
BASICALLY ...
THEY TELL YOU HOW MANY A-HOLES TRIED TO INTERFERE AND GOT KILLED FOR THEIR TROUBLE.
IF YOU WIPE OUT WHATEVER BAD GUYS YOU COME ACROSS, YOUR SOCIAL STANDING'LL KEEP GOIN' UP.
HMPH!
THAT'S JUST *YOUR* DRIVE STYLE.
KEH!

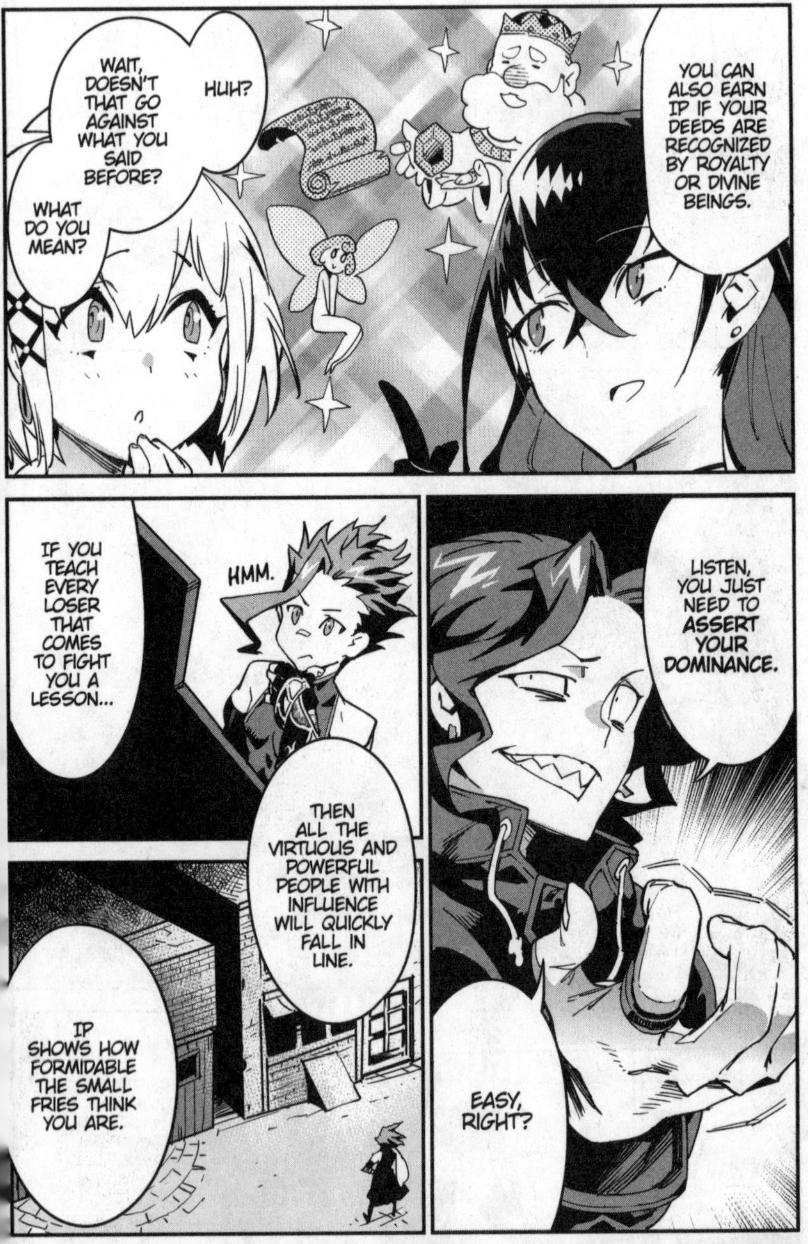
YOU CAN ALSO EARN IP IF YOUR DEEDS ARE RECOGNIZED BY ROYALTY OR DIVINE BEINGS.
HUH?
WAIT, DOESN'T THAT GO AGAINST WHAT YOU SAID BEFORE?
WHAT DO YOU MEAN?
LISTEN, YOU JUST NEED TO ASSERT YOUR DOMINANCE.
EASY, RIGHT?
HMM.
IF YOU TEACH EVERY LOSER THAT COMES TO FIGHT YOU A LESSON...
THEN ALL THE VIRTUOUS AND POWERFUL PEOPLE WITH INFLUENCE WILL QUICKLY FALL IN LINE.
IP SHOWS HOW FORMIDABLE THE SMALL FRIES THINK YOU ARE.

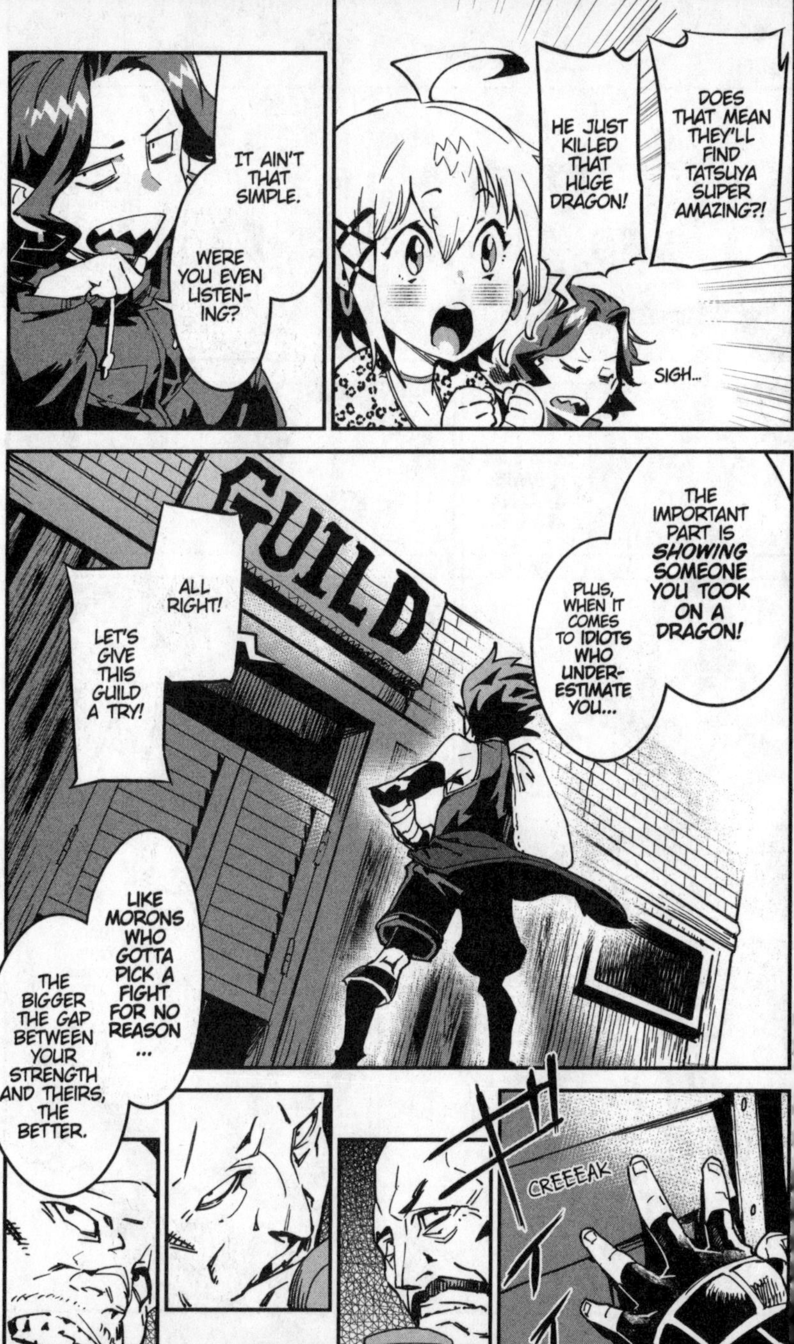
DOES THAT MEAN THEY'LL FIND TATSUYA SUPER AMAZING?!
HE JUST KILLED THAT HUGE DRAGON!
SIGH...
IT AIN'T THAT SIMPLE.
WERE YOU EVEN LISTEN-ING?
THE IMPORTANT PART IS *SHOWING* SOMEONE YOU TOOK ON A DRAGON!
PLUS, WHEN IT COMES TO IDIOTS WHO UNDER-ESTIMATE YOU...
GUILD
ALL RIGHT!
LET'S GIVE THIS GUILD A TRY!
LIKE MORONS WHO GOTTA PICK A FIGHT FOR NO REASON ...
THE BIGGER THE GAP BETWEEN YOUR STRENGTH AND THEIRS, THE BETTER.
CREEEAK

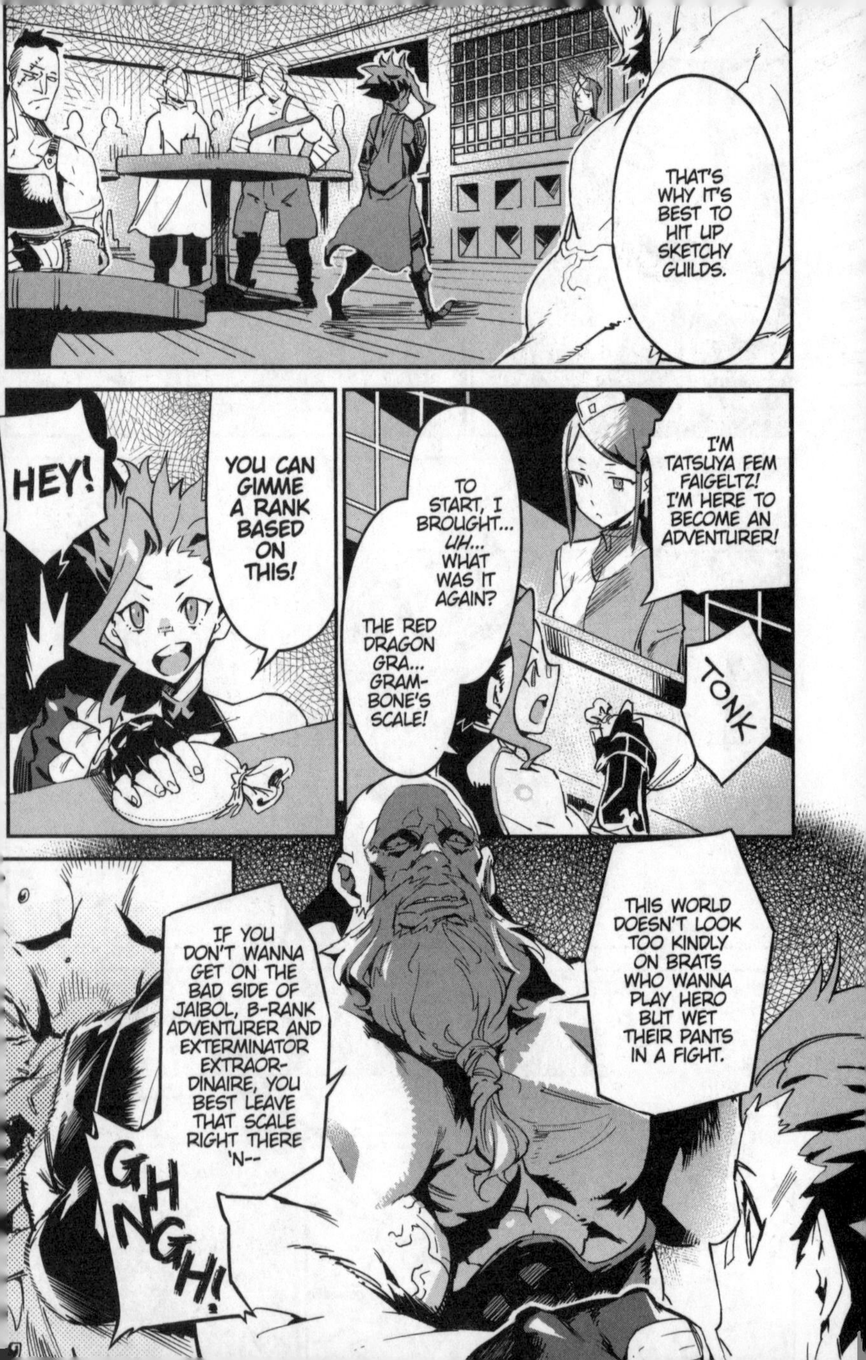
THAT'S WHY IT'S BEST TO HIT UP SKETCHY GUILDS.
I'M TATSUYA FEM FAIGELTZ! I'M HERE TO BECOME AN ADVENTURER!
TONK
TO START, I BROUGHT... UH... WHAT WAS IT AGAIN?
THE RED DRAGON GRA... GRAMBONE'S SCALE!
YOU CAN GIMME A RANK BASED ON THIS!
HEY!
THIS WORLD DOESN'T LOOK TOO KINDLY ON BRATS WHO WANNA PLAY HERO BUT WET THEIR PANTS IN A FIGHT.
IF YOU DON'T WANNA GET ON THE BAD SIDE OF JAIBOL, B-RANK ADVENTURER AND EXTERMINATOR EXTRAOR-DINAIRE, YOU BEST LEAVE THAT SCALE RIGHT THERE 'N--
GHNGH!

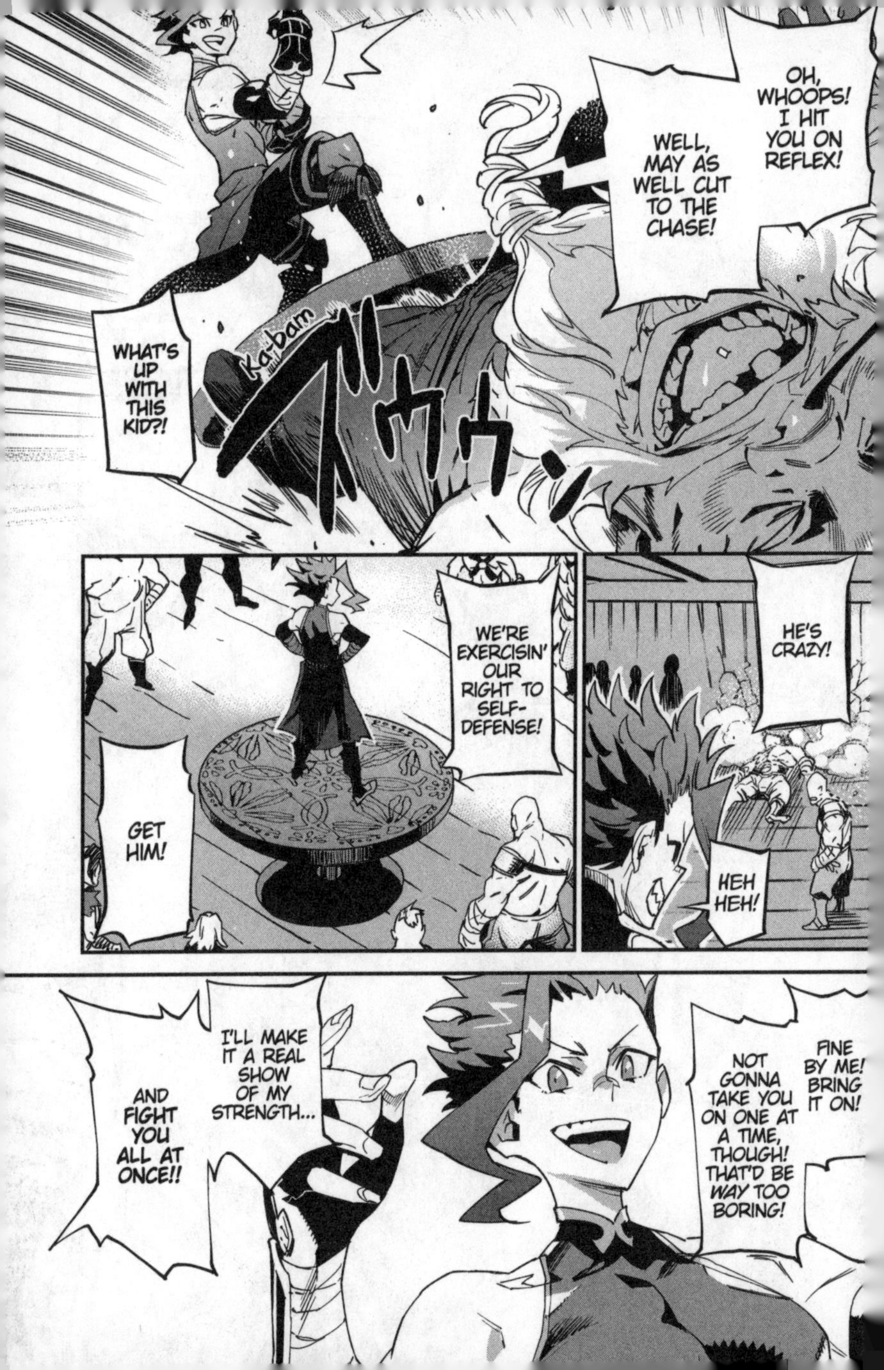
OH, WHOOPS! I HIT YOU ON REFLEX!
WELL, MAY AS WELL CUT TO THE CHASE!
Ka-bam
ズウウン
WHAT'S UP WITH THIS KID?!
HE'S CRAZY!
HEH HEH!
WE'RE EXERCISIN' OUR RIGHT TO SELF-DEFENSE!
GET HIM!
FINE BY ME! BRING IT ON!
NOT GONNA TAKE YOU ON ONE AT A TIME, THOUGH! THAT'D BE WAY TOO BORING!
I'LL MAKE IT A REAL SHOW OF MY STRENGTH...
AND FIGHT YOU ALL AT ONCE!!

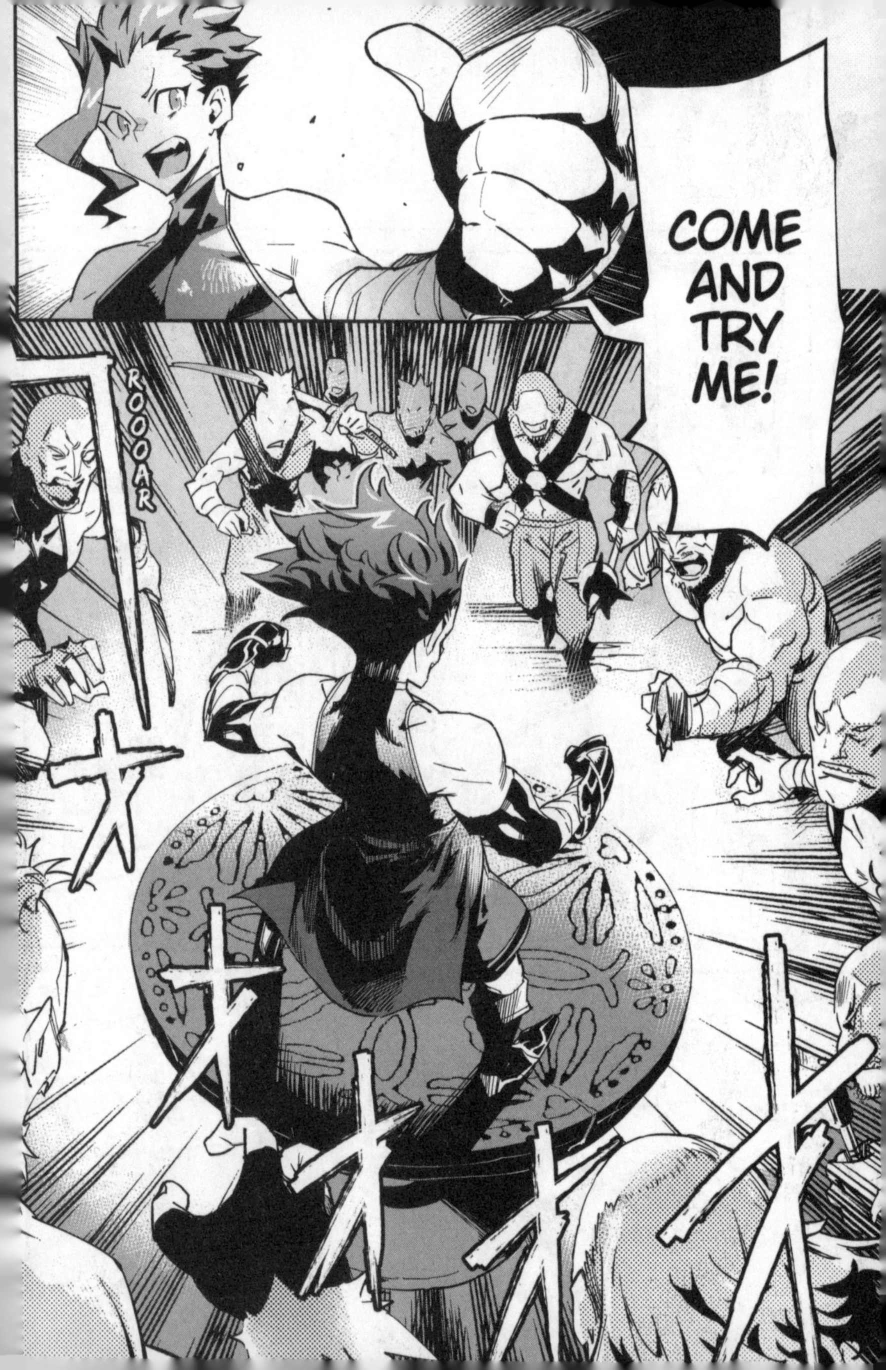
COME AND TRY ME!
ROOOAR

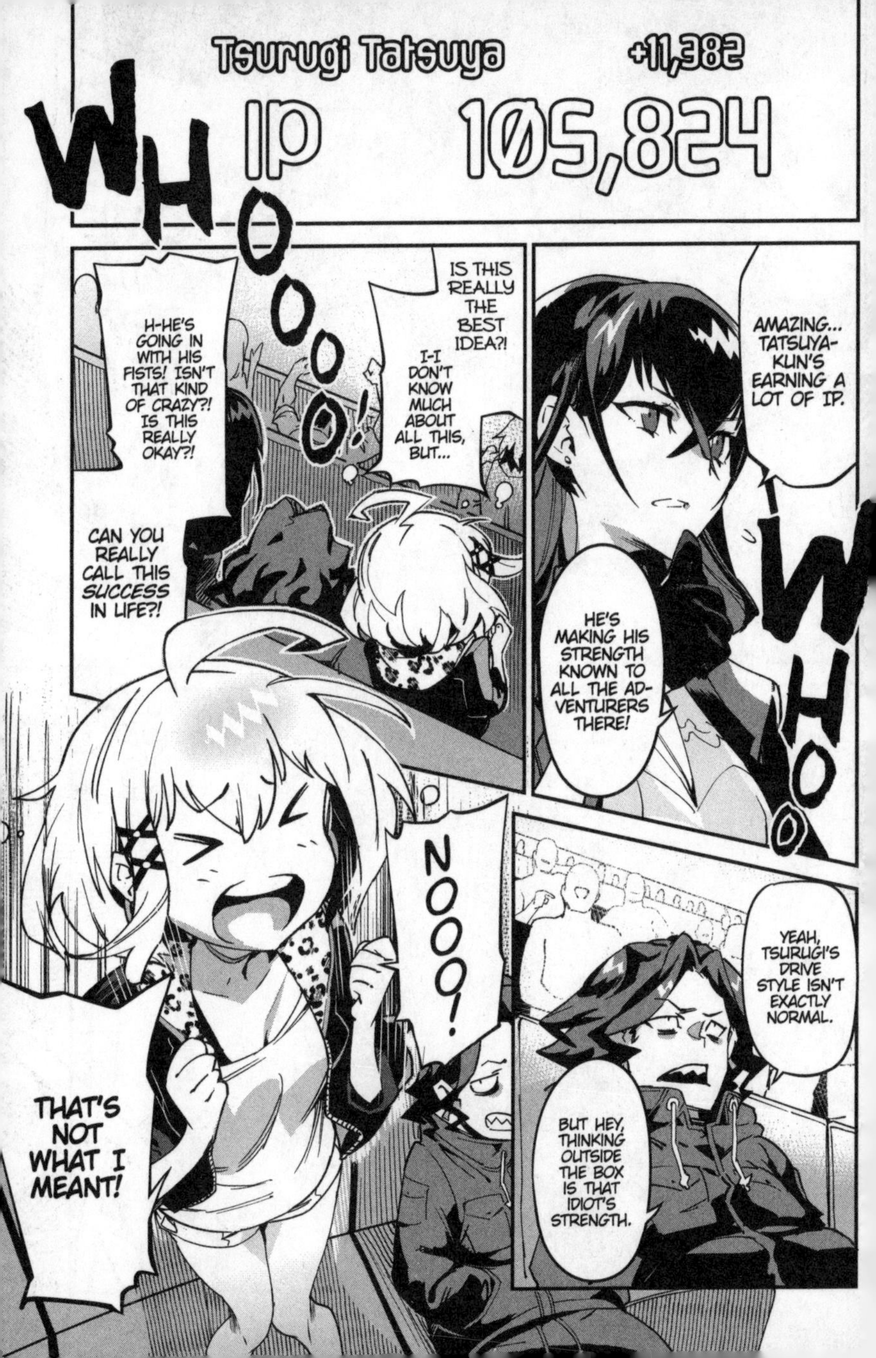

Tsurugi Tatsuya +11,382
IP 105,824
WHOOOOO!
AMAZING... TATSUYA-KUN'S EARNING A LOT OF IP.
HE'S MAKING HIS STRENGTH KNOWN TO ALL THE ADVENTURERS THERE!
WHOO
IS THIS REALLY THE BEST IDEA?!
I-I DON'T KNOW MUCH ABOUT ALL THIS, BUT...
H-HE'S GOING IN WITH HIS FISTS! ISN'T THAT KIND OF CRAZY?! IS THIS REALLY OKAY?!
CAN YOU REALLY CALL THIS SUCCESS IN LIFE?!
YEAH, TSURUGI'S DRIVE STYLE ISN'T EXACTLY NORMAL.
BUT HEY, THINKING OUTSIDE THE BOX IS THAT IDIOT'S STRENGTH.
NOOOO!
THAT'S NOT WHAT I MEANT!

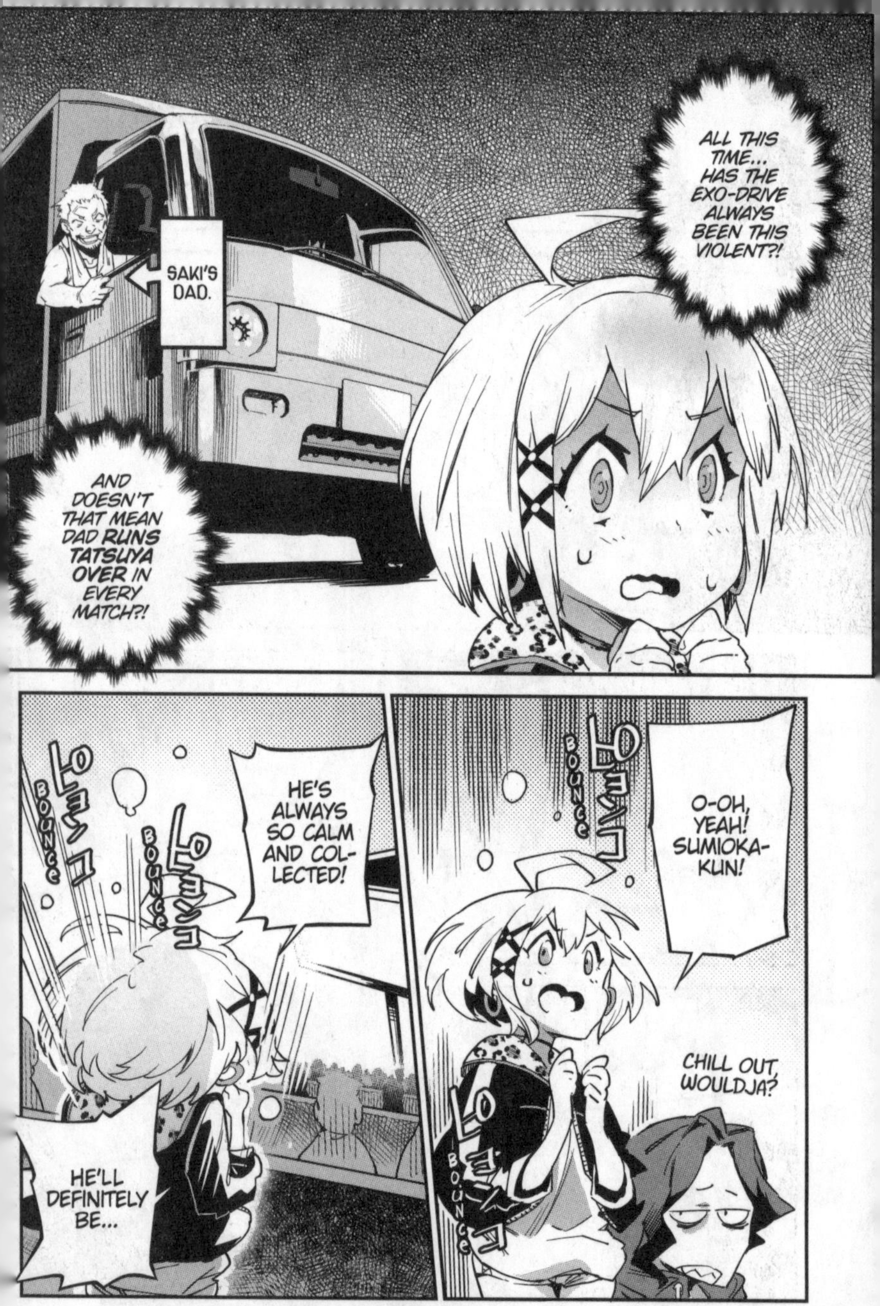
ALL THIS TIME... HAS THE EXO-DRIVE ALWAYS BEEN THIS VIOLENT?!
SAKI'S DAD.
AND DOESN'T THAT MEAN DAD **RUNS TATSUYA OVER** IN EVERY MATCH?!
BOUNCE
O-OH, YEAH! SUMIOKA-KUN!
BOUNCE
CHILL OUT, WOULDJA?
BOUNCE
HE'S ALWAYS SO CALM AND COL-LECTED!
BOUNCE
HE'LL DEFINITELY BE...

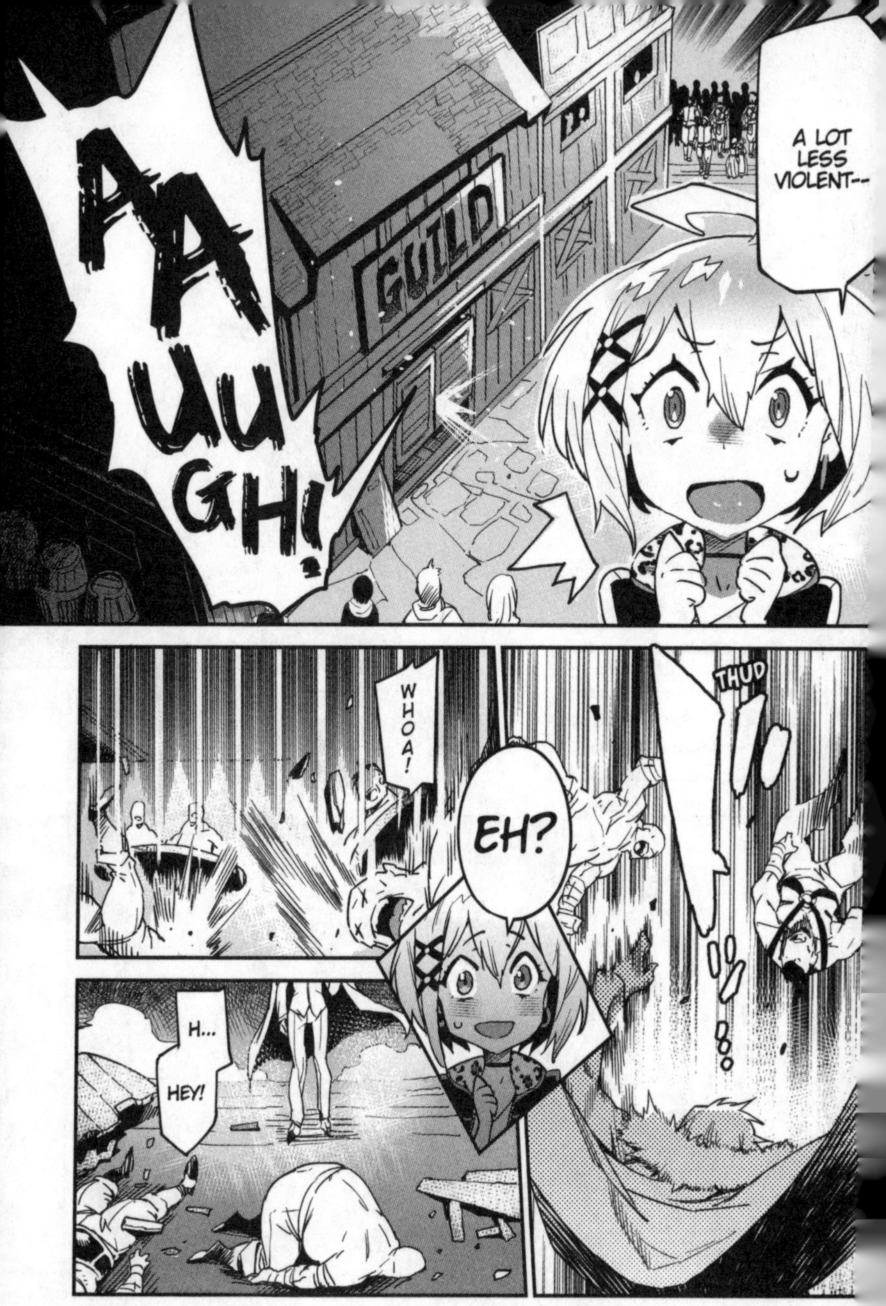
A LOT LESS VIOLENT--
AAUUGH!
THUD
EH?
WHOA!
H... HEY!

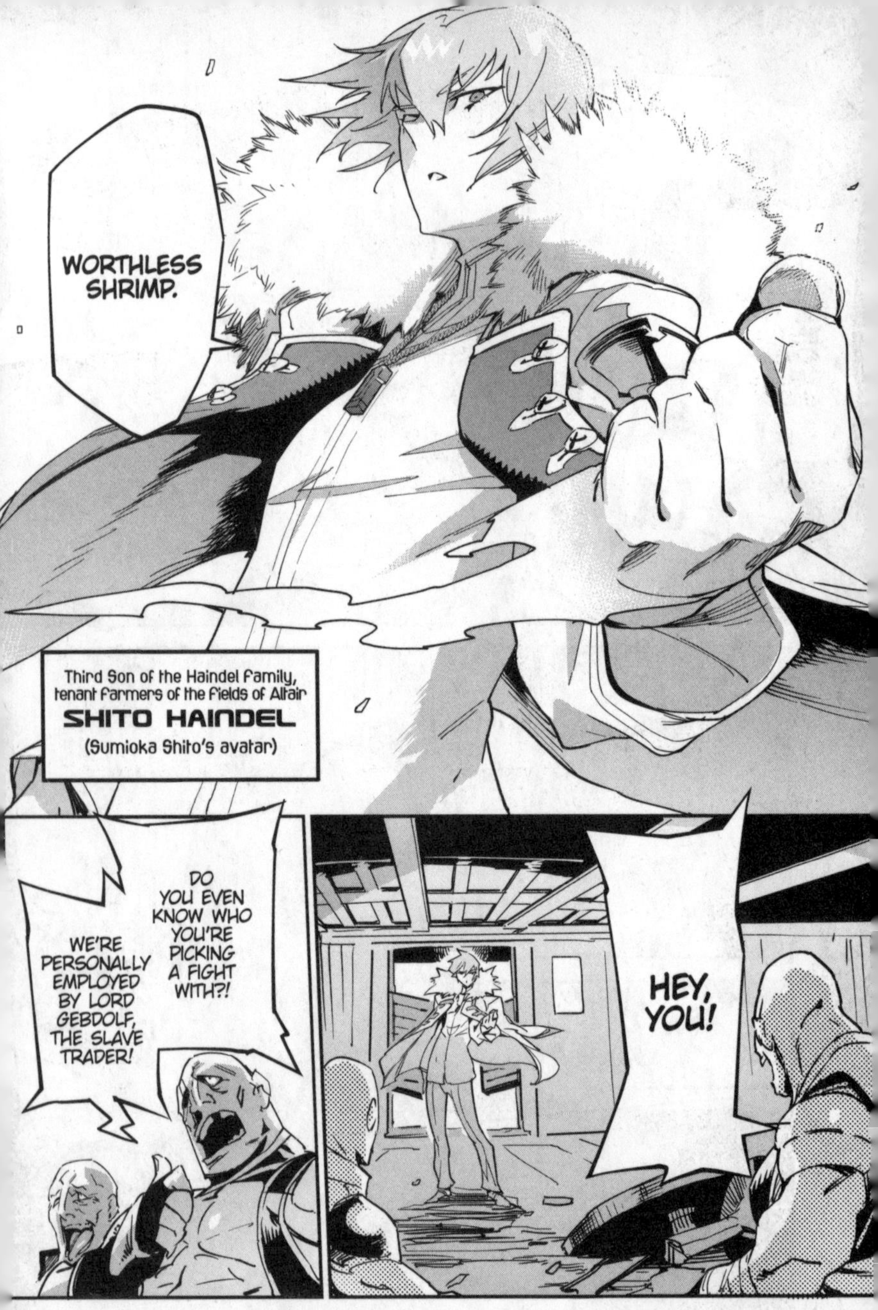
WORTHLESS SHRIMP.
Third Son of the Haindel family, tenant farmers of the fields of Altair
SHITO HAINDEL
(Sumioka Shito's avatar)
HEY, YOU!
DO YOU EVEN KNOW WHO YOU'RE PICKING A FIGHT WITH?!
WE'RE PERSONALLY EMPLOYED BY LORD GEBDOLF, THE SLAVE TRADER!

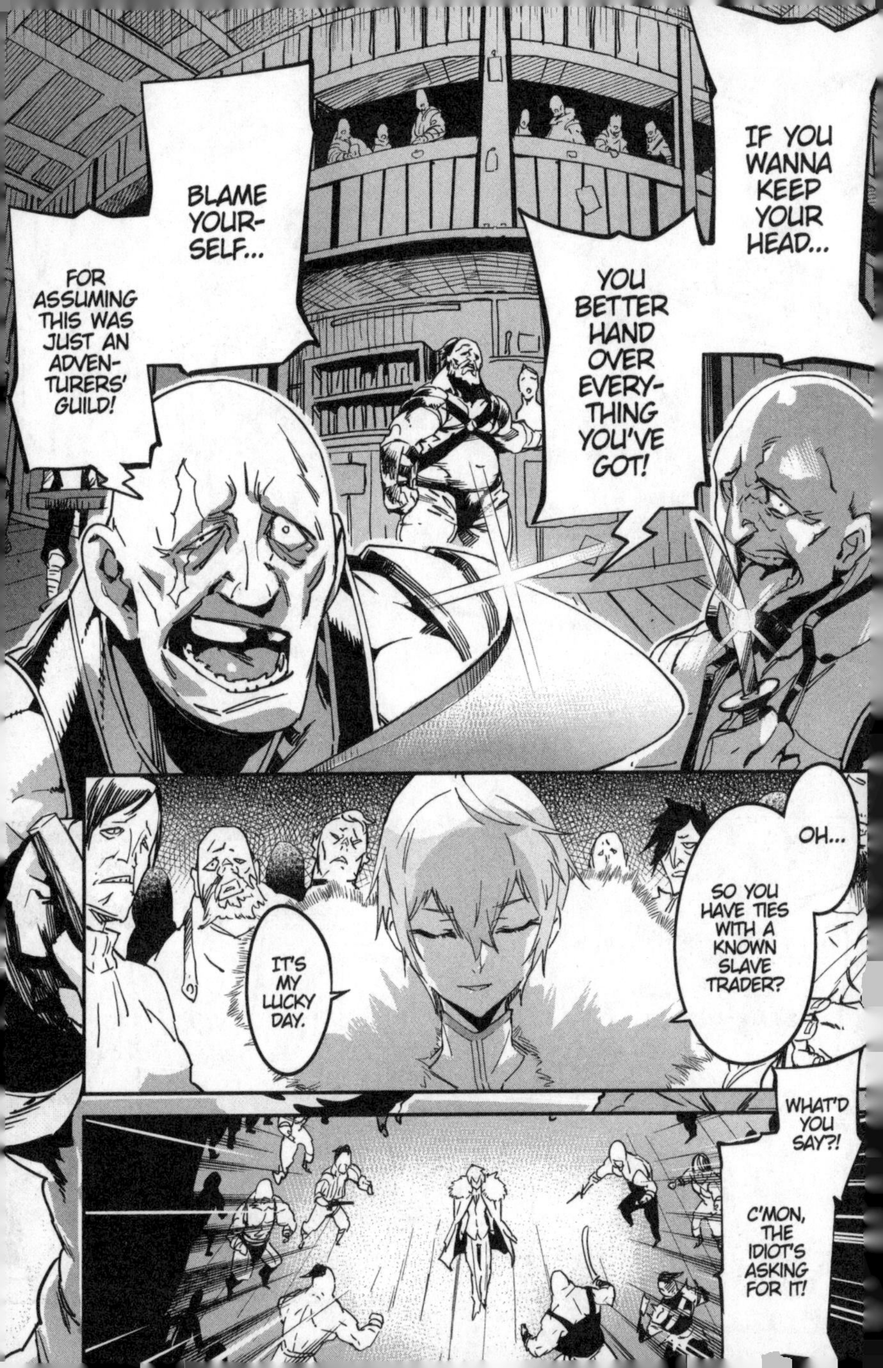
IF YOU WANNA KEEP YOUR HEAD...
YOU BETTER HAND OVER EVERYTHING YOU'VE GOT!
BLAME YOURSELF...
FOR ASSUMING THIS WAS JUST AN ADVENTURERS' GUILD!
OH...
SO YOU HAVE TIES WITH A KNOWN SLAVE TRADER?
IT'S MY LUCKY DAY.
WHAT'D YOU SAY?!
C'MON, THE IDIOT'S ASKING FOR IT!

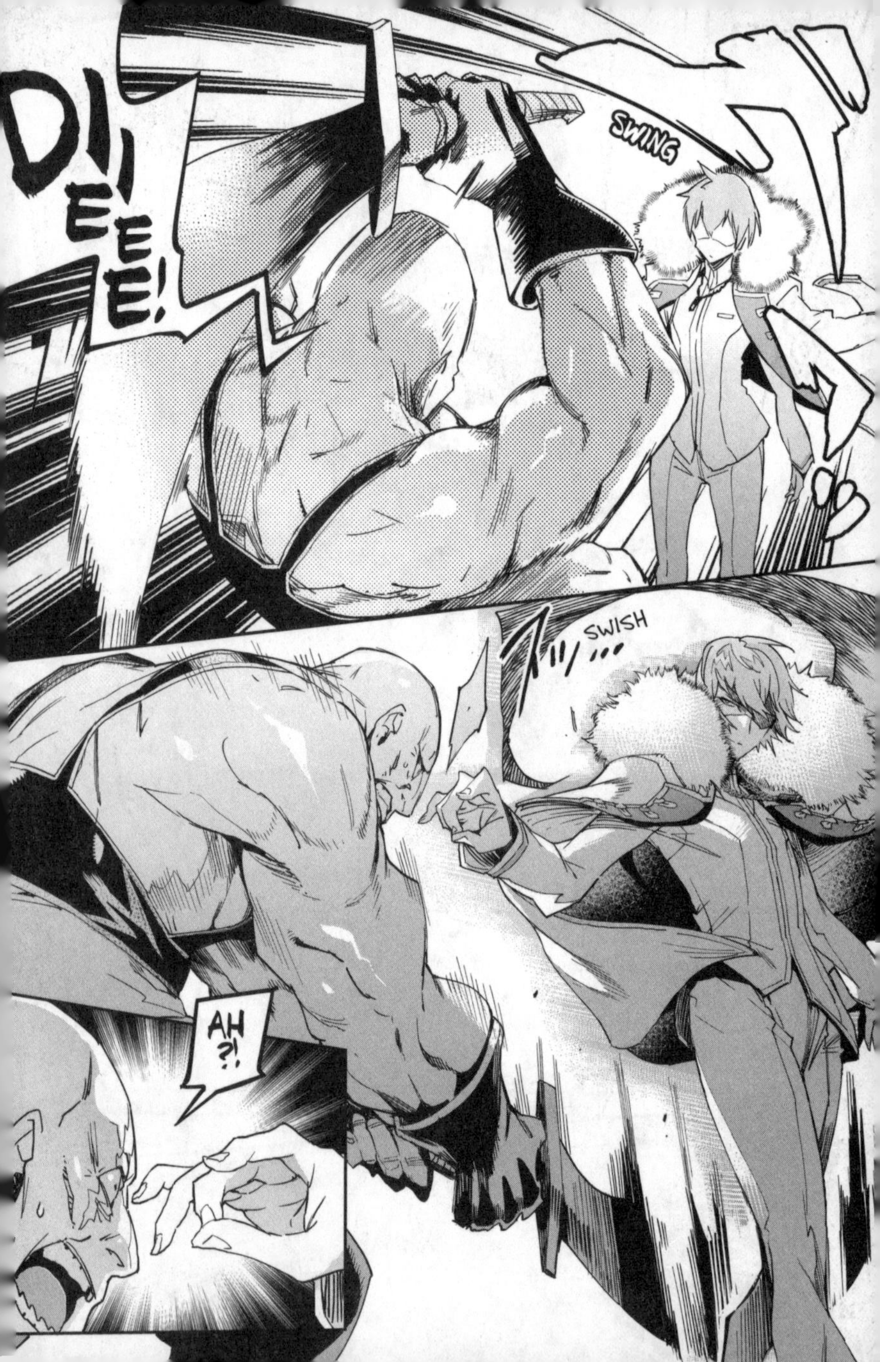
SWING
DIEEEE!
SWISH
AH?!

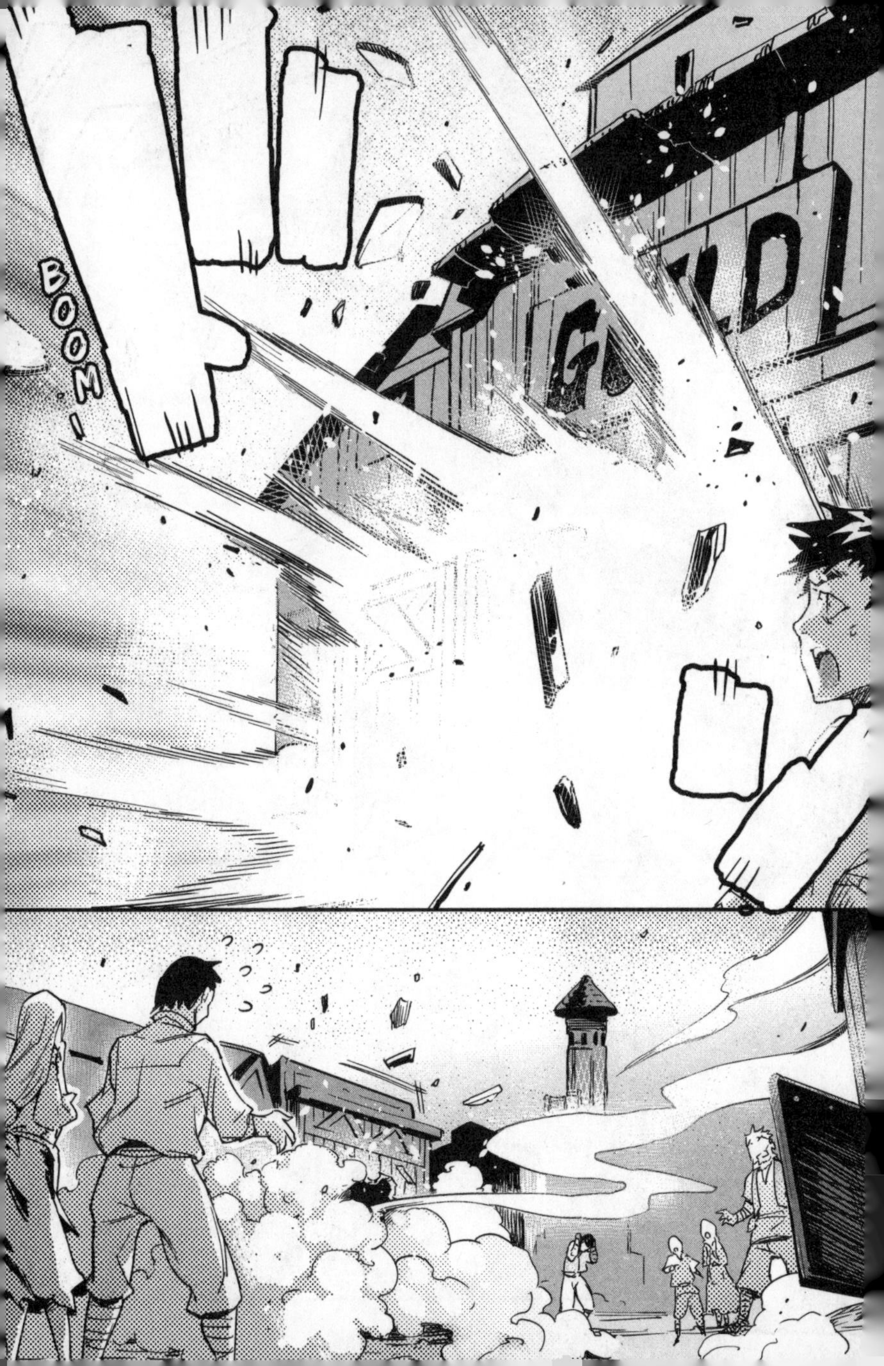
BOOM!

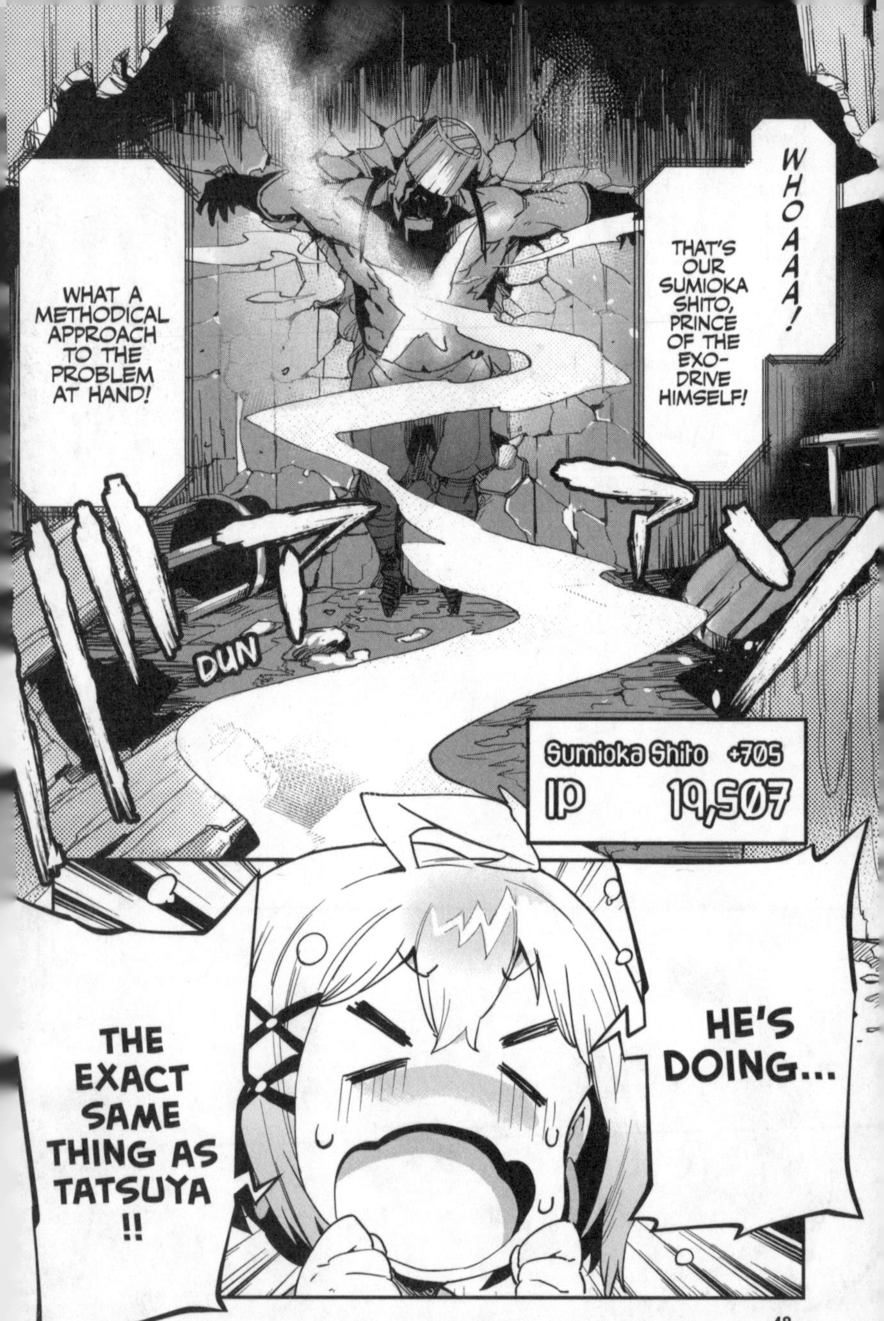
WHOAAAA!
THAT'S OUR SUMIOKA SHITO, PRINCE OF THE EXO-DRIVE HIMSELF!
WHAT A METHODICAL APPROACH TO THE PROBLEM AT HAND!
DUN
Sumioka Shito +705
IP 19,507
HE'S DOING...
THE EXACT SAME THING AS TATSUYA!!

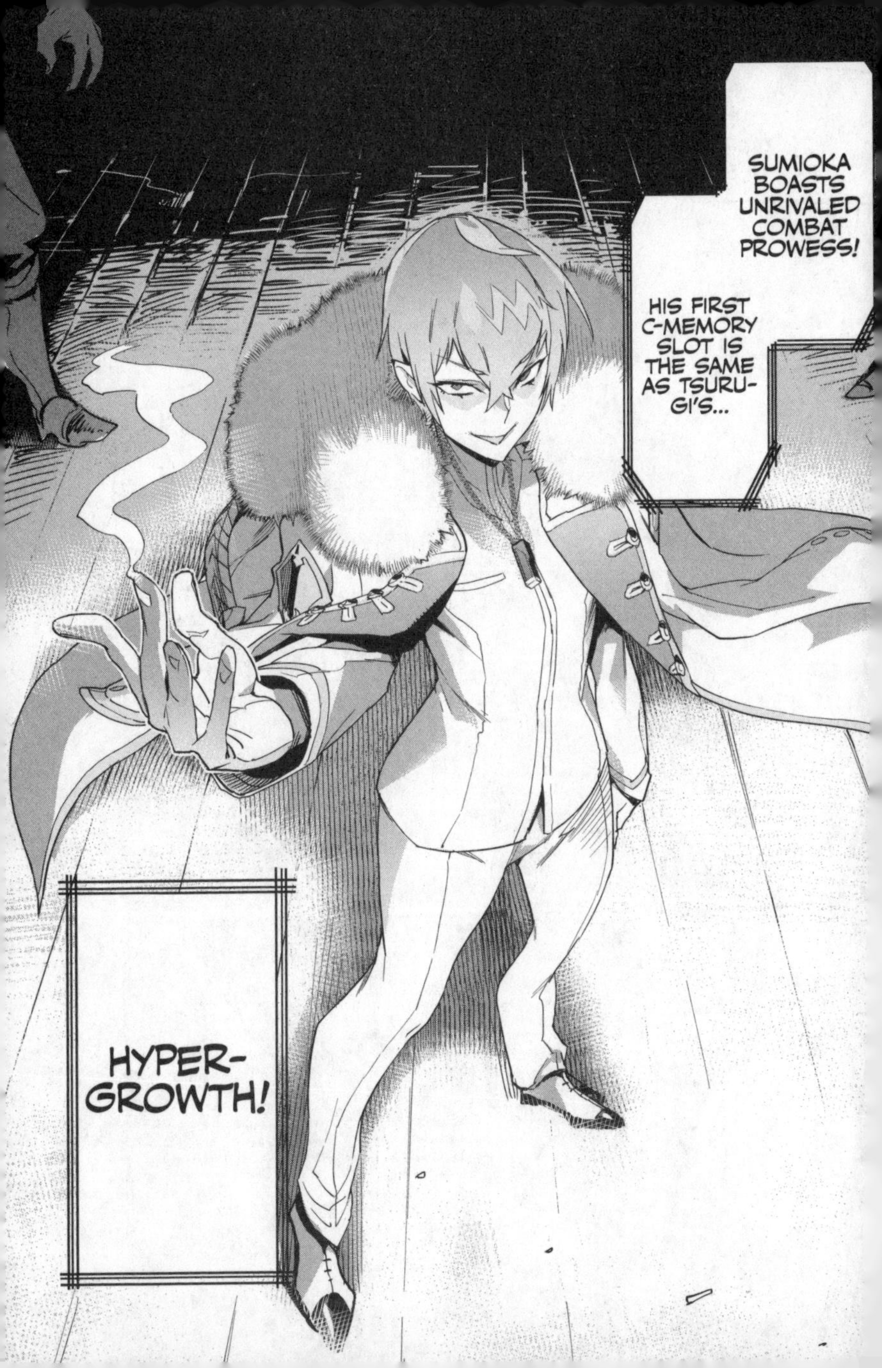
SUMIOKA BOASTS UNRIVALED COMBAT PROWESS!
HIS FIRST C-MEMORY SLOT IS THE SAME AS TSURU-GI'S...
HYPER-GROWTH!

INFORMATION BANK C-MEMORY ①

[HYPER-GROWTH]

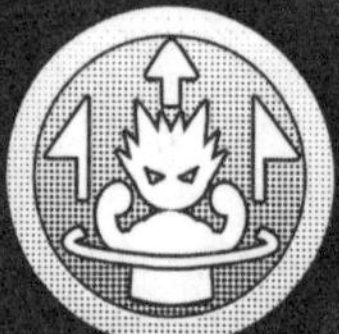

Amplifies IP in proportion to the number of experience points the user earns while in another world, while also drastically amplifying the growth of combat-based skills. Additionally, removes limits on combat skill upgrades and high-tier skill creation, although this is restricted to combat skill branches only. With this single C-memory, becoming the strongest in the Drive world is easy. Since it's possible to gain an advantage against your opponent with Hyper-Growth alone, even Exo-Drive beginners can use it to great effect, while veteran Drivers can easily combine it with other cheat skills to employ advanced tactics. It's a simple but powerful C-memory. Along with Hyper-Knowledge and Hyper-Comms, it's one of the three basic hyper-type cheat skills. A chief user of this skill is Tsurugi Tatsuya.

[ALMIGHTY]

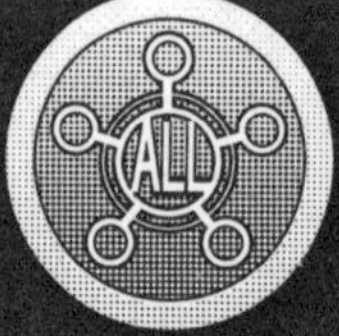
ALL

Ignores a user's original skill tree, allowing them to learn any regular skill. Since the aptitudes of isekai avatars in the Drive are randomly generated, the types of learnable skills accessible and their caps are, to an extent, set from rebirth. Luckily, this C-memory can remove the limit on the number of learnable skills available to Drivers (though *not*, it should be noted, the upper limits of those skills). Whenever experience points are earned using those skills, their levels rise regardless of the originally set aptitude. Additionally, in the Drive worlds, high-tier skills can only be unlocked when the upper limit of a skill is reached *and* all its corresponding skills have been acquired. However, this C-memory can unlock high-tier skills directly without having to acquire any of the preceding lower-tier skills, so long as a Driver has reached the necessary IP quantity.

[E-RANKER]

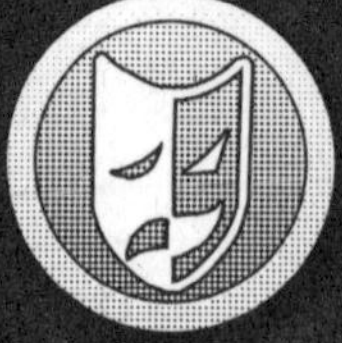

Changes the perception of the Drive world's populace so that they always underestimate and mock the user's true ability. In typical Drives, as reputation and combat ability increase, and a player's true strength is made known, it becomes more likely that any targets fought to gain IP will choose to flee, though this can be affected slightly by the individual Drive world's public order. As a result, picking fights in the opening stages of the Drive can prove problematic. However, so long as this C-memory is in effect, a player's outward appearance as a weakling defeating stronger opponents is maintained, even as far as endgame, and the IP multiplier bonus from maintaining the gap between this outward appearance and a player's true strength will remain constant. On the other hand, although indications of a player's actual skill rank are hidden from other Drivers, Drivers' perceptions remain unaltered, so there is a possibility that opponents may assume E-Ranker is in play. Therefore it is necessary to present one's rank as inherently lower than it truly is.

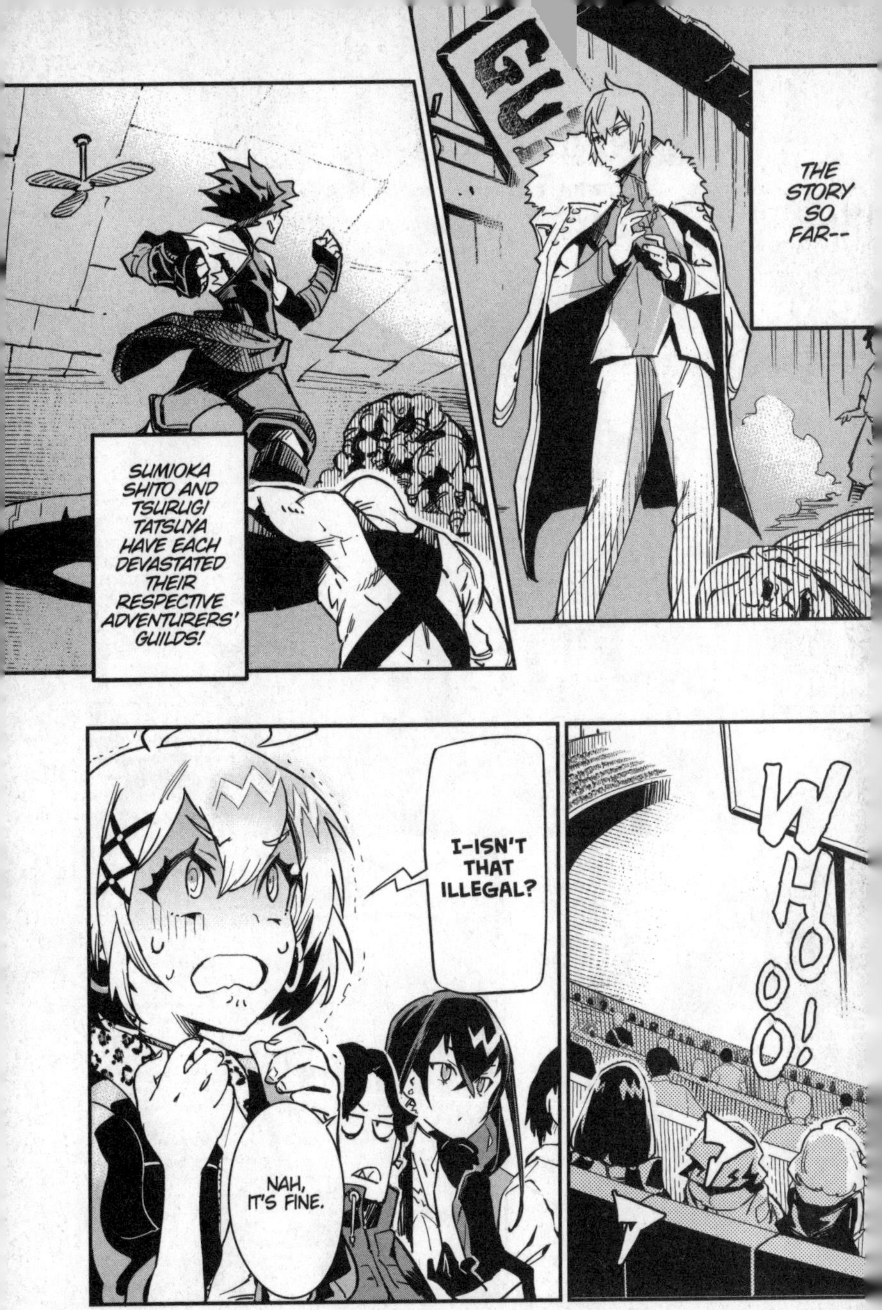
THE STORY SO FAR--
GU
SUMIOKA SHITO AND TSURUGI TATSUYA HAVE EACH DEVASTATED THEIR RESPECTIVE ADVENTURERS' GUILDS!
WHOOOO!
I-ISN'T THAT ILLEGAL?
NAH, IT'S FINE.

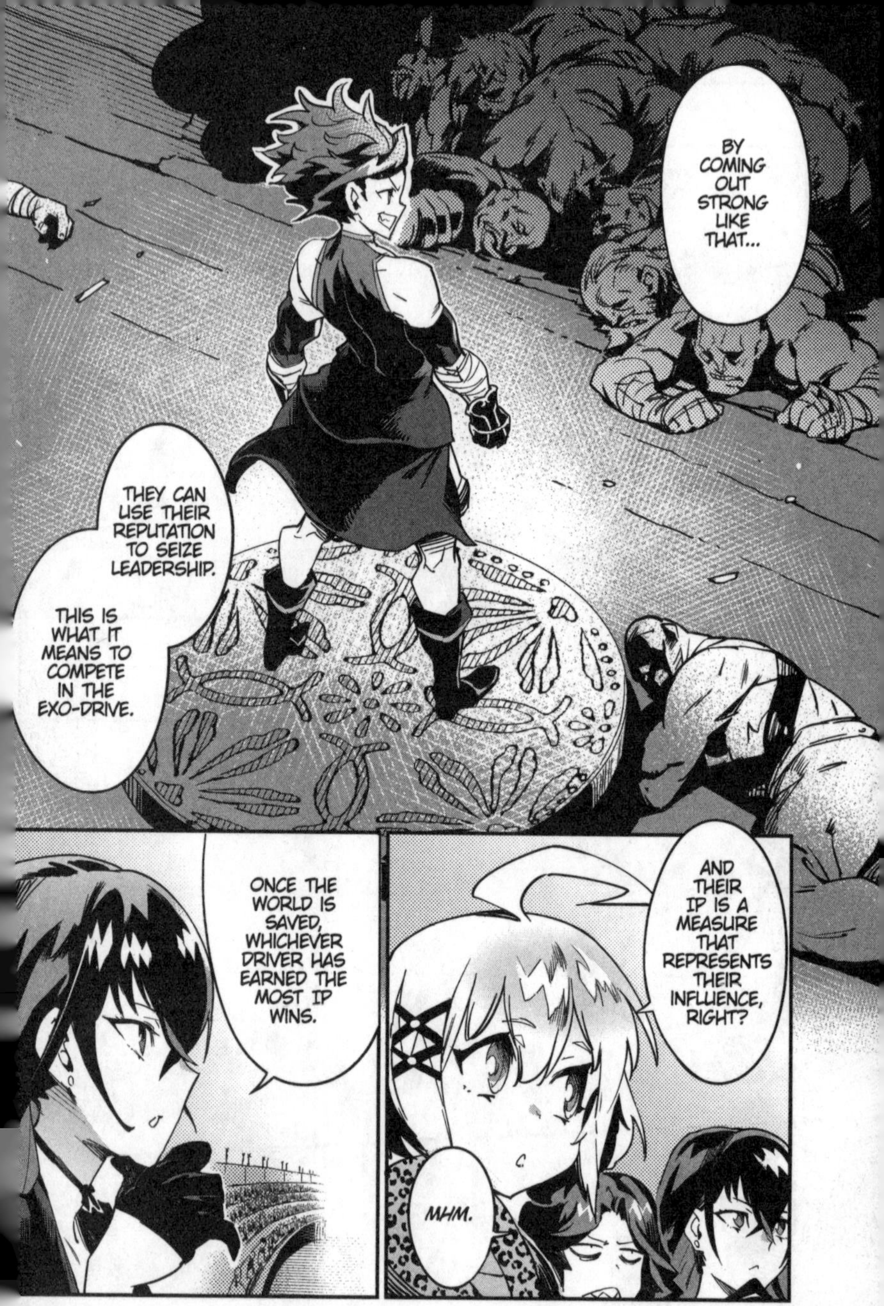
BY COMING OUT STRONG LIKE THAT...
THEY CAN USE THEIR REPUTATION TO SEIZE LEADERSHIP.
THIS IS WHAT IT MEANS TO COMPETE IN THE EXO-DRIVE.
AND THEIR IP IS A MEASURE THAT REPRESENTS THEIR INFLUENCE, RIGHT?
MHM.
ONCE THE WORLD IS SAVED, WHICHEVER DRIVER HAS EARNED THE MOST IP WINS.

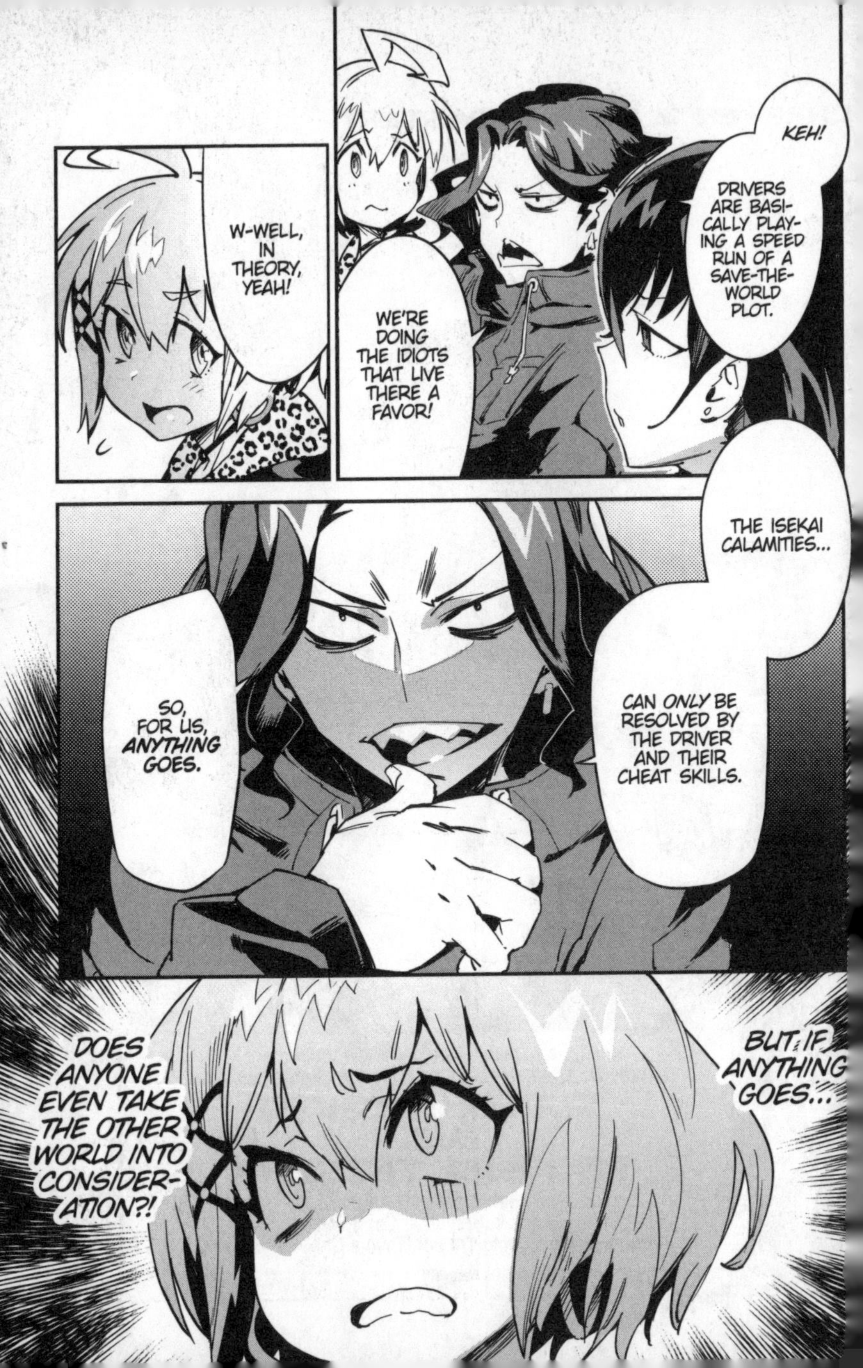
KEH!
DRIVERS ARE BASICALLY PLAYING A SPEED RUN OF A SAVE-THE-WORLD PLOT.
WE'RE DOING THE IDIOTS THAT LIVE THERE A FAVOR!
W-WELL, IN THEORY, YEAH!
THE ISEKAI CALAMITIES...
CAN *ONLY* BE RESOLVED BY THE DRIVER AND THEIR CHEAT SKILLS.
SO, FOR US, **ANYTHING** GOES.
BUT IF ANYTHING GOES...
DOES ANYONE EVEN TAKE THE OTHER WORLD INTO CONSIDERATION?!

CHAPTER 2 [HAREM MASTER]

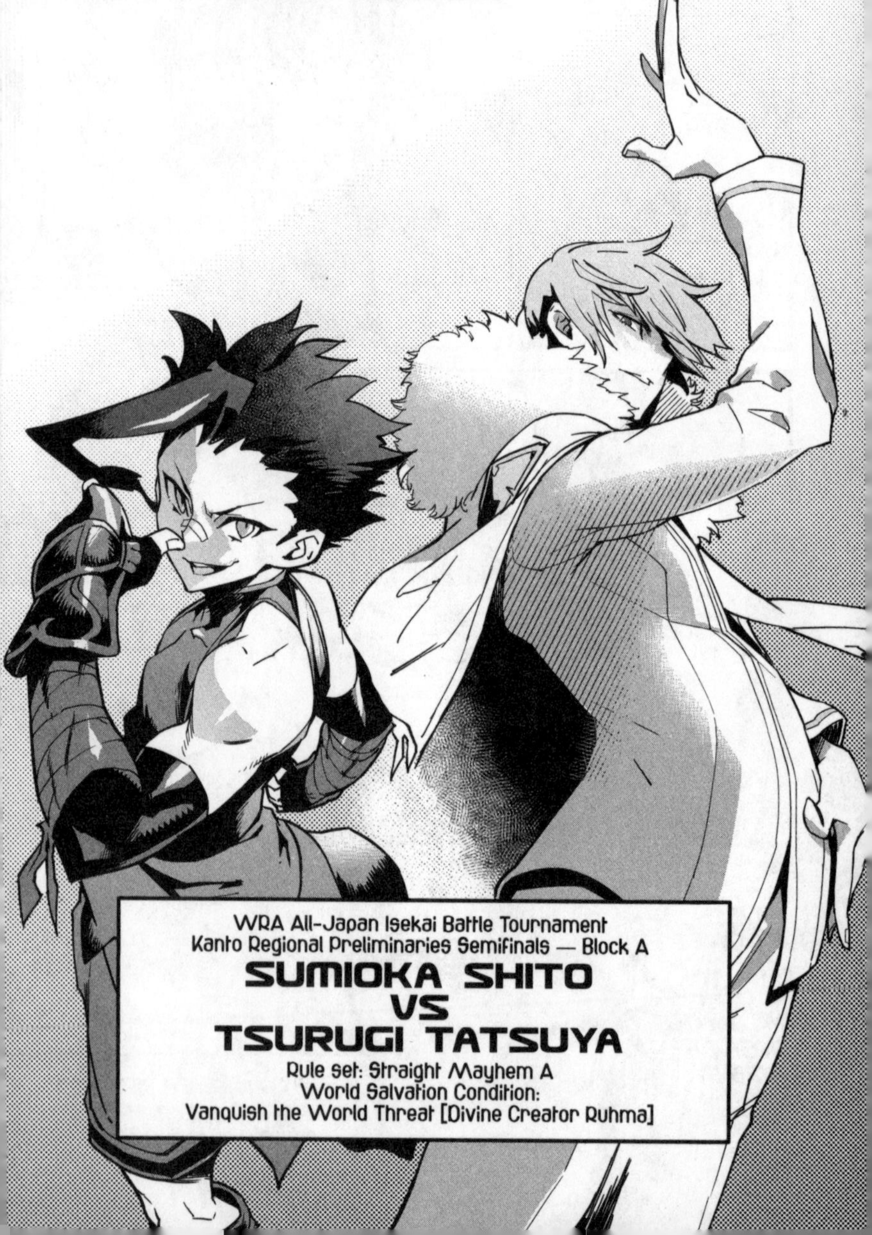

WRA All-Japan Isekai Battle Tournament
Kanto Regional Preliminaries Semifinals — Block A
SUMIOKA SHITO
VS
TSURUGI TATSUYA
Rule set: Straight Mayhem A
World Salvation Condition:
Vanquish the World Threat [Divine Creator Ruhma]

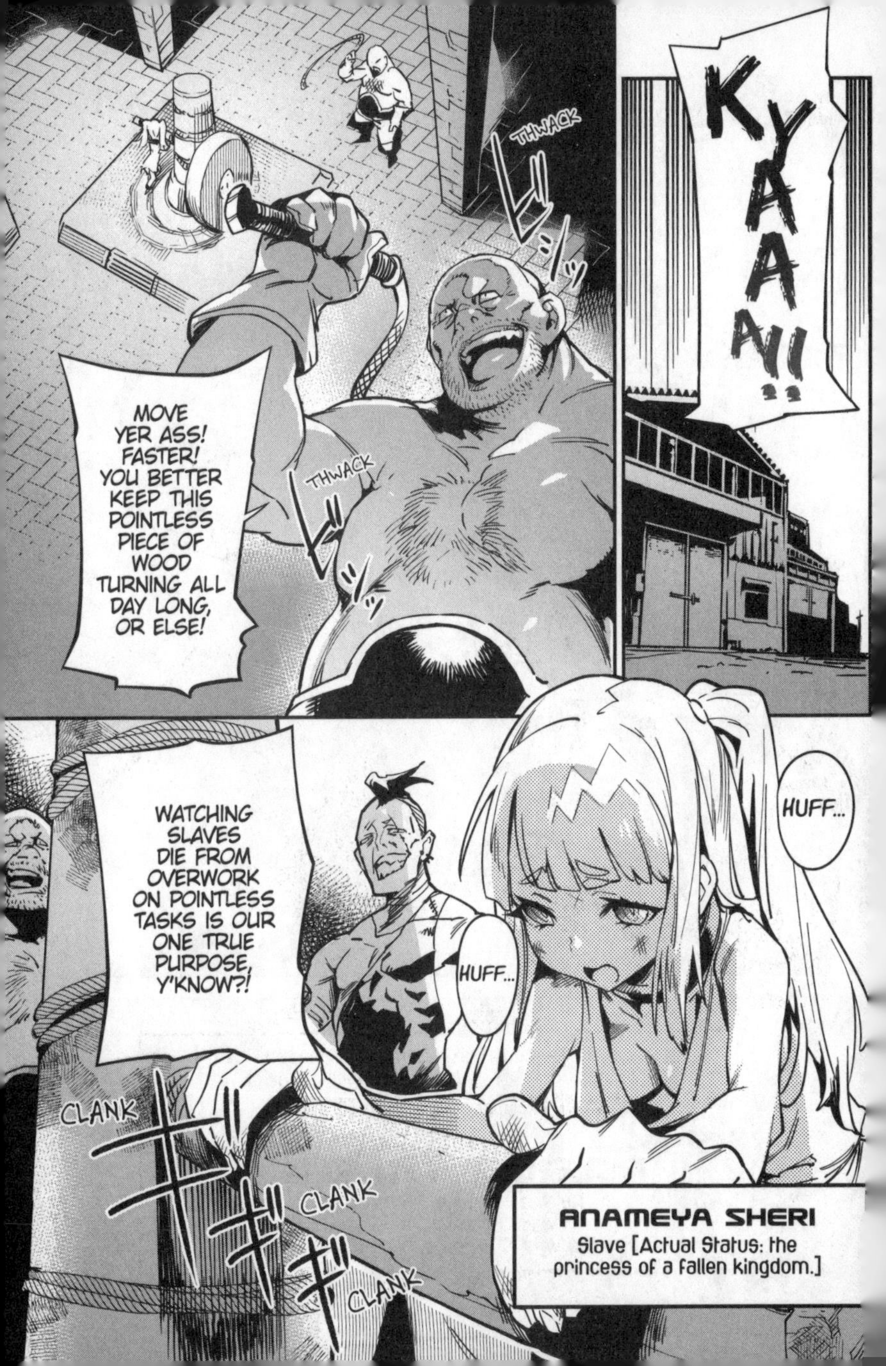
KYAAAN!!
THWACK
MOVE YER ASS! FASTER! YOU BETTER KEEP THIS POINTLESS PIECE OF WOOD TURNING ALL DAY LONG, OR ELSE!
THWACK
HUFF...
WATCHING SLAVES DIE FROM OVERWORK ON POINTLESS TASKS IS OUR ONE TRUE PURPOSE, Y'KNOW?!
HUFF...
CLANK
CLANK
CLANK
ANAMEYA SHERI
Slave [Actual Status: the princess of a fallen kingdom.]

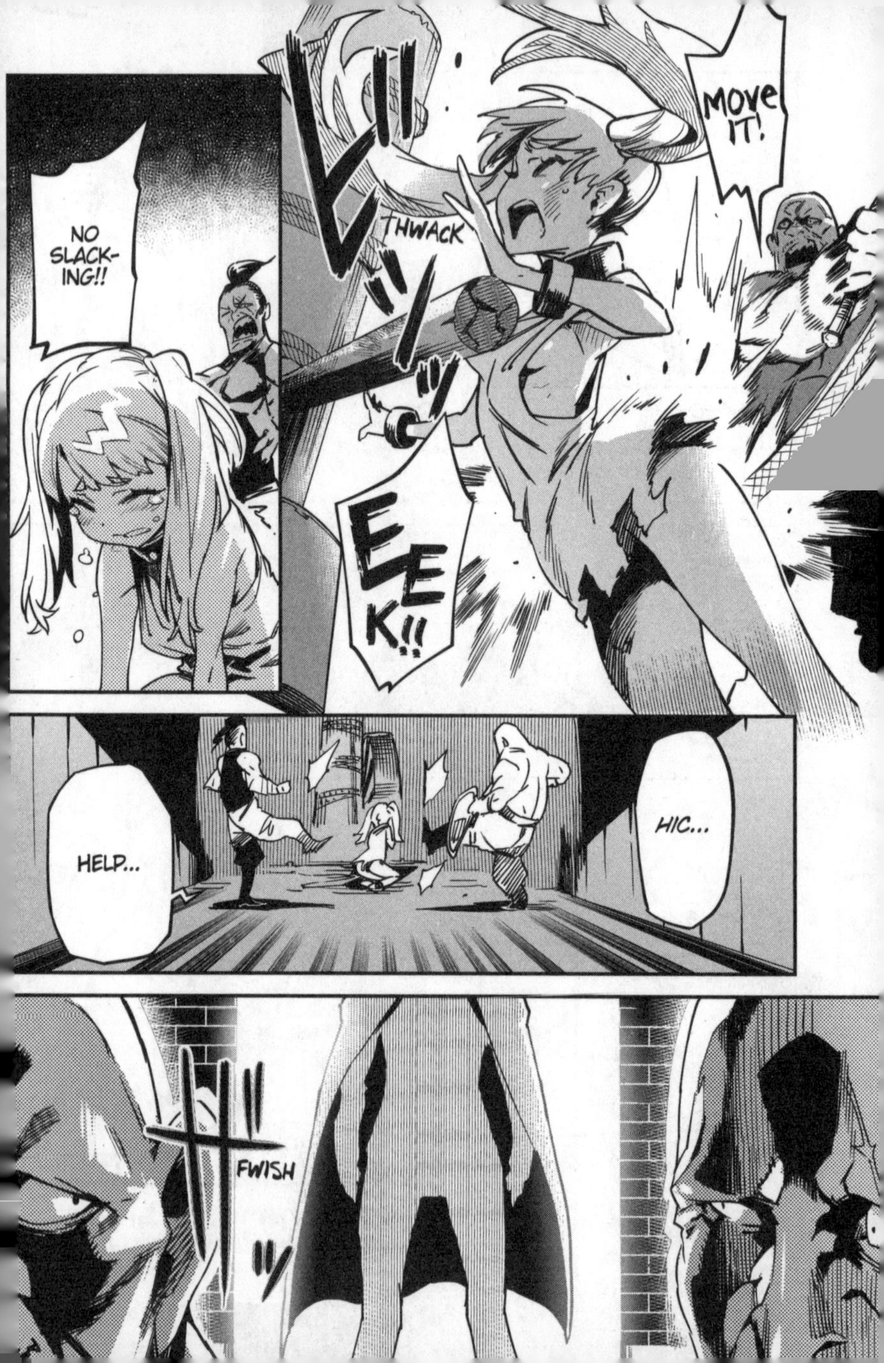
MOVE IT!
THWACK
EEEK!!
NO SLACK-ING!!
HIC...
HELP...
FWISH

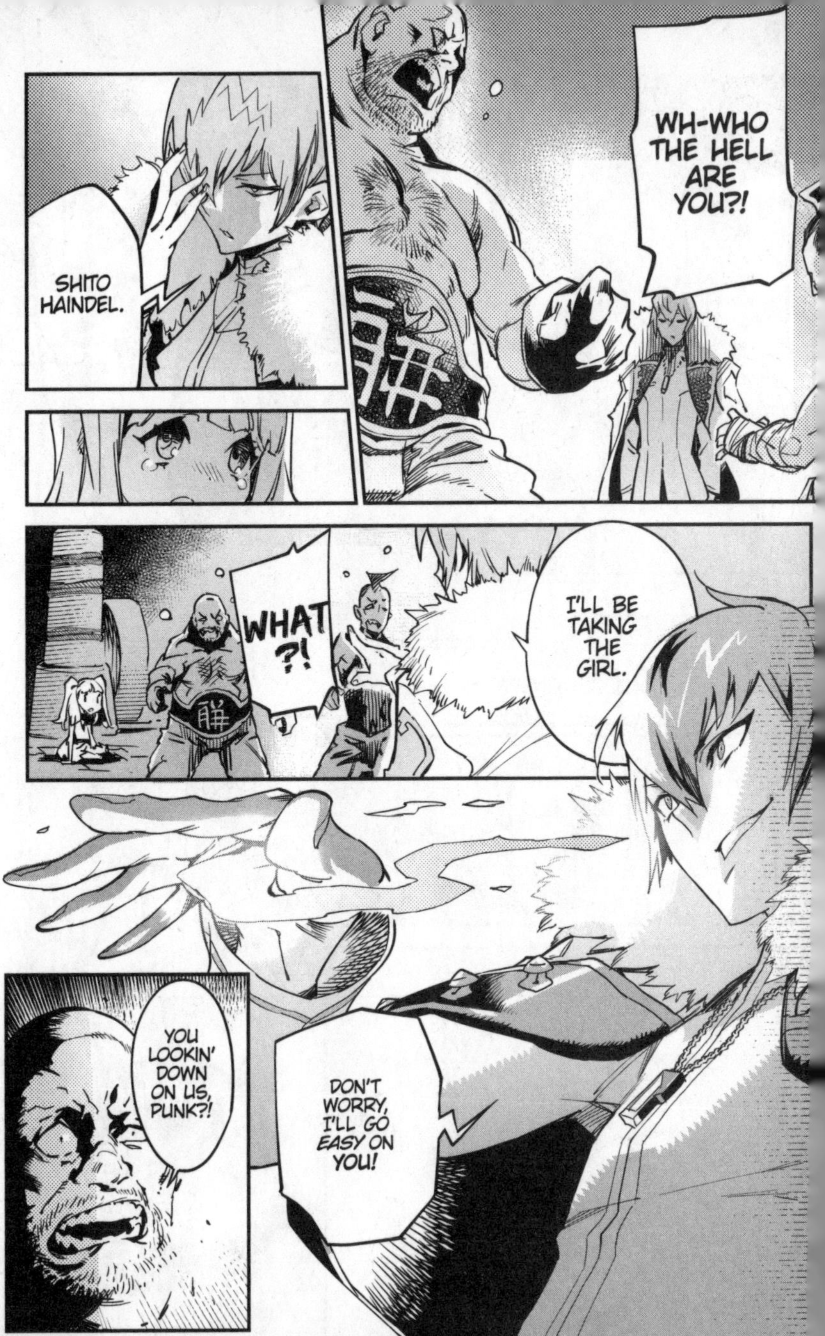
WH-WHO THE HELL ARE YOU?!
SHITO HAINDEL.
I'LL BE TAKING THE GIRL.
WHAT ?!
DON'T WORRY, I'LL GO *EASY* ON YOU!
YOU LOOKIN' DOWN ON US, PUNK?!

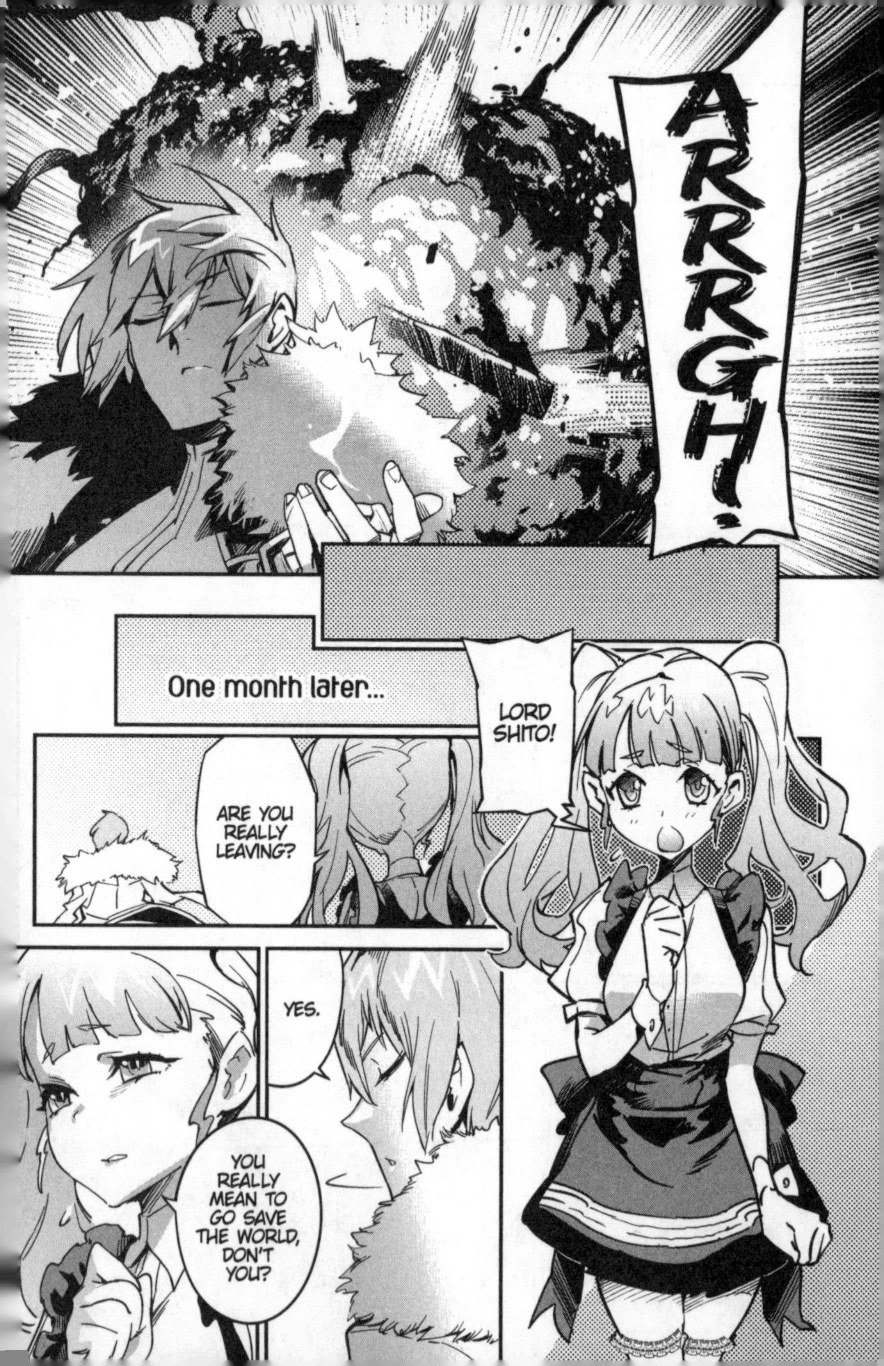
ARRRGH!
One month later...
LORD SHITO!
ARE YOU REALLY LEAVING?
YES.
YOU REALLY MEAN TO GO SAVE THE WORLD, DON'T YOU?

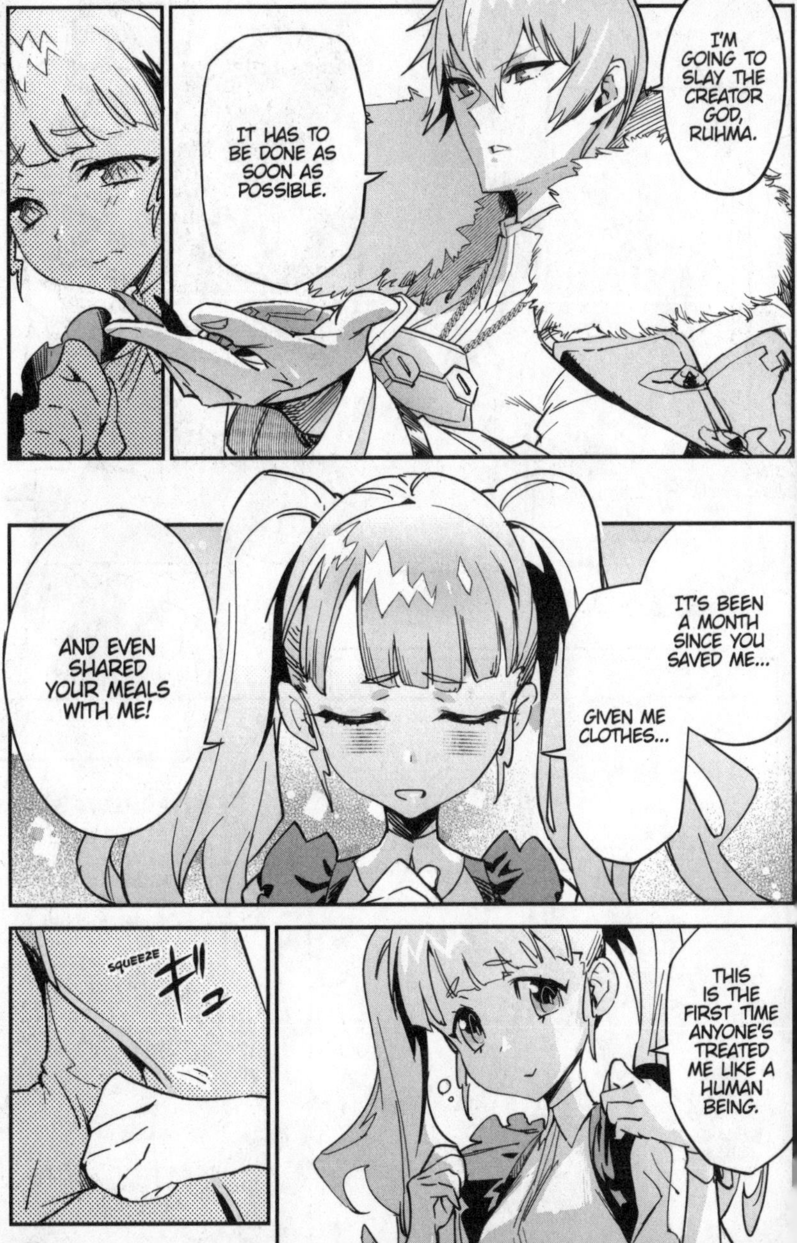
I'M GOING TO SLAY THE CREATOR GOD, RUHMA.
IT HAS TO BE DONE AS SOON AS POSSIBLE.
IT'S BEEN A MONTH SINCE YOU SAVED ME...
GIVEN ME CLOTHES...
AND EVEN SHARED YOUR MEALS WITH ME!
THIS IS THE FIRST TIME ANYONE'S TREATED ME LIKE A HUMAN BEING.
SQUEEZE
ギュ

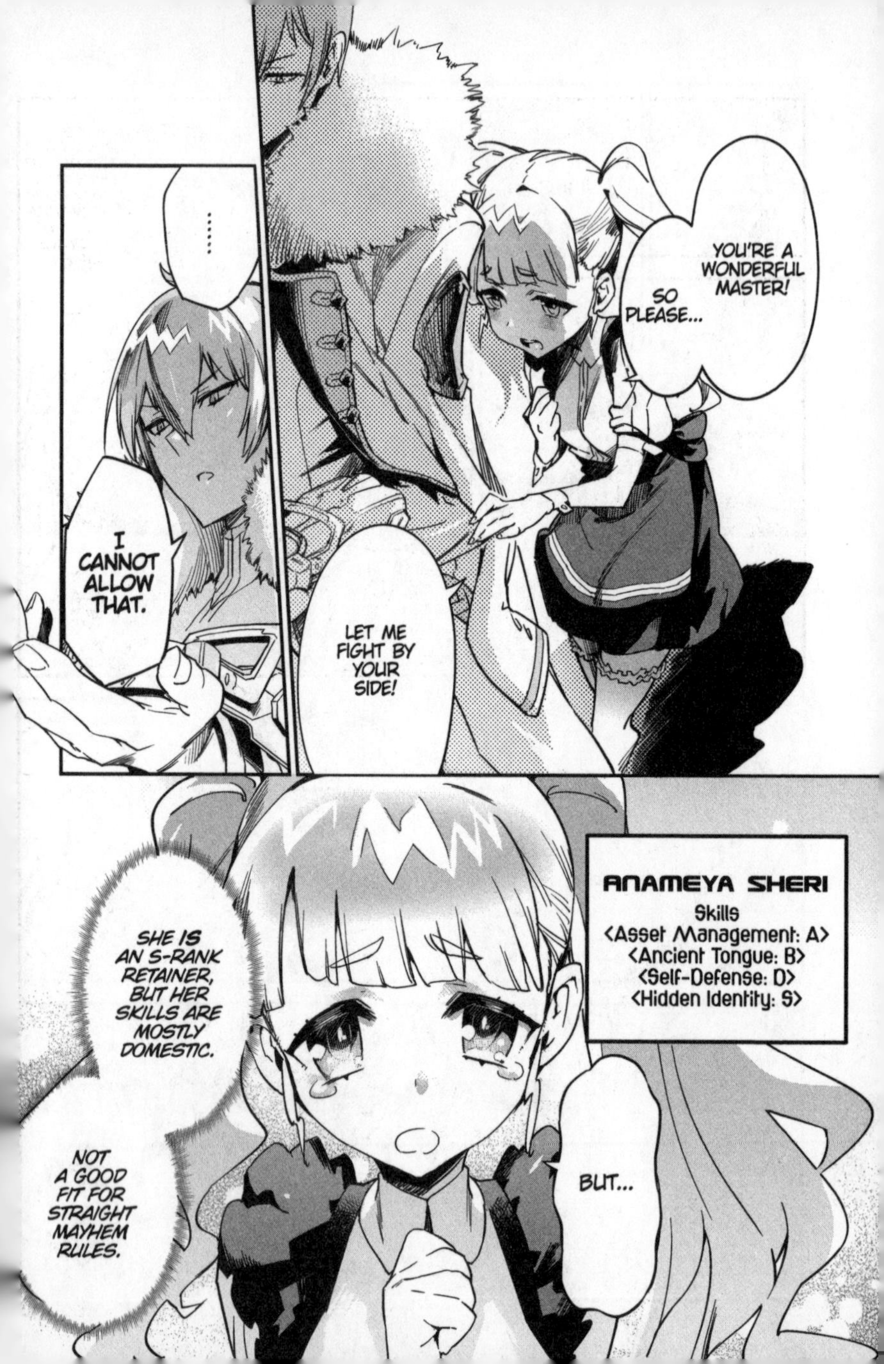
YOU'RE A WONDERFUL MASTER!
SO PLEASE...
LET ME FIGHT BY YOUR SIDE!
......
I CANNOT ALLOW THAT.
ANAMEYA SHERI
Skills
<Asset Management: A>
<Ancient Tongue: B>
<Self-Defense: D>
<Hidden Identity: S>
BUT...
SHE IS AN S-RANK RETAINER, BUT HER SKILLS ARE MOSTLY DOMESTIC.
NOT A GOOD FIT FOR STRAIGHT MAYHEM RULES.

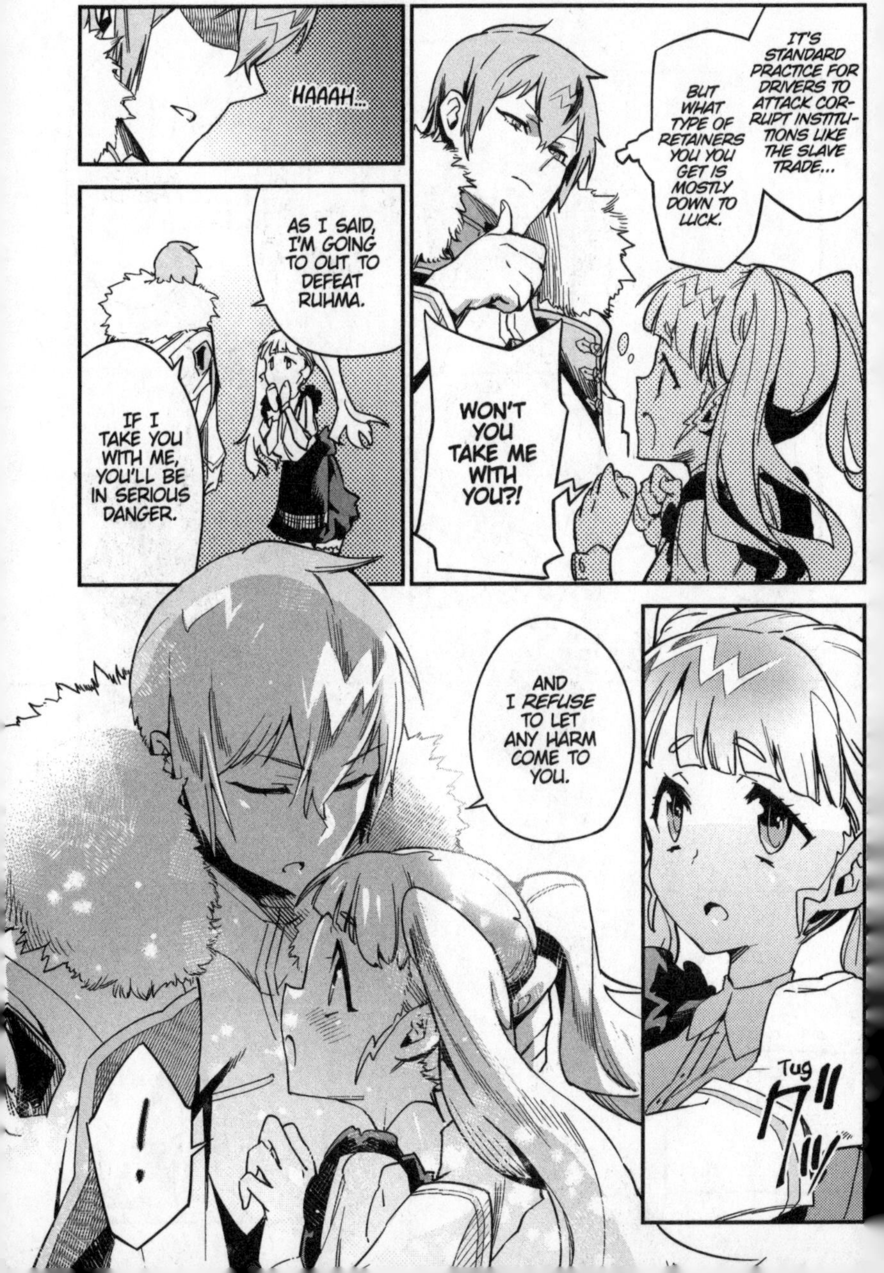
IT'S STANDARD PRACTICE FOR DRIVERS TO ATTACK CORRUPT INSTITUTIONS LIKE THE SLAVE TRADE...
BUT WHAT TYPE OF RETAINERS YOU YOU GET IS MOSTLY DOWN TO LUCK.
WON'T YOU TAKE ME WITH YOU?!
HAAAH...
AS I SAID, I'M GOING TO OUT TO DEFEAT RUHMA.
IF I TAKE YOU WITH ME, YOU'LL BE IN SERIOUS DANGER.
Tug
AND I *REFUSE* TO LET ANY HARM COME TO YOU.

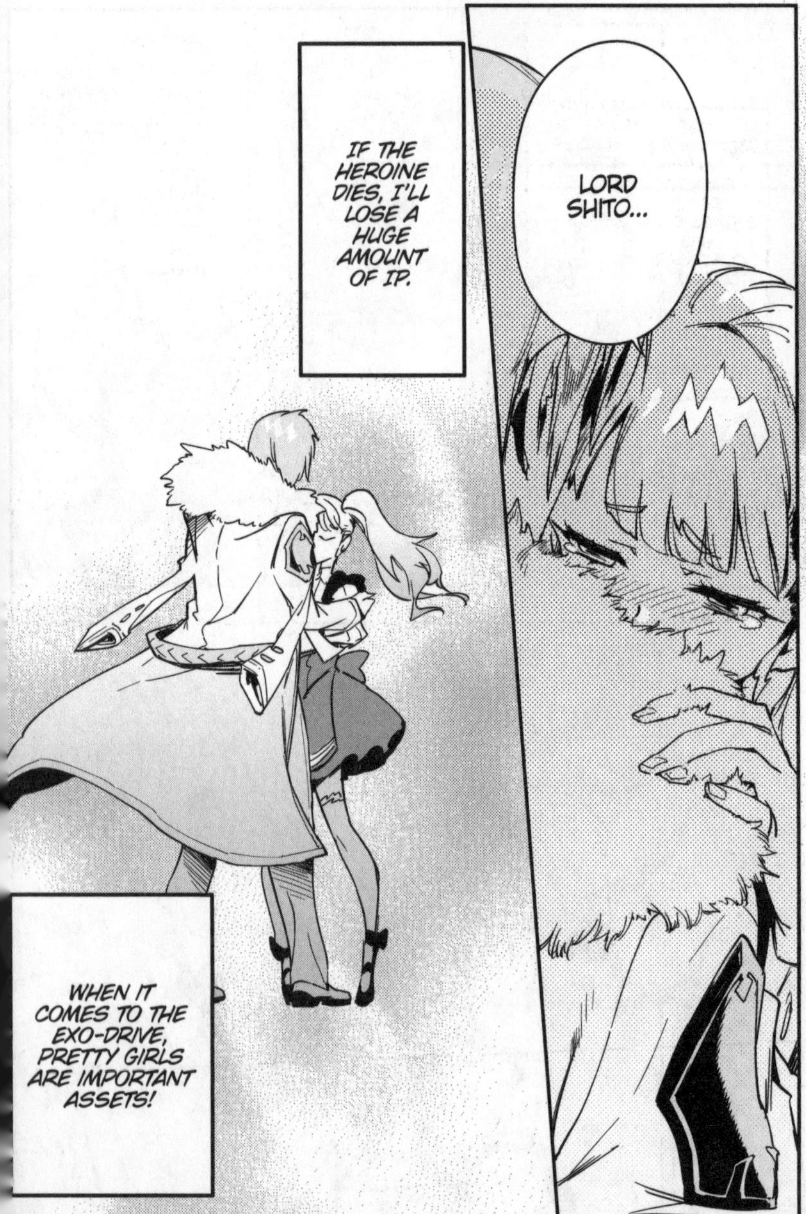
LORD SHITO...
IF THE HEROINE DIES, I'LL LOSE A HUGE AMOUNT OF IP.
WHEN IT COMES TO THE EXO-DRIVE, PRETTY GIRLS ARE IMPORTANT ASSETS!

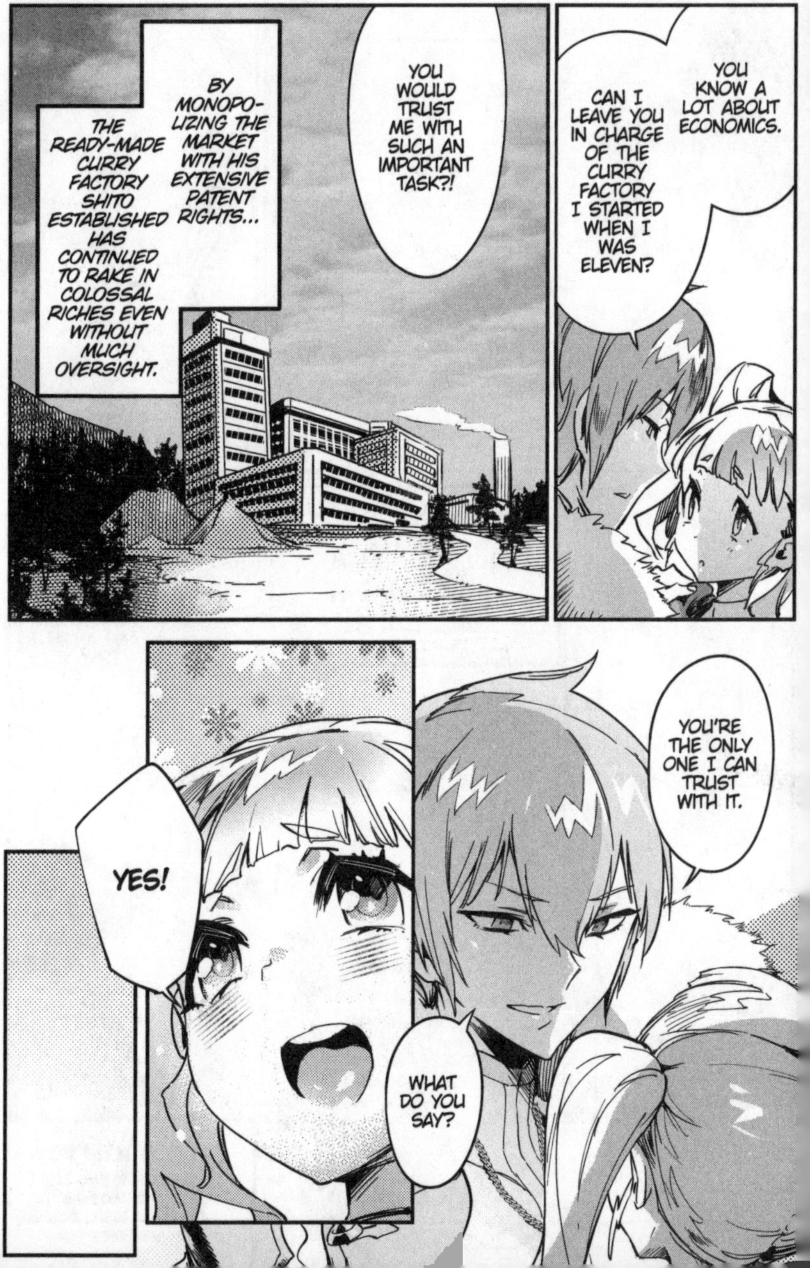
YOU KNOW A LOT ABOUT ECONOMICS.
CAN I LEAVE YOU IN CHARGE OF THE CURRY FACTORY I STARTED WHEN I WAS ELEVEN?
YOU WOULD TRUST ME WITH SUCH AN IMPORTANT TASK?!
BY MONOPOLIZING THE MARKET WITH HIS EXTENSIVE PATENT RIGHTS...
THE READY-MADE CURRY FACTORY SHITO ESTABLISHED HAS CONTINUED TO RAKE IN COLOSSAL RICHES EVEN WITHOUT MUCH OVERSIGHT.
YOU'RE THE ONLY ONE I CAN TRUST WITH IT.
WHAT DO YOU SAY?
YES!

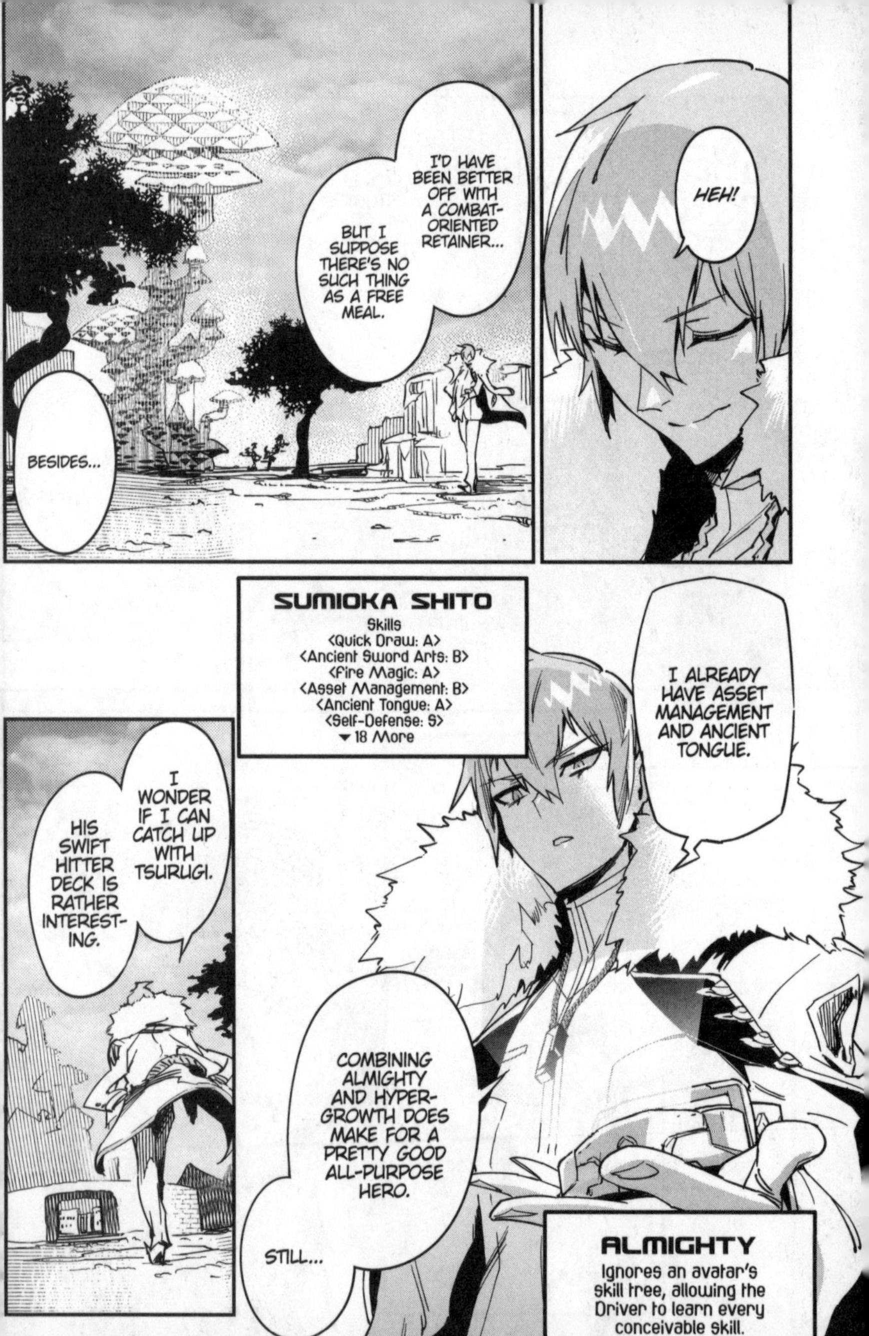
HEH!
I'D HAVE BEEN BETTER OFF WITH A COMBAT-ORIENTED RETAINER...
BUT I SUPPOSE THERE'S NO SUCH THING AS A FREE MEAL.
BESIDES...
SUMIOKA SHITO
Skills
<Quick Draw: A>
<Ancient Sword Arts: B>
<Fire Magic: A>
<Asset Management: B>
<Ancient Tongue: A>
<Self-Defense: S>
▼18 More
I ALREADY HAVE ASSET MANAGEMENT AND ANCIENT TONGUE.
COMBINING ALMIGHTY AND HYPER-GROWTH DOES MAKE FOR A PRETTY GOOD ALL-PURPOSE HERO.
STILL...
ALMIGHTY
Ignores an avatar's skill tree, allowing the Driver to learn every conceivable skill.
I WONDER IF I CAN CATCH UP WITH TSURUGI.
HIS SWIFT HITTER DECK IS RATHER INTERESTING.

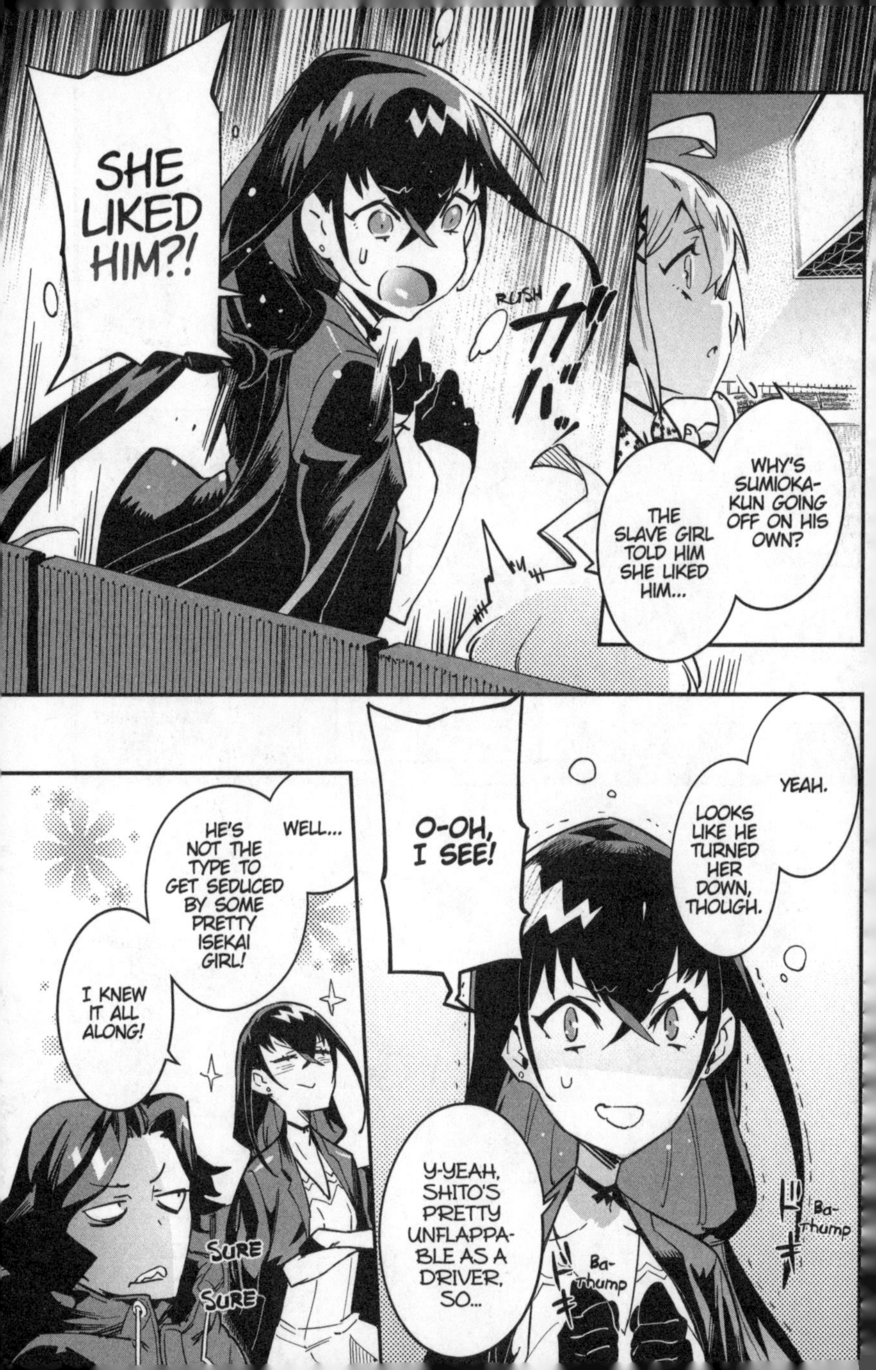
WHY'S SUMIOKA-KUN GOING OFF ON HIS OWN?
THE SLAVE GIRL TOLD HIM SHE LIKED HIM...
RUSH
SHE LIKED HIM?!
YEAH.
LOOKS LIKE HE TURNED HER DOWN, THOUGH.
O-OH, I SEE!
Y-YEAH, SHITO'S PRETTY UNFLAPPABLE AS A DRIVER, SO...
Ba-thump
Ba-thump
WELL...
HE'S NOT THE TYPE TO GET SEDUCED BY SOME PRETTY ISEKAI GIRL!
I KNEW IT ALL ALONG!
SURE
SURE

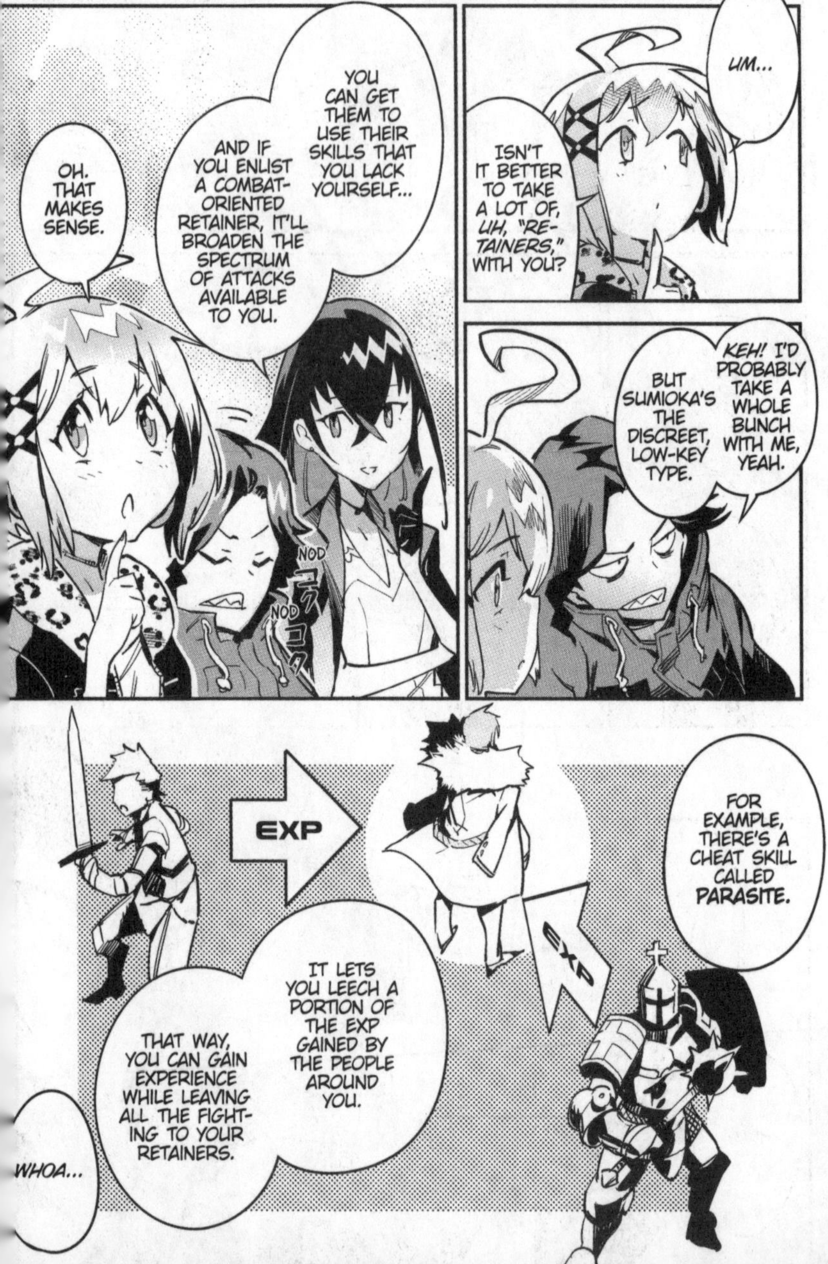
UM...
ISN'T IT BETTER TO TAKE A LOT OF, UH, "RE-TAINERS," WITH YOU?
KEH! I'D PROBABLY TAKE A WHOLE BUNCH WITH ME, YEAH.
BUT SUMIOKA'S THE DISCREET, LOW-KEY TYPE.
YOU CAN GET THEM TO USE THEIR SKILLS THAT YOU LACK YOURSELF...
AND IF YOU ENLIST A COMBAT-ORIENTED RETAINER, IT'LL BROADEN THE SPECTRUM OF ATTACKS AVAILABLE TO YOU.
OH. THAT MAKES SENSE.
NOD
NOD
FOR EXAMPLE, THERE'S A CHEAT SKILL CALLED PARASITE.
EXP
EXP
IT LETS YOU LEECH A PORTION OF THE EXP GAINED BY THE PEOPLE AROUND YOU.
THAT WAY, YOU CAN GAIN EXPERIENCE WHILE LEAVING ALL THE FIGHT-ING TO YOUR RETAINERS.
WHOA...

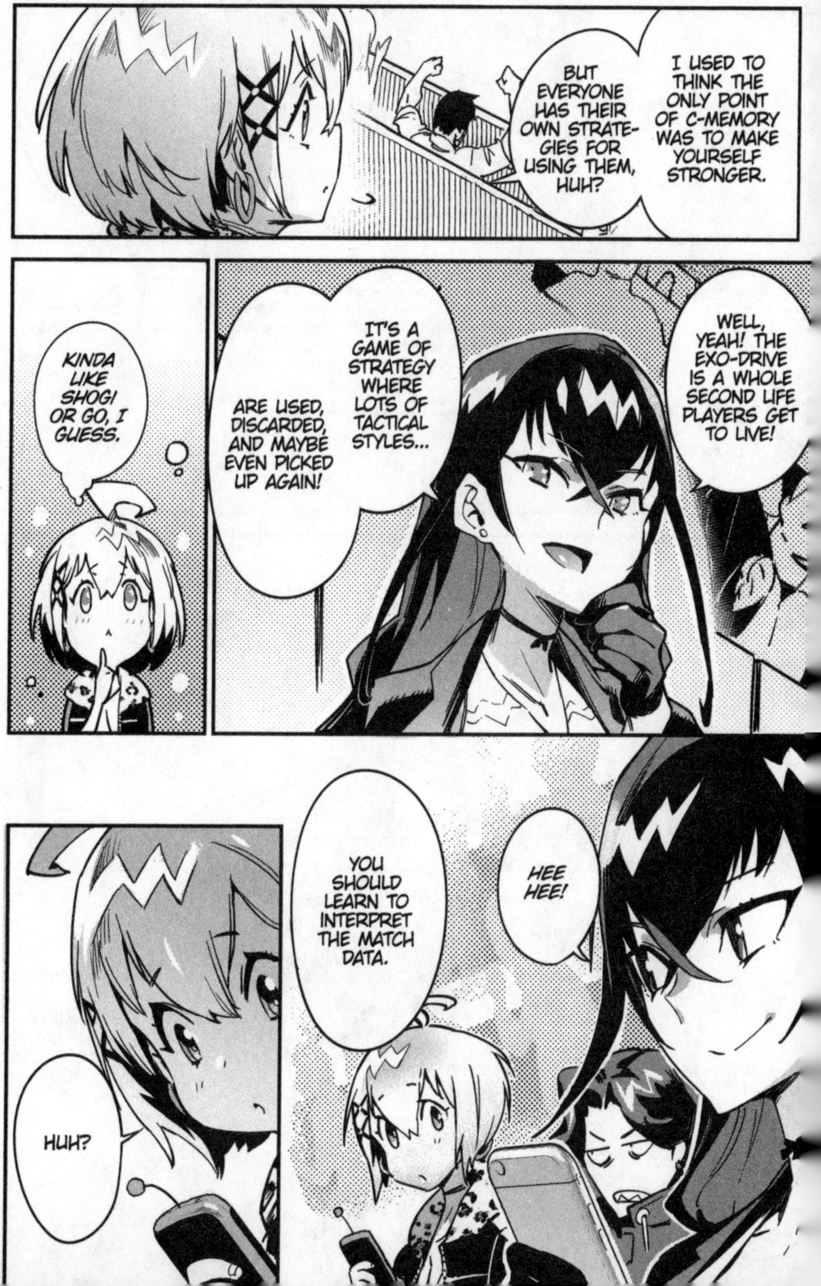
I USED TO THINK THE ONLY POINT OF C-MEMORY WAS TO MAKE YOURSELF STRONGER.
BUT EVERYONE HAS THEIR OWN STRATE-GIES FOR USING THEM, HUH?
WELL, YEAH! THE EXO-DRIVE IS A WHOLE SECOND LIFE PLAYERS GET TO LIVE!
IT'S A GAME OF STRATEGY WHERE LOTS OF TACTICAL STYLES...
ARE USED, DISCARDED, AND MAYBE EVEN PICKED UP AGAIN!
KINDA LIKE SHOGI OR GO, I GUESS.
HEE HEE!
YOU SHOULD LEARN TO INTERPRET THE MATCH DATA.
HUH?

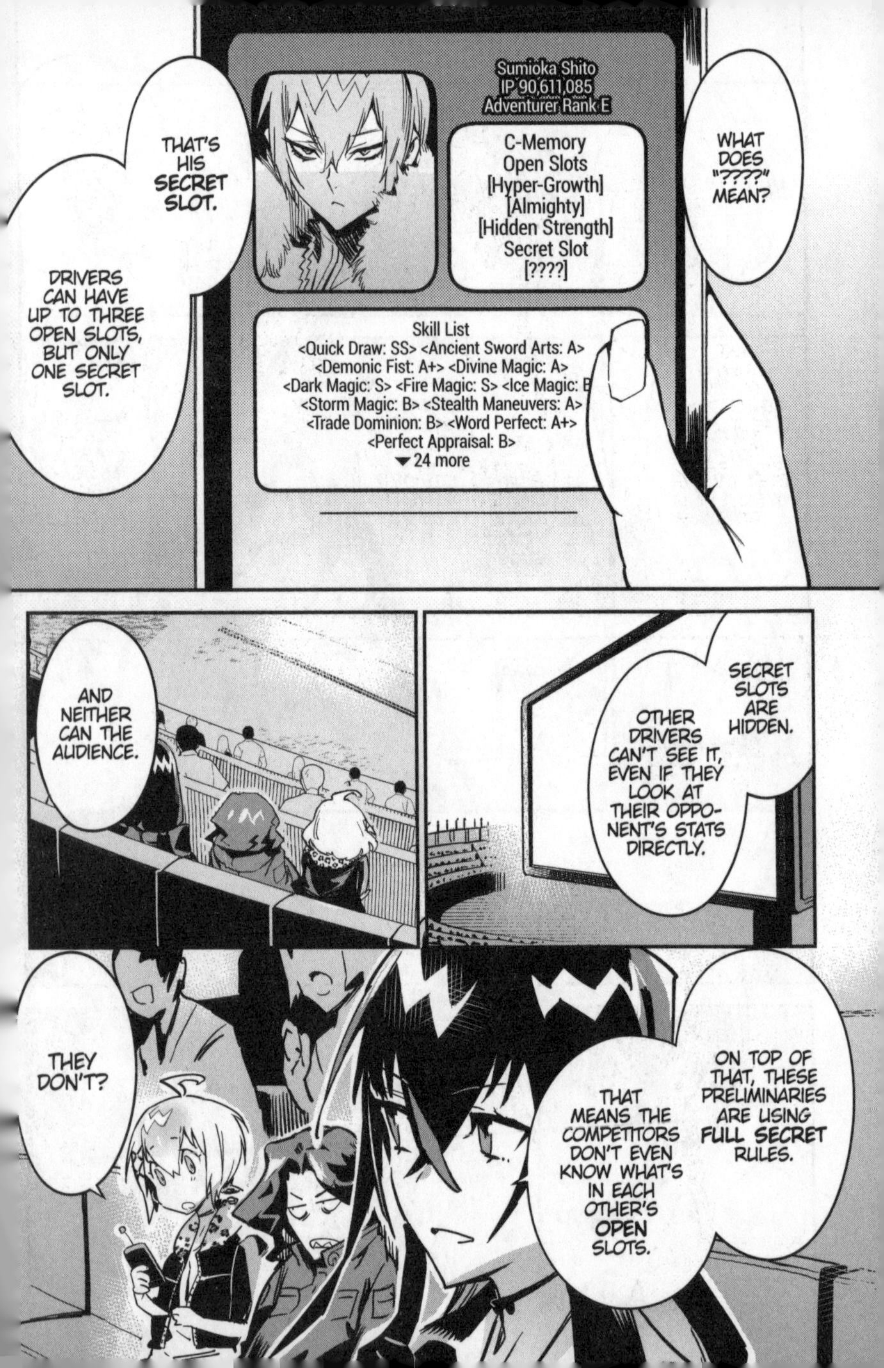
WHAT DOES "????" MEAN?
Sumioka Shito
IP 90,611,085
Adventurer Rank E
C-Memory
Open Slots
[Hyper-Growth]
[Almighty]
[Hidden Strength]
Secret Slot
[????]
Skill List
<Quick Draw: SS> <Ancient Sword Arts: A>
<Demonic Fist: A+> <Divine Magic: A>
<Dark Magic: S> <Fire Magic: S> <Ice Magic: B
<Storm Magic: B> <Stealth Maneuvers: A>
<Trade Dominion: B> <Word Perfect: A+>
<Perfect Appraisal: B>
▼24 more
THAT'S HIS SECRET SLOT.
DRIVERS CAN HAVE UP TO THREE OPEN SLOTS, BUT ONLY ONE SECRET SLOT.
SECRET SLOTS ARE HIDDEN.
OTHER DRIVERS CAN'T SEE IT, EVEN IF THEY LOOK AT THEIR OPPO-NENT'S STATS DIRECTLY.
AND NEITHER CAN THE AUDIENCE.
ON TOP OF THAT, THESE PRELIMINARIES ARE USING **FULL SECRET** RULES.
THAT MEANS THE COMPETITORS DON'T EVEN KNOW WHAT'S IN EACH OTHER'S **OPEN** SLOTS.
THEY DON'T?

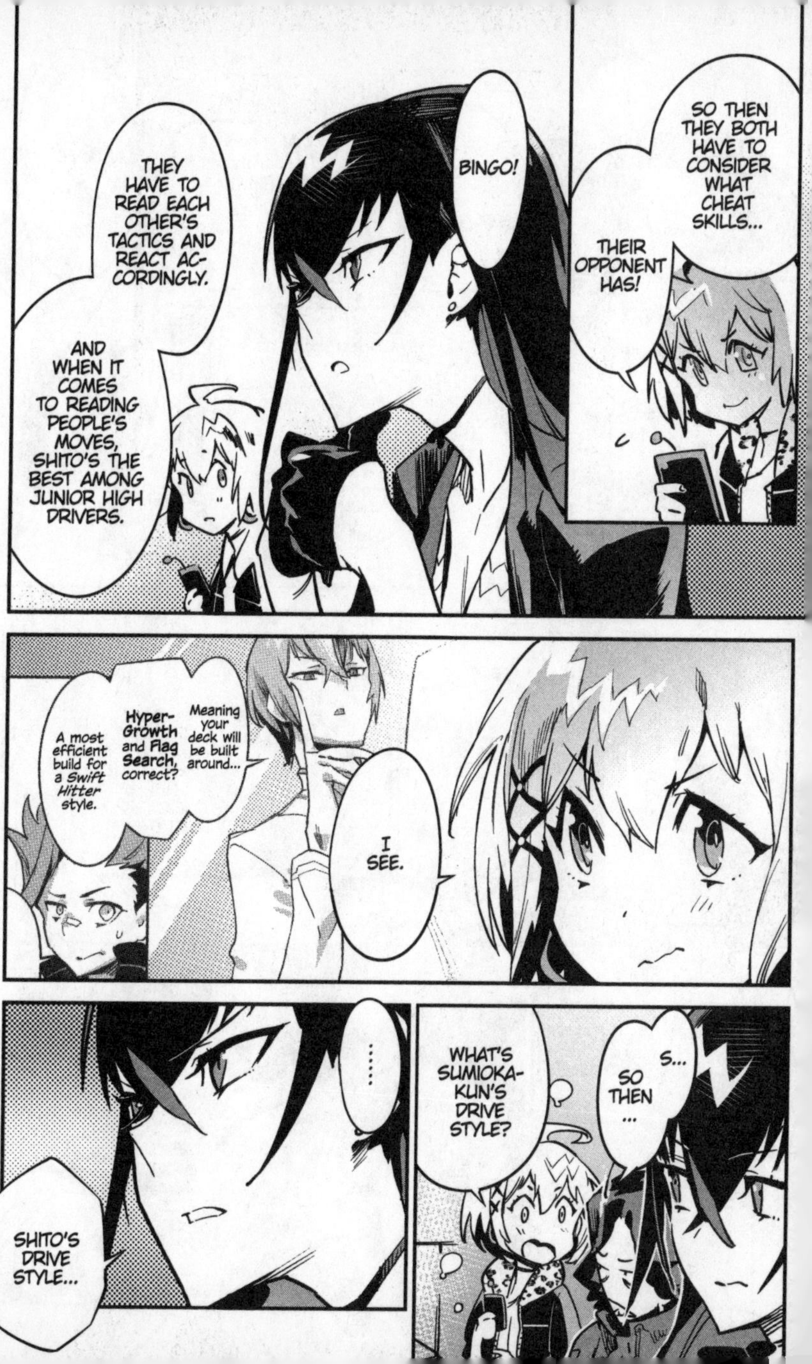
SO THEN THEY BOTH HAVE TO CONSIDER WHAT CHEAT SKILLS...
THEIR OPPONENT HAS!
BINGO!
THEY HAVE TO READ EACH OTHER'S TACTICS AND REACT AC-CORDINGLY.
AND WHEN IT COMES TO READING PEOPLE'S MOVES, SHITO'S THE BEST AMONG JUNIOR HIGH DRIVERS.
I SEE.
Meaning your deck will be built around... Hyper-Growth and Flag Search, correct? A most efficient build for a Swift Hitter style.
S... SO THEN...
WHAT'S SUMIOKA-KUN'S DRIVE STYLE?
......
SHITO'S DRIVE STYLE...

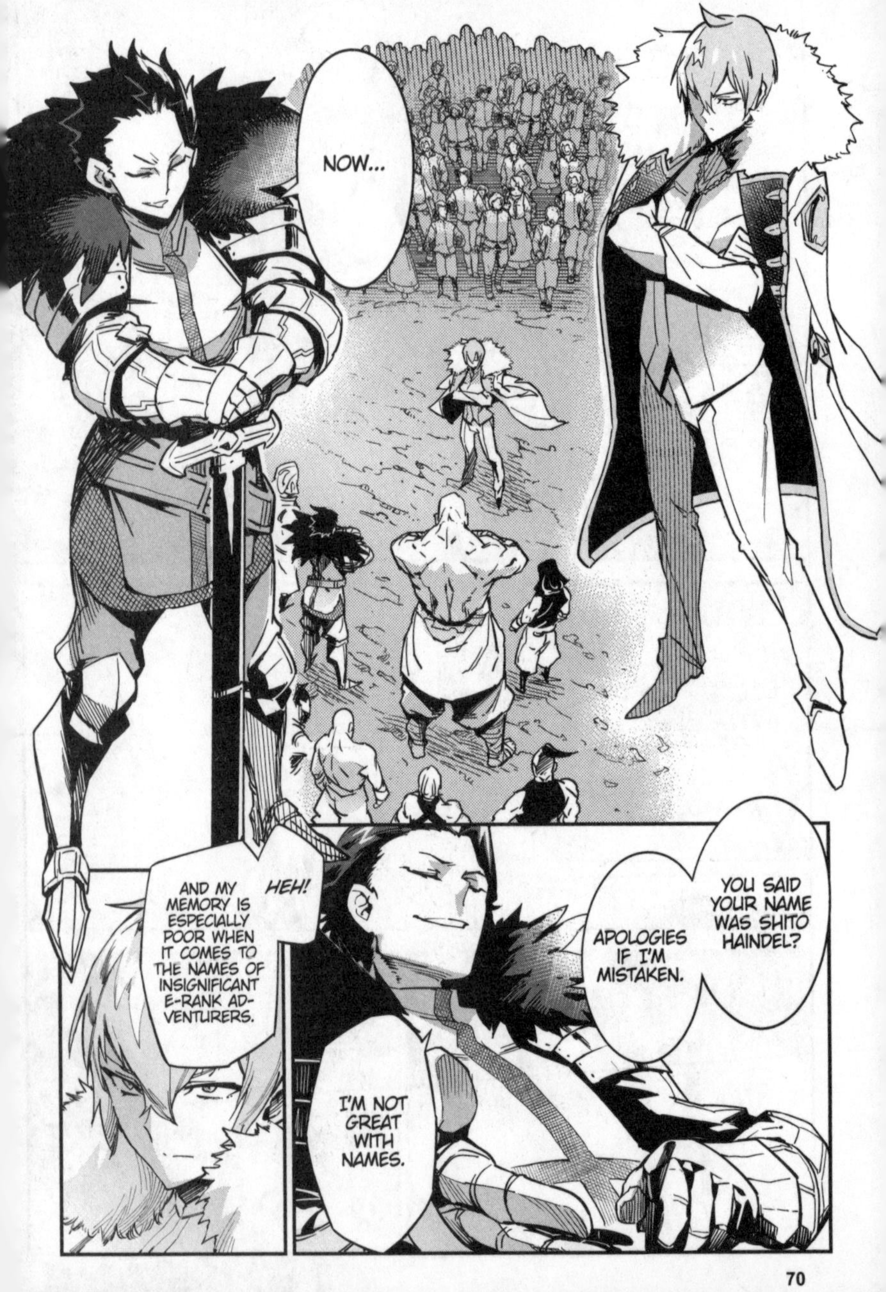
NOW...
YOU SAID YOUR NAME WAS SHITO HAINDEL?
APOLOGIES IF I'M MISTAKEN.
I'M NOT GREAT WITH NAMES.
HEH!
AND MY MEMORY IS ESPECIALLY POOR WHEN IT COMES TO THE NAMES OF INSIGNIFICANT E-RANK ADVENTURERS.

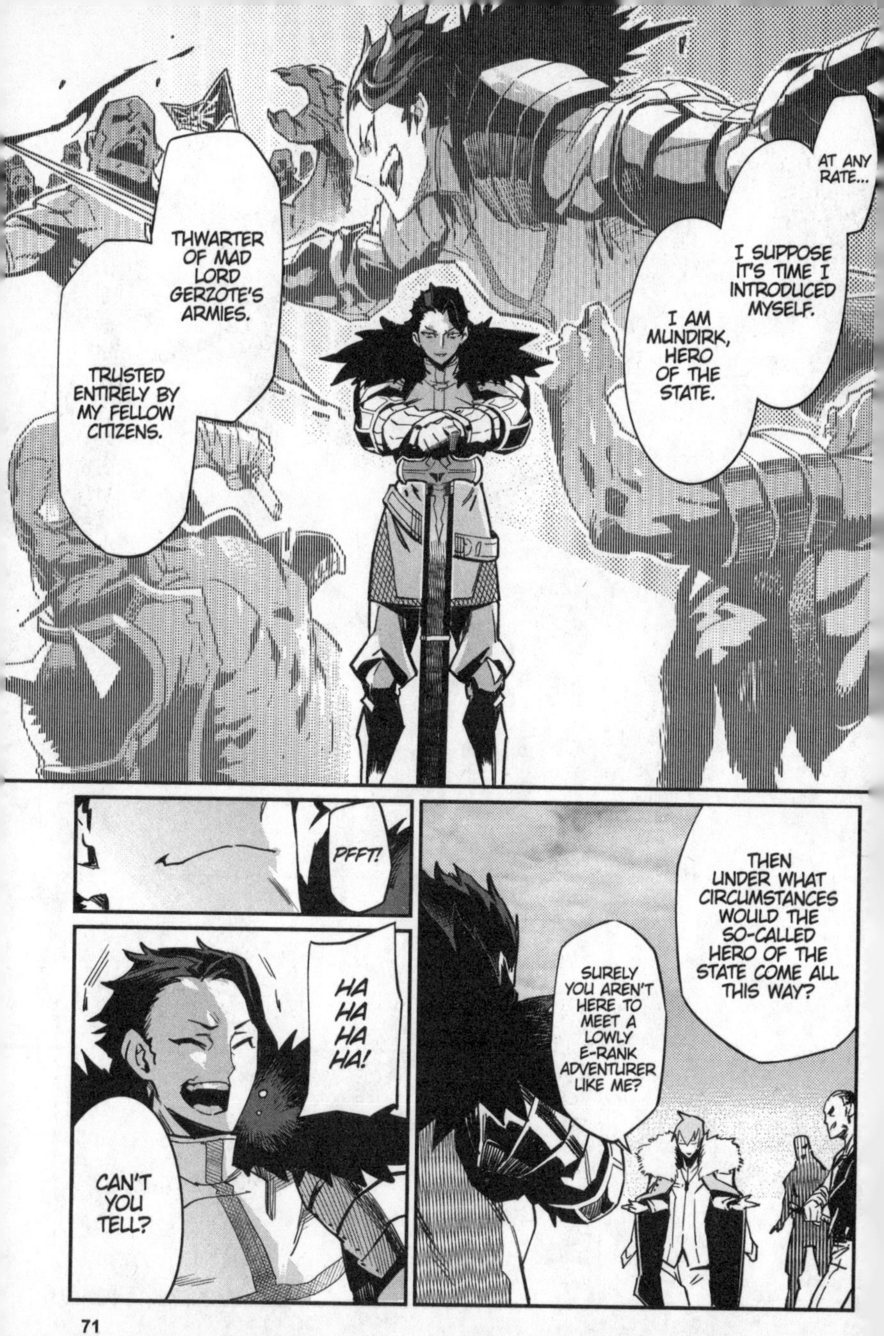
AT ANY RATE...
I SUPPOSE IT'S TIME I INTRODUCED MYSELF.
I AM MUNDIRK, HERO OF THE STATE.
THWARTER OF MAD LORD GERZOTE'S ARMIES.
TRUSTED ENTIRELY BY MY FELLOW CITIZENS.
THEN UNDER WHAT CIRCUMSTANCES WOULD THE SO-CALLED HERO OF THE STATE COME ALL THIS WAY?
SURELY YOU AREN'T HERE TO MEET A LOWLY E-RANK ADVENTURER LIKE ME?
PFFT!
HA HA HA HA!
CAN'T YOU TELL?

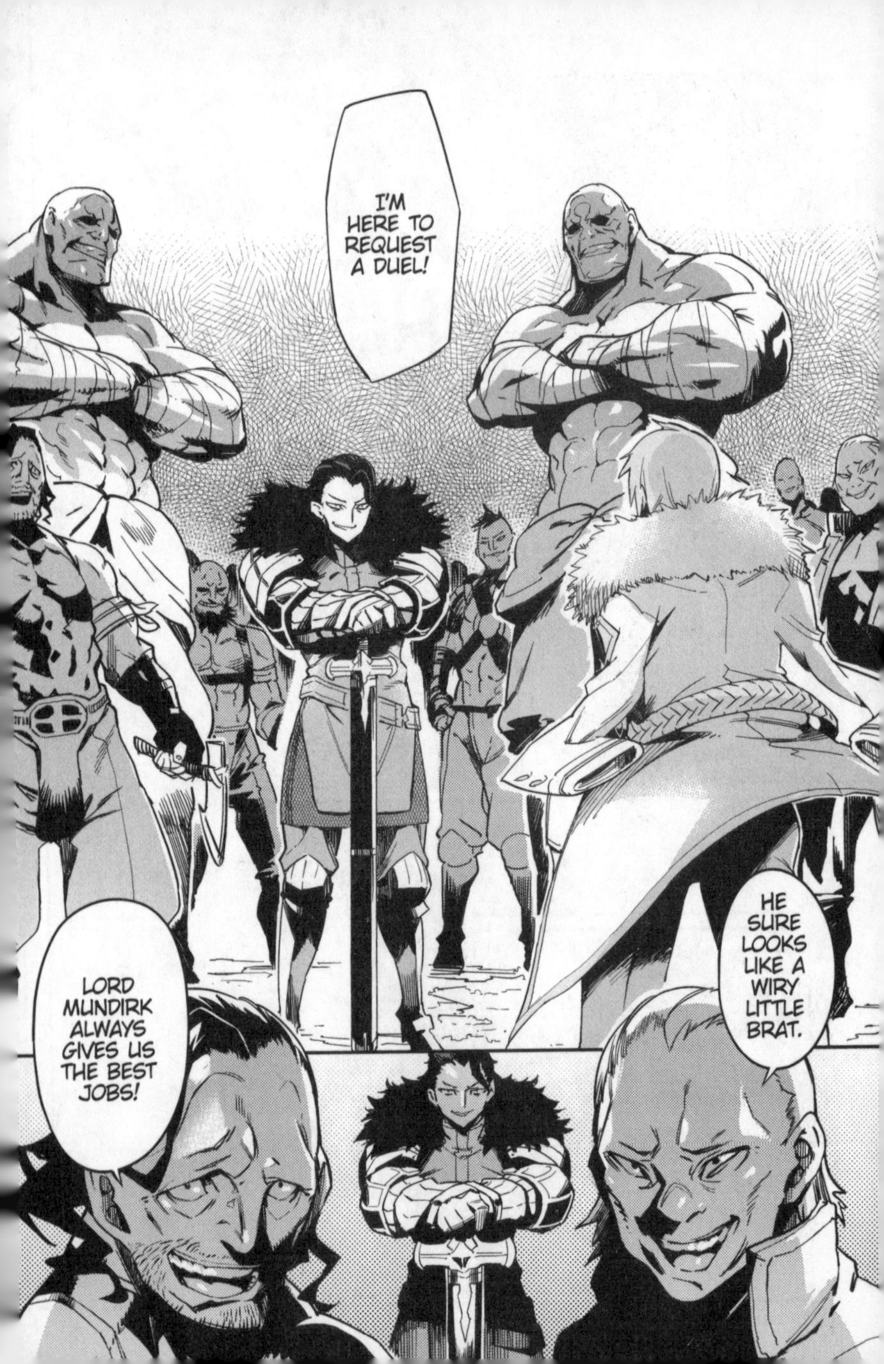
I'M HERE TO REQUEST A DUEL!
HE SURE LOOKS LIKE A WIRY LITTLE BRAT.
LORD MUNDIRK ALWAYS GIVES US THE BEST JOBS!

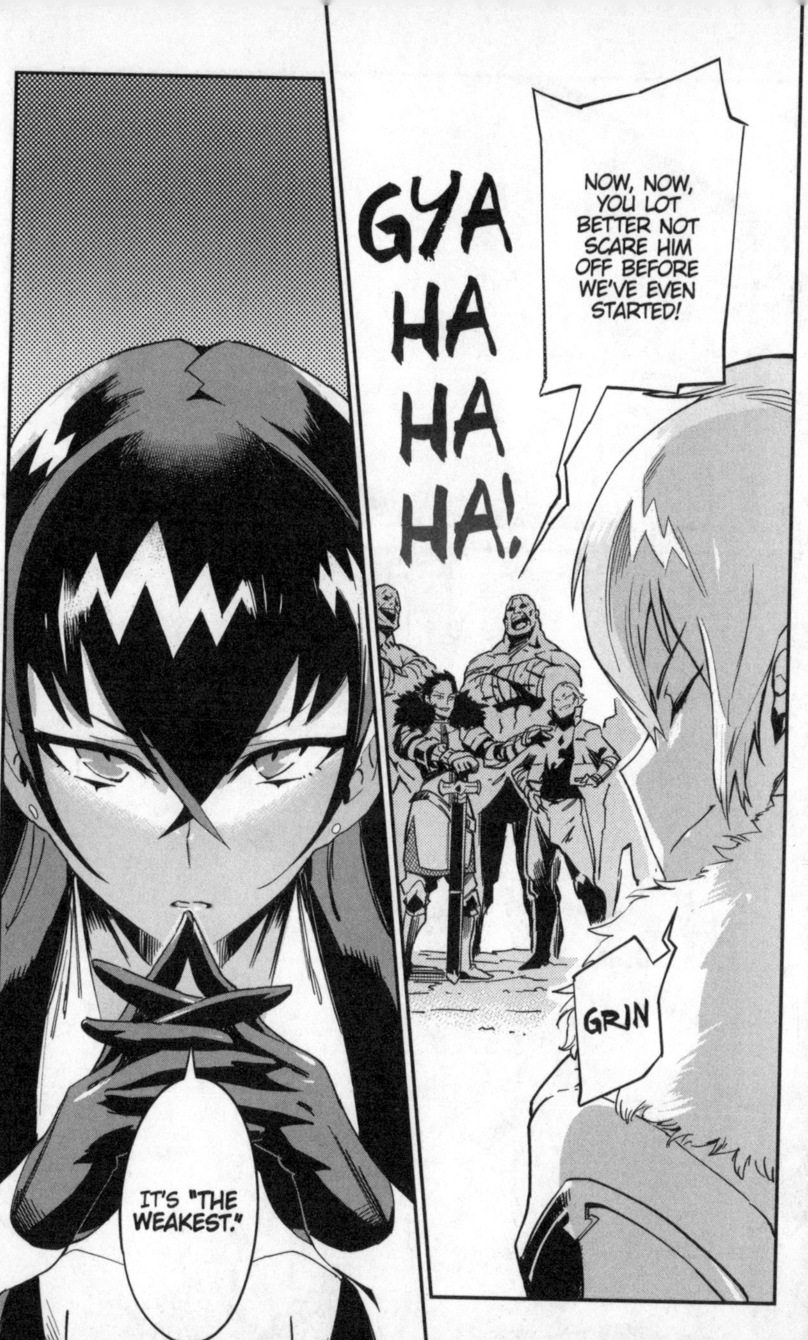
NOW, NOW, YOU LOT BETTER NOT SCARE HIM OFF BEFORE WE'VE EVEN STARTED!
GYA HA HA HA HA!
GRIN
IT'S "THE WEAKEST."

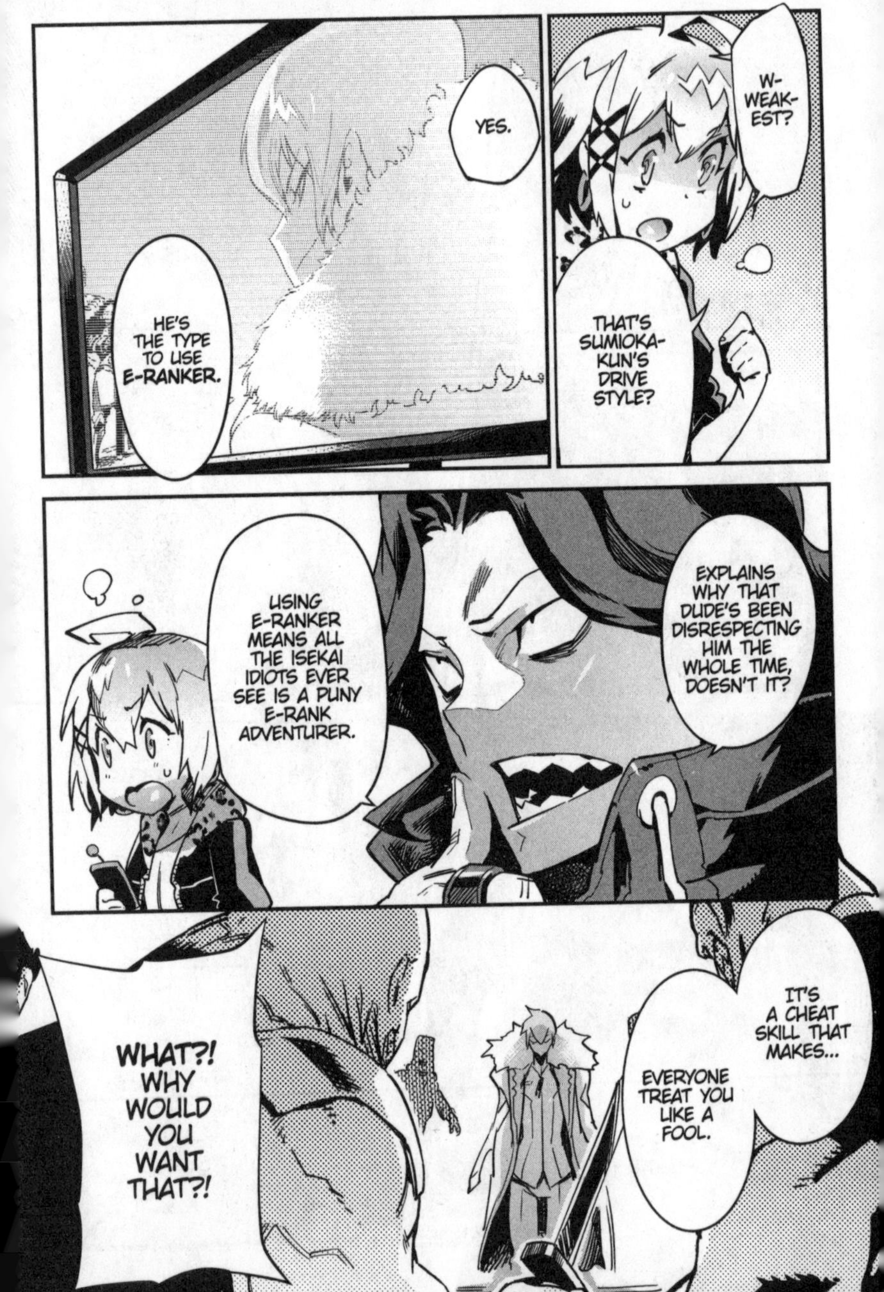
W-WEAKEST?
THAT'S SUMIOKA-KUN'S DRIVE STYLE?
YES.
HE'S THE TYPE TO USE E-RANKER.
EXPLAINS WHY THAT DUDE'S BEEN DISRESPECTING HIM THE WHOLE TIME, DOESN'T IT?
USING E-RANKER MEANS ALL THE ISEKAI IDIOTS EVER SEE IS A PUNY E-RANK ADVENTURER.
IT'S A CHEAT SKILL THAT MAKES...
EVERYONE TREAT YOU LIKE A FOOL.
WHAT?! WHY WOULD YOU WANT THAT?!

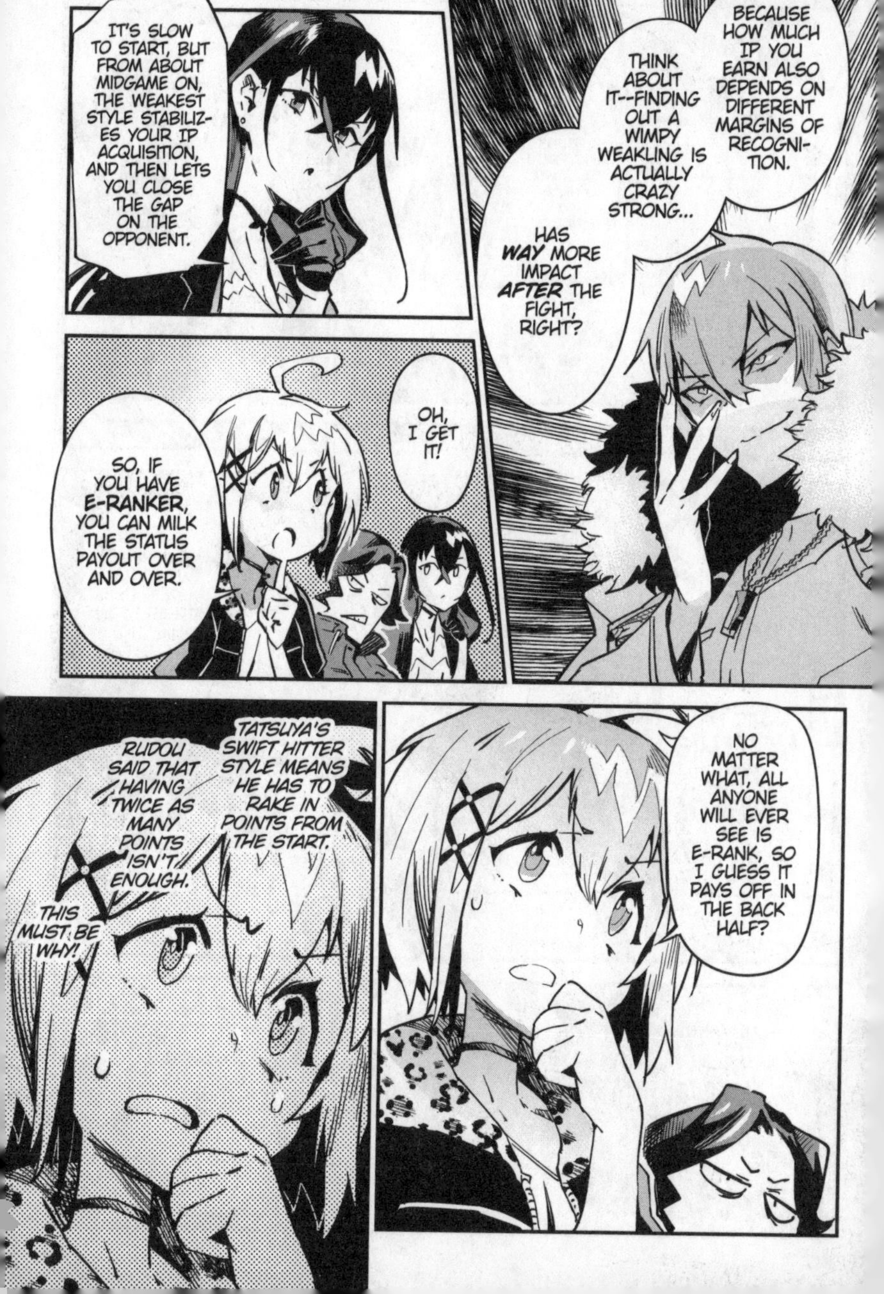
BECAUSE HOW MUCH IP YOU EARN ALSO DEPENDS ON DIFFERENT MARGINS OF RECOGNITION.
THINK ABOUT IT--FINDING OUT A WIMPY WEAKLING IS ACTUALLY CRAZY STRONG...
HAS **WAY** MORE IMPACT **AFTER** THE FIGHT, RIGHT?
IT'S SLOW TO START, BUT FROM ABOUT MIDGAME ON, THE WEAKEST STYLE STABILIZES YOUR IP ACQUISITION, AND THEN LETS YOU CLOSE THE GAP ON THE OPPONENT.
OH, I GET IT!
SO, IF YOU HAVE **E-RANKER**, YOU CAN MILK THE STATUS PAYOUT OVER AND OVER.
NO MATTER WHAT, ALL ANYONE WILL EVER SEE IS E-RANK, SO I GUESS IT PAYS OFF IN THE BACK HALF?
TATSUYA'S SWIFT HITTER STYLE MEANS HE HAS TO RAKE IN POINTS FROM THE START.
RUDOU SAID THAT HAVING TWICE AS MANY POINTS ISN'T ENOUGH.
THIS MUST BE WHY!

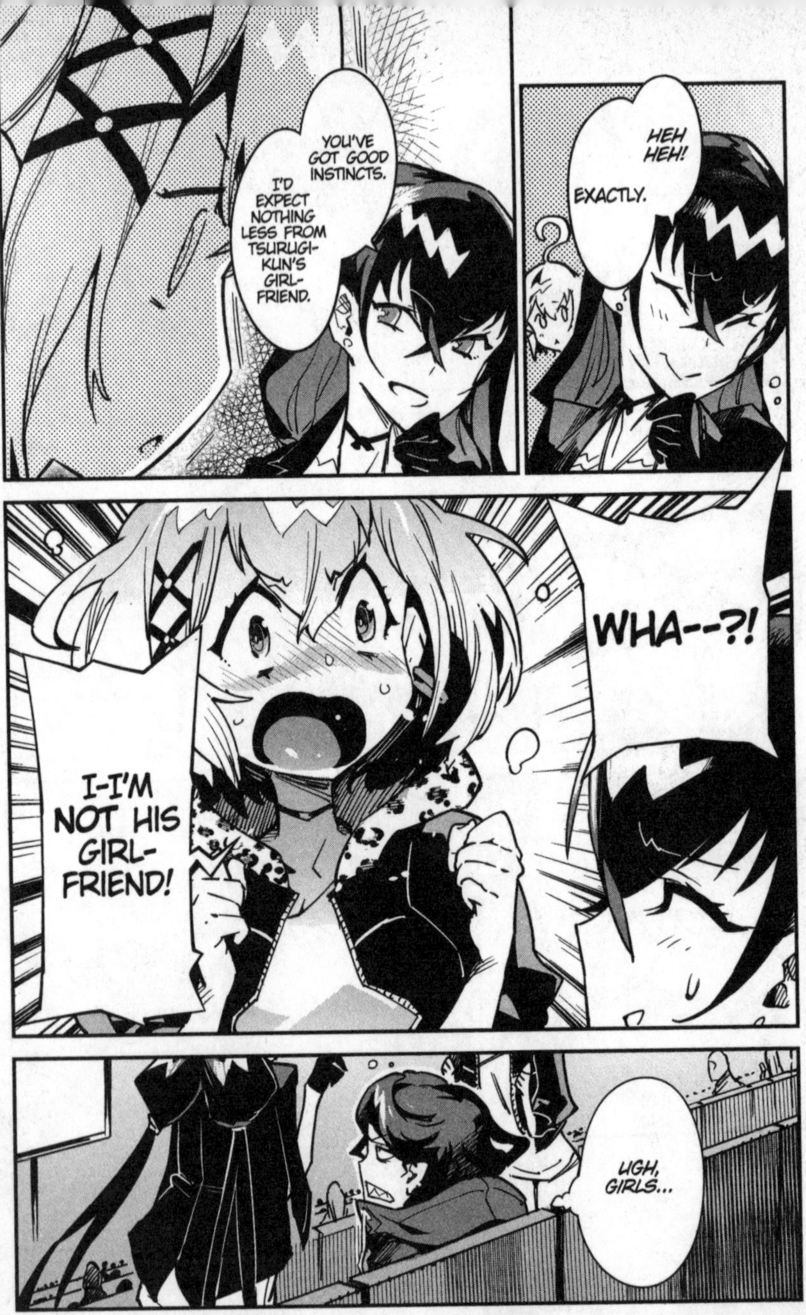
HEH HEH!
EXACTLY.
YOU'VE GOT GOOD INSTINCTS.
I'D EXPECT NOTHING LESS FROM TSURUGI-KUN'S GIRLFRIEND.
WHA--?!
I-I'M NOT HIS GIRLFRIEND!
UGH, GIRLS...

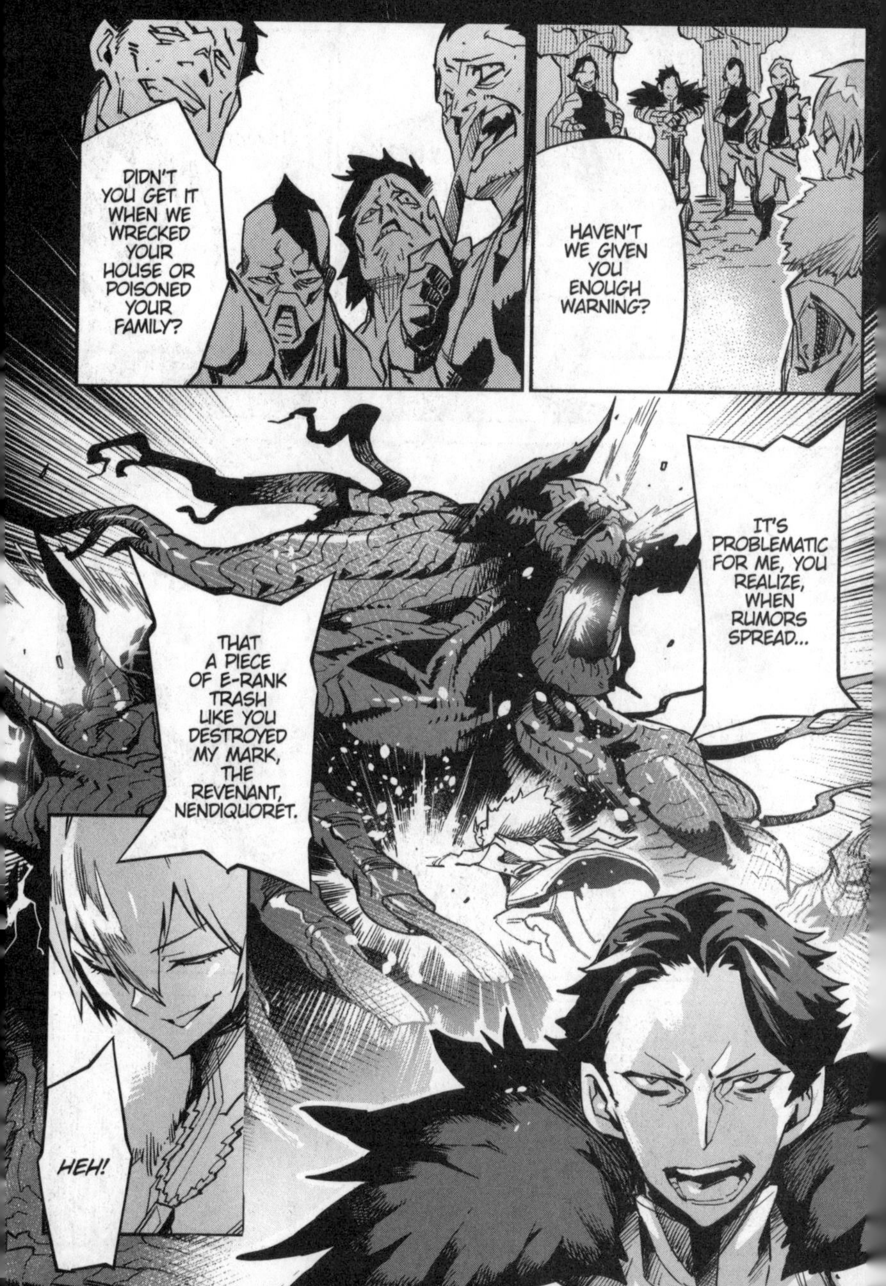
HAVEN'T WE GIVEN YOU ENOUGH WARNING?
DIDN'T YOU GET IT WHEN WE WRECKED YOUR HOUSE OR POISONED YOUR FAMILY?
IT'S PROBLEMATIC FOR ME, YOU REALIZE, WHEN RUMORS SPREAD...
THAT A PIECE OF E-RANK TRASH LIKE YOU DESTROYED MY MARK, THE REVENANT, NENDIQUORET.
HEH!

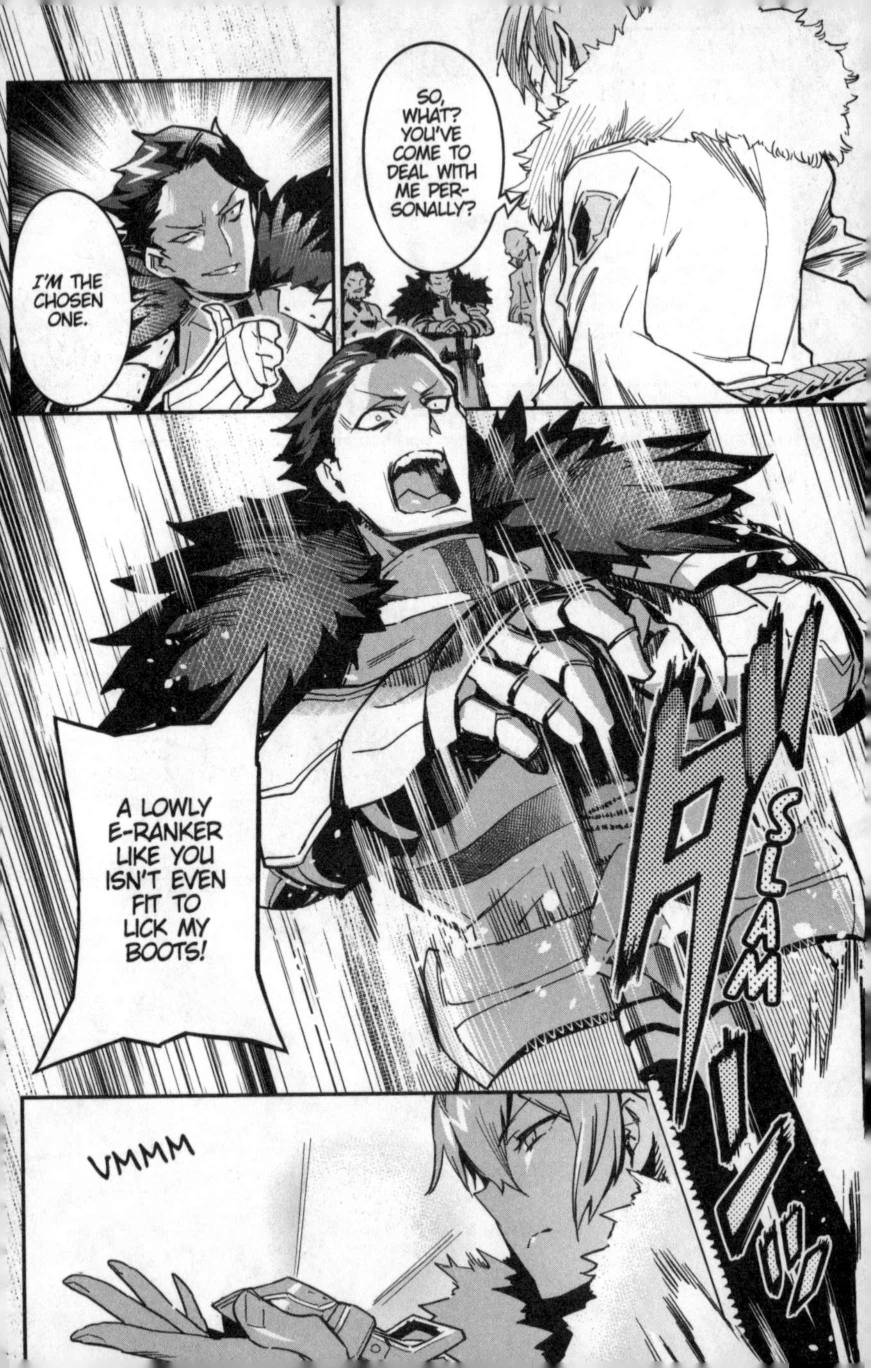
SO, WHAT? YOU'VE COME TO DEAL WITH ME PER-SONALLY?
I'M THE CHOSEN ONE.
A LOWLY E-RANKER LIKE YOU ISN'T EVEN FIT TO LICK MY BOOTS!
SLAM
VMMM

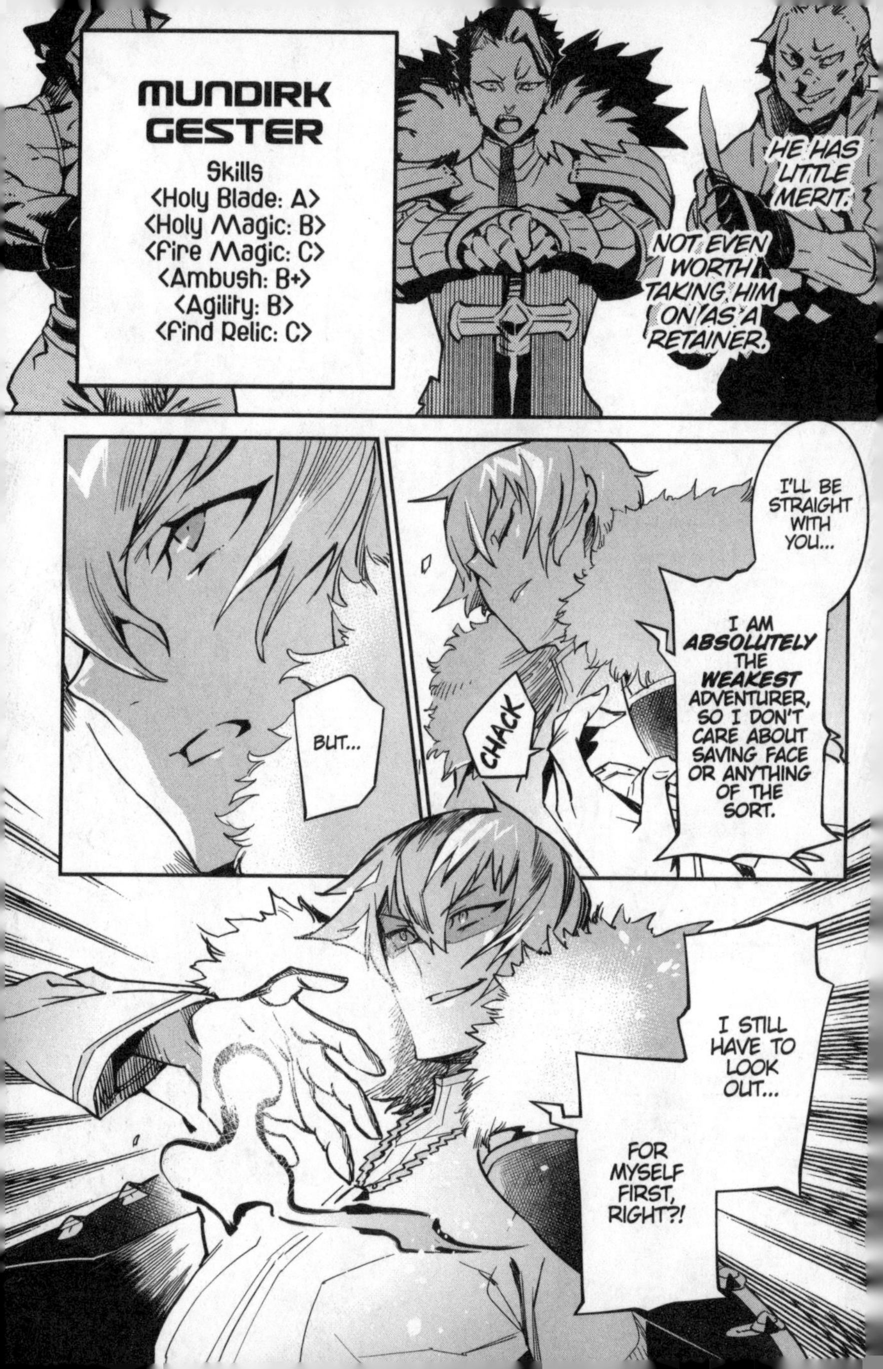
HE HAS LITTLE MERIT.
NOT EVEN WORTH TAKING HIM ON AS A RETAINER.
MUNDIRK GESTER
Skills
<Holy Blade: A>
<Holy Magic: B>
<Fire Magic: C>
<Ambush: B+>
<Agility: B>
<Find Relic: C>
I'LL BE STRAIGHT WITH YOU...
I AM ABSOLUTELY THE WEAKEST ADVENTURER, SO I DON'T CARE ABOUT SAVING FACE OR ANYTHING OF THE SORT.
CHACK
BUT...
I STILL HAVE TO LOOK OUT...
FOR MYSELF FIRST, RIGHT?!

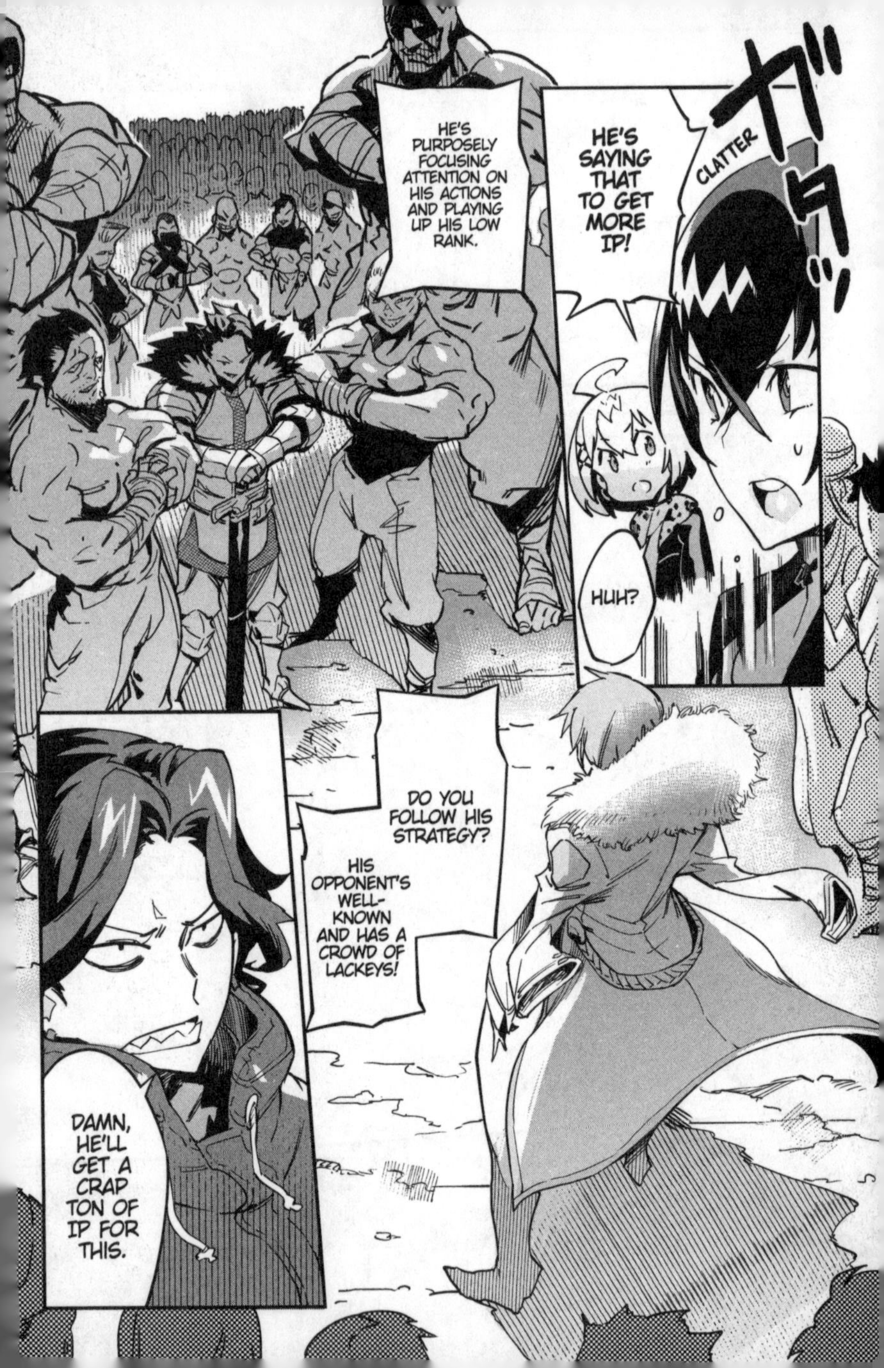
CLATTER
HE'S SAYING THAT TO GET MORE IP!
HUH?
HE'S PURPOSELY FOCUSING ATTENTION ON HIS ACTIONS AND PLAYING UP HIS LOW RANK.
DO YOU FOLLOW HIS STRATEGY?
HIS OPPONENT'S WELL-KNOWN AND HAS A CROWD OF LACKEYS!
DAMN, HE'LL GET A CRAP TON OF IP FOR THIS.

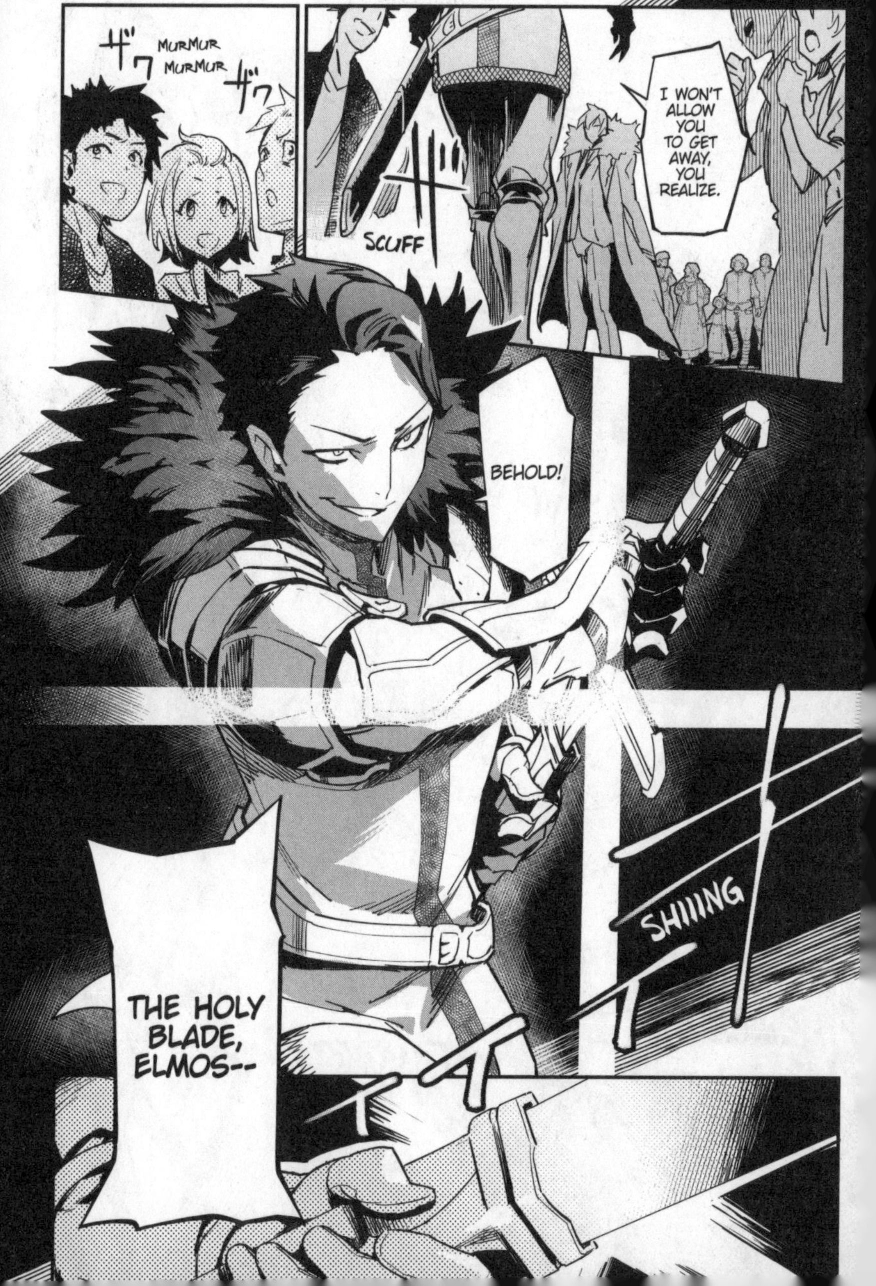
I WON'T ALLOW YOU TO GET AWAY, YOU REALIZE.
SCUFF
MURMUR MURMUR
BEHOLD!
SHIIING
THE HOLY BLADE, ELMOS--

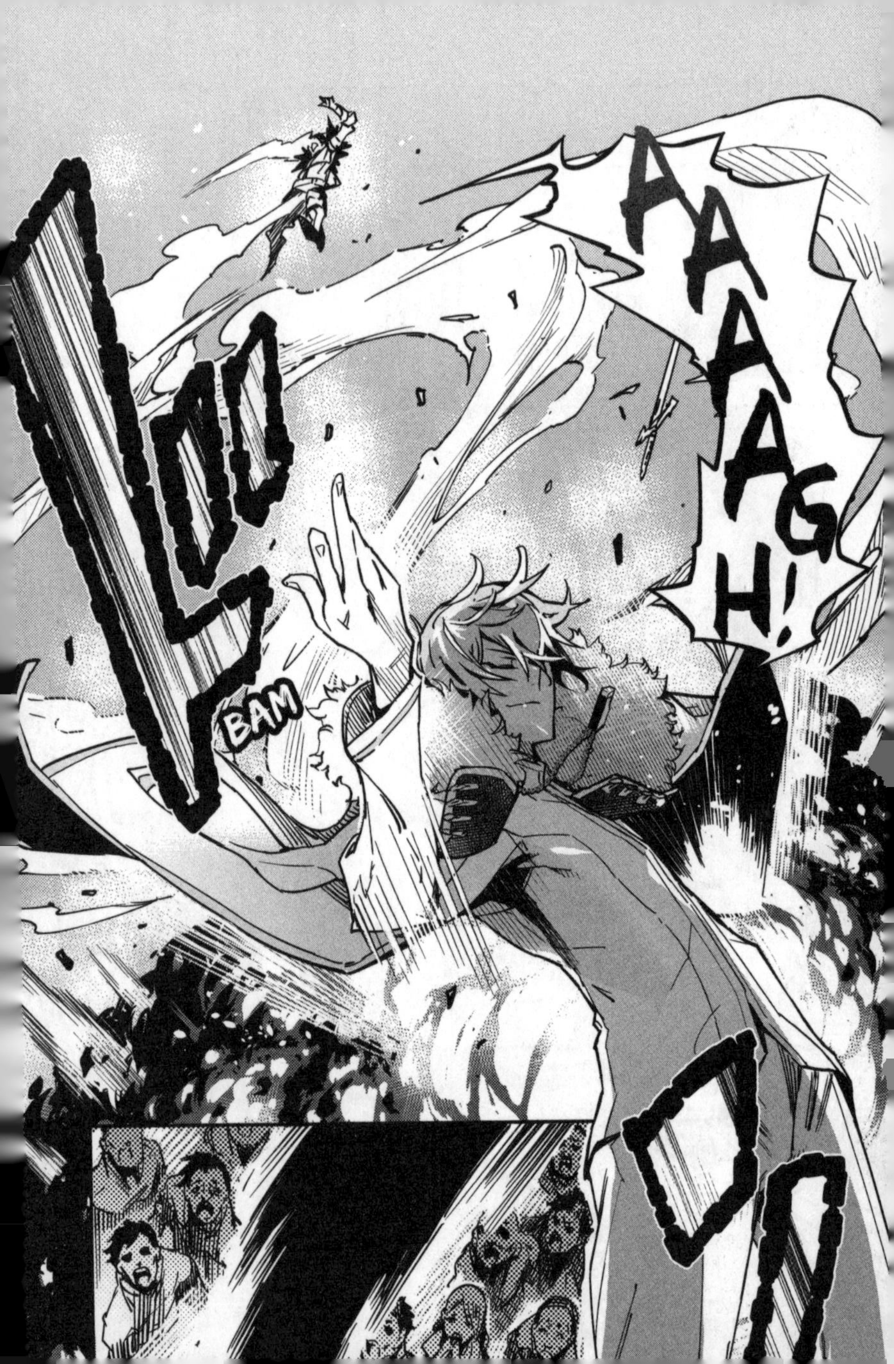
AAAAAGH!
BAM

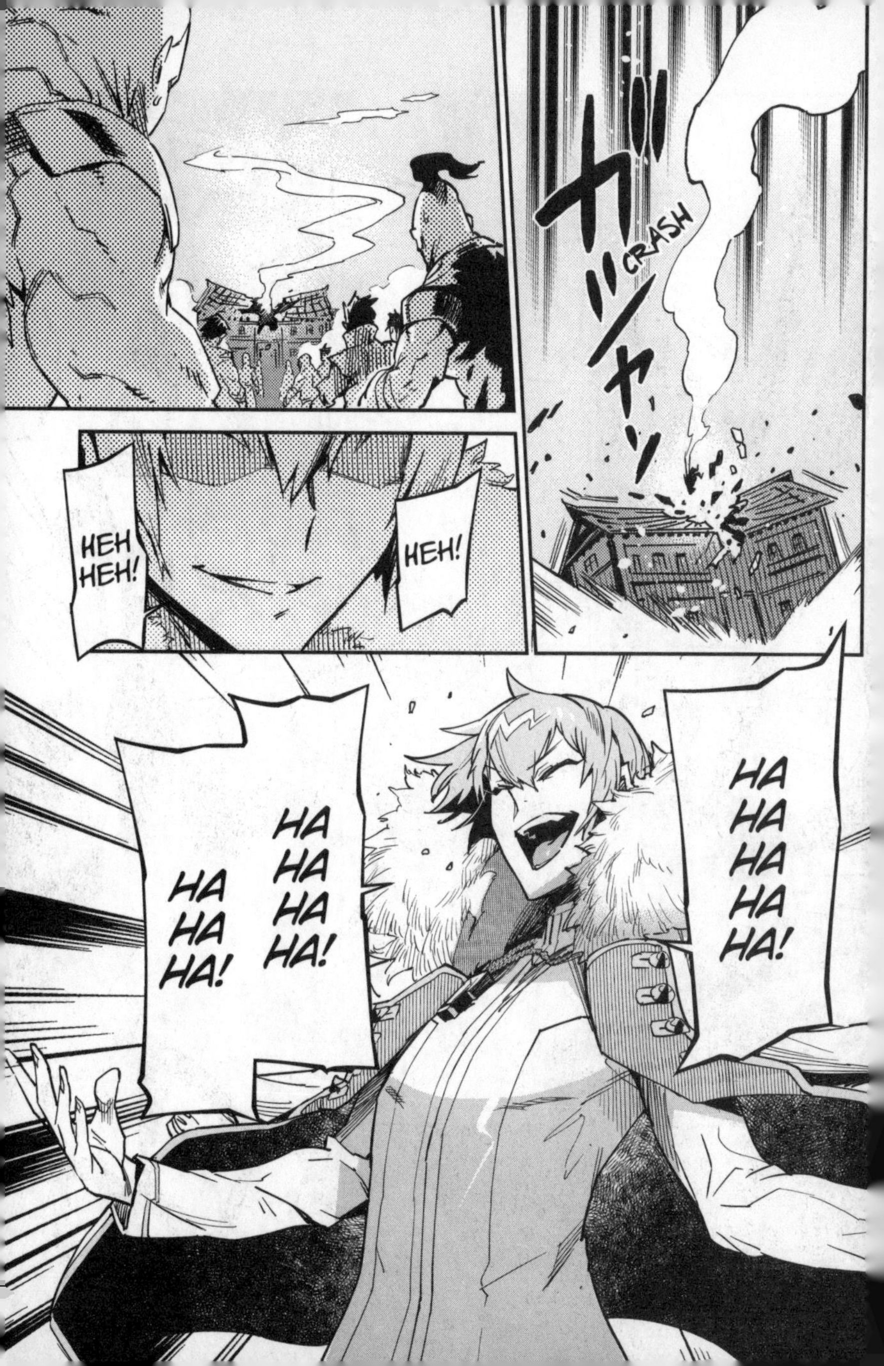
ガシャンッ
CRASH
HEH!
HEH HEH!
HA HA HA HA HA HA!
HA HA HA HA HA!
HA HA HA!

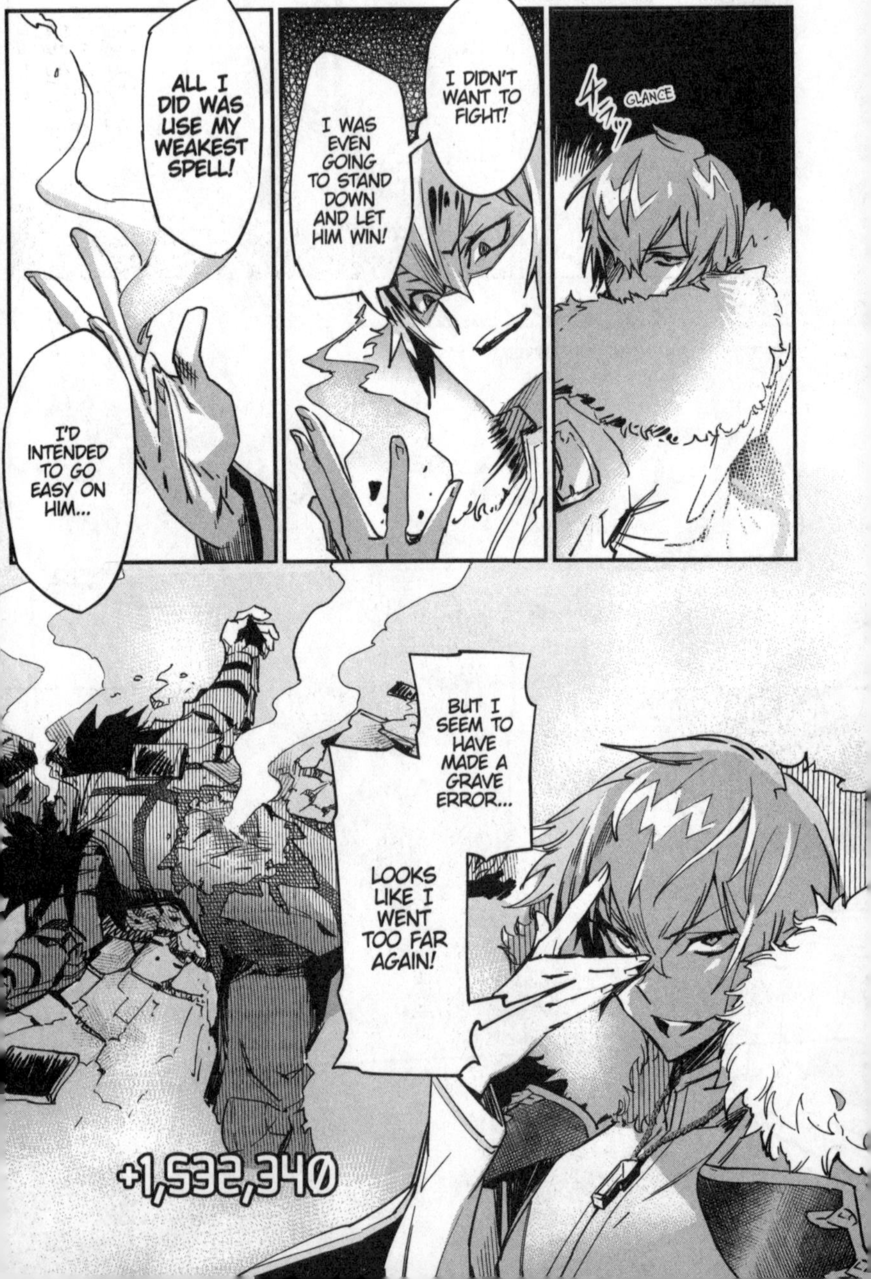
GLANCE
I DIDN'T WANT TO FIGHT!
I WAS EVEN GOING TO STAND DOWN AND LET HIM WIN!
ALL I DID WAS USE MY WEAKEST SPELL!
I'D INTENDED TO GO EASY ON HIM...
BUT I SEEM TO HAVE MADE A GRAVE ERROR...
LOOKS LIKE I WENT TOO FAR AGAIN!
+1,532,340

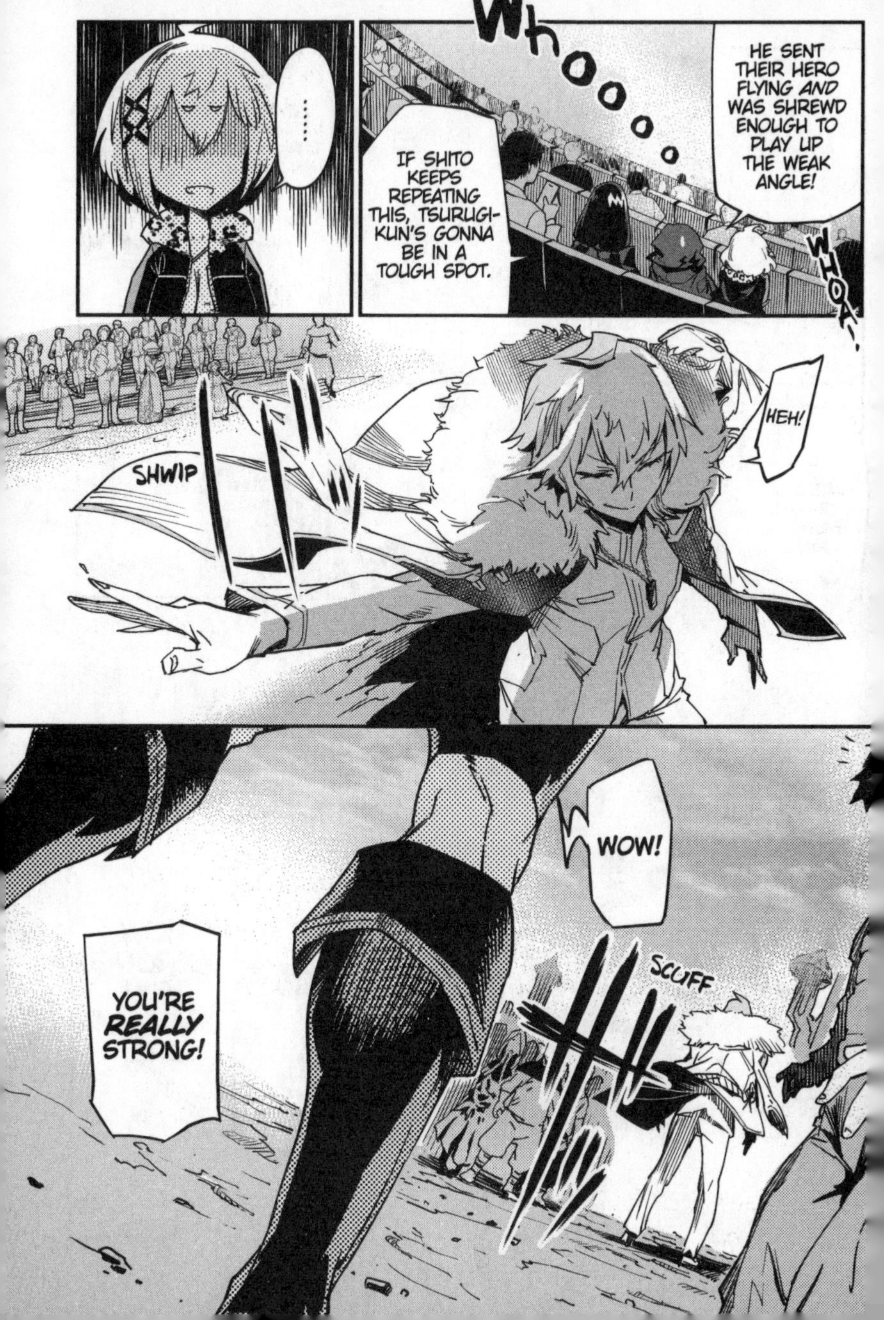
HE SENT THEIR HERO FLYING *AND* WAS SHREWD ENOUGH TO PLAY UP THE WEAK ANGLE!
Whoooo
WHOA...
IF SHITO KEEPS REPEATING THIS, TSURUGI-KUN'S GONNA BE IN A TOUGH SPOT.
......
HEH!
SHWIP
WOW!
YOU'RE *REALLY* STRONG!
SCUFF

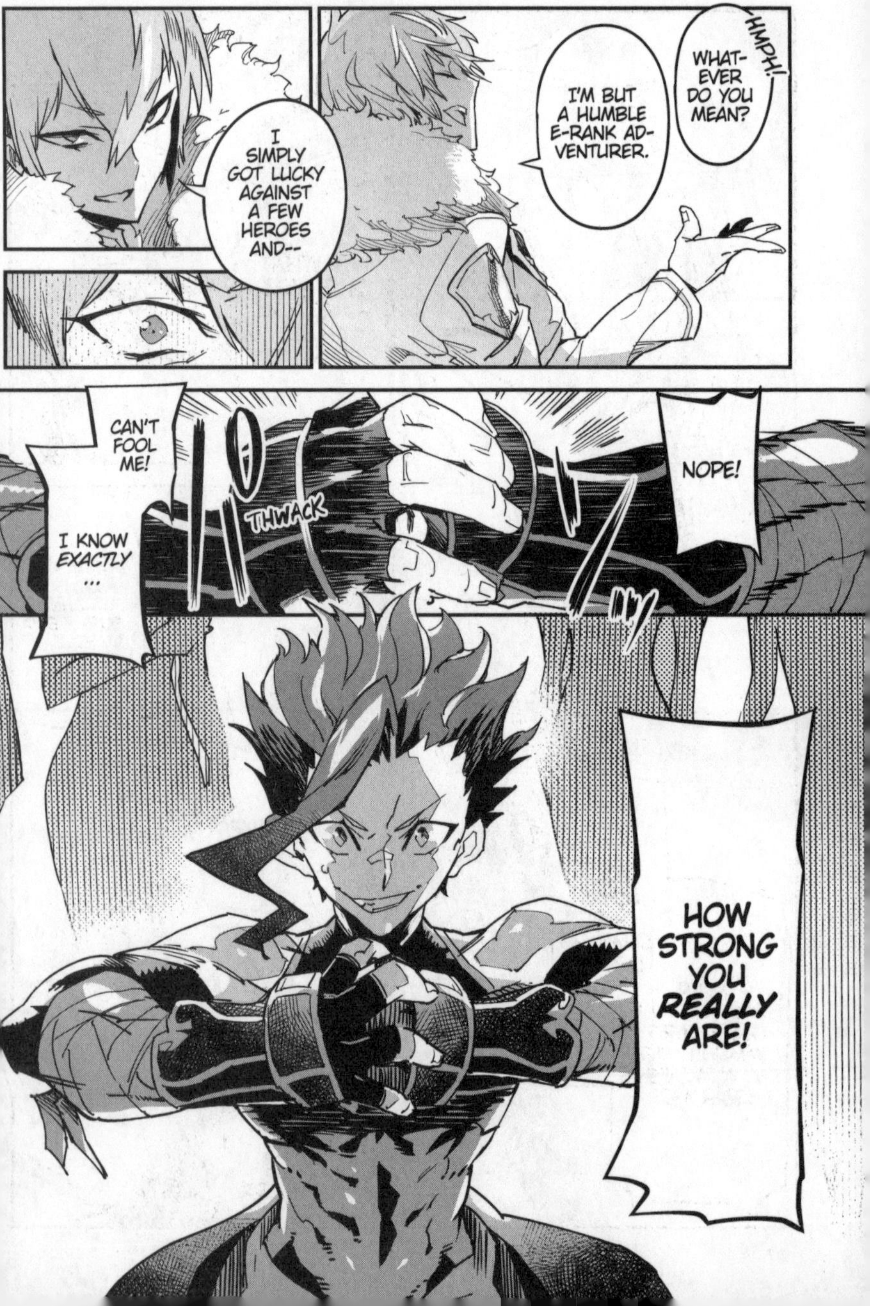
HMPH!
WHAT-EVER DO YOU MEAN?
I'M BUT A HUMBLE E-RANK AD-VENTURER.
I SIMPLY GOT LUCKY AGAINST A FEW HEROES AND--
NOPE!
THWACK
CAN'T FOOL ME!
I KNOW *EXACTLY* ...
HOW STRONG YOU *REALLY* ARE!

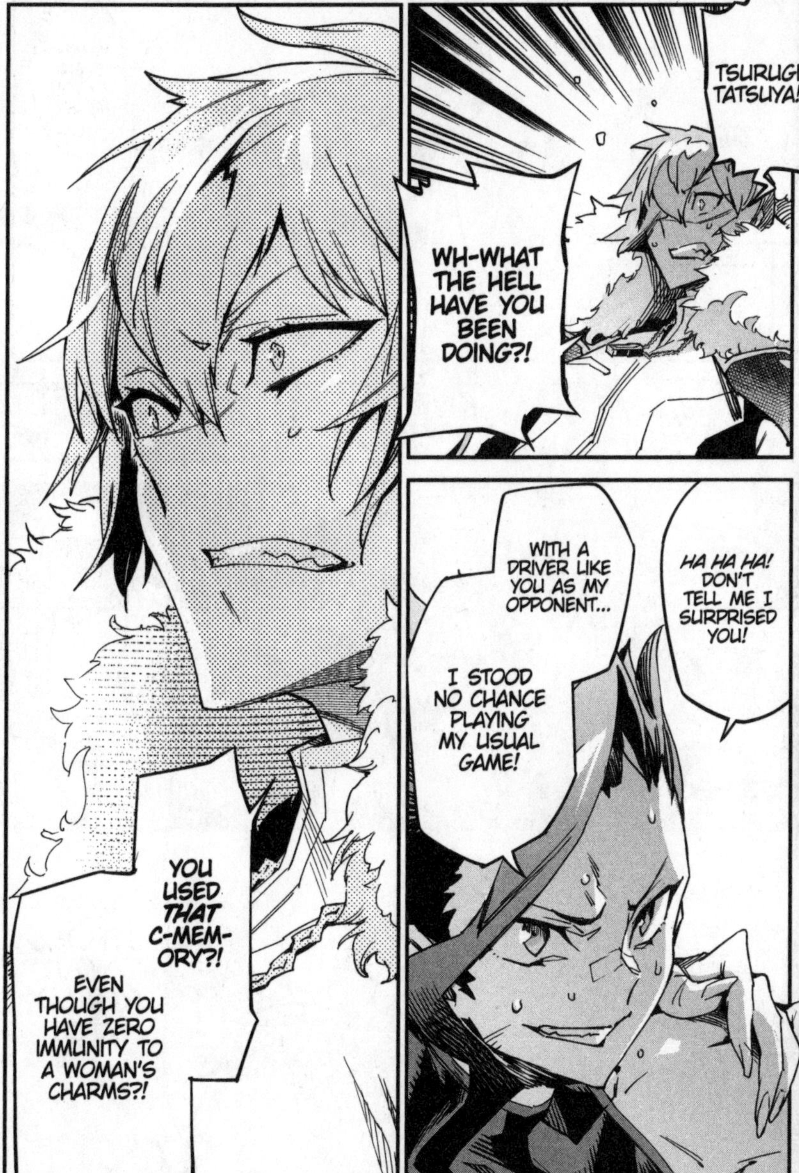
TSURUGI TATSUYA!
WH-WHAT THE HELL HAVE YOU BEEN DOING?!
HA HA HA! DON'T TELL ME I SURPRISED YOU!
WITH A DRIVER LIKE YOU AS MY OPPONENT...
I STOOD NO CHANCE PLAYING MY USUAL GAME!
YOU USED *THAT* C-MEMORY?!
EVEN THOUGH YOU HAVE ZERO IMMUNITY TO A WOMAN'S CHARMS?!

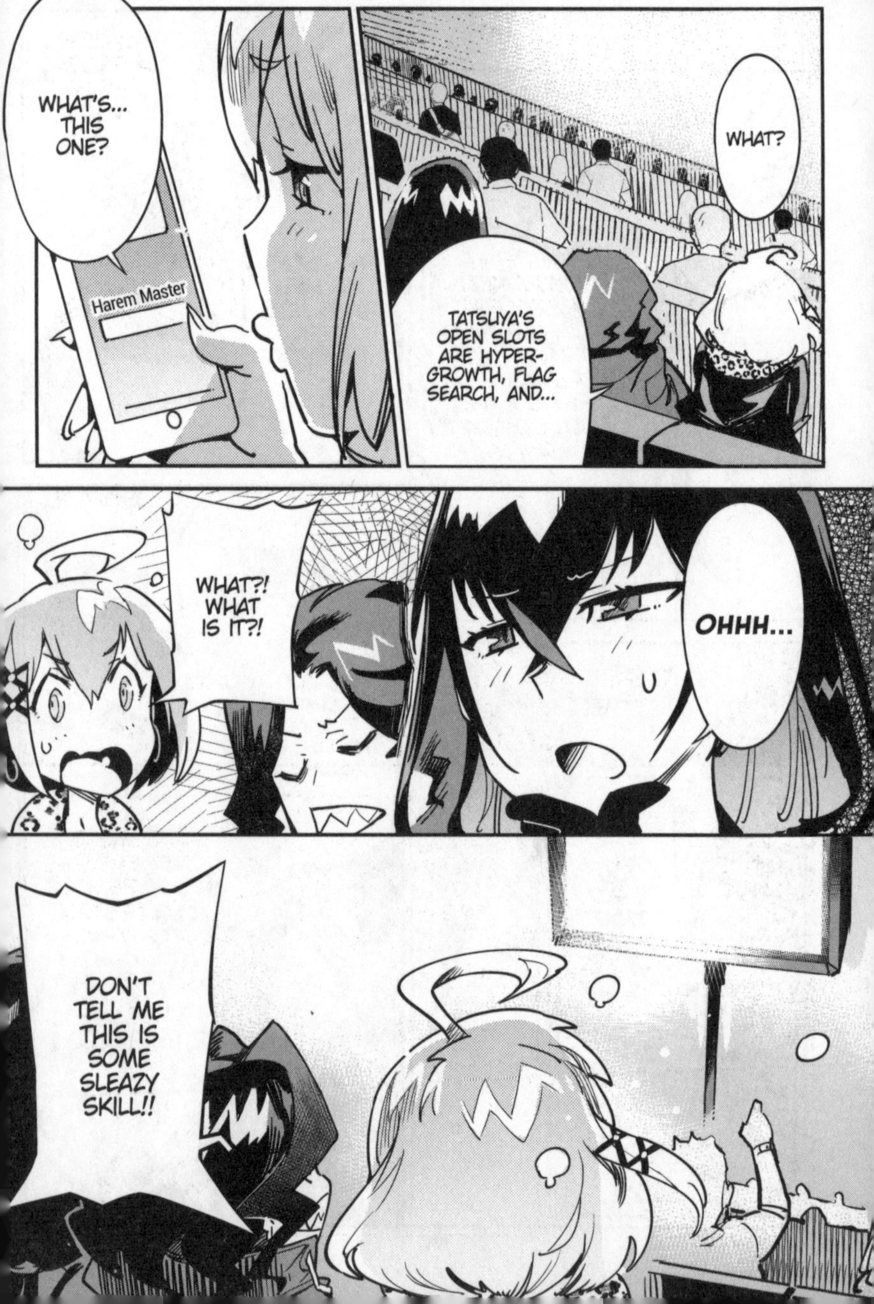
WHAT?
TATSUYA'S OPEN SLOTS ARE HYPER-GROWTH, FLAG SEARCH, AND...
WHAT'S... THIS ONE?
Harem Master
OHHH...
WHAT?! WHAT IS IT?!
DON'T TELL ME THIS IS SOME SLEAZY SKILL!!

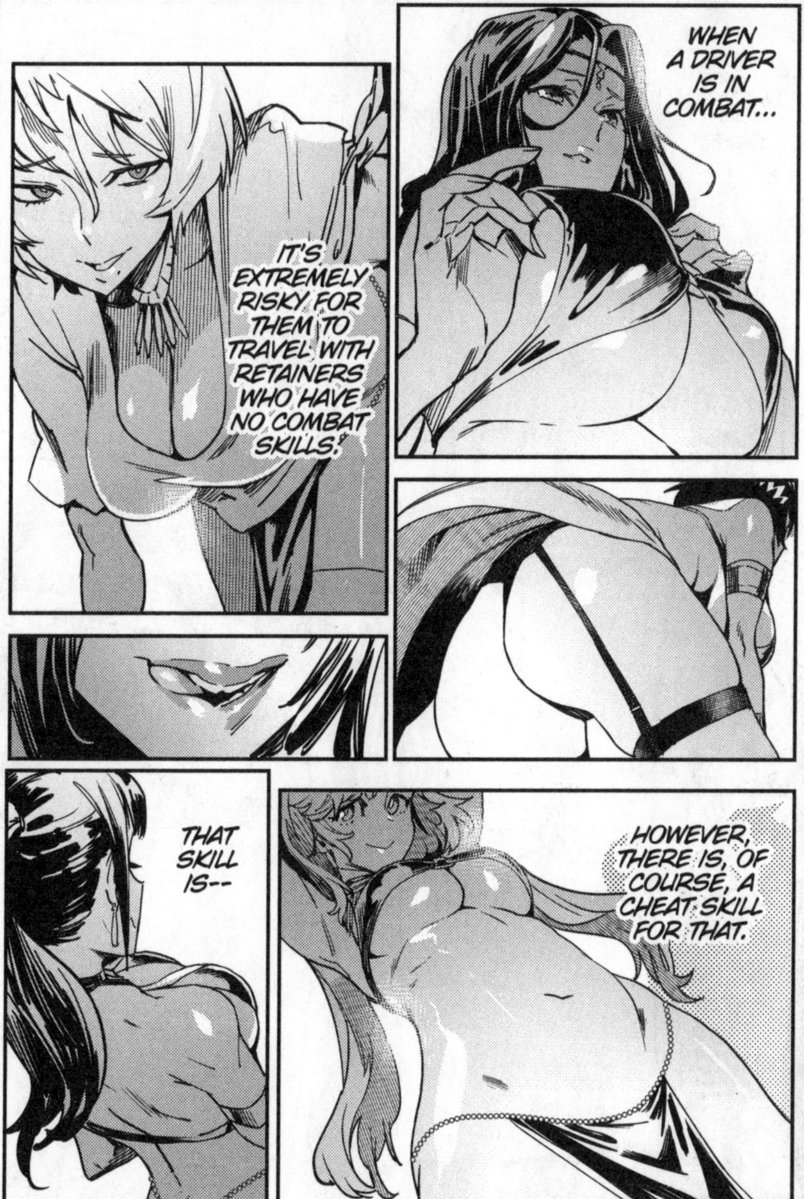
WHEN A DRIVER IS IN COMBAT...
IT'S EXTREMELY RISKY FOR THEM TO TRAVEL WITH RETAINERS WHO HAVE NO COMBAT SKILLS.
HOWEVER, THERE IS, OF COURSE, A CHEAT SKILL FOR THAT.
THAT SKILL IS--

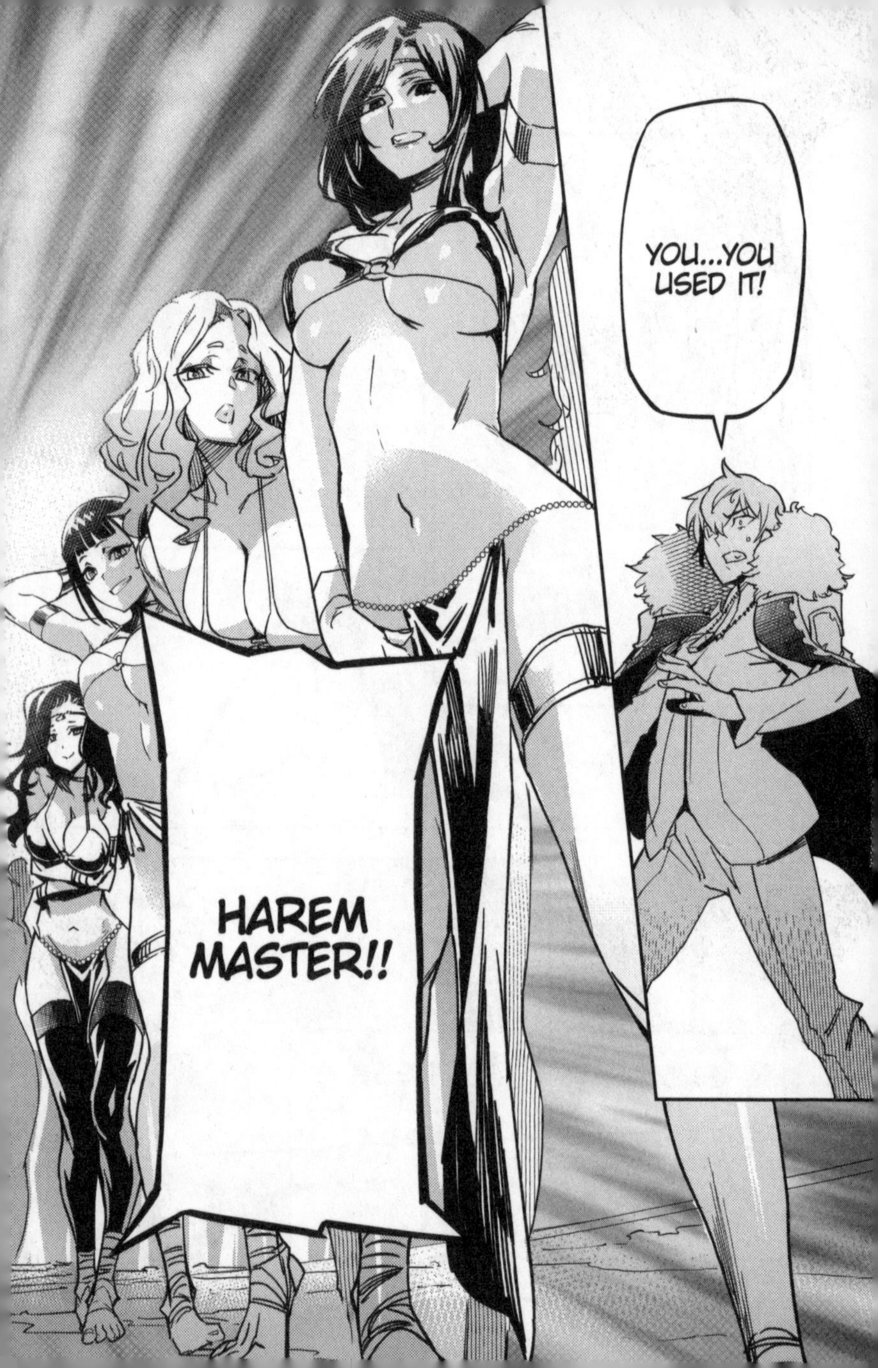
YOU...YOU USED IT!
HAREM MASTER!!

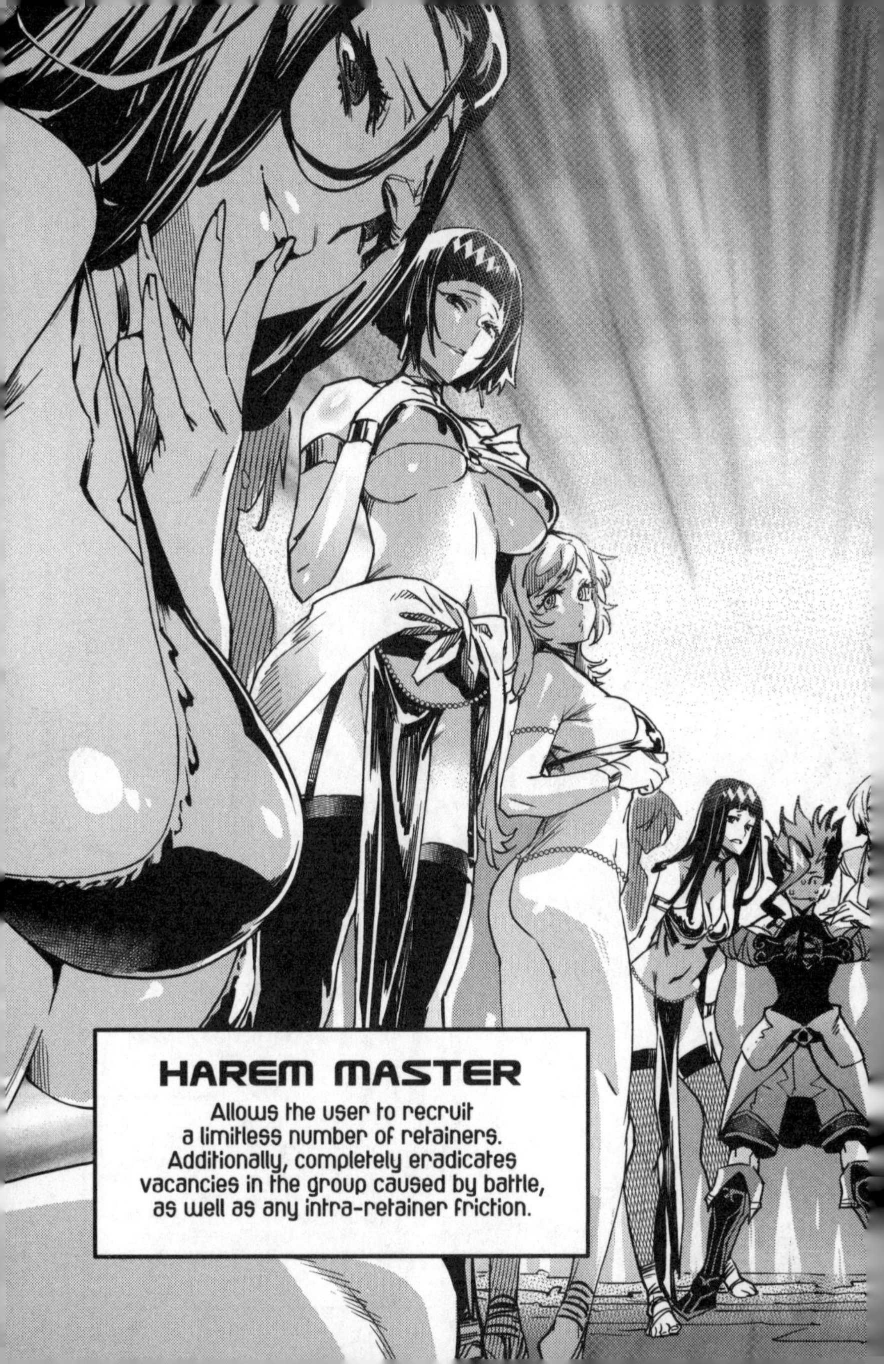
HAREM MASTER
Allows the user to recruit a limitless number of retainers. Additionally, completely eradicates vacancies in the group caused by battle, as well as any intra-retainer friction.

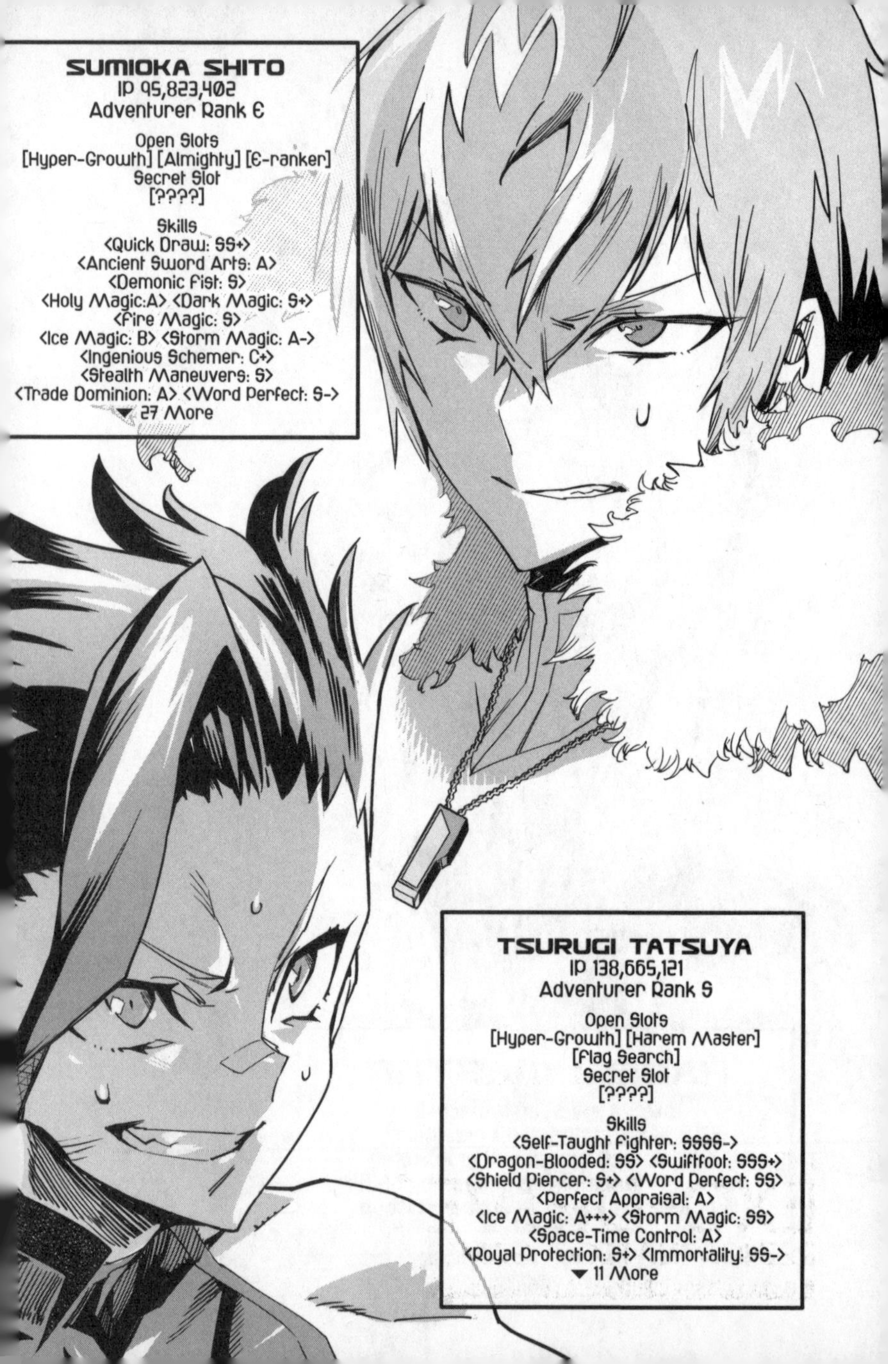
SUMIOKA SHITO
IP 95,823,402
Adventurer Rank E
Open Slots
[Hyper-Growth] [Almighty] [E-ranker]
Secret Slot
[????]
Skills
<Quick Draw: SS+>
<Ancient Sword Arts: A>
<Demonic Fist: S>
<Holy Magic:A> <Dark Magic: S+>
<Fire Magic: S>
<Ice Magic: B> <Storm Magic: A->
<Ingenious Schemer: C+>
<Stealth Maneuvers: S>
<Trade Dominion: A> <Word Perfect: S->
▼ 27 More
TSURUGI TATSUYA
IP 138,665,121
Adventurer Rank S
Open Slots
[Hyper-Growth] [Harem Master]
[Flag Search]
Secret Slot
[????]
Skills
<Self-Taught Fighter: SSSS->
<Dragon-Blooded: SS> <Swiftfoot: SSS+>
<Shield Piercer: S+> <Word Perfect: SS>
<Perfect Appraisal: A>
<Ice Magic: A+++> <Storm Magic: SS>
<Space-Time Control: A>
<Royal Protection: S+> <Immortality: SS->
▼ 11 More

THE
EXO-DRIVE
REINCARNATION GAMES
ALL-JAPAN ISEKAI BATTLE TOURNAMENT!

THE
EXO-DRIVE
REINCARNATION GAMES
ALL-JAPAN ISEKAI BATTLE TOURNAMENT!

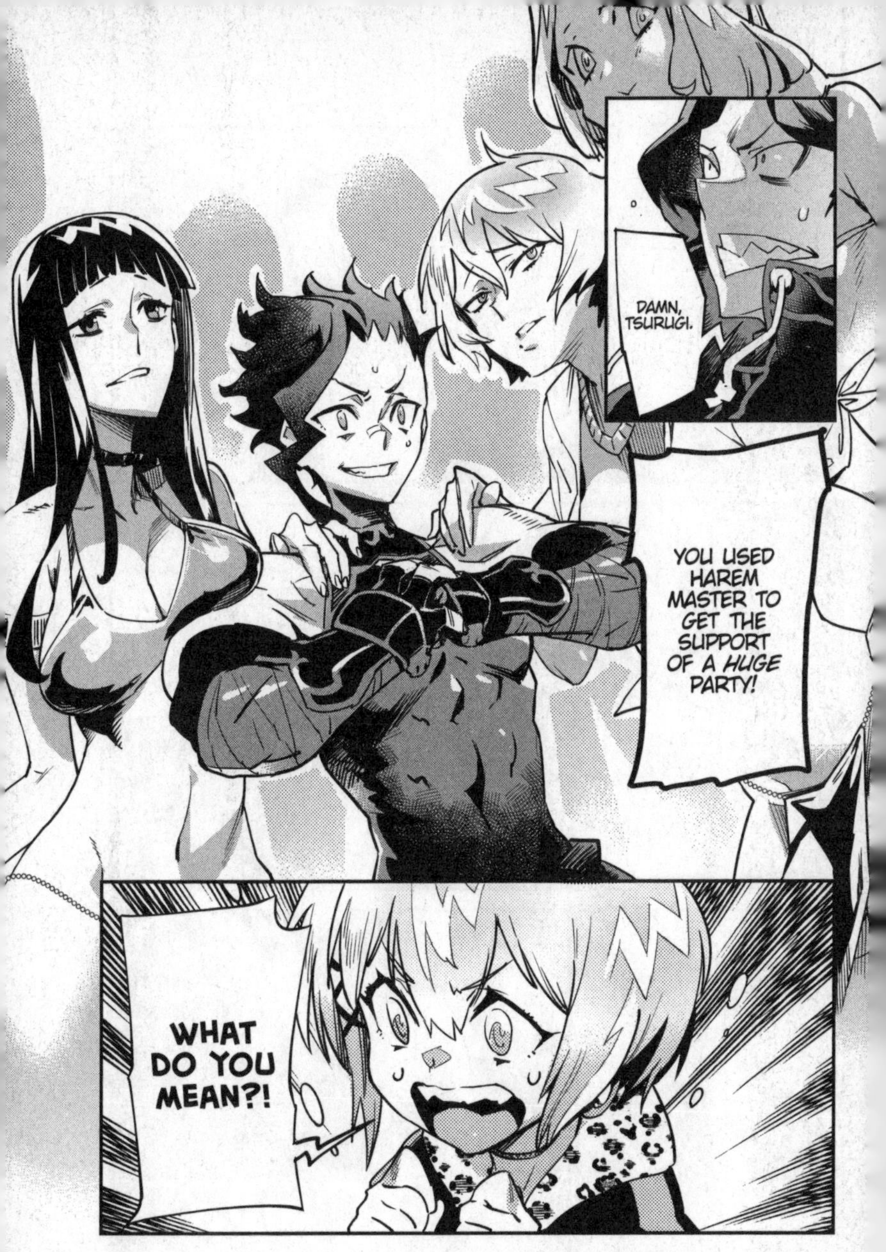
DAMN, TSURUGI.
YOU USED HAREM MASTER TO GET THE SUPPORT OF A *HUGE* PARTY!
WHAT DO YOU MEAN?!

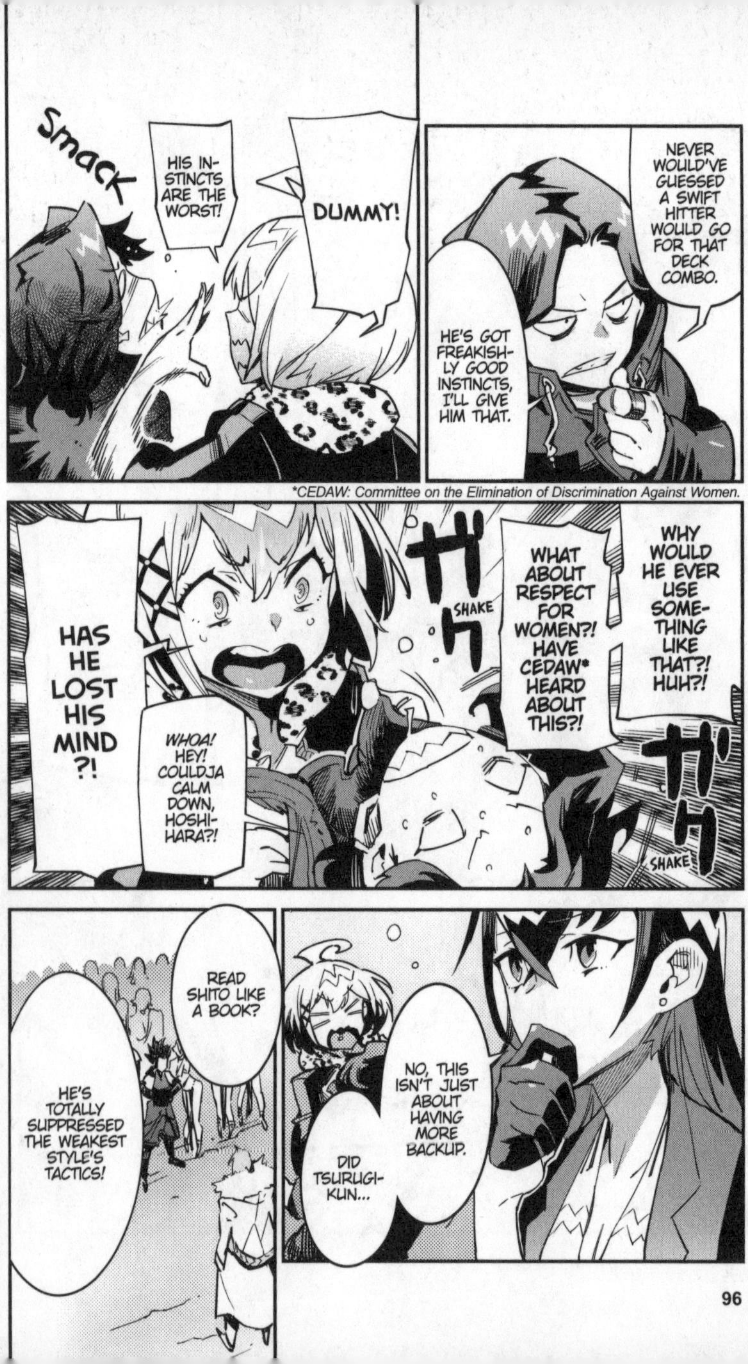

NEVER WOULD'VE GUESSED A SWIFT HITTER WOULD GO FOR THAT DECK COMBO.
HE'S GOT FREAKISHLY GOOD INSTINCTS, I'LL GIVE HIM THAT.
DUMMY!
HIS INSTINCTS ARE THE WORST!
Smack
WHY WOULD HE EVER USE SOMETHING LIKE THAT?! HUH?!
ガク
SHAKE
WHAT ABOUT RESPECT FOR WOMEN?! HAVE CEDAW* HEARD ABOUT THIS?!
ガク
SHAKE
HAS HE LOST HIS MIND?!
WHOA! HEY! COULDJA CALM DOWN, HOSHIHARA?!
NO, THIS ISN'T JUST ABOUT HAVING MORE BACKUP.
DID TSURUGI-KUN...
READ SHITO LIKE A BOOK?
HE'S TOTALLY SUPPRESSED THE WEAKEST STYLE'S TACTICS!

*CEDAW: Committee on the Elimination of Discrimination Against Women.

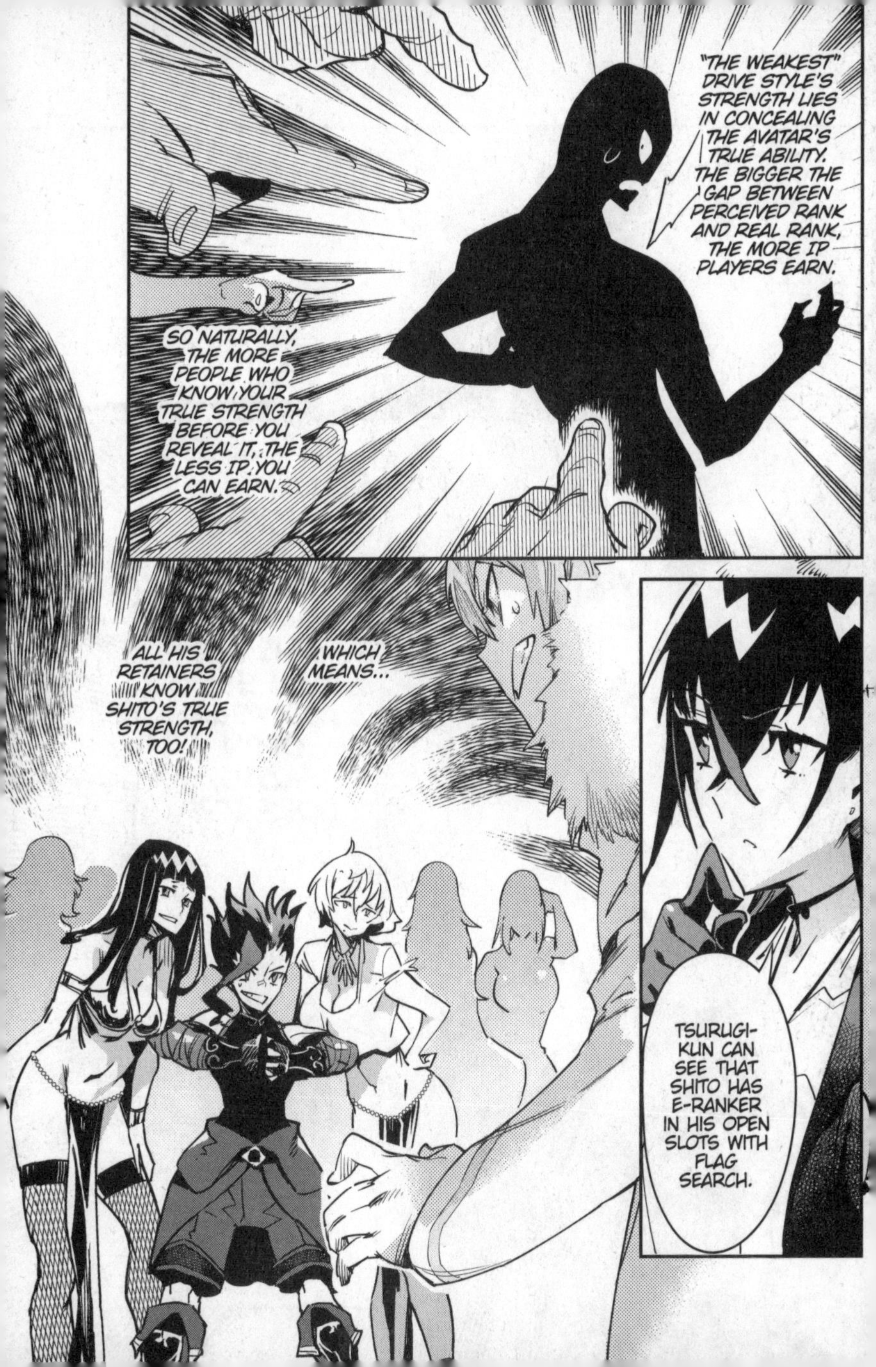
"THE WEAKEST" DRIVE STYLE'S STRENGTH LIES IN CONCEALING THE AVATAR'S TRUE ABILITY. THE BIGGER THE GAP BETWEEN PERCEIVED RANK AND REAL RANK, THE MORE IP PLAYERS EARN.
SO NATURALLY, THE MORE PEOPLE WHO KNOW YOUR TRUE STRENGTH BEFORE YOU REVEAL IT, THE LESS IP YOU CAN EARN.
TSURUGI-KUN CAN SEE THAT SHITO HAS E-RANKER IN HIS OPEN SLOTS WITH FLAG SEARCH.
...WHICH MEANS...
ALL HIS RETAINERS KNOW SHITO'S TRUE STRENGTH, TOO!

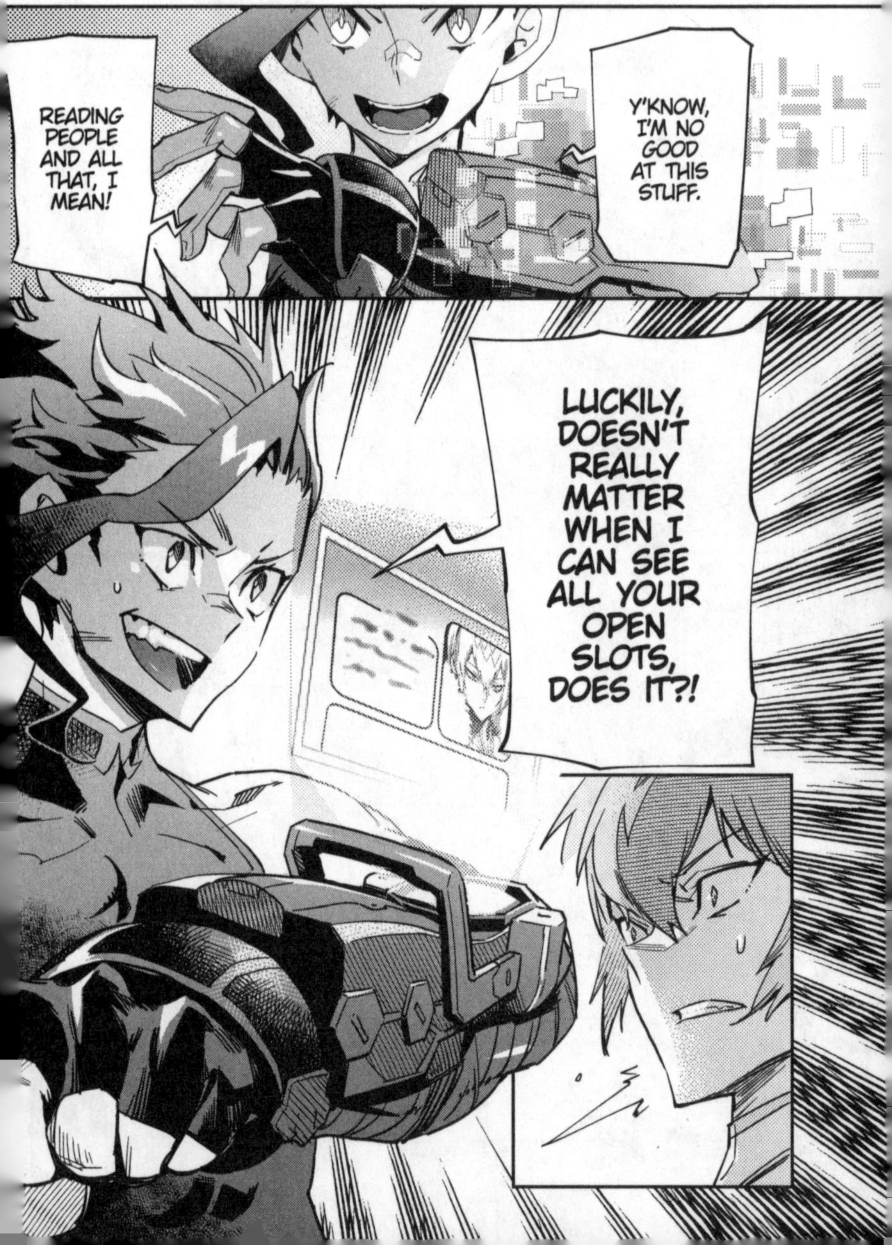
Y'KNOW, I'M NO GOOD AT THIS STUFF.
READING PEOPLE AND ALL THAT, I MEAN!
LUCKILY, DOESN'T REALLY MATTER WHEN I CAN SEE ALL YOUR OPEN SLOTS, DOES IT?!

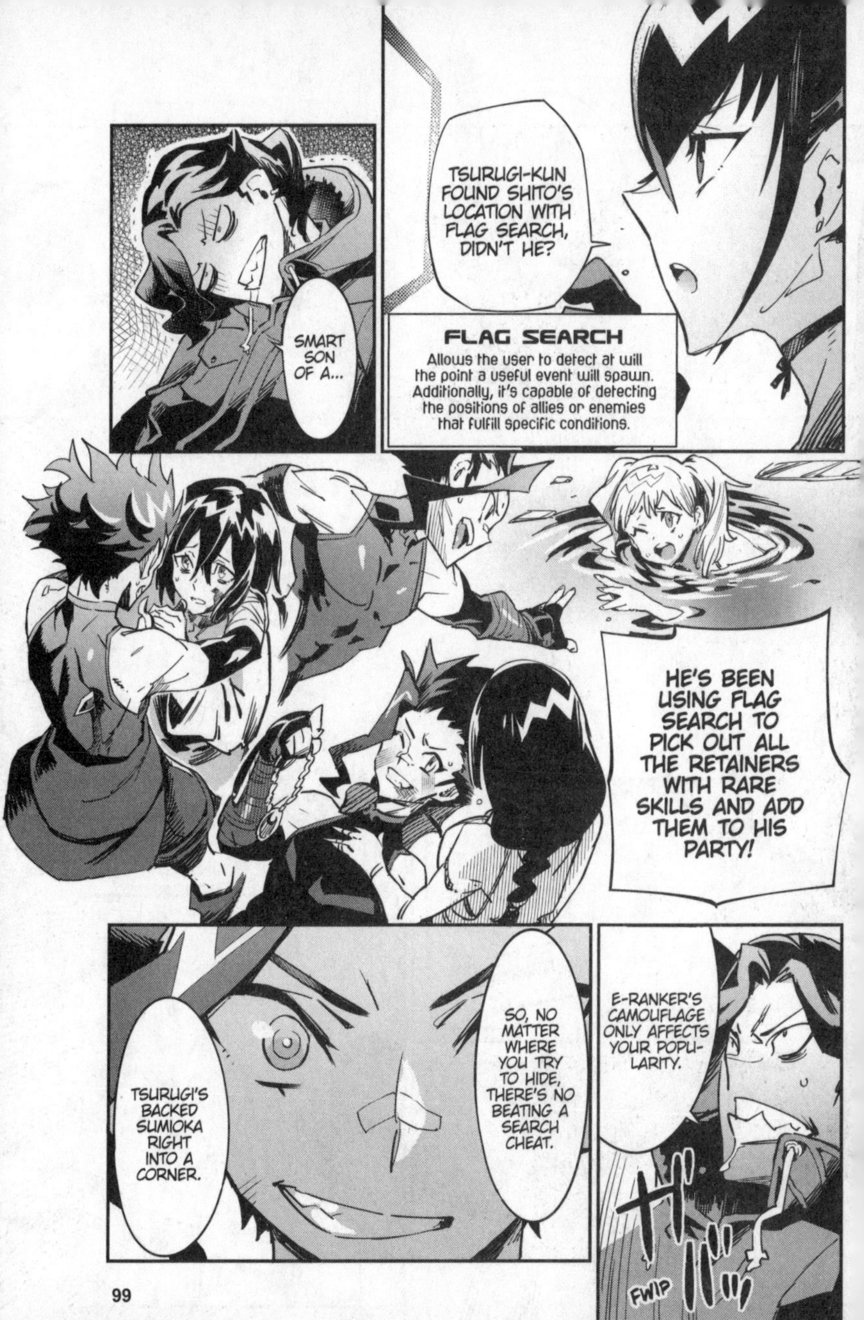

TSURUGI-KUN FOUND SHITO'S LOCATION WITH FLAG SEARCH, DIDN'T HE?
FLAG SEARCH
Allows the user to detect at will the point a useful event will spawn. Additionally, it's capable of detecting the positions of allies or enemies that fulfill specific conditions.
SMART SON OF A...
HE'S BEEN USING FLAG SEARCH TO PICK OUT ALL THE RETAINERS WITH RARE SKILLS AND ADD THEM TO HIS PARTY!
E-RANKER'S CAMOUFLAGE ONLY AFFECTS YOUR POPULARITY.
FWIP
SO, NO MATTER WHERE YOU TRY TO HIDE, THERE'S NO BEATING A SEARCH CHEAT.
TSURUGI'S BACKED SUMIOKA RIGHT INTO A CORNER.

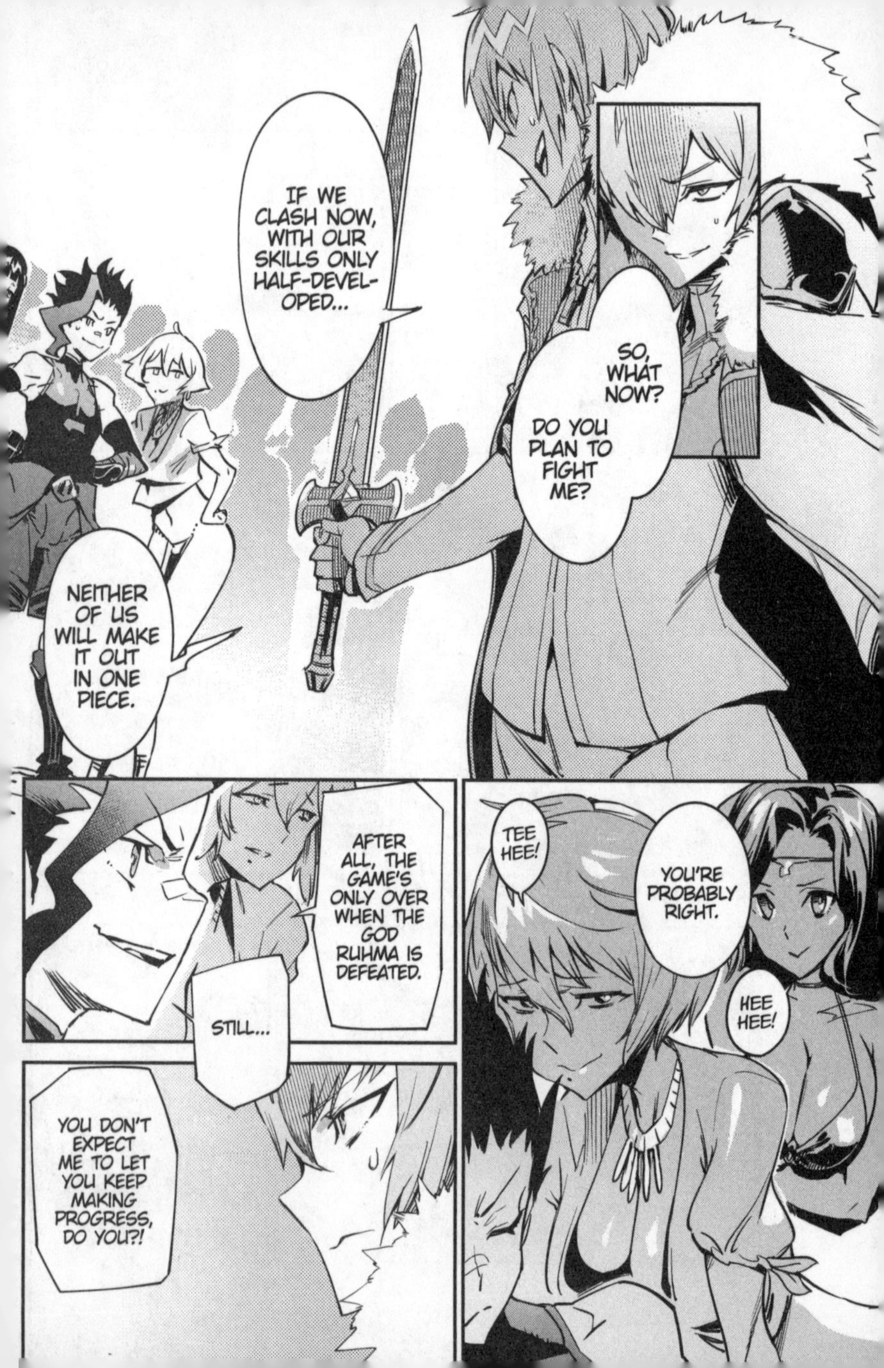
SO, WHAT NOW?
DO YOU PLAN TO FIGHT ME?
IF WE CLASH NOW, WITH OUR SKILLS ONLY HALF-DEVEL-OPED...
NEITHER OF US WILL MAKE IT OUT IN ONE PIECE.
YOU'RE PROBABLY RIGHT.
TEE HEE!
HEE HEE!
AFTER ALL, THE GAME'S ONLY OVER WHEN THE GOD RUHMA IS DEFEATED.
STILL...
YOU DON'T EXPECT ME TO LET YOU KEEP MAKING PROGRESS, DO YOU?!

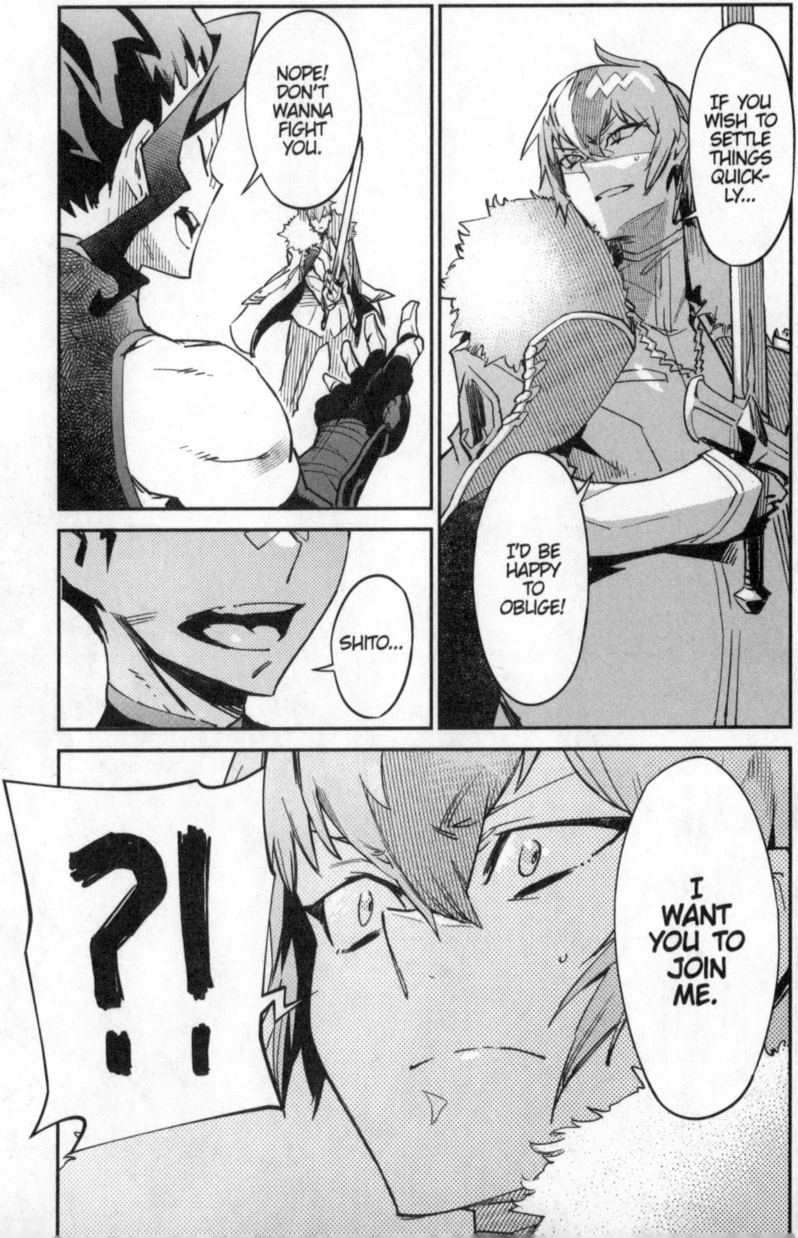
IF YOU WISH TO SETTLE THINGS QUICK-LY...
I'D BE HAPPY TO OBLIGE!
NOPE! DON'T WANNA FIGHT YOU.
SHITO...
I WANT YOU TO JOIN ME.
?!!

CHAPTER 3 [FLAG SEARCH]

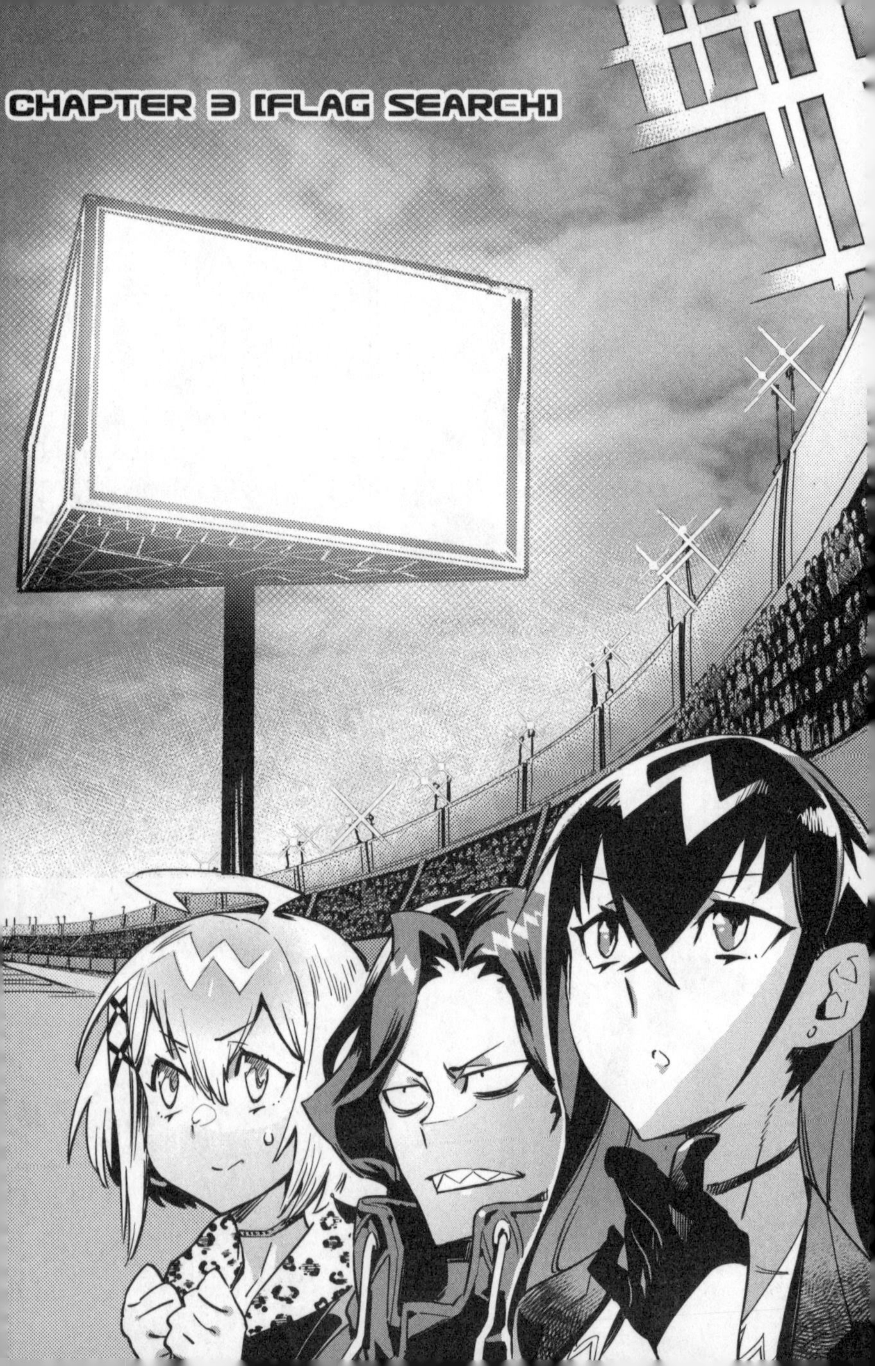

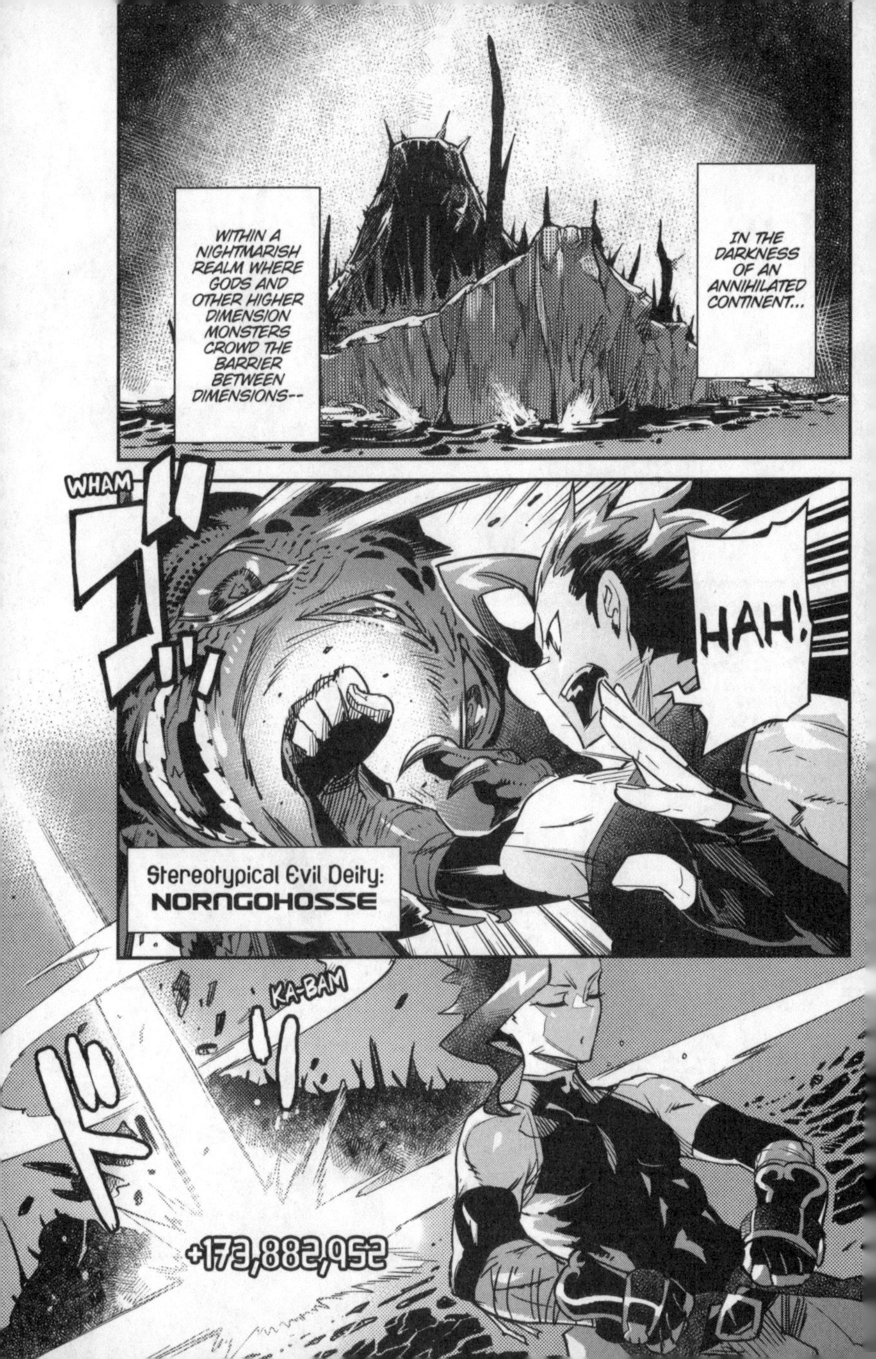
IN THE DARKNESS OF AN ANNIHILATED CONTINENT...
WITHIN A NIGHTMARISH REALM WHERE GODS AND OTHER HIGHER DIMENSION MONSTERS CROWD THE BARRIER BETWEEN DIMENSIONS--
HAH!
WHAM
Stereotypical Evil Deity:
NORNGOHOSSE
KA-BAM
+173,882,952

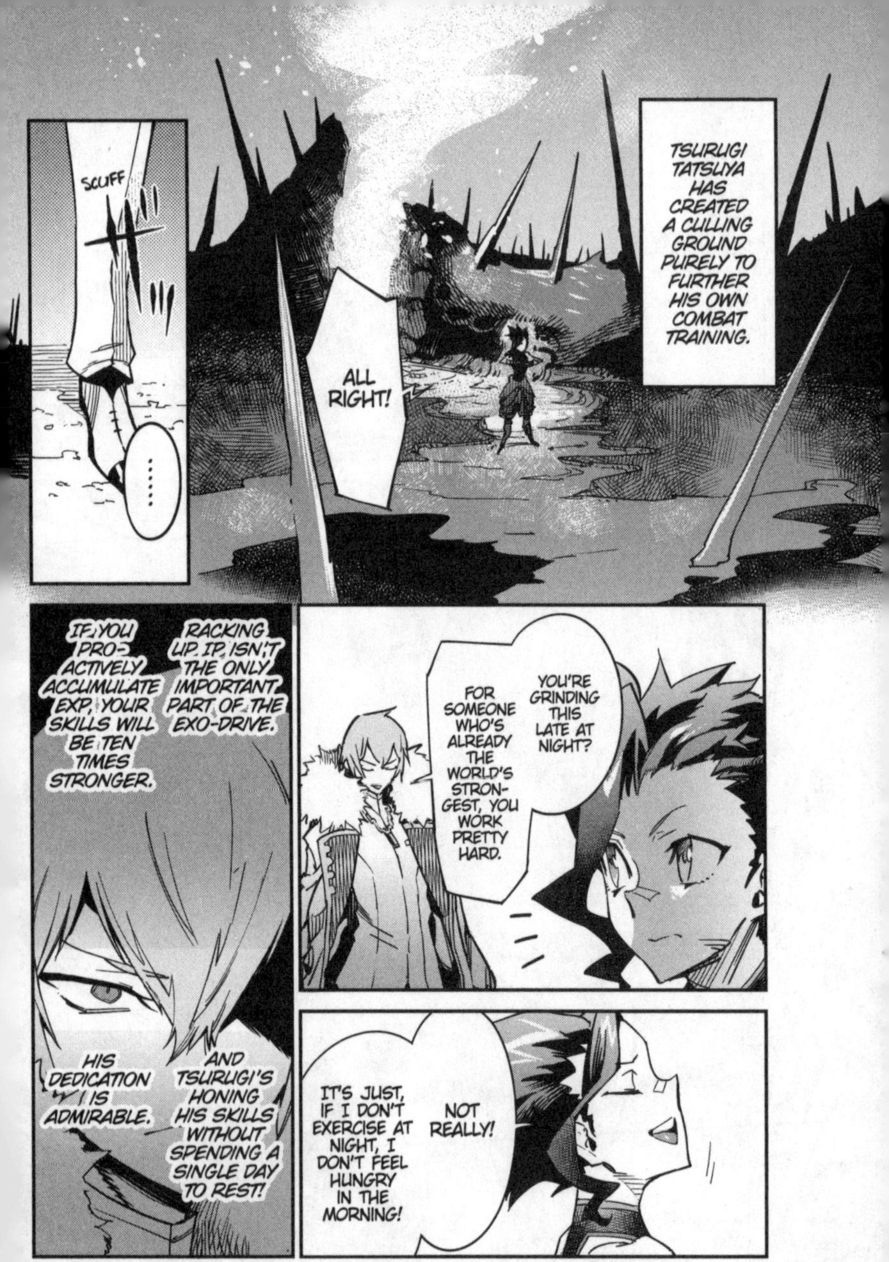
TSURUGI TATSUYA HAS CREATED A CULLING GROUND PURELY TO FURTHER HIS OWN COMBAT TRAINING.
ALL RIGHT!
SCUFF
......
YOU'RE GRINDING THIS LATE AT NIGHT?
FOR SOMEONE WHO'S ALREADY THE WORLD'S STRON-GEST, YOU WORK PRETTY HARD.
NOT REALLY!
IT'S JUST, IF I DON'T EXERCISE AT NIGHT, I DON'T FEEL HUNGRY IN THE MORNING!
RACKING UP IP ISN'T THE ONLY IMPORTANT PART OF THE EXO-DRIVE.
IF YOU PRO-ACTIVELY ACCUMULATE EXP, YOUR SKILLS WILL BE TEN TIMES STRONGER.
AND TSURUGI'S HONING HIS SKILLS WITHOUT SPENDING A SINGLE DAY TO REST!
HIS DEDICATION IS ADMIRABLE.

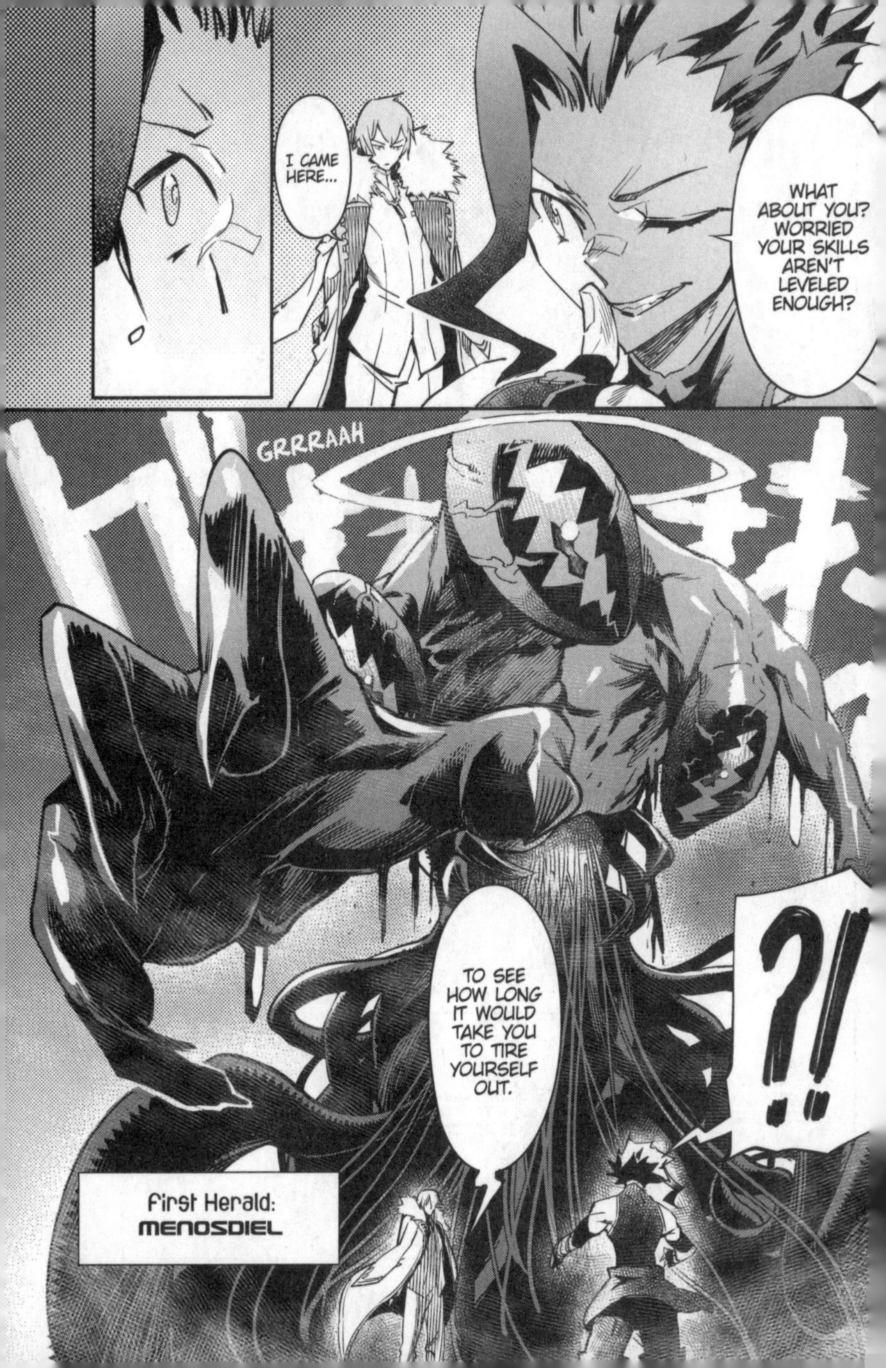
WHAT ABOUT YOU? WORRIED YOUR SKILLS AREN'T LEVELED ENOUGH?
I CAME HERE...
GRRRAAH
?!!
TO SEE HOW LONG IT WOULD TAKE YOU TO TIRE YOURSELF OUT.
First Herald:
MENOSDIEL

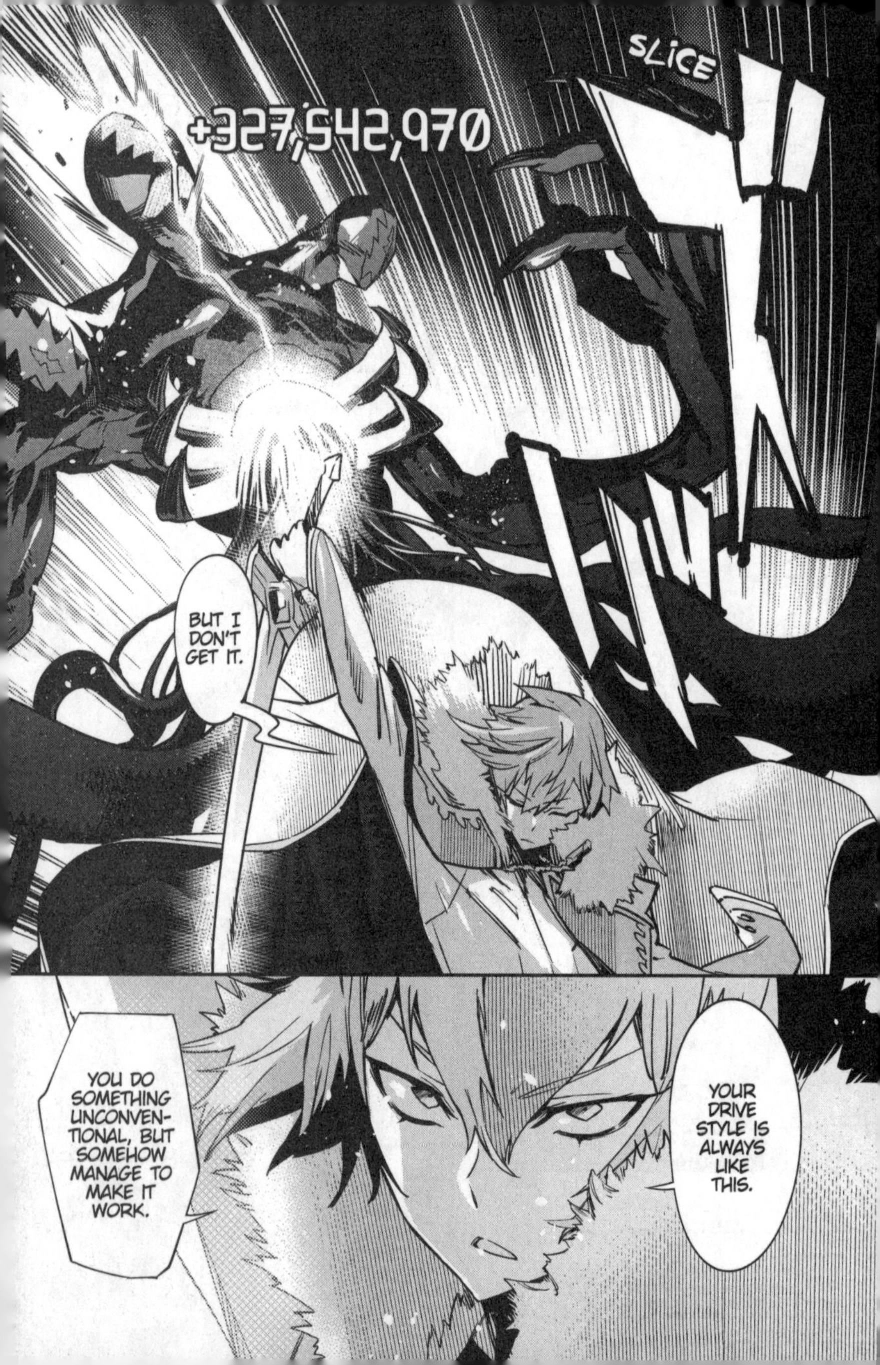
SLICE
+327,542,970
BUT I DON'T GET IT.
YOUR DRIVE STYLE IS ALWAYS LIKE THIS.
YOU DO SOMETHING UNCONVENTIONAL, BUT SOMEHOW MANAGE TO MAKE IT WORK.

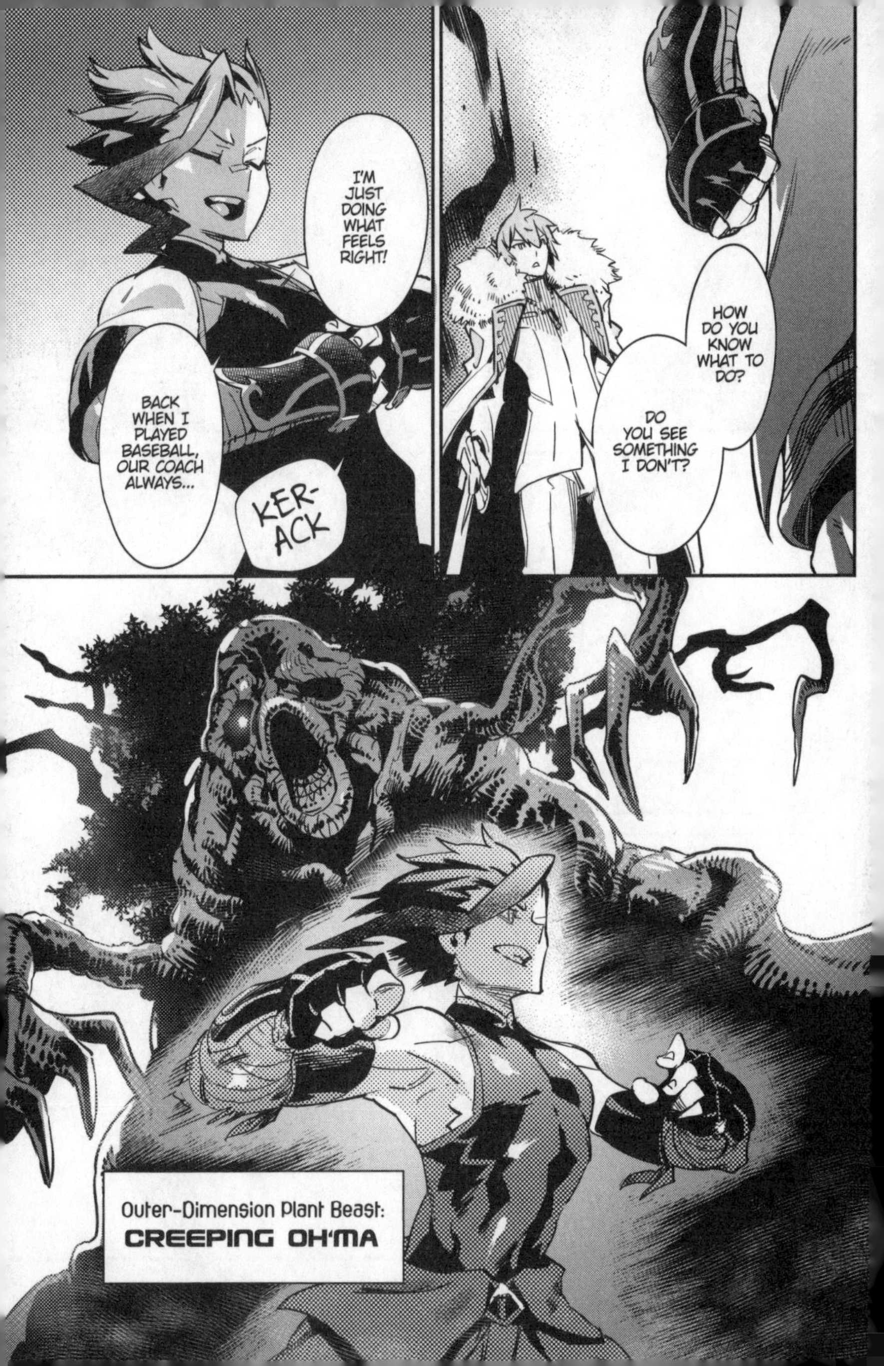
HOW DO YOU KNOW WHAT TO DO?
DO YOU SEE SOMETHING I DON'T?
I'M JUST DOING WHAT FEELS RIGHT!
BACK WHEN I PLAYED BASEBALL, OUR COACH ALWAYS...
KER-ACK
Outer-Dimension Plant Beast:
CREEPING OH'MA

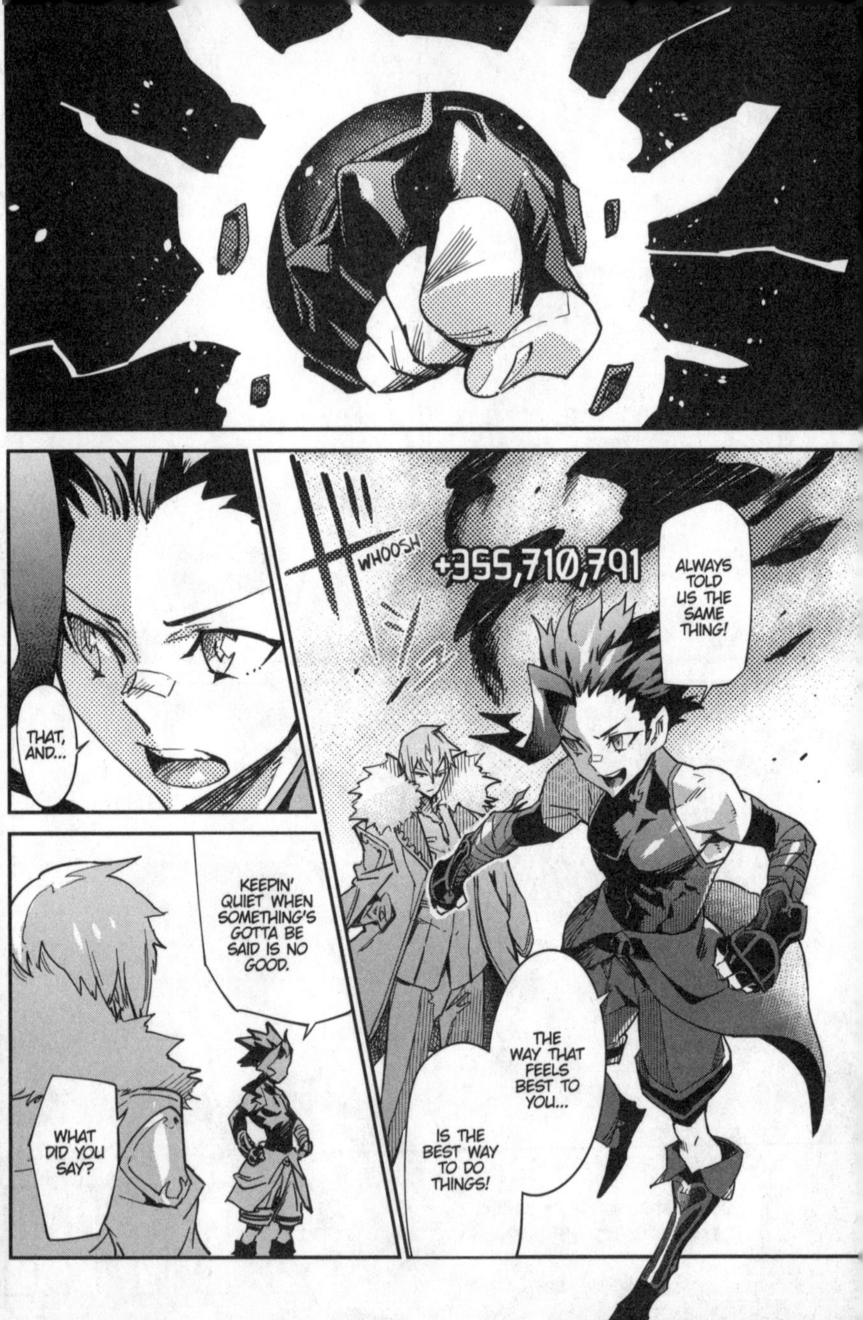
WHOOSH
+355,710,791
ALWAYS TOLD US THE SAME THING!
THE WAY THAT FEELS BEST TO YOU...
IS THE BEST WAY TO DO THINGS!
THAT, AND...
KEEPIN' QUIET WHEN SOMETHING'S GOTTA BE SAID IS NO GOOD.
WHAT DID YOU SAY?

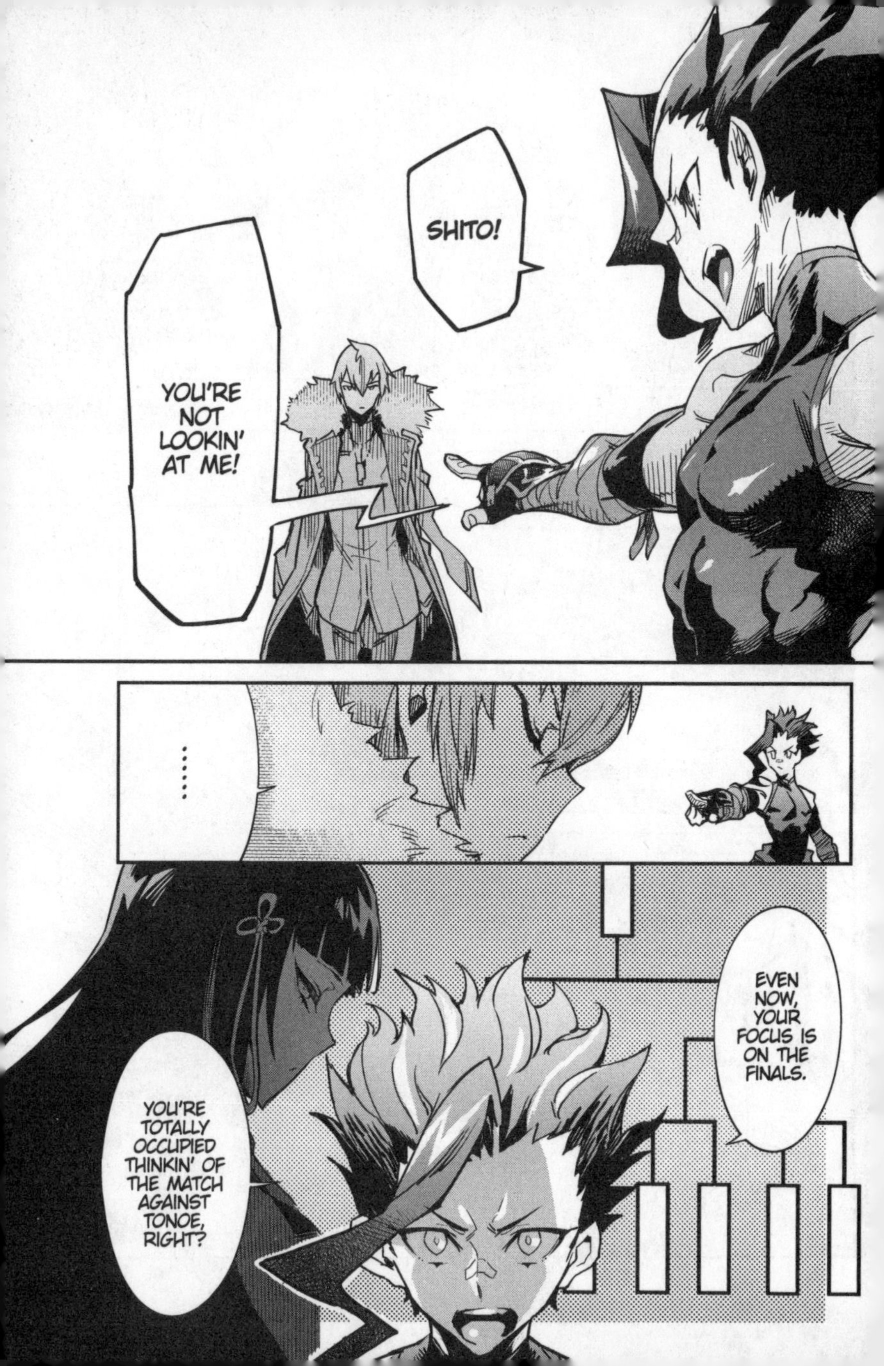
SHITO!
YOU'RE NOT LOOKIN' AT ME!
......
EVEN NOW, YOUR FOCUS IS ON THE FINALS.
YOU'RE TOTALLY OCCUPIED THINKIN' OF THE MATCH AGAINST TONOE, RIGHT?

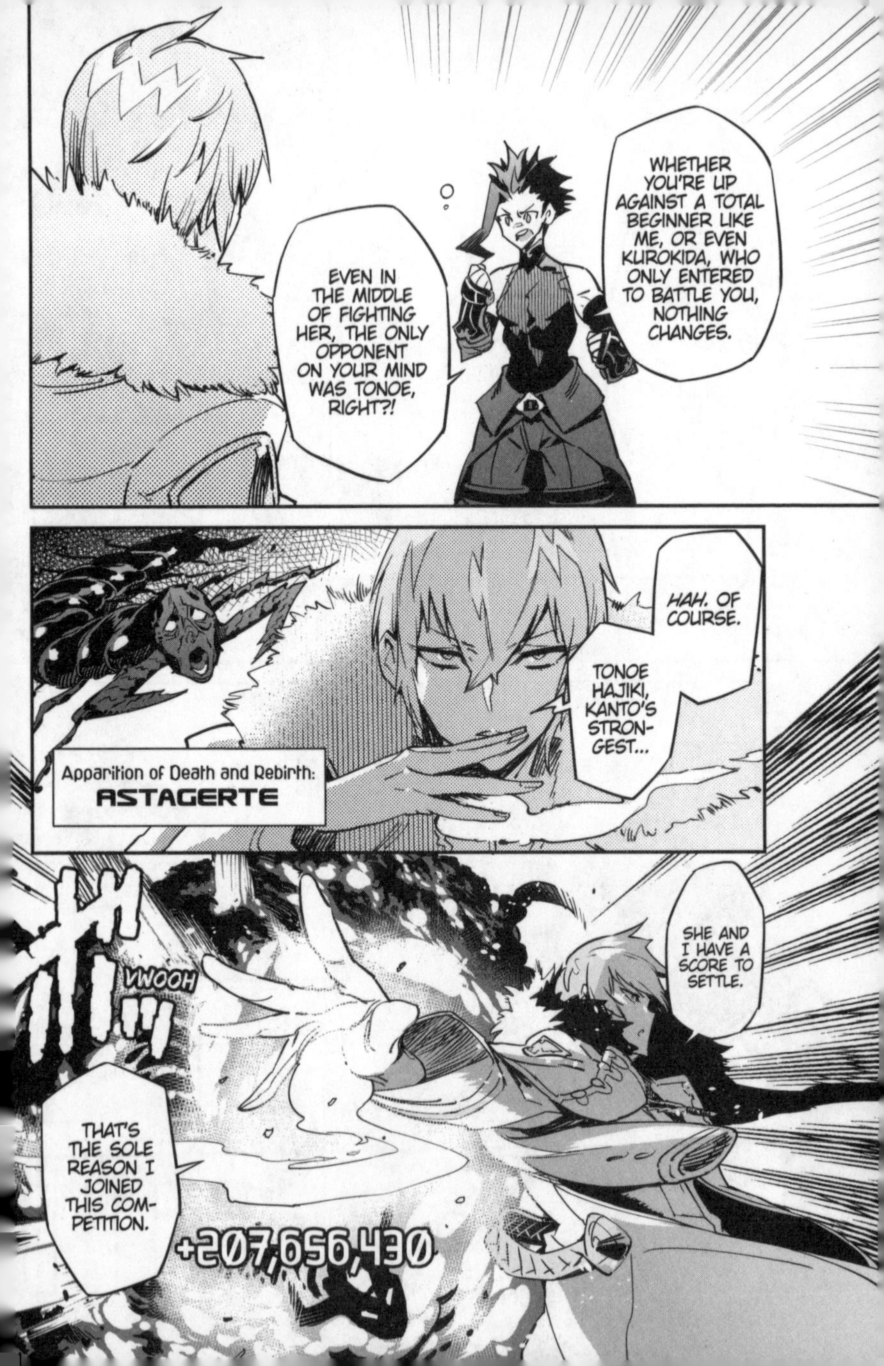

WHETHER YOU'RE UP AGAINST A TOTAL BEGINNER LIKE ME, OR EVEN KUROKIDA, WHO ONLY ENTERED TO BATTLE YOU, NOTHING CHANGES.
EVEN IN THE MIDDLE OF FIGHTING HER, THE ONLY OPPONENT ON YOUR MIND WAS TONOE, RIGHT?!
HAH. OF COURSE.
TONOE HAJIKI, KANTO'S STRONGEST...
Apparition of Death and Rebirth:
ASTAGERTE
SHE AND I HAVE A SCORE TO SETTLE.
VWOOH
THAT'S THE SOLE REASON I JOINED THIS COMPETITION.
+207,656,430

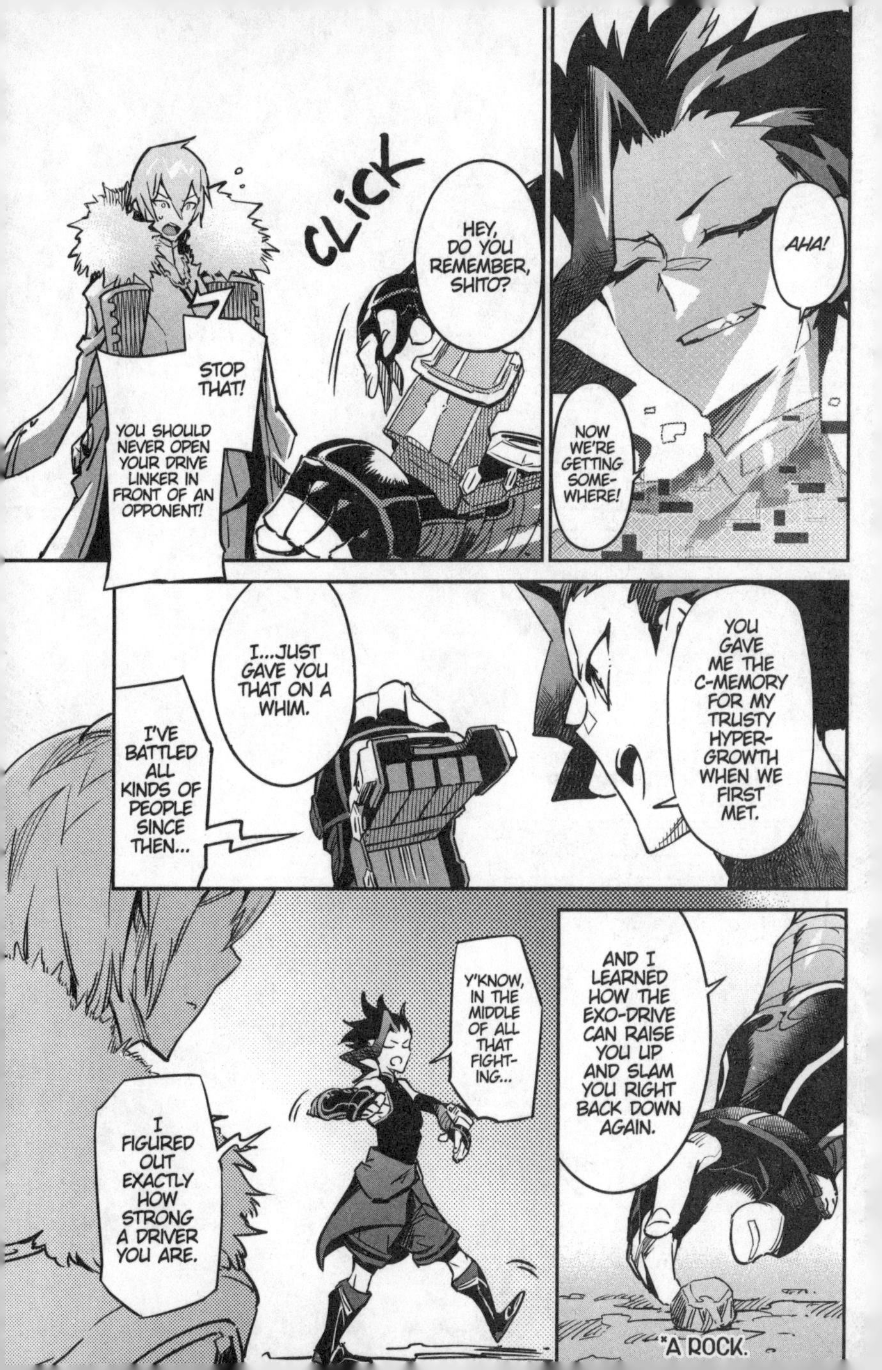
AHA!
NOW WE'RE GETTING SOME-WHERE!
CLICK
HEY, DO YOU REMEMBER, SHITO?
STOP THAT!
YOU SHOULD NEVER OPEN YOUR DRIVE LINKER IN FRONT OF AN OPPONENT!
YOU GAVE ME THE C-MEMORY FOR MY TRUSTY HYPER-GROWTH WHEN WE FIRST MET.
I...JUST GAVE YOU THAT ON A WHIM.
I'VE BATTLED ALL KINDS OF PEOPLE SINCE THEN...
AND I LEARNED HOW THE EXO-DRIVE CAN RAISE YOU UP AND SLAM YOU RIGHT BACK DOWN AGAIN.
*A ROCK.
Y'KNOW, IN THE MIDDLE OF ALL THAT FIGHT-ING...
I FIGURED OUT EXACTLY HOW STRONG A DRIVER YOU ARE.

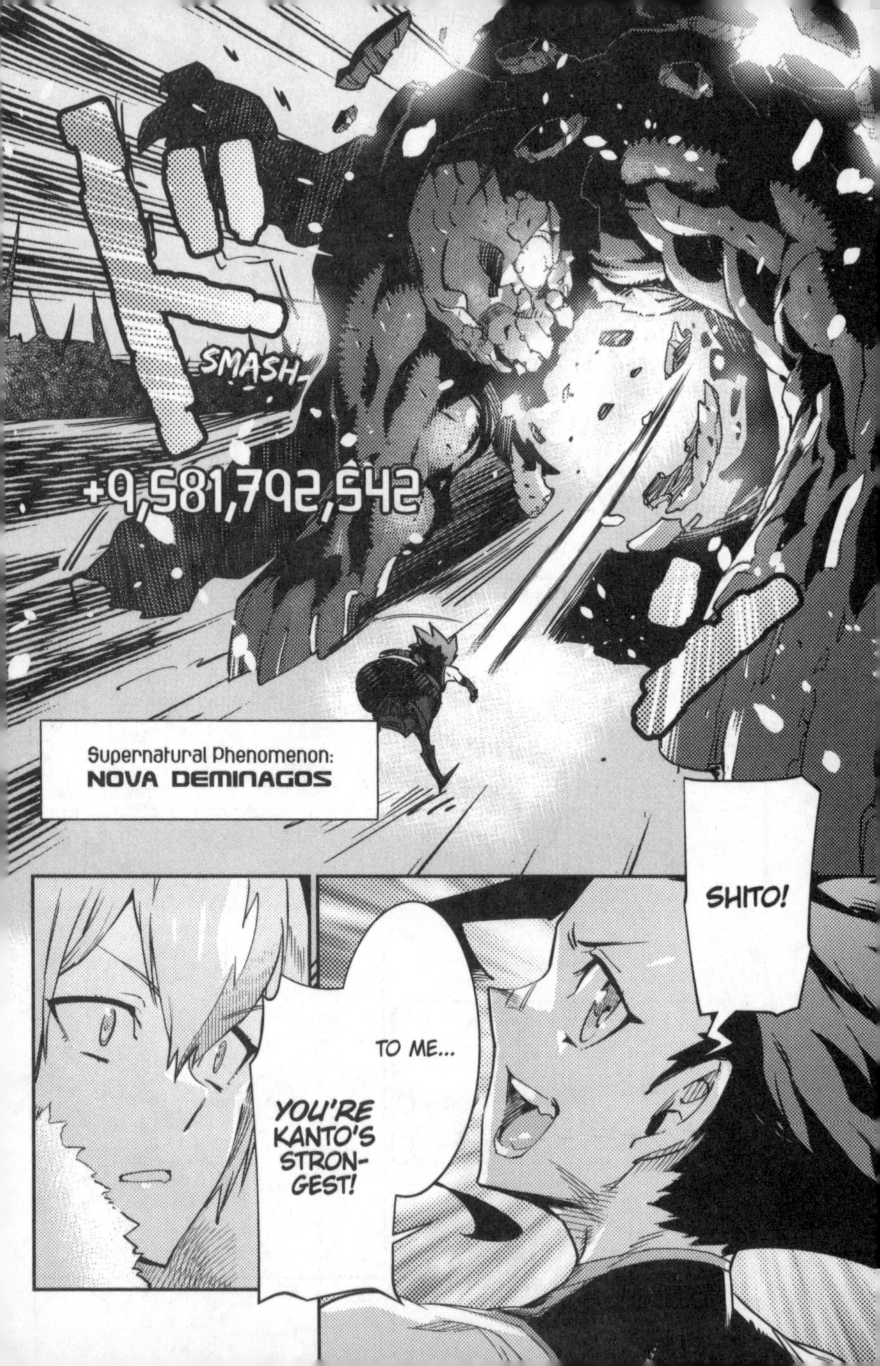
SMASH
+9,581,792,542
Supernatural Phenomenon:
NOVA DEMINAGOS
SHITO!
TO ME...
YOU'RE KANTO'S STRONG-EST!

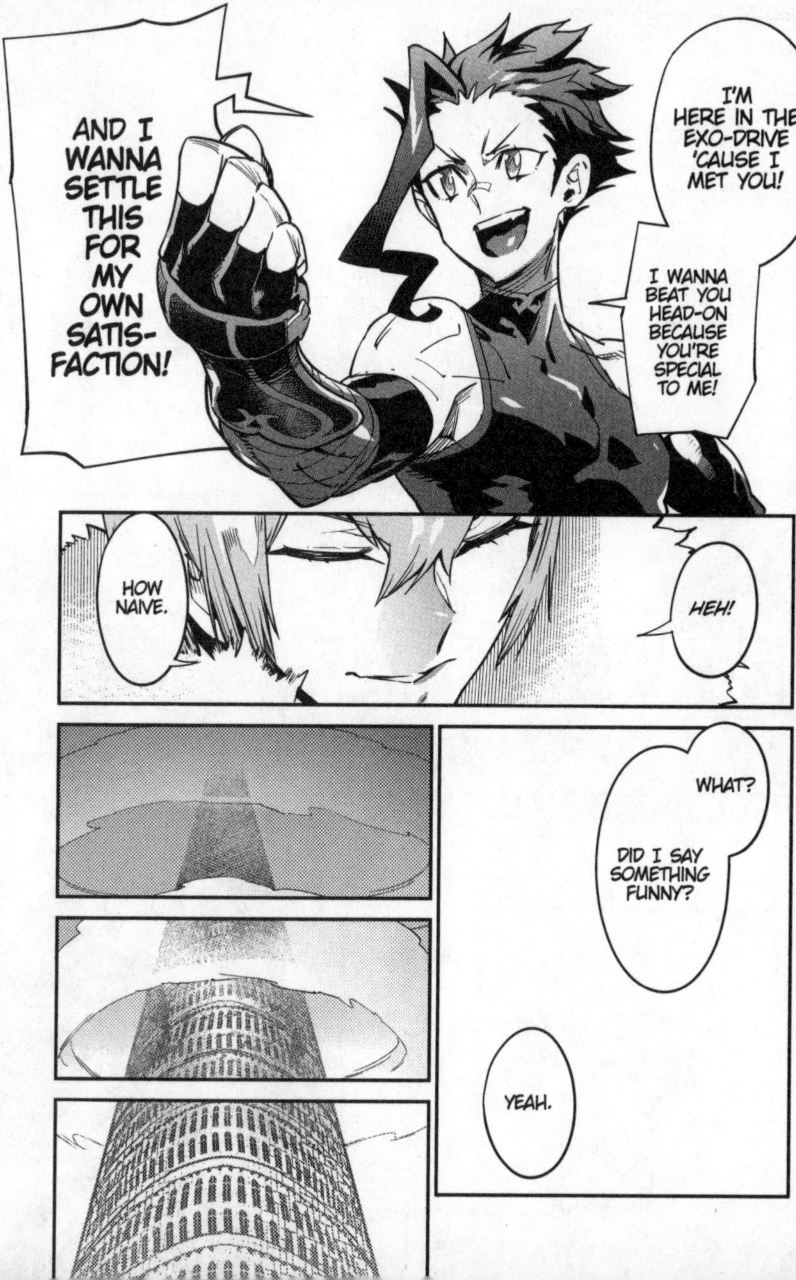
I'M HERE IN THE EXO-DRIVE 'CAUSE I MET YOU!
I WANNA BEAT YOU HEAD-ON BECAUSE YOU'RE SPECIAL TO ME!
AND I WANNA SETTLE THIS FOR MY OWN SATIS-FACTION!
HEH!
HOW NAIVE.
WHAT?
DID I SAY SOMETHING FUNNY?
YEAH.

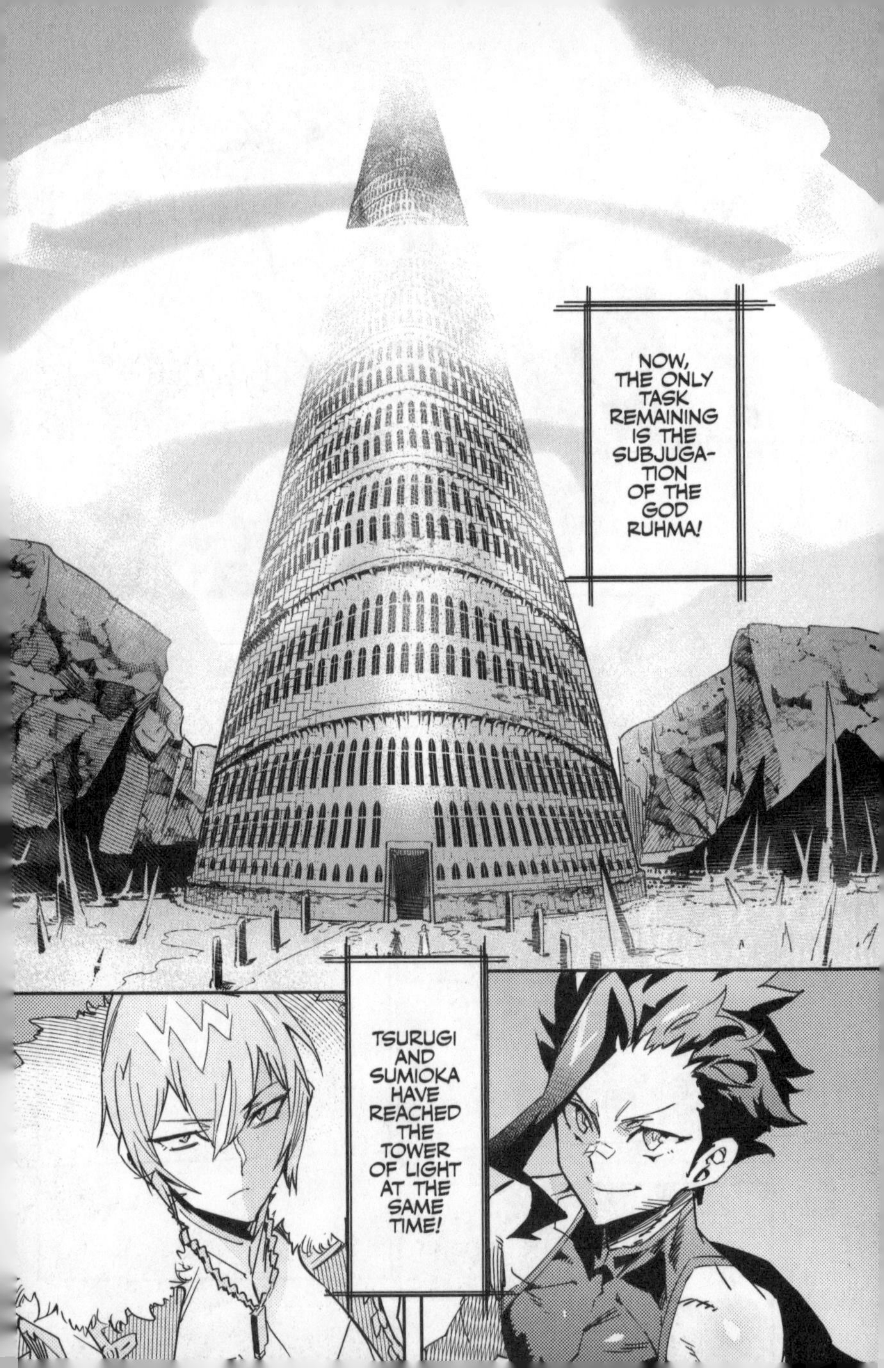
NOW, THE ONLY TASK REMAINING IS THE SUBJUGATION OF THE GOD RUHMA!
TSURUGI AND SUMIOKA HAVE REACHED THE TOWER OF LIGHT AT THE SAME TIME!

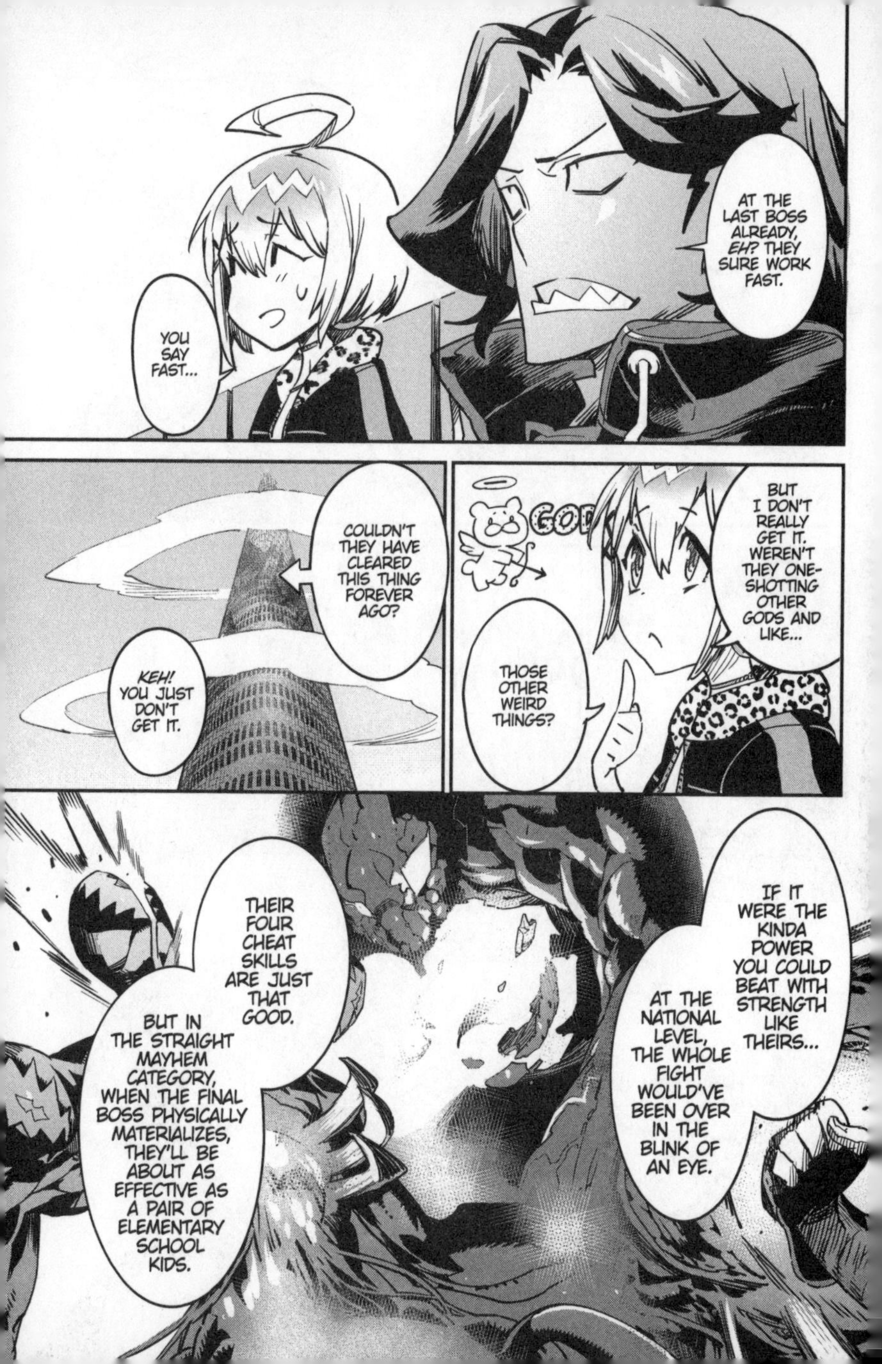
AT THE LAST BOSS ALREADY, *EH?* THEY SURE WORK FAST.
YOU SAY FAST...
BUT I DON'T REALLY GET IT. WEREN'T THEY ONE-SHOTTING OTHER GODS AND LIKE...
GOD
THOSE OTHER WEIRD THINGS?
COULDN'T THEY HAVE CLEARED THIS THING FOREVER AGO?
KEH! YOU JUST DON'T GET IT.
IF IT WERE THE KINDA POWER YOU COULD BEAT WITH STRENGTH LIKE THEIRS...
AT THE NATIONAL LEVEL, THE WHOLE FIGHT WOULD'VE BEEN OVER IN THE BLINK OF AN EYE.
THEIR FOUR CHEAT SKILLS ARE JUST THAT GOOD.
BUT IN THE STRAIGHT MAYHEM CATEGORY, WHEN THE FINAL BOSS PHYSICALLY MATERIALIZES, THEY'LL BE ABOUT AS EFFECTIVE AS A PAIR OF ELEMENTARY SCHOOL KIDS.

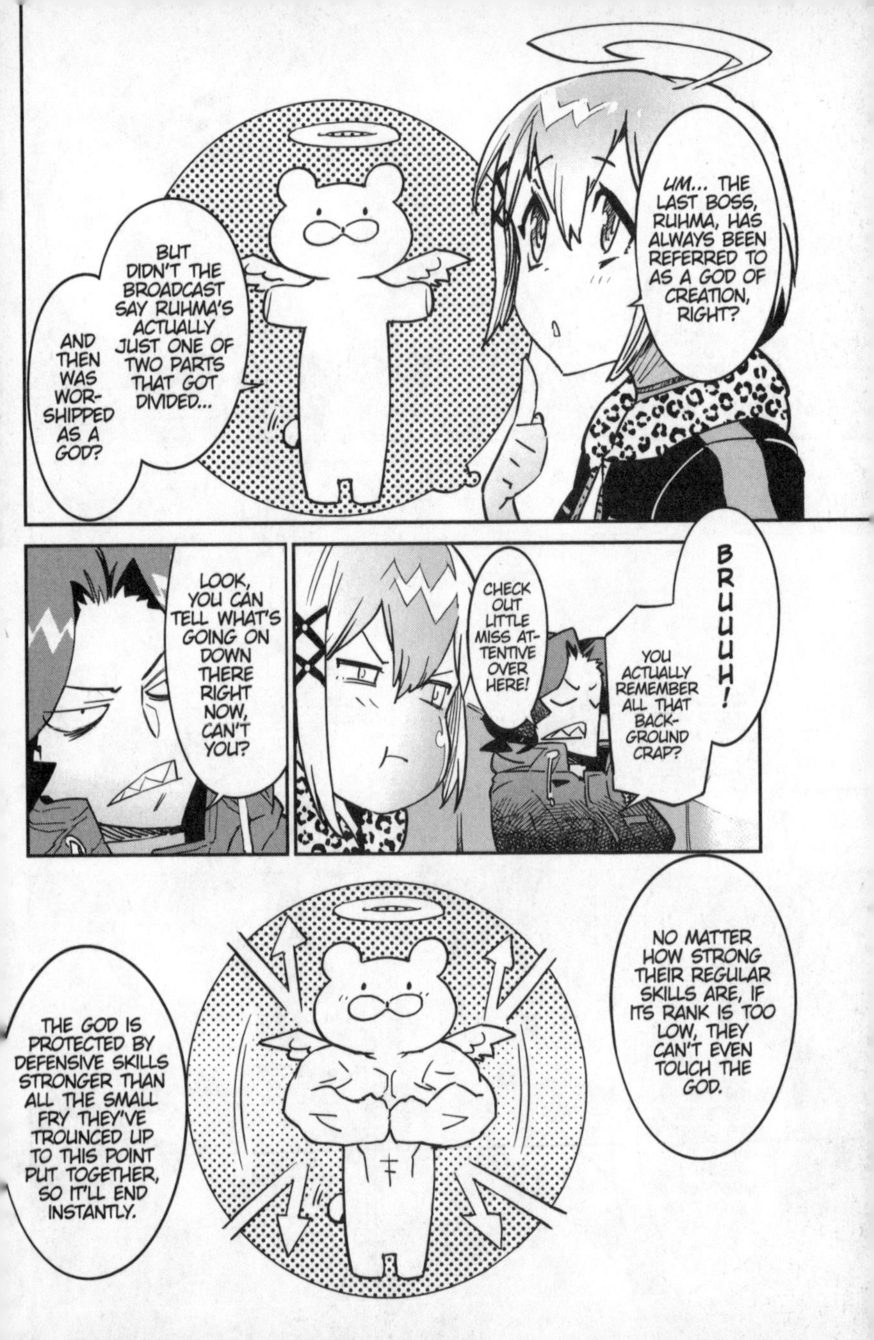
UM... THE LAST BOSS, RUHMA, HAS ALWAYS BEEN REFERRED TO AS A GOD OF CREATION, RIGHT?
BUT DIDN'T THE BROADCAST SAY RUHMA'S ACTUALLY JUST ONE OF TWO PARTS THAT GOT DIVIDED...
AND THEN WAS WOR-SHIPPED AS A GOD?
BRUUUH!
YOU ACTUALLY REMEMBER ALL THAT BACK-GROUND CRAP?
CHECK OUT LITTLE MISS AT-TENTIVE OVER HERE!
LOOK, YOU CAN TELL WHAT'S GOING ON DOWN THERE RIGHT NOW, CAN'T YOU?
NO MATTER HOW STRONG THEIR REGULAR SKILLS ARE, IF ITS RANK IS TOO LOW, THEY CAN'T EVEN TOUCH THE GOD.
THE GOD IS PROTECTED BY DEFENSIVE SKILLS STRONGER THAN ALL THE SMALL FRY THEY'VE TROUNCED UP TO THIS POINT PUT TOGETHER, SO IT'LL END INSTANTLY.

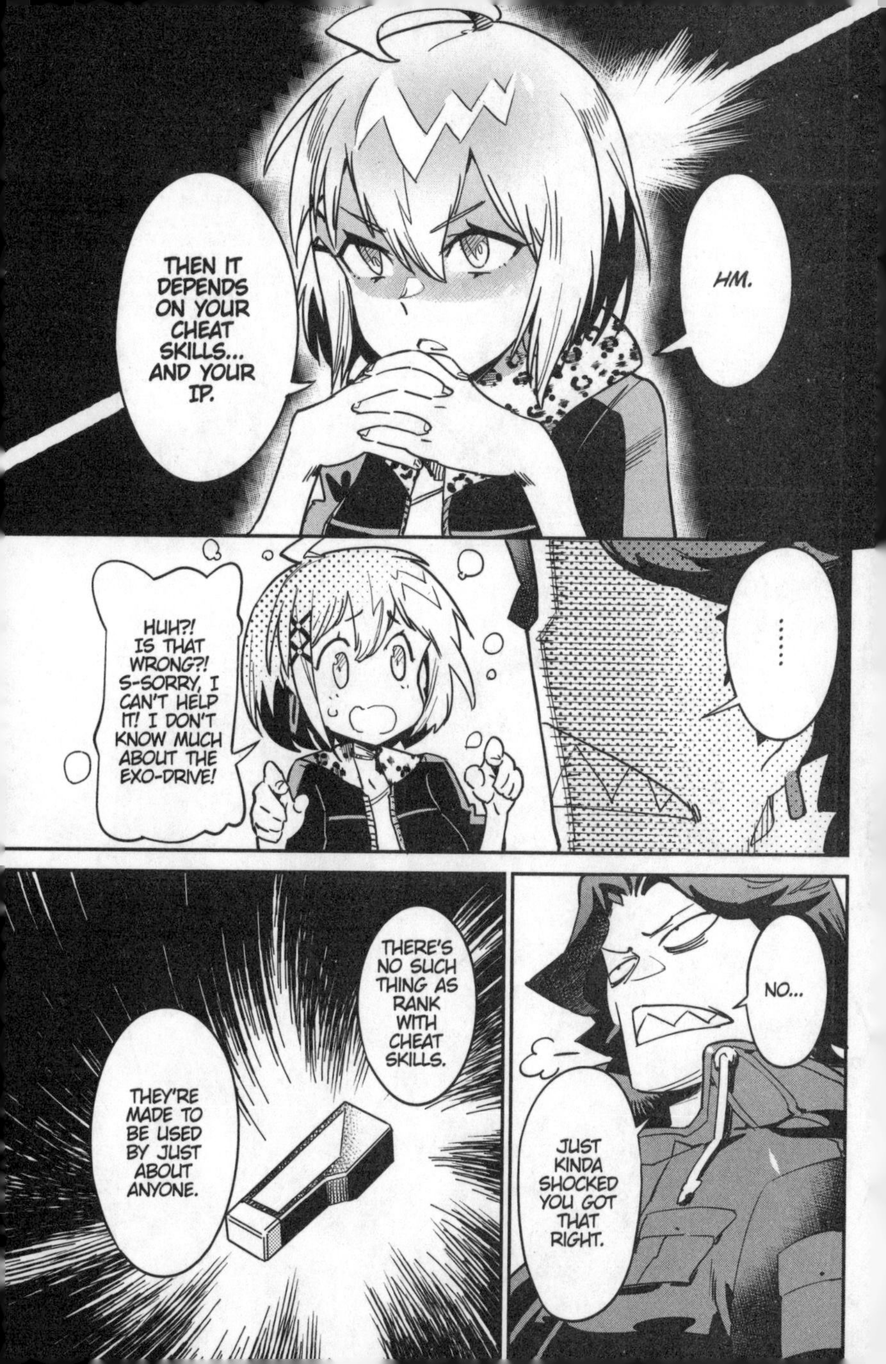
HM.
THEN IT DEPENDS ON YOUR CHEAT SKILLS... AND YOUR IP.
......
HUH?! IS THAT WRONG?! S-SORRY, I CAN'T HELP IT! I DON'T KNOW MUCH ABOUT THE EXO-DRIVE!
NO...
JUST KINDA SHOCKED YOU GOT THAT RIGHT.
THERE'S NO SUCH THING AS RANK WITH CHEAT SKILLS.
THEY'RE MADE TO BE USED BY JUST ABOUT ANYONE.

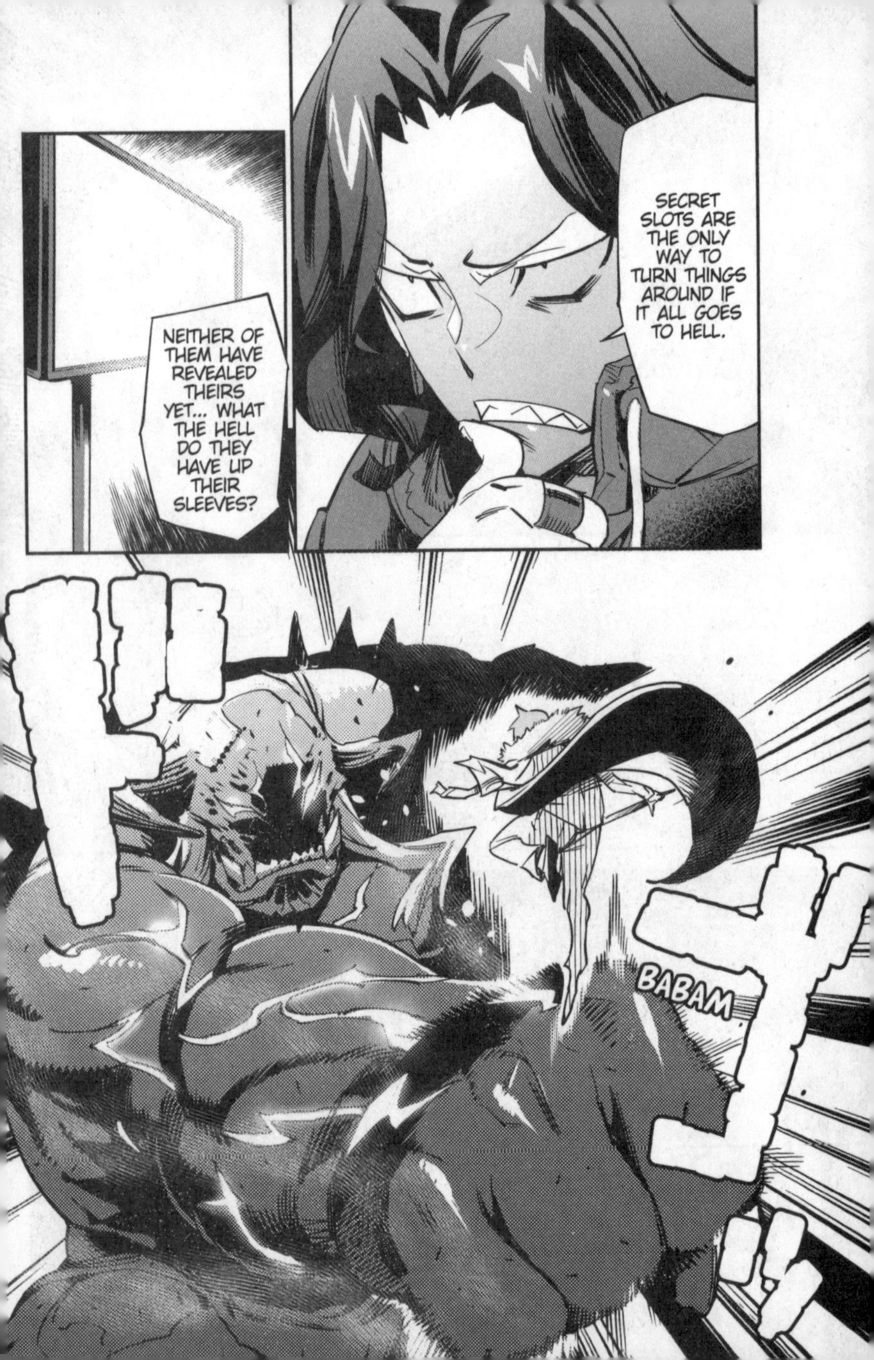
SECRET SLOTS ARE THE ONLY WAY TO TURN THINGS AROUND IF IT ALL GOES TO HELL.
NEITHER OF THEM HAVE REVEALED THEIRS YET... WHAT THE HELL DO THEY HAVE UP THEIR SLEEVES?
BABAM

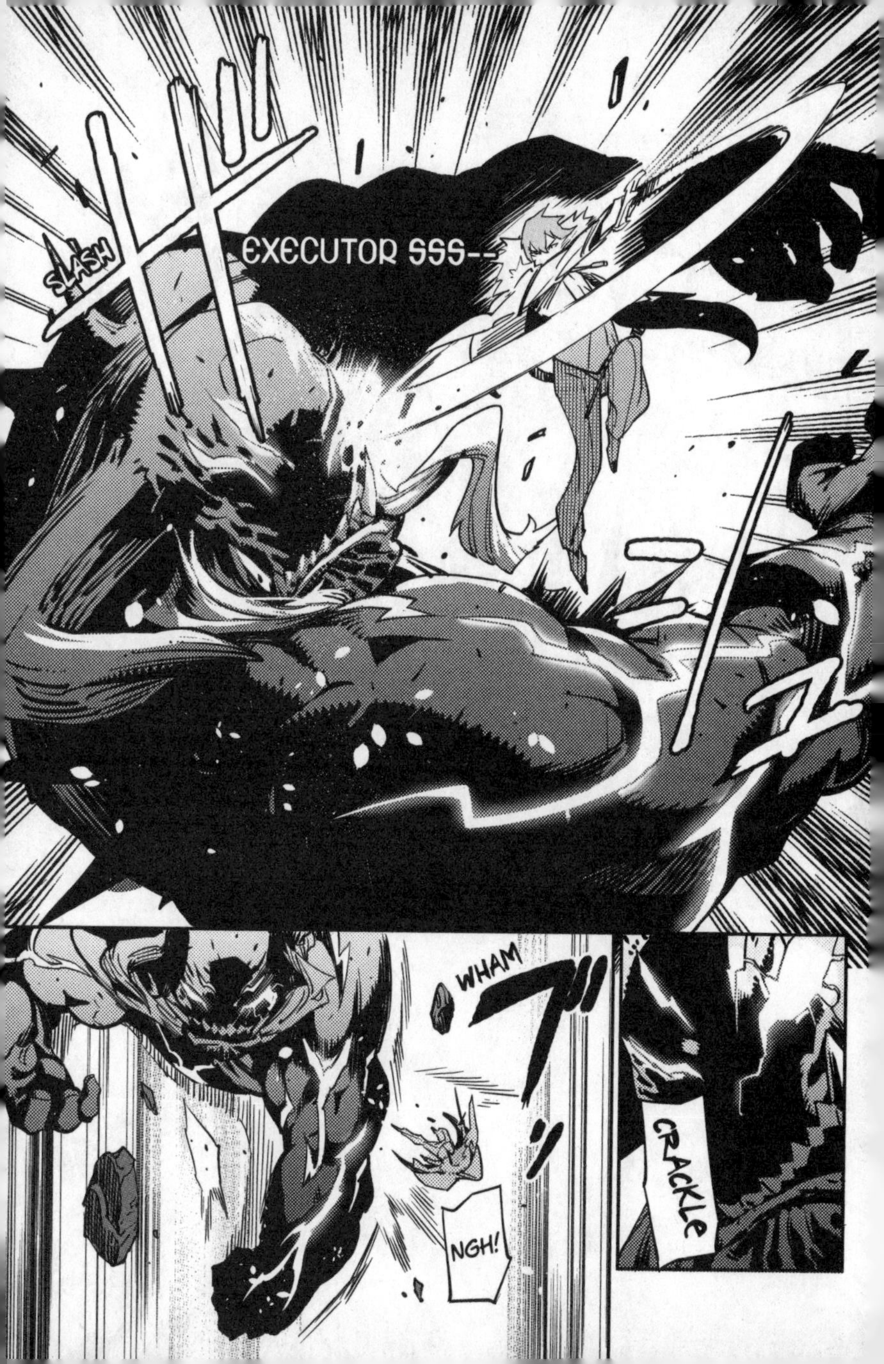
EXECUTOR SSS--
SLASH
CRACKLE
WHAM
NGH!

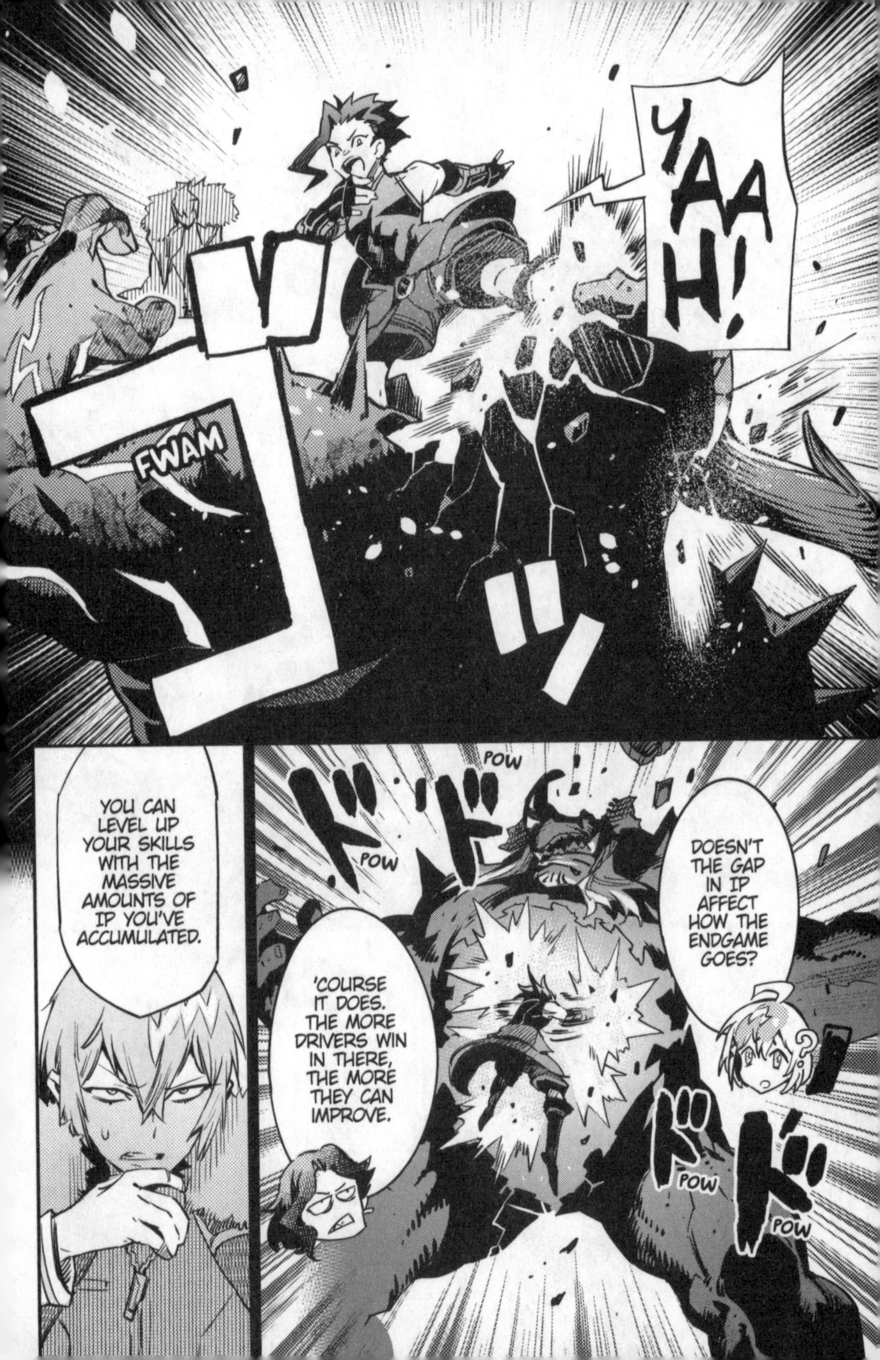
YAAAH!
FWAM
POW
DOESN'T THE GAP IN IP AFFECT HOW THE ENDGAME GOES?
POW
'COURSE IT DOES. THE MORE DRIVERS WIN IN THERE, THE MORE THEY CAN IMPROVE.
POW
POW
YOU CAN LEVEL UP YOUR SKILLS WITH THE MASSIVE AMOUNTS OF IP YOU'VE ACCUMULATED.

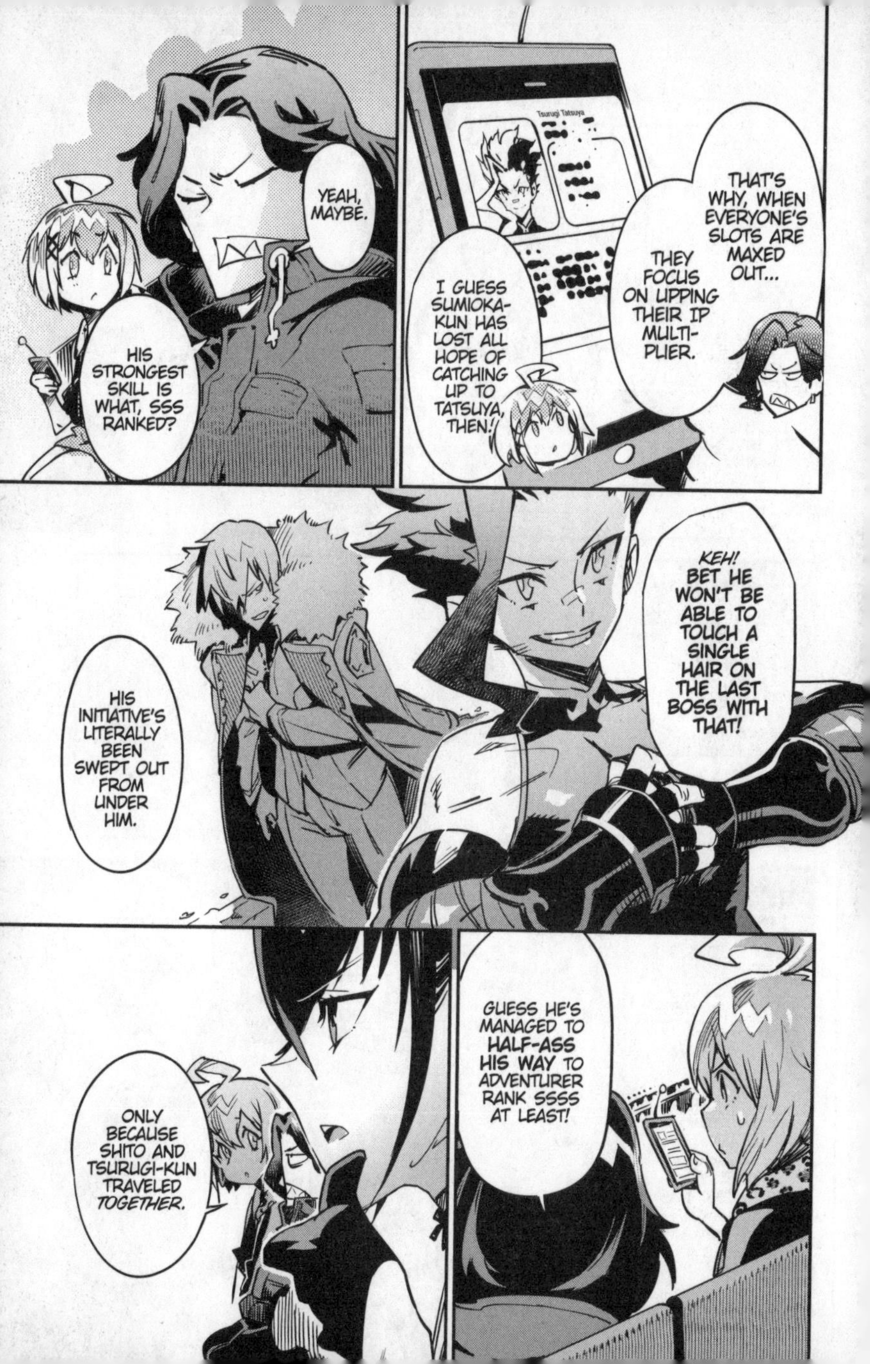
Tsurugi Tatsuya
THAT'S WHY, WHEN EVERYONE'S SLOTS ARE MAXED OUT...
THEY FOCUS ON UPPING THEIR IP MULTIPLIER.
I GUESS SUMIOKA-KUN HAS LOST ALL HOPE OF CATCHING UP TO TATSUYA, THEN!
YEAH, MAYBE.
HIS STRONGEST SKILL IS WHAT, SSS RANKED?
KEH! BET HE WON'T BE ABLE TO TOUCH A SINGLE HAIR ON THE LAST BOSS WITH THAT!
HIS INITIATIVE'S LITERALLY BEEN SWEPT OUT FROM UNDER HIM.
GUESS HE'S MANAGED TO **HALF-ASS HIS WAY** TO ADVENTURER RANK SSSS AT LEAST!
ONLY BECAUSE SHITO AND TSURUGI-KUN TRAVELED *TOGETHER*.

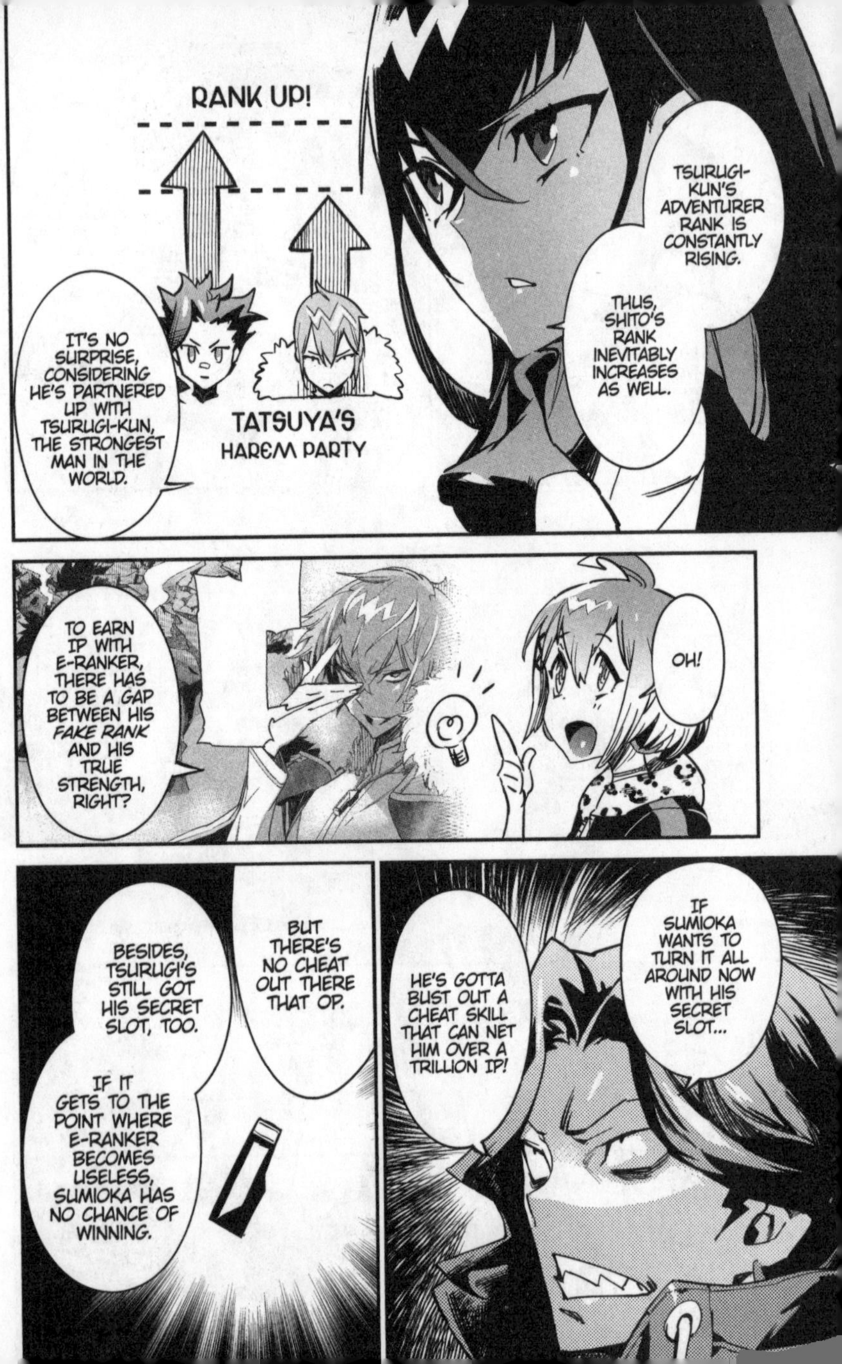
TSURUGI-KUN'S ADVENTURER RANK IS CONSTANTLY RISING.
THUS, SHITO'S RANK INEVITABLY INCREASES AS WELL.
RANK UP!
TATSUYA'S HAREM PARTY
IT'S NO SURPRISE, CONSIDERING HE'S PARTNERED UP WITH TSURUGI-KUN, THE STRONGEST MAN IN THE WORLD.
OH!
TO EARN IP WITH E-RANKER, THERE HAS TO BE A GAP BETWEEN HIS *FAKE RANK* AND HIS TRUE STRENGTH, RIGHT?
IF SUMIOKA WANTS TO TURN IT ALL AROUND NOW WITH HIS SECRET SLOT...
HE'S GOTTA BUST OUT A CHEAT SKILL THAT CAN NET HIM OVER A TRILLION IP!
BUT THERE'S NO CHEAT OUT THERE THAT OP.
BESIDES, TSURUGI'S STILL GOT HIS SECRET SLOT, TOO.
IF IT GETS TO THE POINT WHERE E-RANKER BECOMES USELESS, SUMIOKA HAS NO CHANCE OF WINNING.

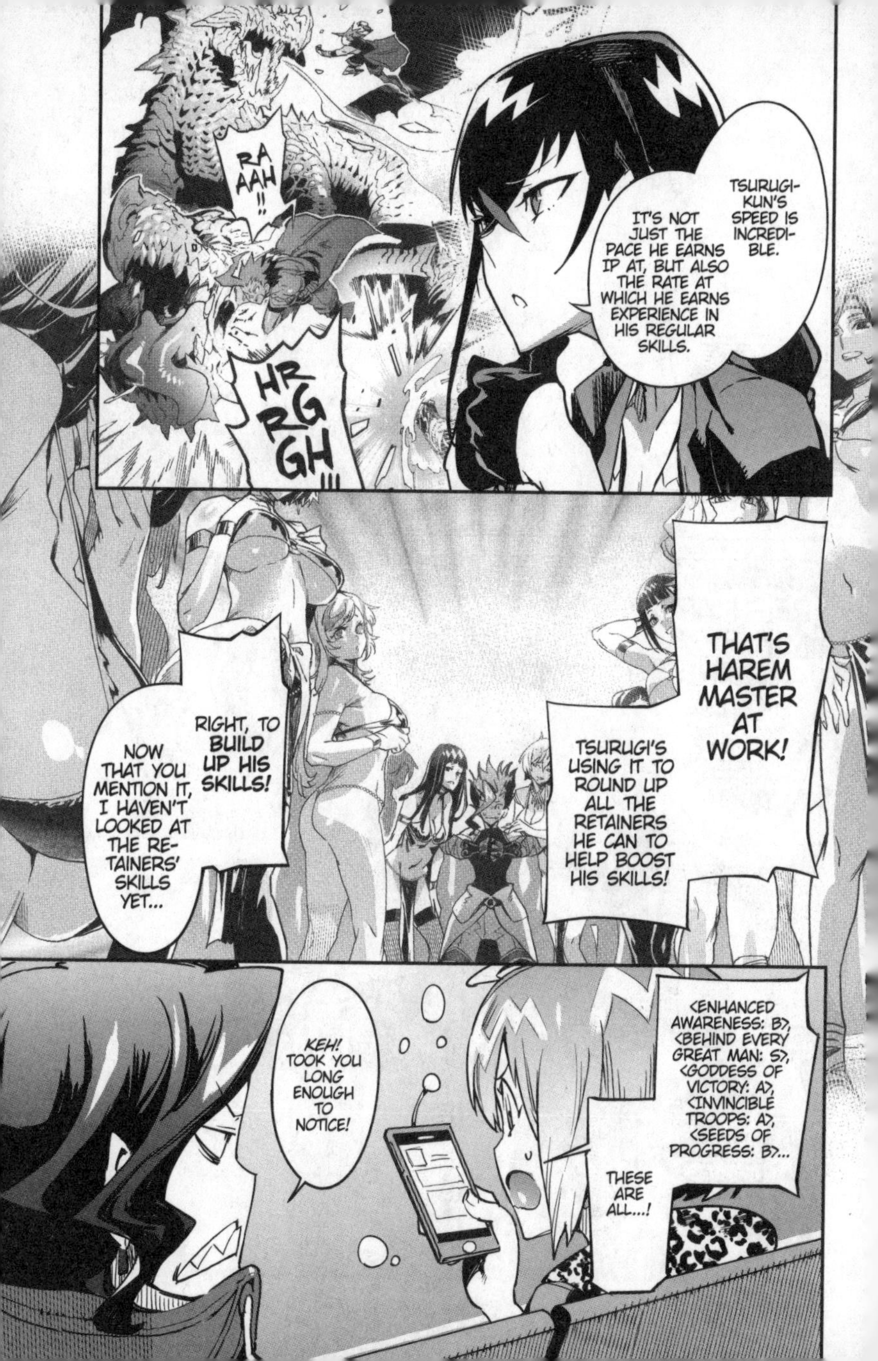
TSURUGI-KUN'S SPEED IS INCREDIBLE.
IT'S NOT JUST THE PACE HE EARNS IP AT, BUT ALSO THE RATE AT WHICH HE EARNS EXPERIENCE IN HIS REGULAR SKILLS.
RA AAH!!
HRRGGH!!!
THAT'S HAREM MASTER AT WORK!
TSURUGI'S USING IT TO ROUND UP ALL THE RETAINERS HE CAN TO HELP BOOST HIS SKILLS!
RIGHT, TO BUILD UP HIS SKILLS!
NOW THAT YOU MENTION IT, I HAVEN'T LOOKED AT THE RETAINERS' SKILLS YET...
<ENHANCED AWARENESS: B>, <BEHIND EVERY GREAT MAN: S>, <GODDESS OF VICTORY: A>, <INVINCIBLE TROOPS: A>, <SEEDS OF PROGRESS: B>...
THESE ARE ALL...!
KEH! TOOK YOU LONG ENOUGH TO NOTICE!

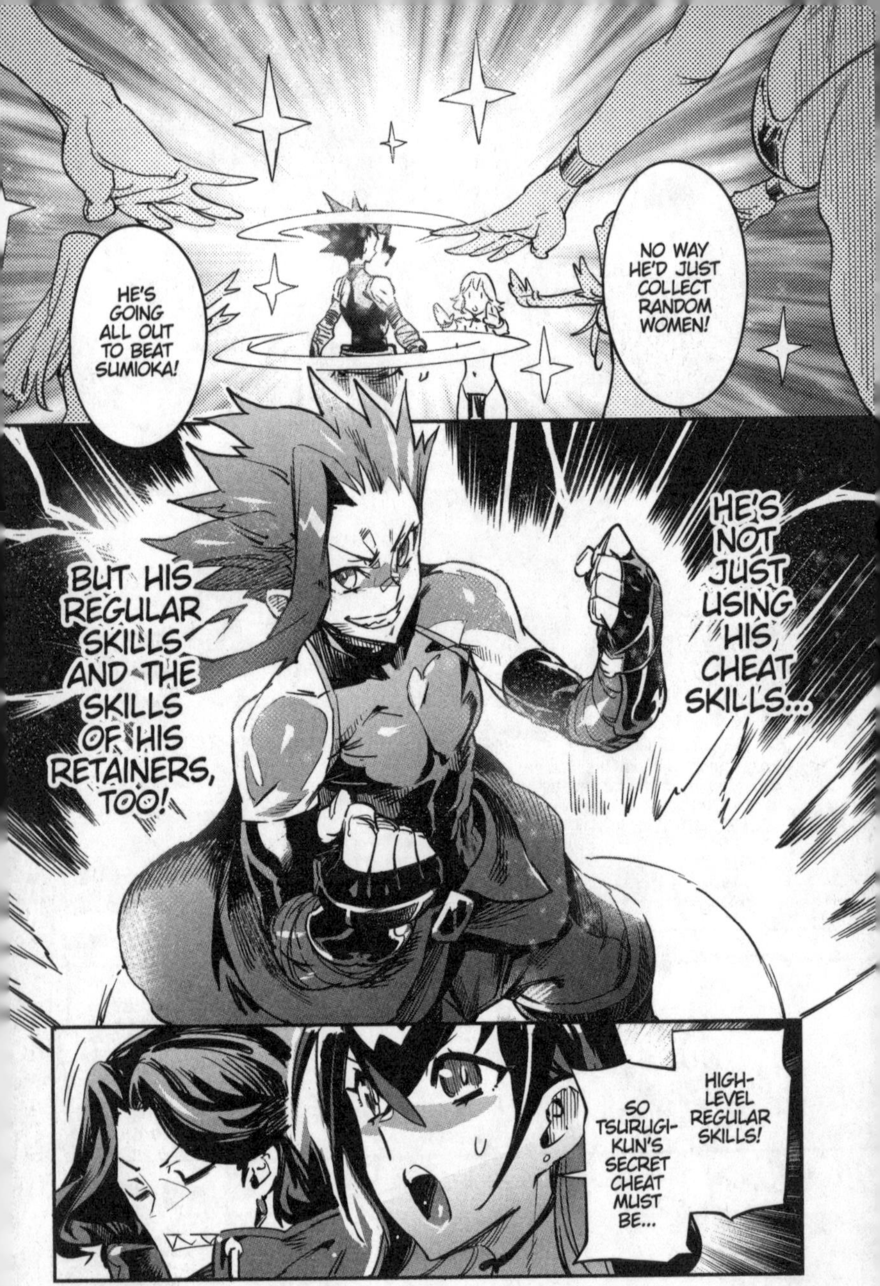
NO WAY HE'D JUST COLLECT RANDOM WOMEN!
HE'S GOING ALL OUT TO BEAT SUMIOKA!
HE'S NOT JUST USING HIS CHEAT SKILLS...
BUT HIS REGULAR SKILLS AND THE SKILLS OF HIS RETAINERS, TOO!
HIGH-LEVEL REGULAR SKILLS!
SO TSURUGI-KUN'S SECRET CHEAT MUST BE...

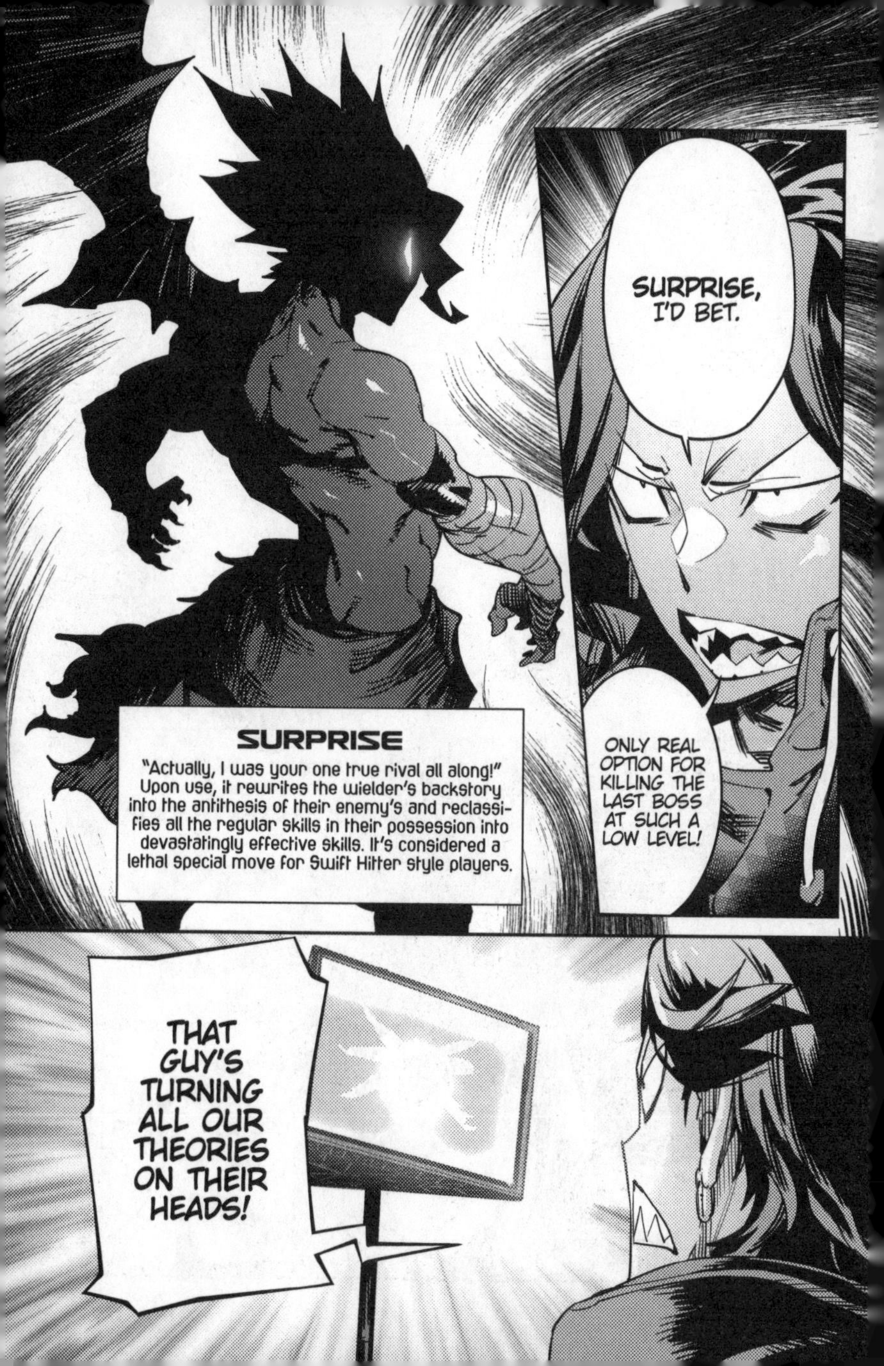

SURPRISE, I'D BET.
ONLY REAL OPTION FOR KILLING THE LAST BOSS AT SUCH A LOW LEVEL!
SURPRISE
"Actually, I was your one true rival all along!" Upon use, it rewrites the wielder's backstory into the antithesis of their enemy's and reclassifies all the regular skills in their possession into devastatingly effective skills. It's considered a lethal special move for Swift Hitter style players.
THAT GUY'S TURNING ALL OUR THEORIES ON THEIR HEADS!

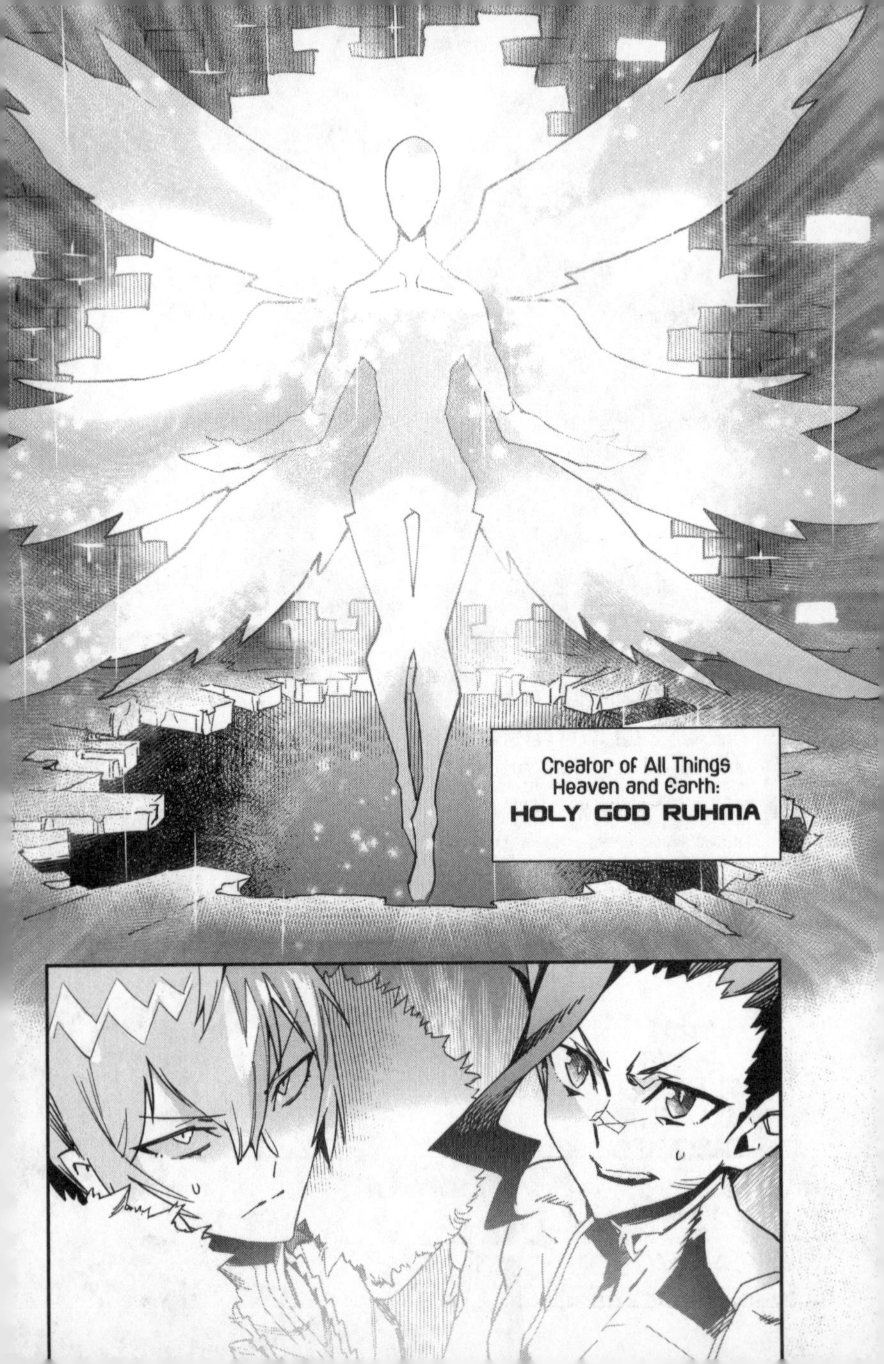
Creator of All Things
Heaven and Earth:
HOLY GOD RUHMA

THE
EXO-DRIVE
REINCARNATION GAMES
ALL-JAPAN ISEKAI BATTLE TOURNAMENT!

THE
EXO-DRIVE
REINCARNATION GAMES
ALL-JAPAN ISEKAI BATTLE TOURNAMENT!

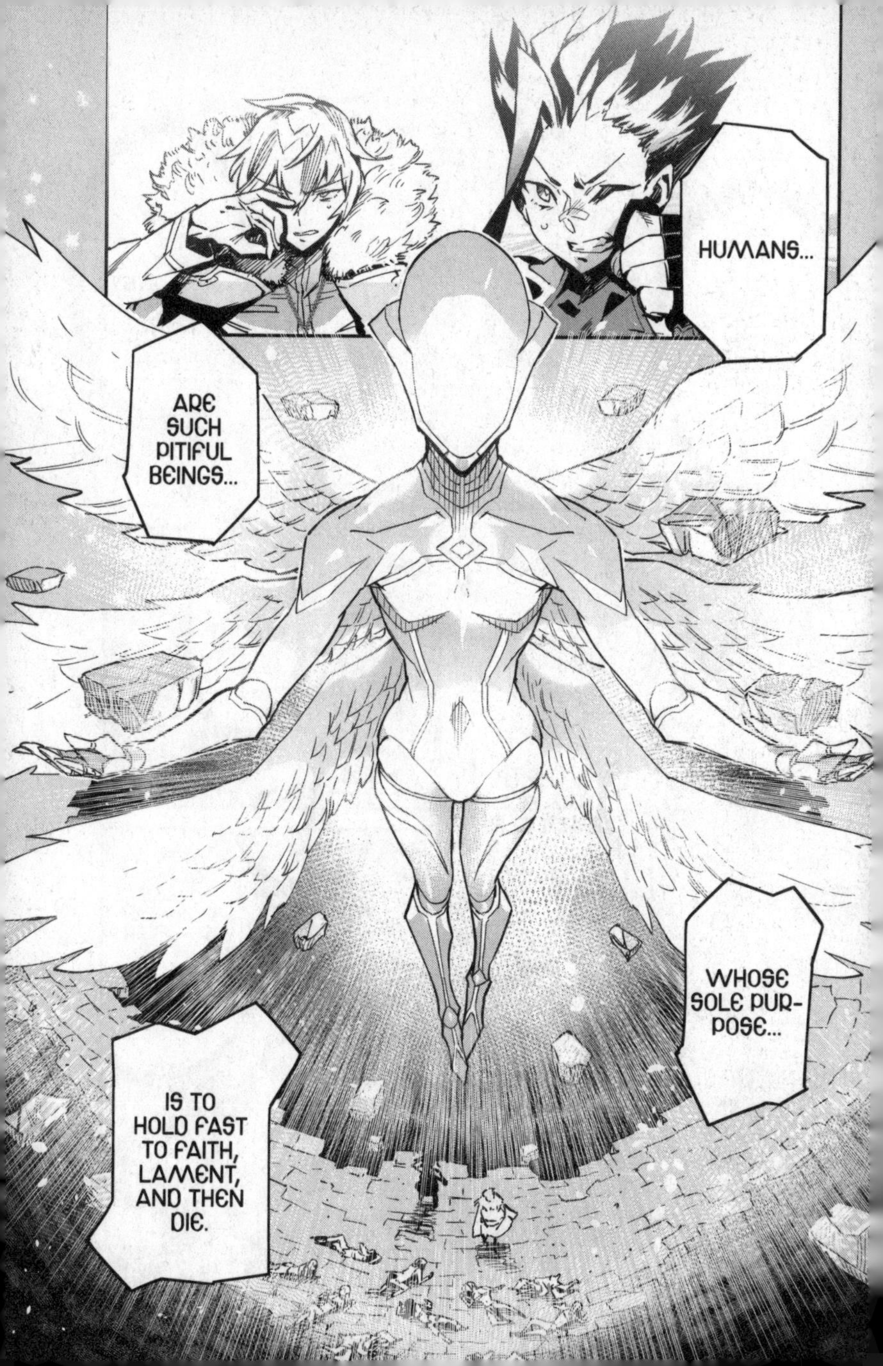
HUMANS...
ARE SUCH PITIFUL BEINGS...
WHOSE SOLE PUR-POSE...
IS TO HOLD FAST TO FAITH, LAMENT, AND THEN DIE.

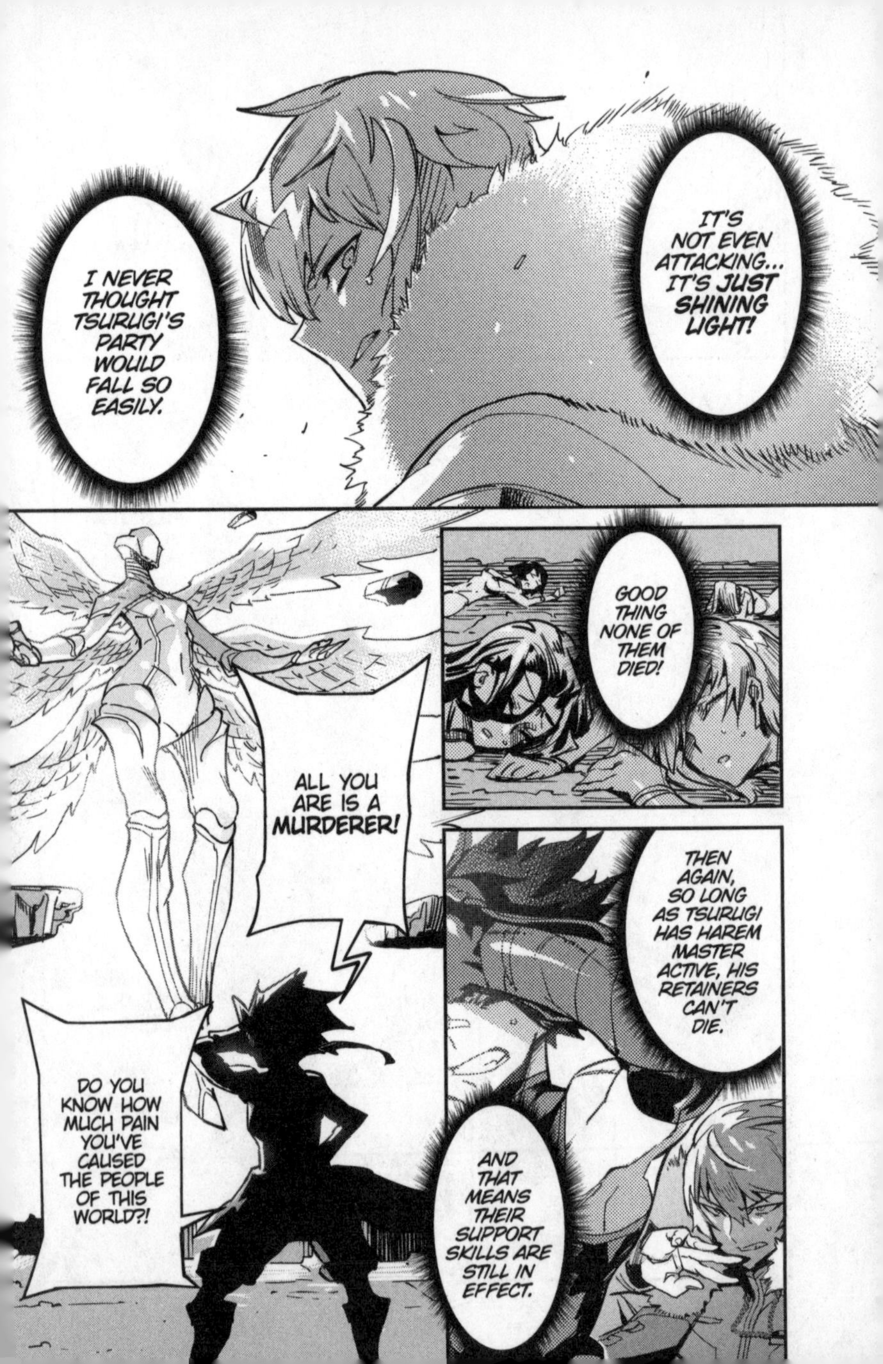
IT'S NOT EVEN ATTACKING... IT'S JUST SHINING LIGHT!
I NEVER THOUGHT TSURUGI'S PARTY WOULD FALL SO EASILY.
GOOD THING NONE OF THEM DIED!
THEN AGAIN, SO LONG AS TSURUGI HAS HAREM MASTER ACTIVE, HIS RETAINERS CAN'T DIE.
AND THAT MEANS THEIR SUPPORT SKILLS ARE STILL IN EFFECT.
ALL YOU ARE IS A MURDERER!
DO YOU KNOW HOW MUCH PAIN YOU'VE CAUSED THE PEOPLE OF THIS WORLD?!

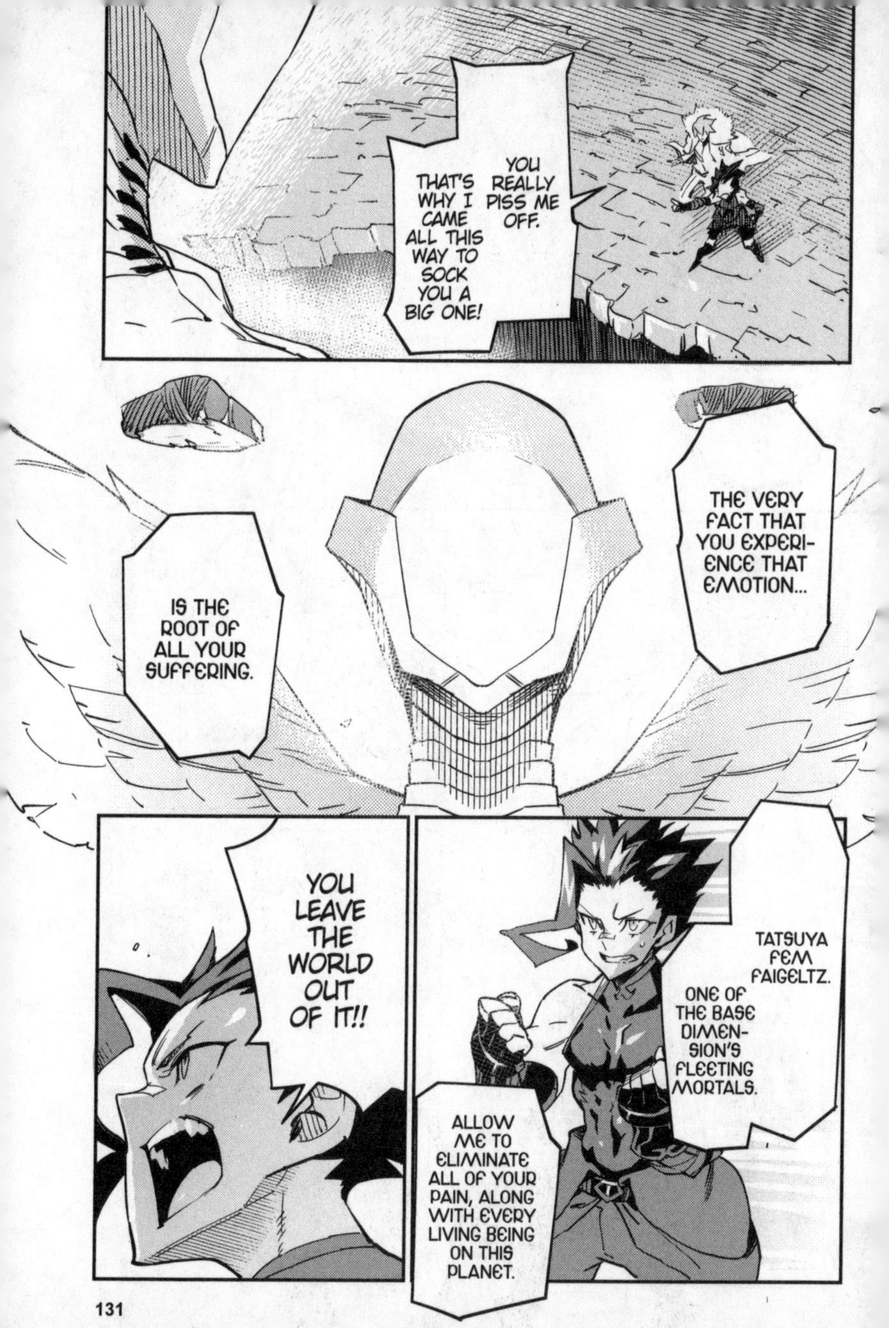
YOU REALLY PISS ME OFF.
THAT'S WHY I CAME ALL THIS WAY TO SOCK YOU A BIG ONE!
THE VERY FACT THAT YOU EXPERI-ENCE THAT EMOTION...
IS THE ROOT OF ALL YOUR SUFFERING.
TATSUYA FEM FAIGELTZ.
ONE OF THE BASE DIMEN-SION'S FLEETING MORTALS.
ALLOW ME TO ELIMINATE ALL OF YOUR PAIN, ALONG WITH EVERY LIVING BEING ON THIS PLANET.
YOU LEAVE THE WORLD OUT OF IT!!

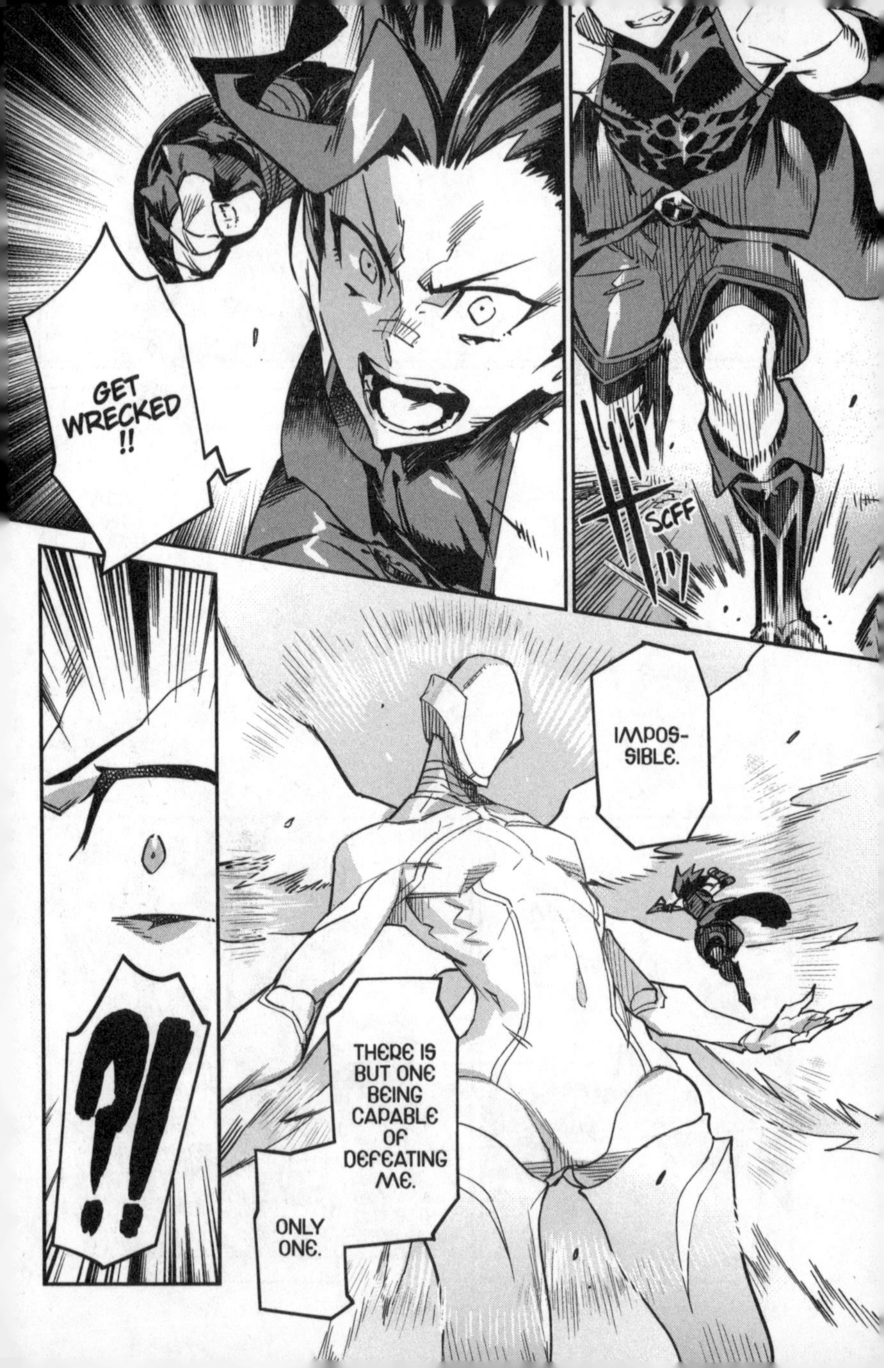
SCFF
GET WRECKED!!
IMPOSSIBLE.
THERE IS BUT ONE BEING CAPABLE OF DEFEATING ME.
ONLY ONE.
?!

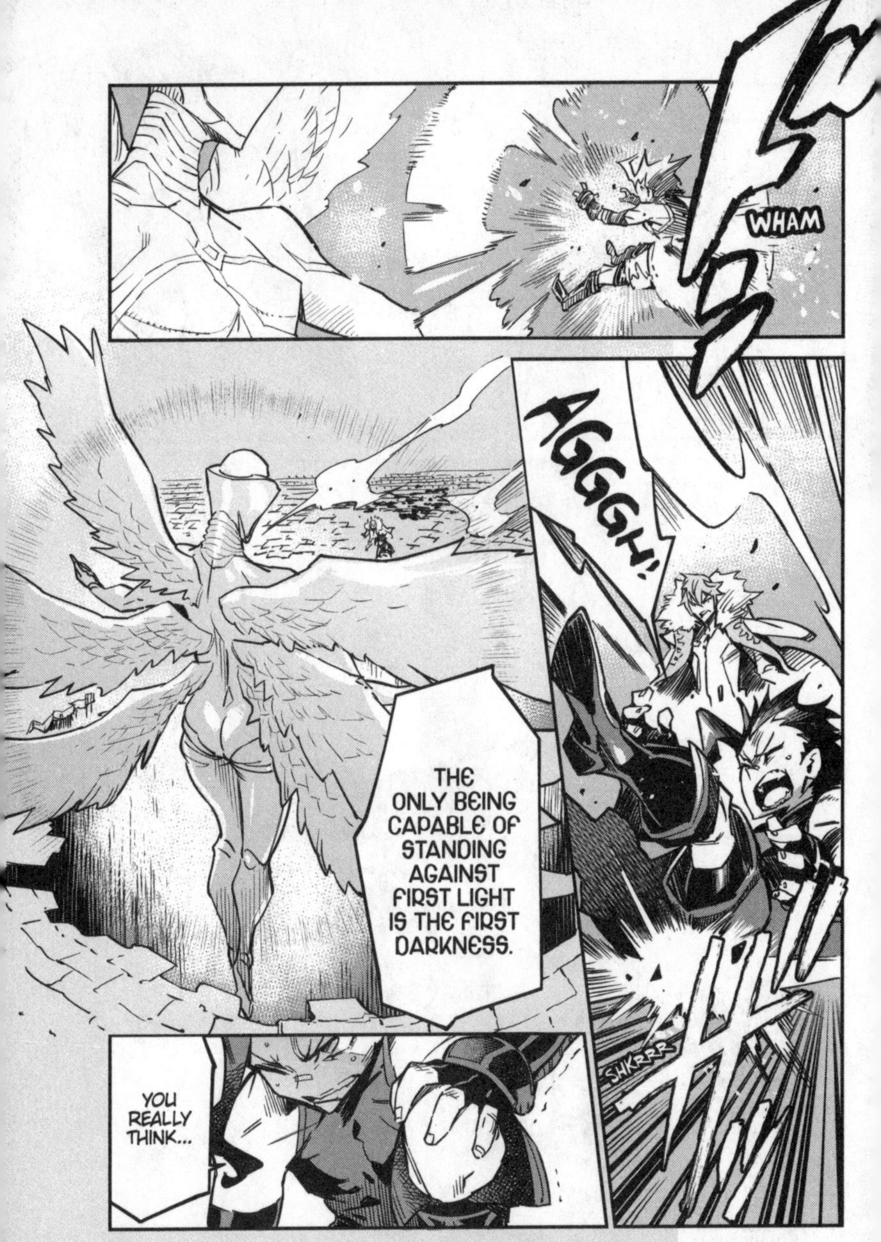
WHAM
AGGGH!!
SHKRRR
THE ONLY BEING CAPABLE OF STANDING AGAINST FIRST LIGHT IS THE FIRST DARKNESS.
YOU REALLY THINK...

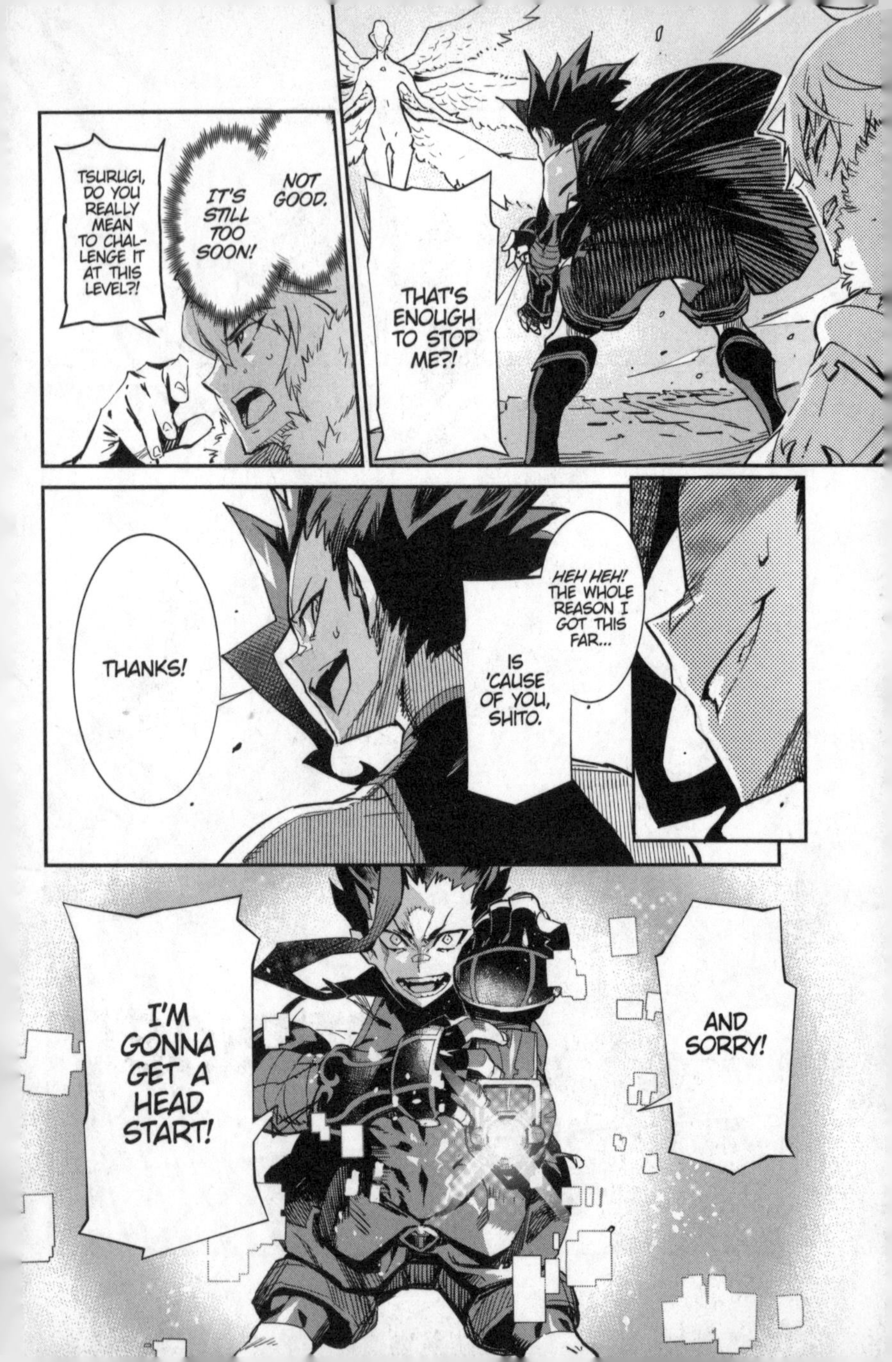
THAT'S ENOUGH TO STOP ME?!
NOT GOOD.
IT'S STILL TOO SOON!
TSURUGI, DO YOU REALLY MEAN TO CHAL-LENGE IT AT THIS LEVEL?!
HEH HEH! THE WHOLE REASON I GOT THIS FAR...
IS 'CAUSE OF YOU, SHITO.
THANKS!
AND SORRY!
I'M GONNA GET A HEAD START!

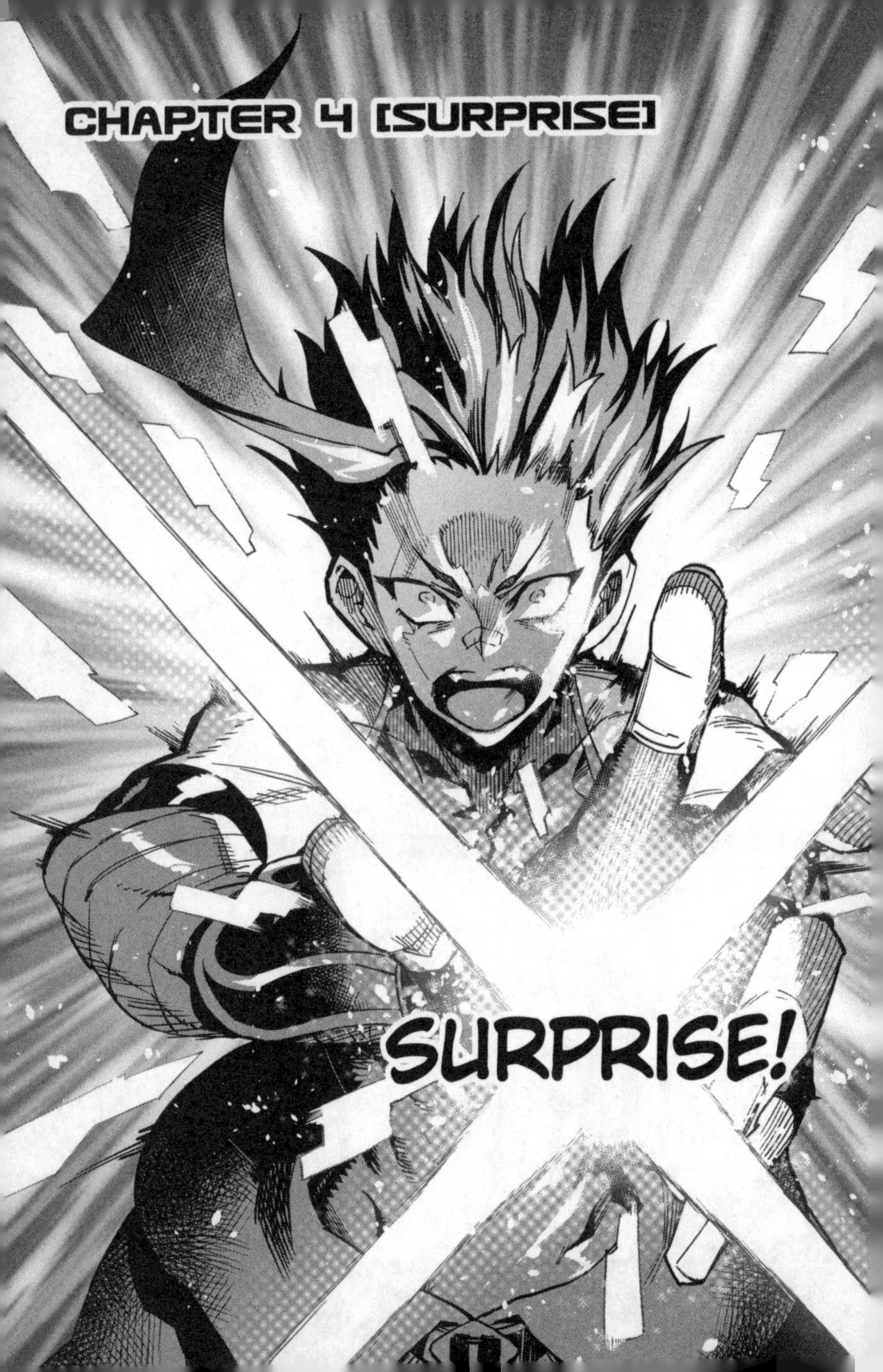
CHAPTER 4 [SURPRISE]
SURPRISE!

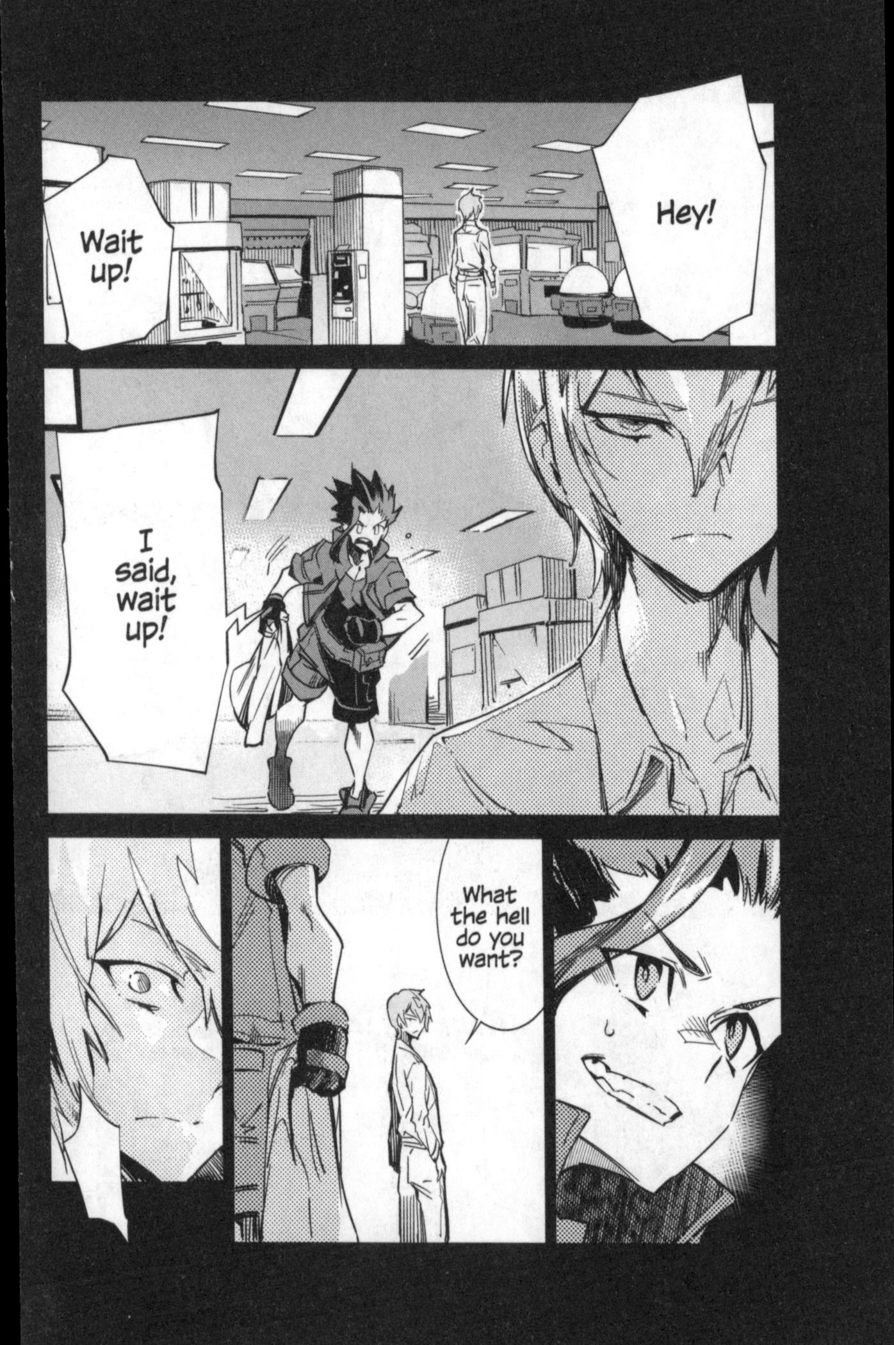
Hey!
Wait up!
I said, wait up!
What the hell do you want?

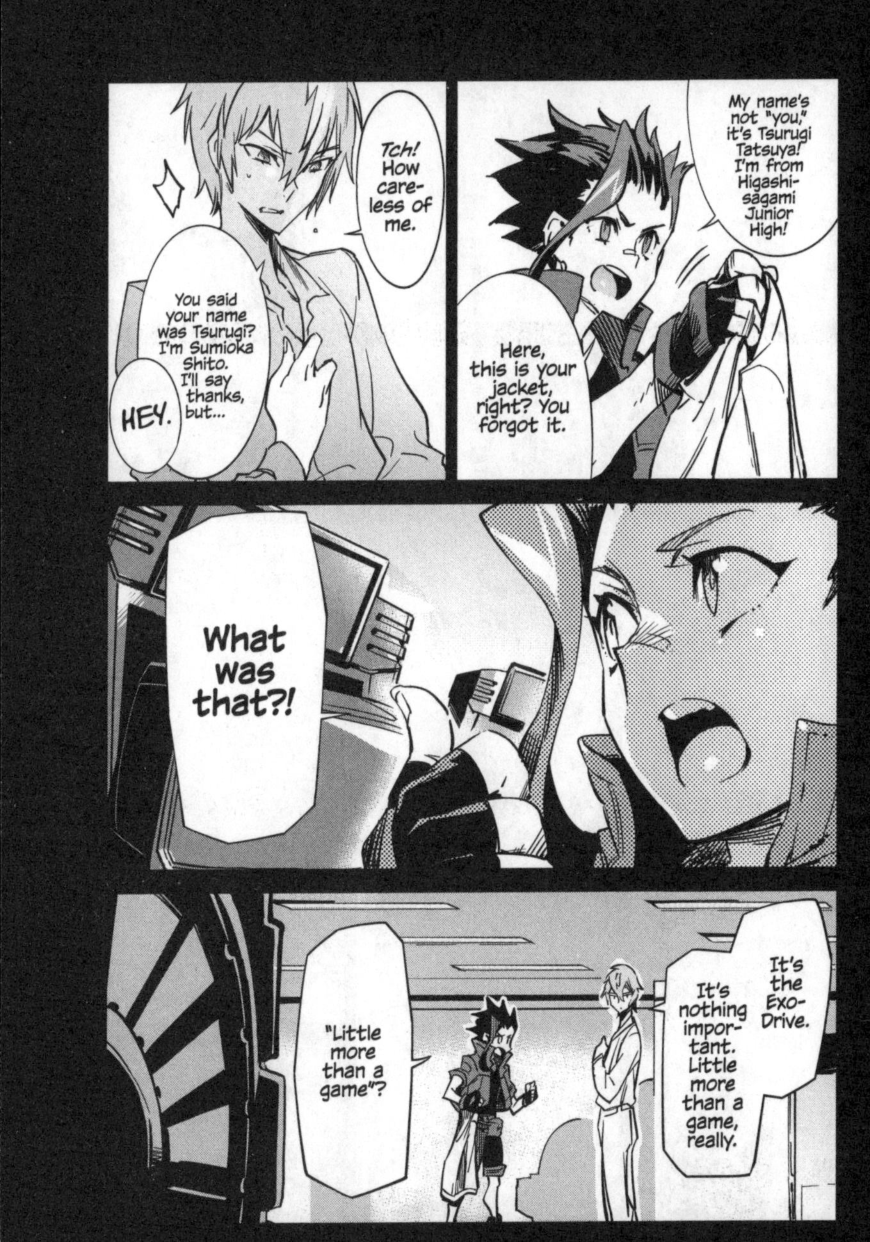
My name's not "you," it's Tsurugi Tatsuya! I'm from Higashi-sagami Junior High!
Here, this is your jacket, right? You forgot it.
Tch! How care-less of me.
You said your name was Tsurugi? I'm Sumioka Shito. I'll say thanks, but...
HEY.
What was that?!
It's the Exo-Drive.
It's nothing impor-tant. Little more than a game, really.
"Little more than a game"?

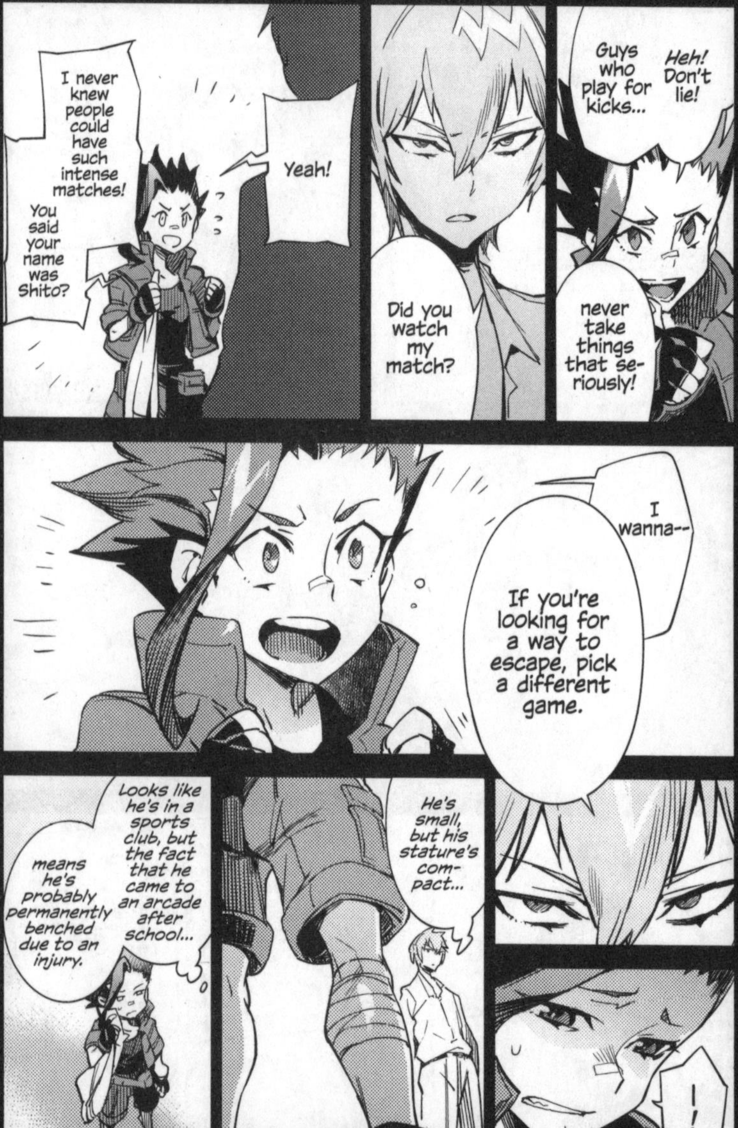
Heh! Don't lie!
Guys who play for kicks...
never take things that seriously!
Did you watch my match?
Yeah!
I never knew people could have such intense matches!
You said your name was Shito?
I wanna--
If you're looking for a way to escape, pick a different game.
!
He's small, but his stature's compact...
Looks like he's in a sports club, but the fact that he came to an arcade after school...
means he's probably permanently benched due to an injury.

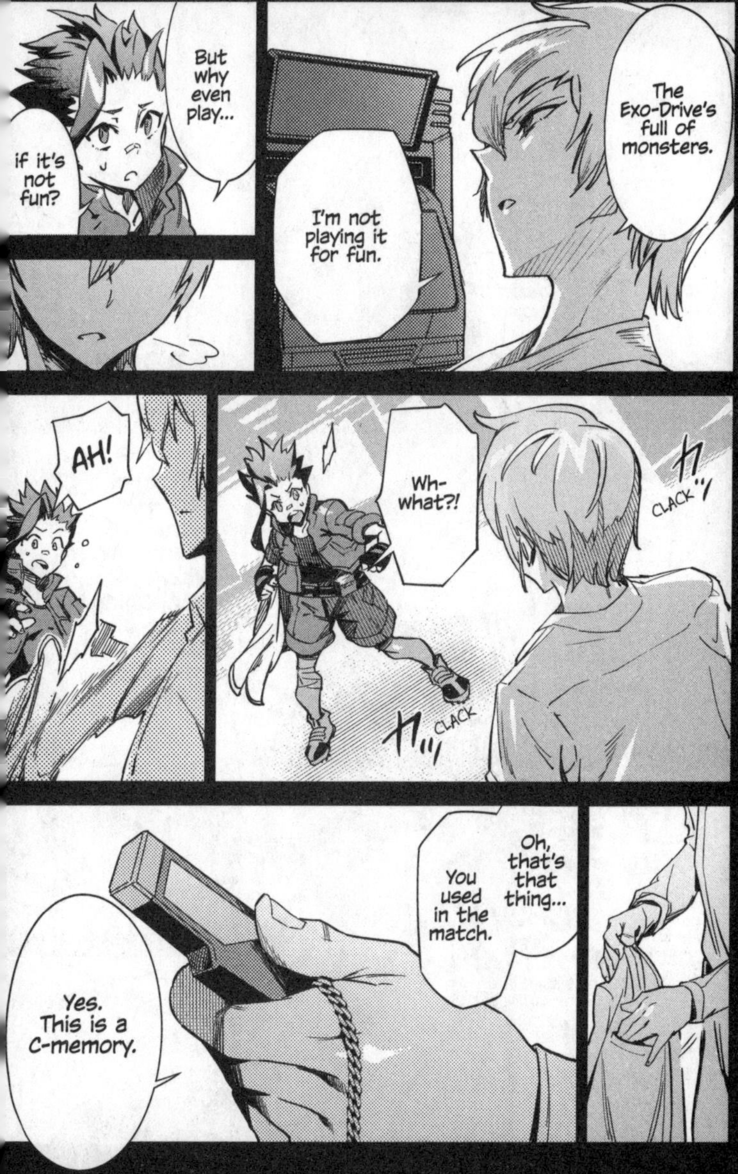
The Exo-Drive's full of monsters.
I'm not playing it for fun.
But why even play...
if it's not fun?
CLACK
Wh-what?!
CLACK
AH!
Oh, that's that thing...
You used in the match.
Yes. This is a C-memory.

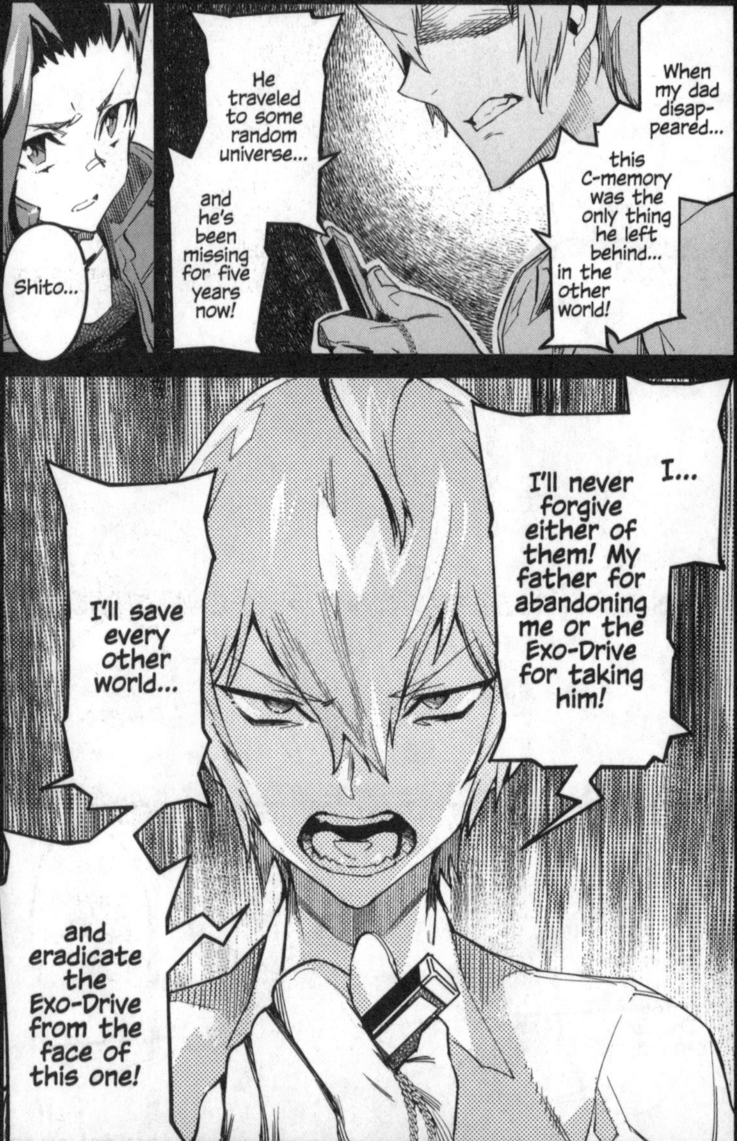
When my dad disappeared...
this C-memory was the only thing he left behind... in the other world!
He traveled to some random universe...
and he's been missing for five years now!
Shito...
I...
I'll never forgive either of them! My father for abandoning me or the Exo-Drive for taking him!
I'll save every other world...
and eradicate the Exo-Drive from the face of this one!

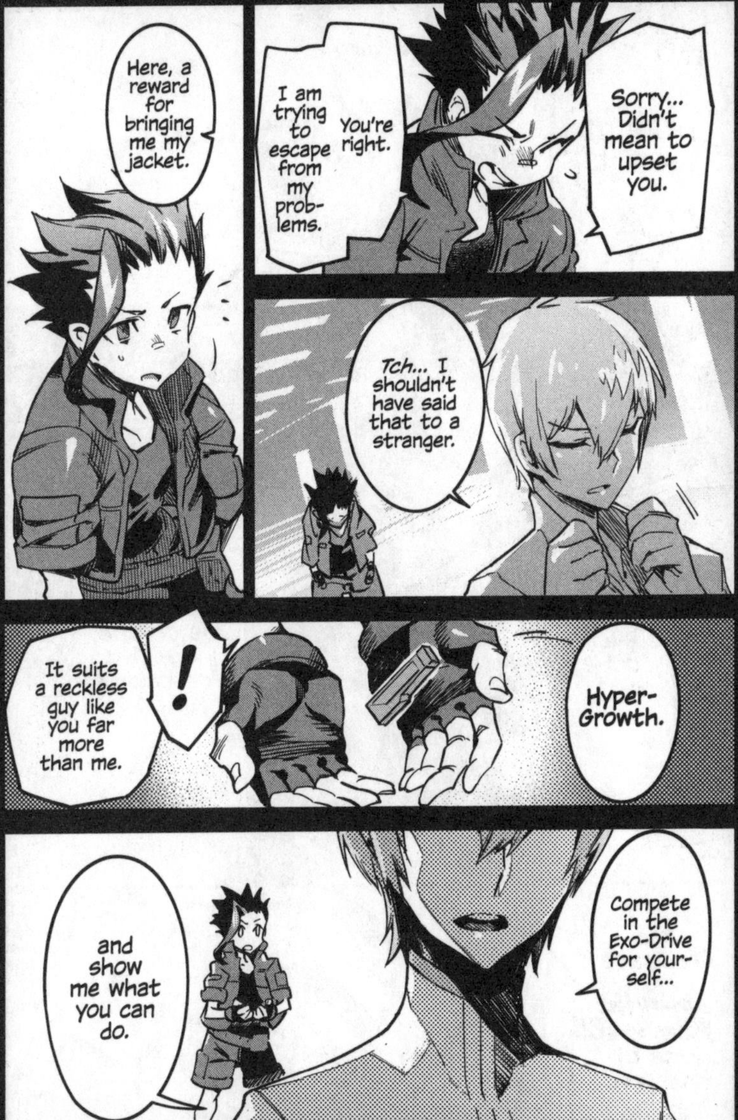
Sorry... Didn't mean to upset you.
You're right.
I am trying to escape from my problems.
Tch... I shouldn't have said that to a stranger.
Here, a reward for bringing me my jacket.
Hyper-Growth.
!
It suits a reckless guy like you far more than me.
Compete in the Exo-Drive for yourself...
and show me what you can do.

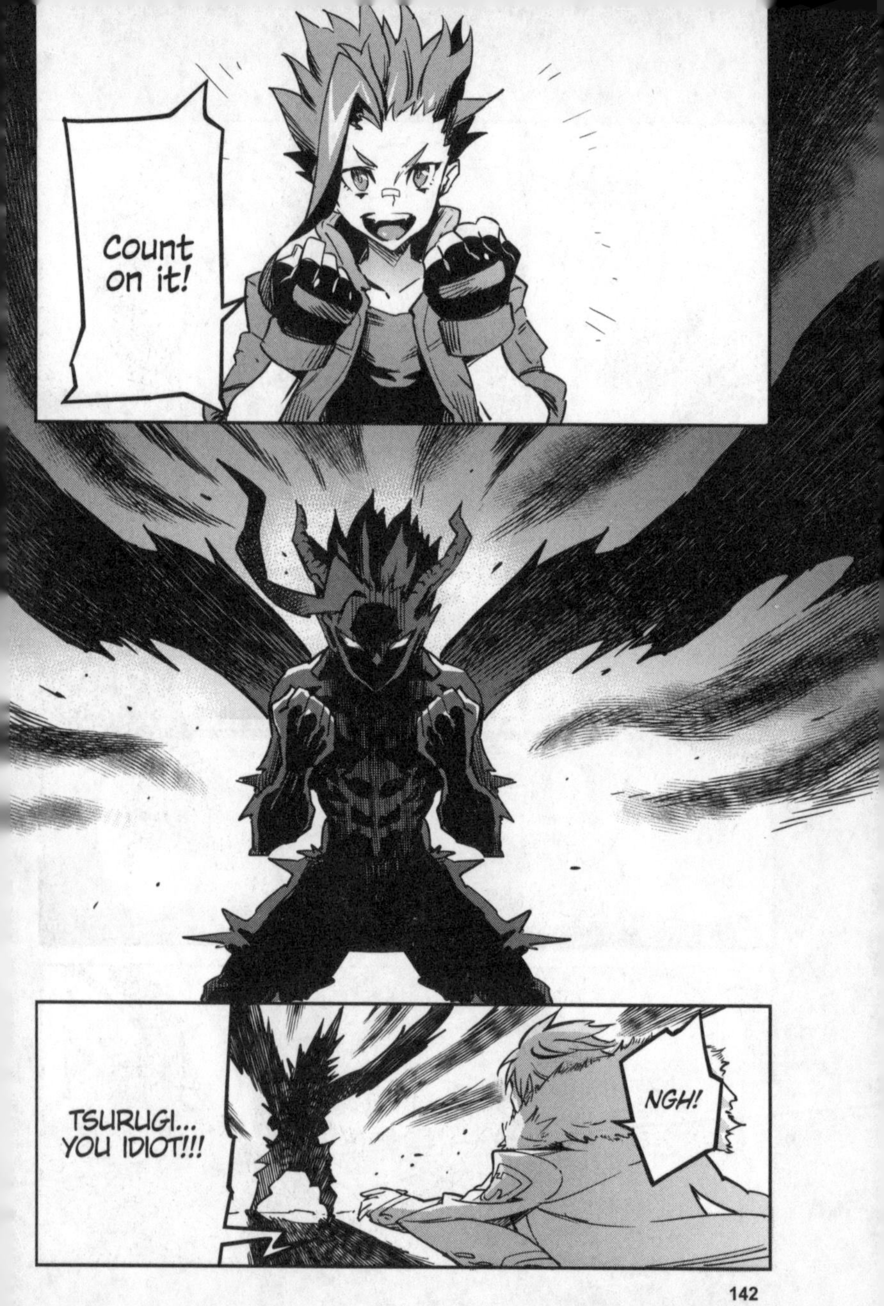
Count on it!
NGH!
TSURUGI... YOU IDIOT!!!

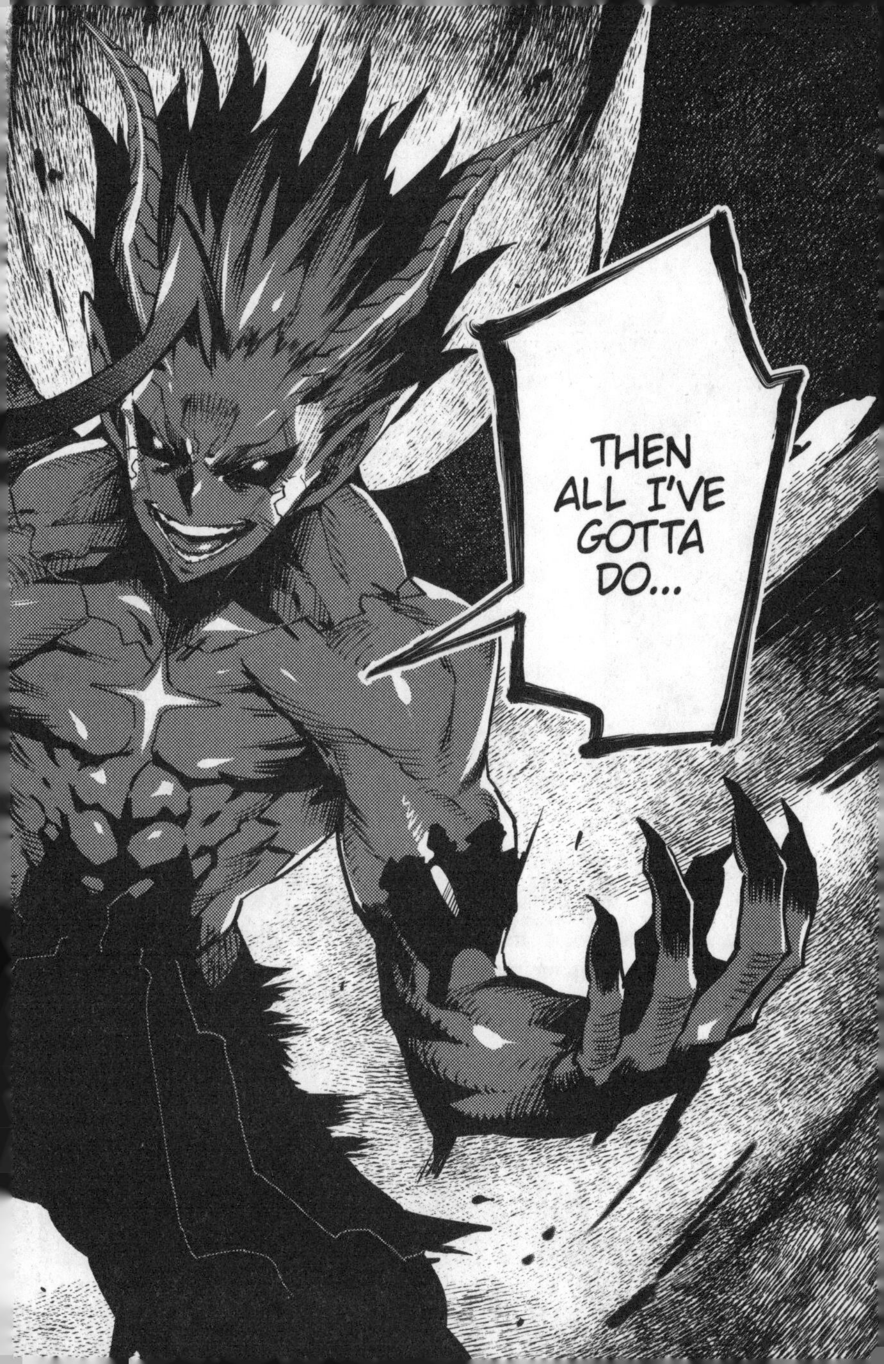
THEN ALL I'VE GOTTA DO...

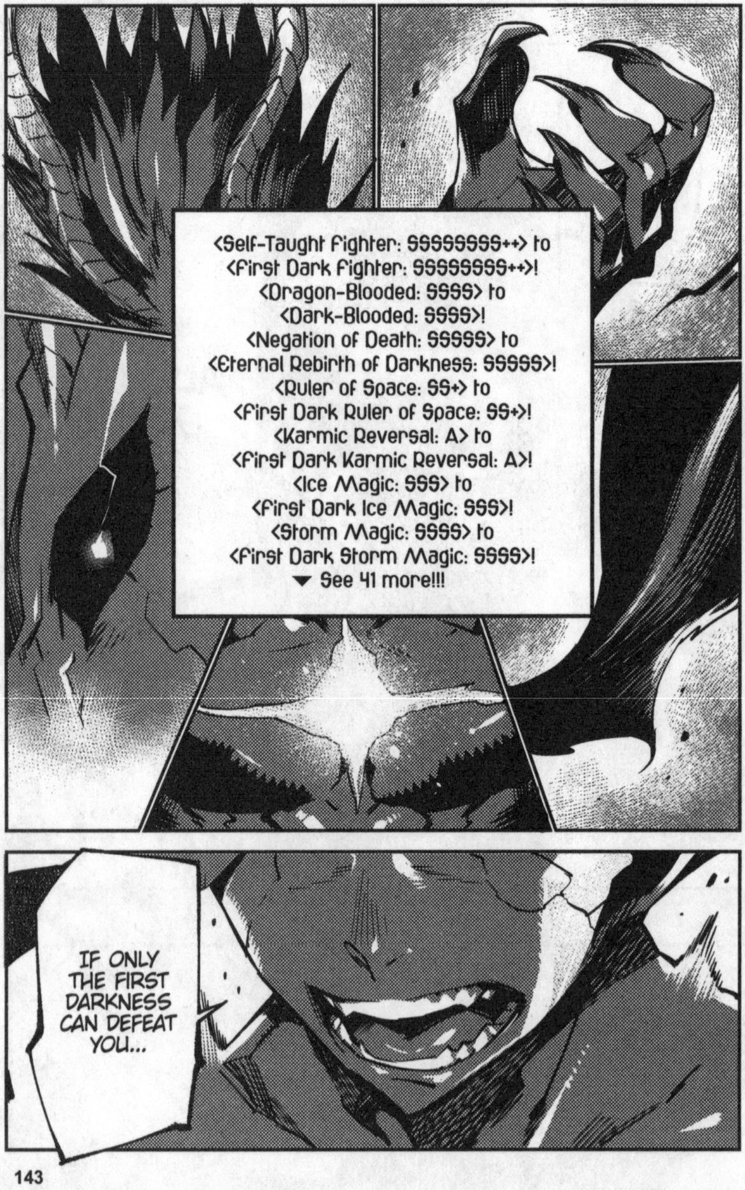
<Self-Taught Fighter: SSSSSSSS++> to
<First Dark Fighter: SSSSSSSS++>!
<Dragon-Blooded: SSSS> to
<Dark-Blooded: SSSS>!
<Negation of Death: SSSSS> to
<Eternal Rebirth of Darkness: SSSSS>!
<Ruler of Space: SS+> to
<First Dark Ruler of Space: SS+>!
<Karmic Reversal: A> to
<First Dark Karmic Reversal: A>!
<Ice Magic: SSS> to
<First Dark Ice Magic: SSS>!
<Storm Magic: SSSS> to
<First Dark Storm Magic: SSSS>!
▼ See 41 more!!!
IF ONLY THE FIRST DARKNESS CAN DEFEAT YOU...

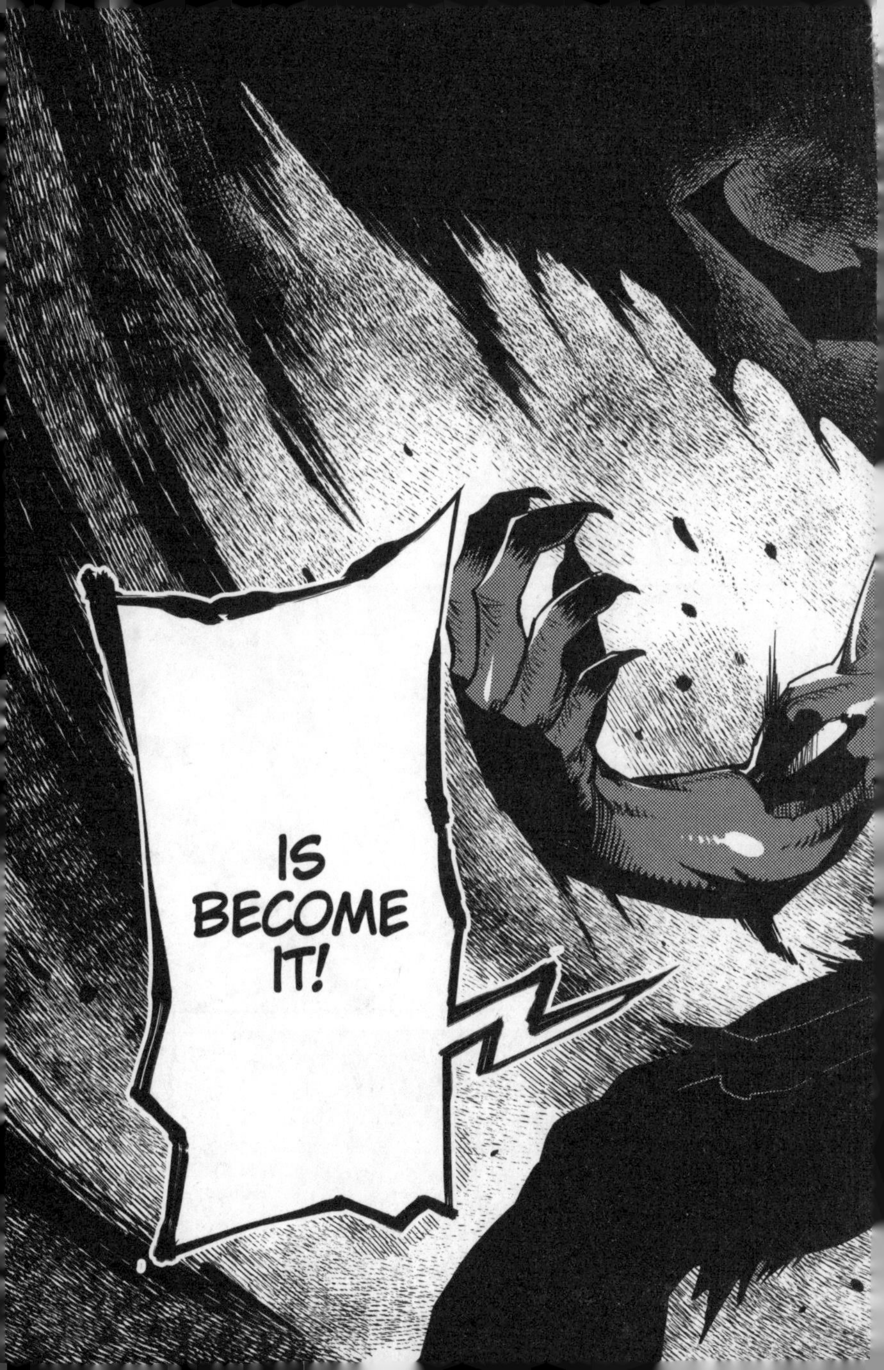
IS BECOME IT!

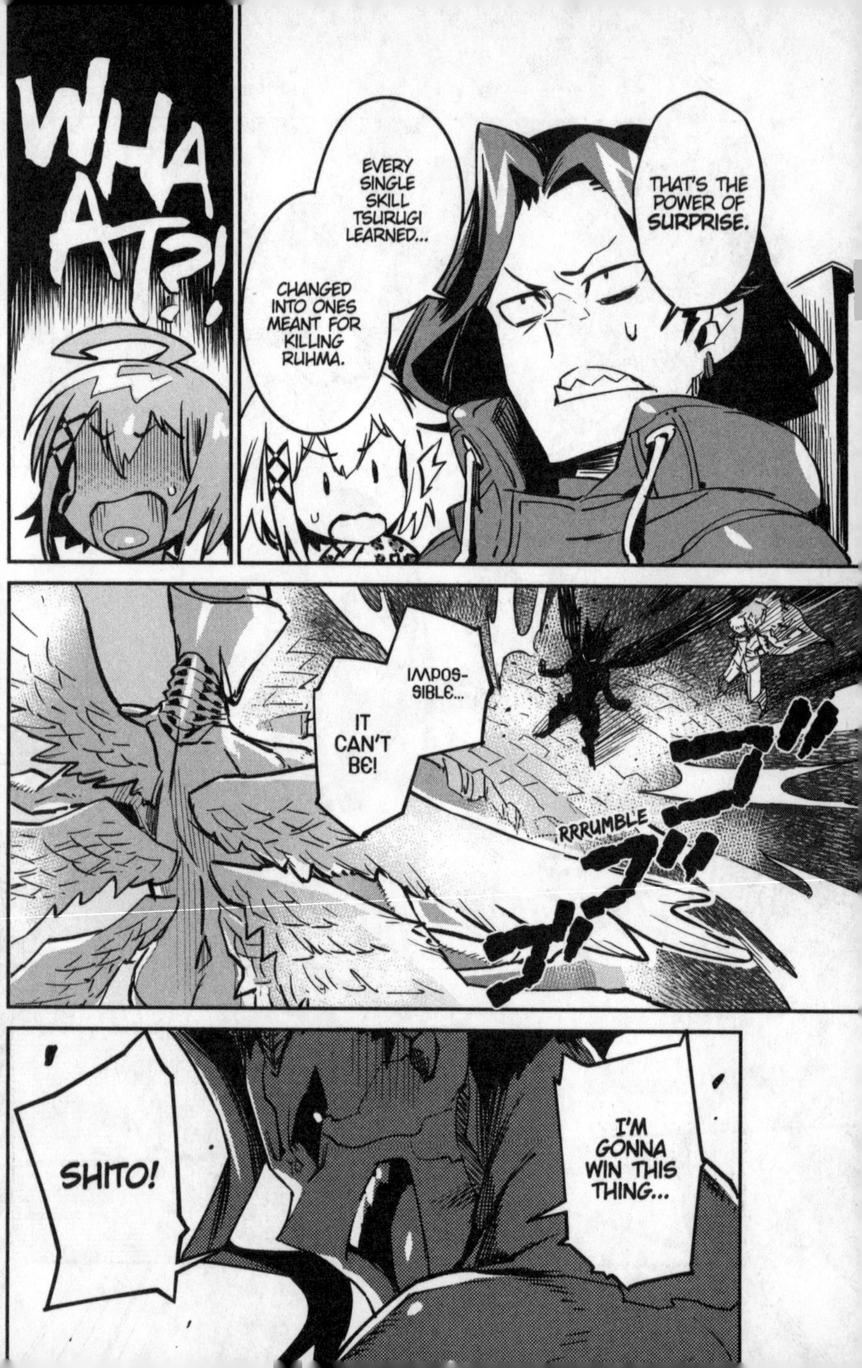
THAT'S THE POWER OF SURPRISE.
EVERY SINGLE SKILL TSURUGI LEARNED...
CHANGED INTO ONES MEANT FOR KILLING RUHMA.
WHAAT?!
IMPOSSIBLE...
IT CAN'T BE!
RRRUMBLE
I'M GONNA WIN THIS THING...
SHITO!

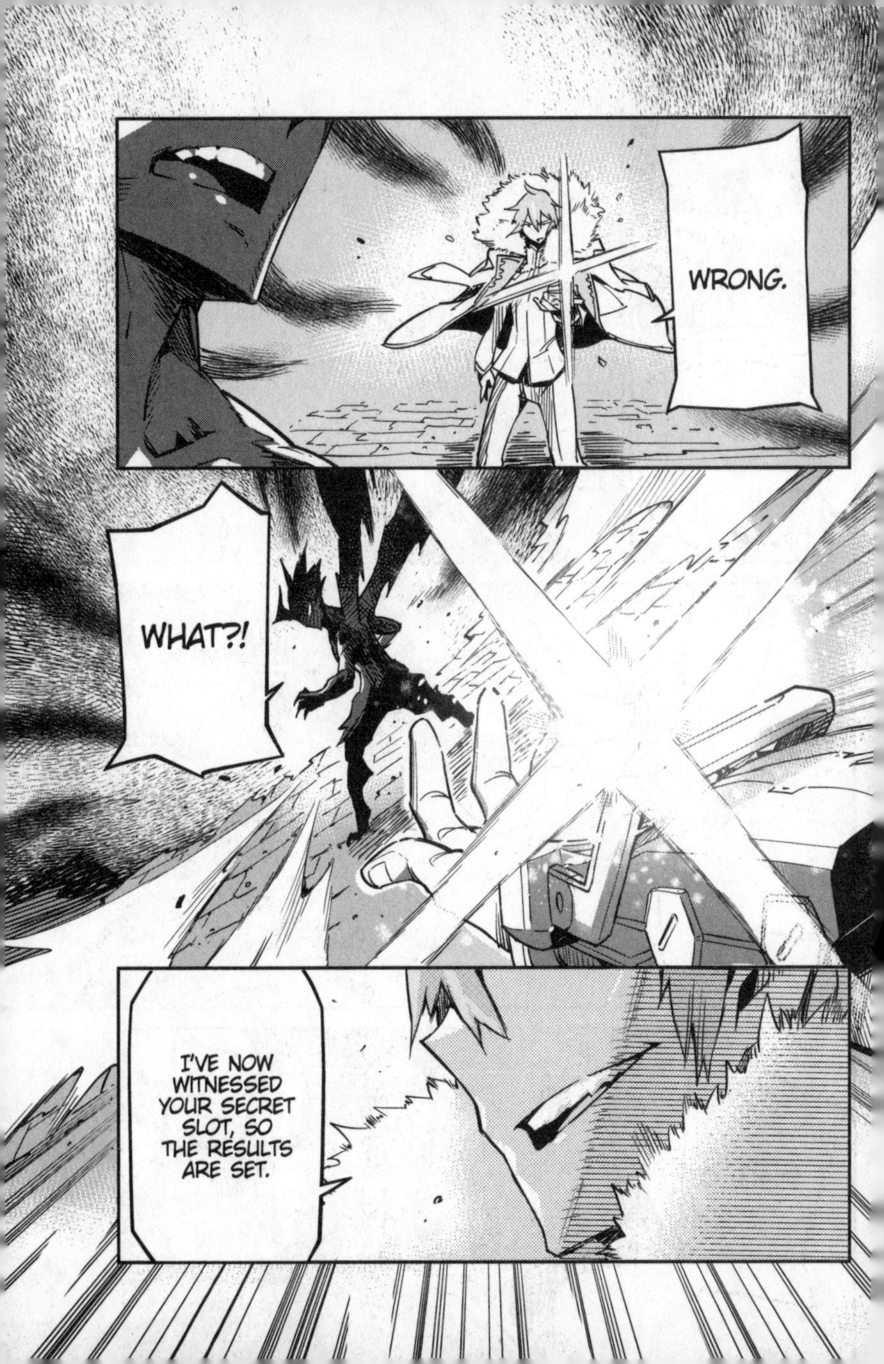

WRONG.
WHAT?!
I'VE NOW WITNESSED YOUR SECRET SLOT, SO THE RESULTS ARE SET.

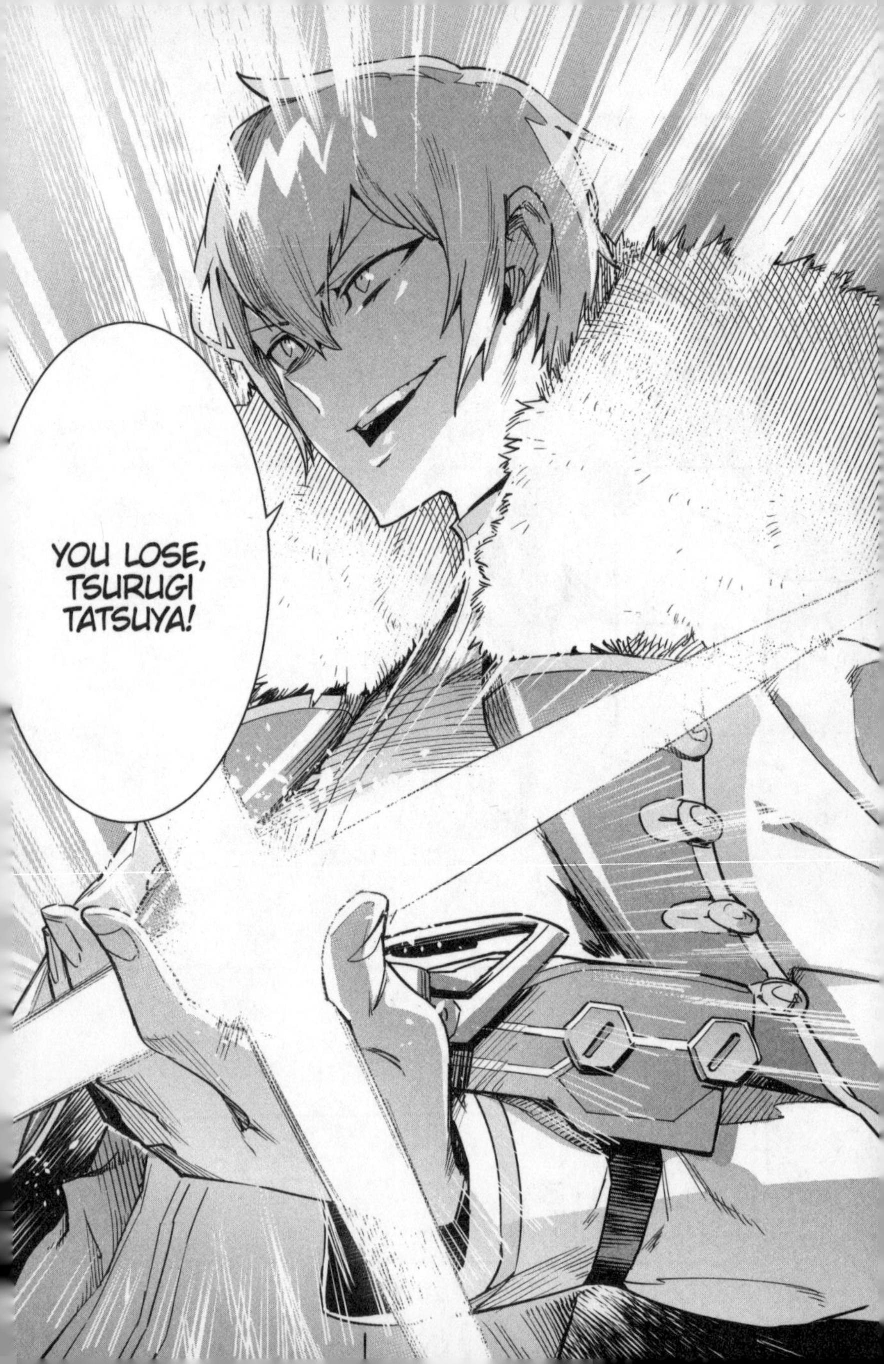
YOU LOSE, TSURUGI TATSUYA!

THE
EXO-DRIVE
REINCARNATION GAMES
ALL-JAPAN ISEKAI BATTLE TOURNAMENT!

THE
EXO-DRIVE
REINCARNATION GAMES
ALL-JAPAN ISEKAI BATTLE TOURNAMENT!

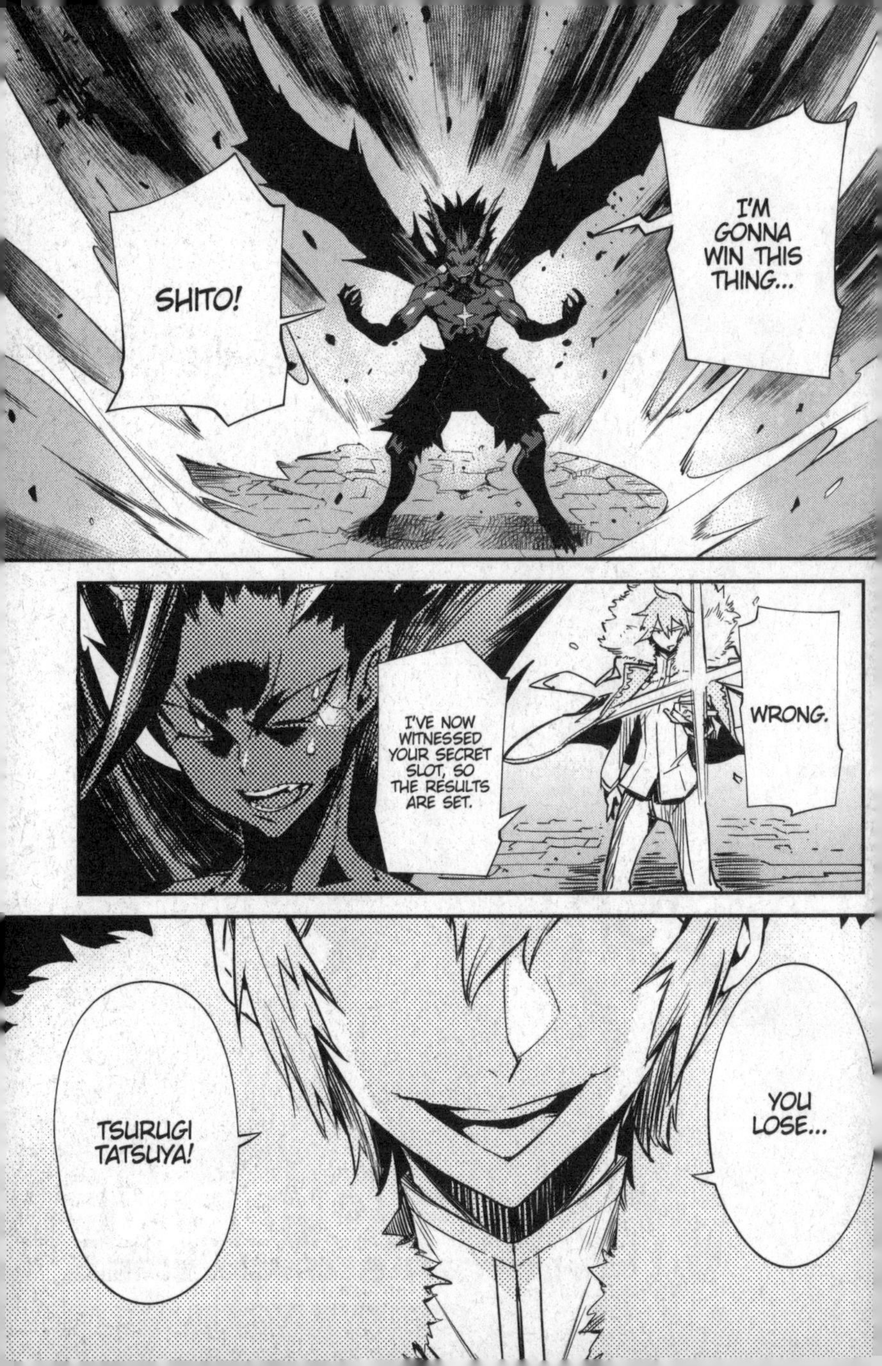
I'M GONNA WIN THIS THING...
SHITO!
WRONG.
I'VE NOW WITNESSED YOUR SECRET SLOT, SO THE RESULTS ARE SET.
YOU LOSE...
TSURUGI TATSUYA!

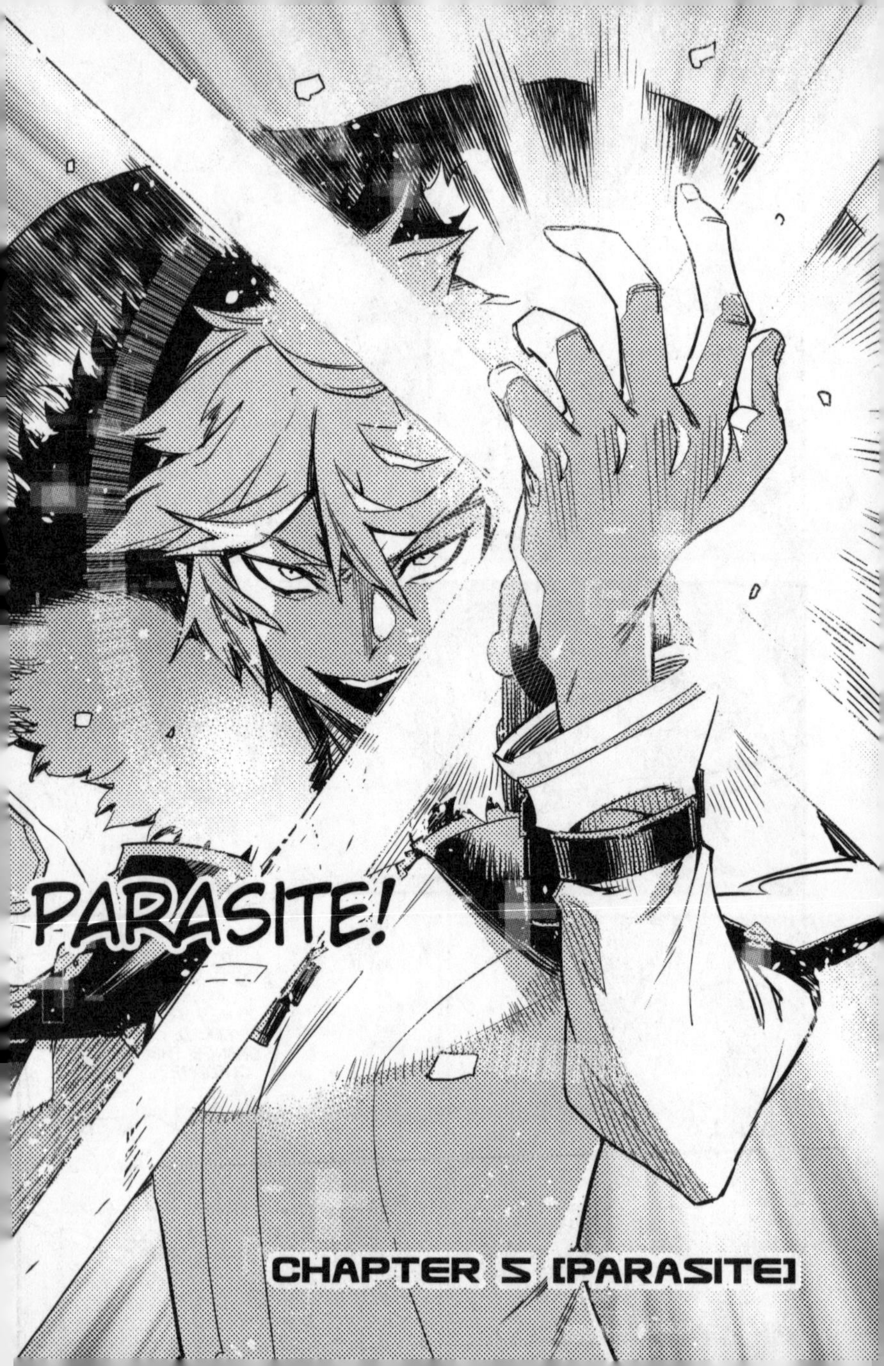
PARASITE!
CHAPTER 5 [PARASITE]

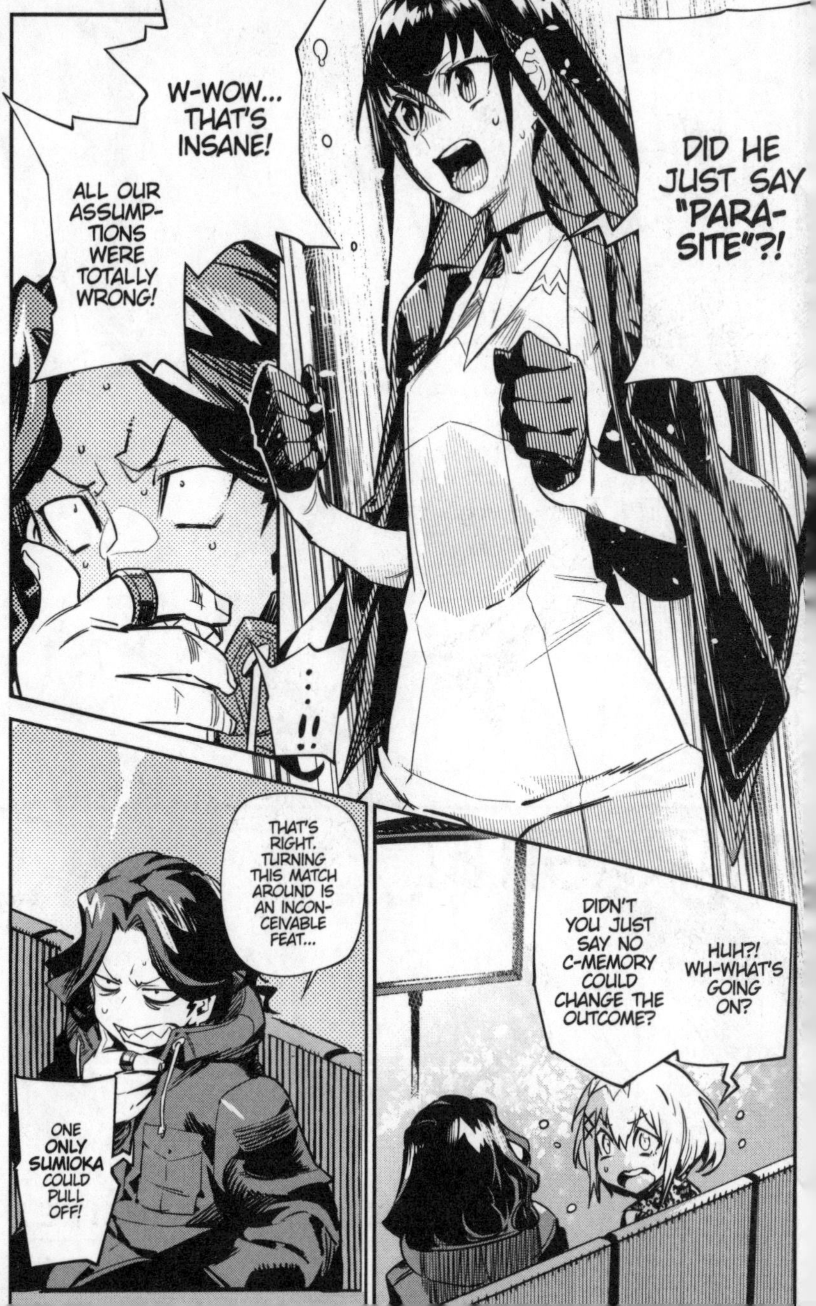
DID HE JUST SAY "PARA-SITE"?!
W-WOW... THAT'S INSANE!
ALL OUR ASSUMP-TIONS WERE TOTALLY WRONG!
...!!
HUH?! WH-WHAT'S GOING ON?
DIDN'T YOU JUST SAY NO C-MEMORY COULD CHANGE THE OUTCOME?
THAT'S RIGHT. TURNING THIS MATCH AROUND IS AN INCON-CEIVABLE FEAT...
ONE ONLY SUMIOKA COULD PULL OFF!

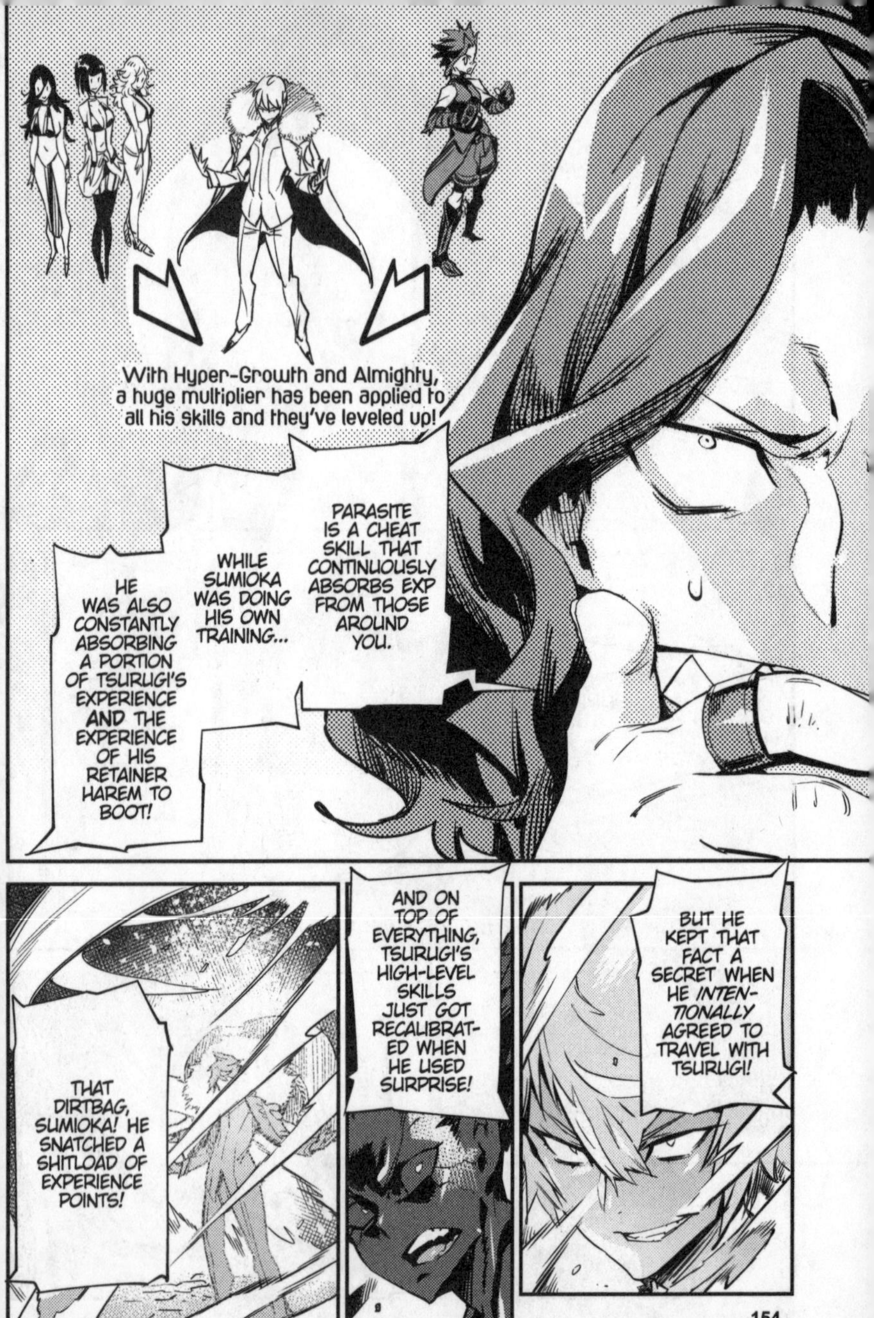

PARASITE IS A CHEAT SKILL THAT CONTINUOUSLY ABSORBS EXP FROM THOSE AROUND YOU.
WHILE SUMIOKA WAS DOING HIS OWN TRAINING...
HE WAS ALSO CONSTANTLY ABSORBING A PORTION OF TSURUGI'S EXPERIENCE AND THE EXPERIENCE OF HIS RETAINER HAREM TO BOOT!
With Hyper-Growth and Almighty, a huge multiplier has been applied to all his skills and they've leveled up!
BUT HE KEPT THAT FACT A SECRET WHEN HE *INTENTIONALLY* AGREED TO TRAVEL WITH TSURUGI!
AND ON TOP OF EVERYTHING, TSURUGI'S HIGH-LEVEL SKILLS JUST GOT RECALIBRATED WHEN HE USED SURPRISE!
THAT DIRTBAG, SUMIOKA! HE SNATCHED A SHITLOAD OF EXPERIENCE POINTS!

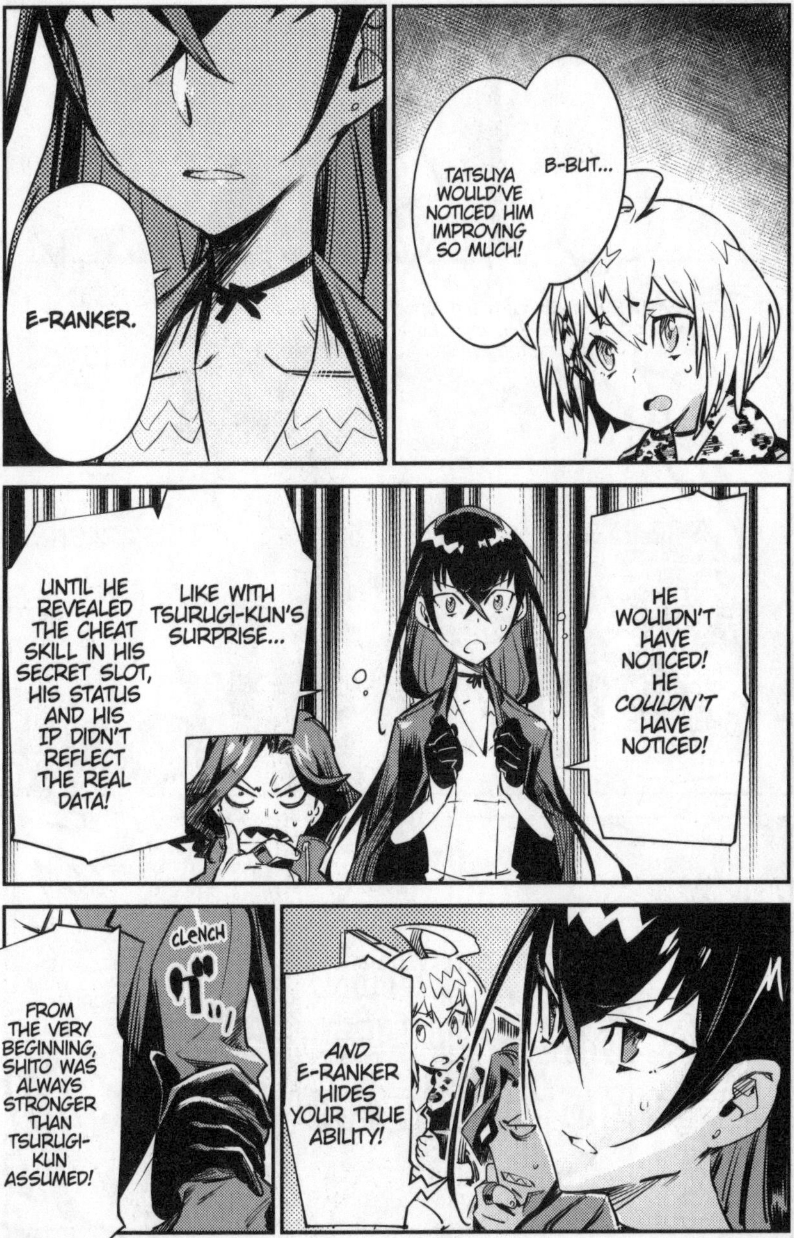
B-BUT...
TATSUYA WOULD'VE NOTICED HIM IMPROVING SO MUCH!
E-RANKER.
HE WOULDN'T HAVE NOTICED! HE COULDN'T HAVE NOTICED!
LIKE WITH TSURUGI-KUN'S SURPRISE...
UNTIL HE REVEALED THE CHEAT SKILL IN HIS SECRET SLOT, HIS STATUS AND HIS IP DIDN'T REFLECT THE REAL DATA!
AND E-RANKER HIDES YOUR TRUE ABILITY!
CLENCH
FROM THE VERY BEGINNING, SHITO WAS ALWAYS STRONGER THAN TSURUGI-KUN ASSUMED!

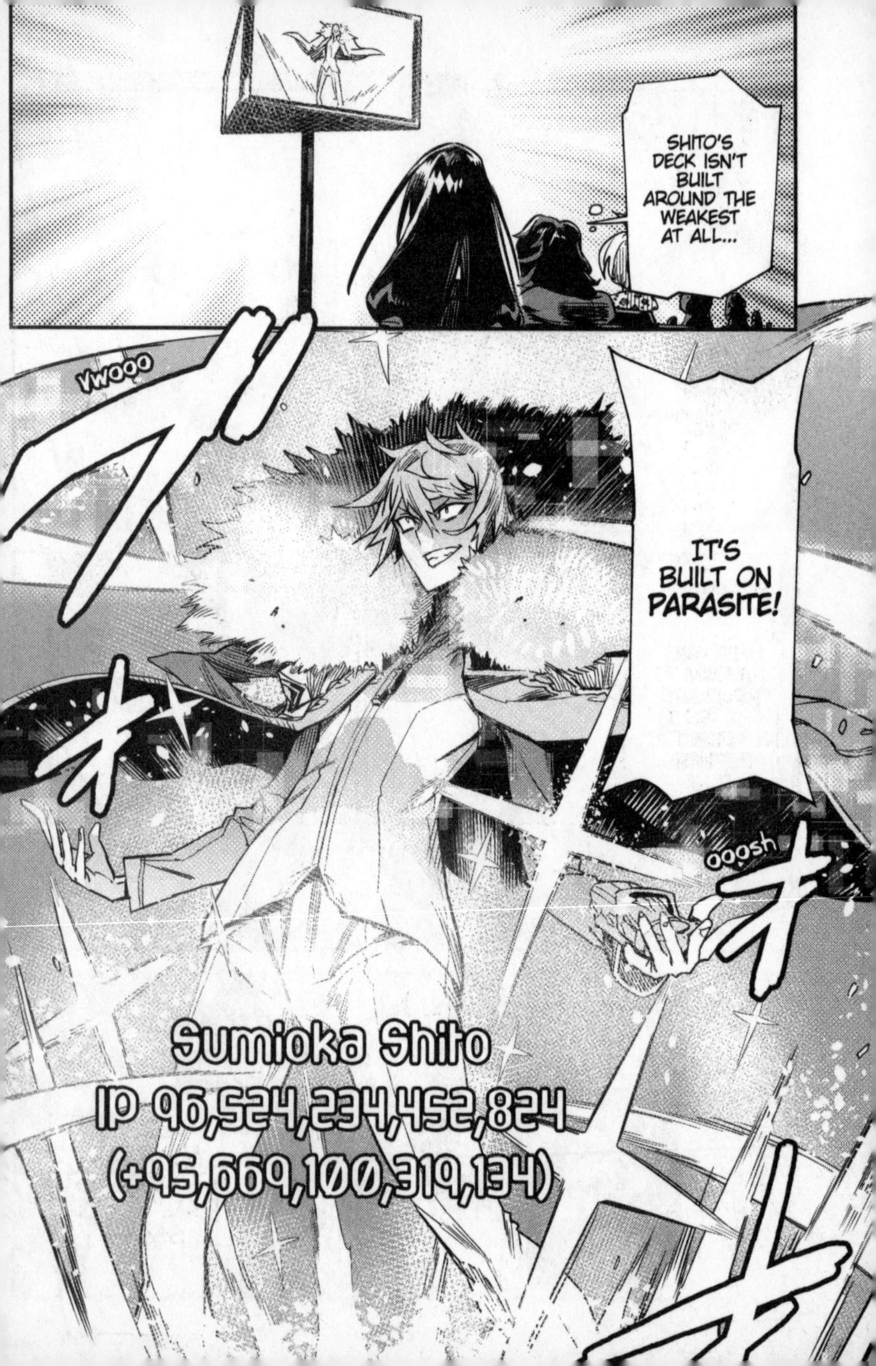
SHITO'S DECK ISN'T BUILT AROUND THE WEAKEST AT ALL...
IT'S BUILT ON PARASITE!
Ywooo
ooosh
Sumioka Shito
IP 96,524,234,452,824
(+95,669,100,319,134)

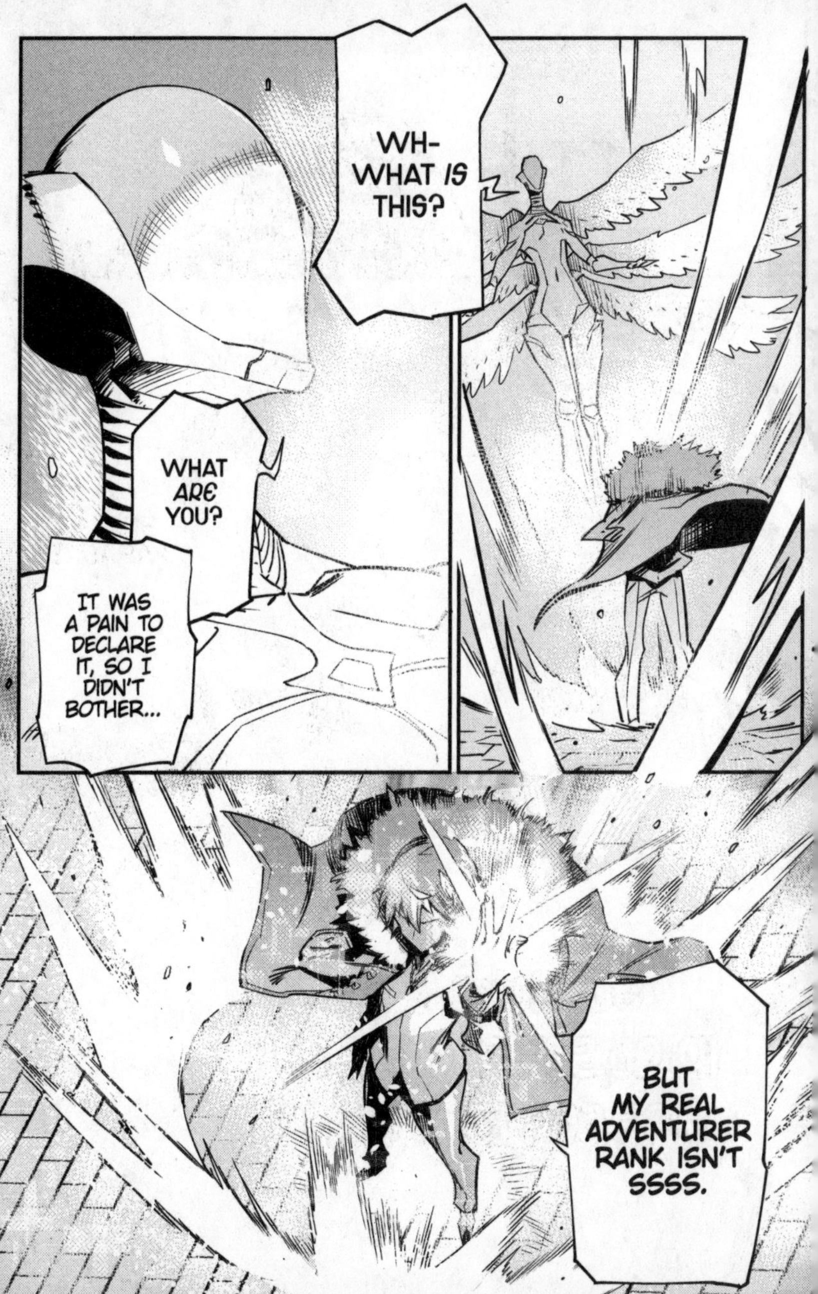
WH- WHAT IS THIS?
WHAT ARE YOU?
IT WAS A PAIN TO DECLARE IT, SO I DIDN'T BOTHER...
BUT MY REAL ADVENTURER RANK ISN'T SSSS.

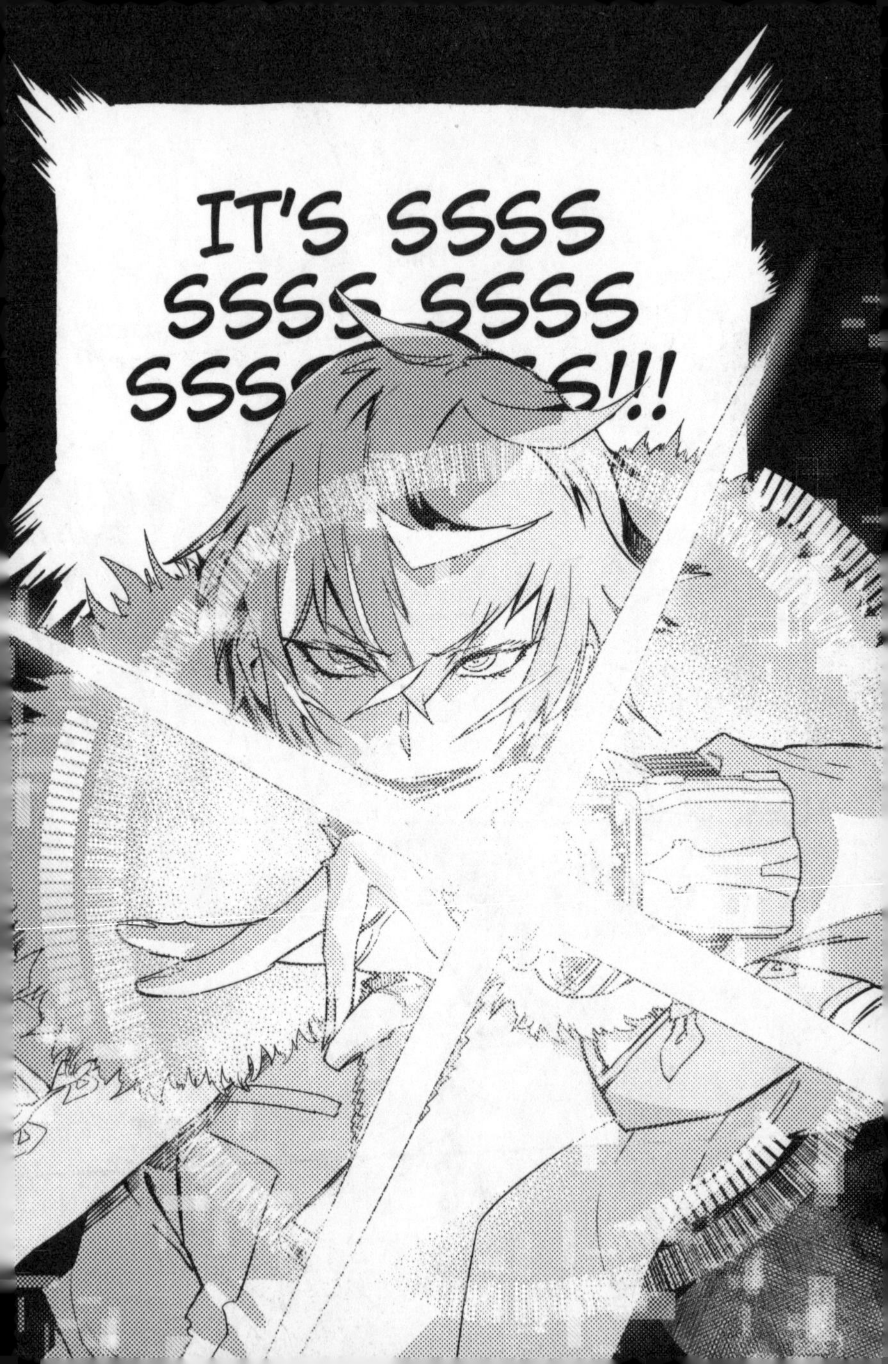
IT'S SSSS
SSSS SSSS
SSS S!!!

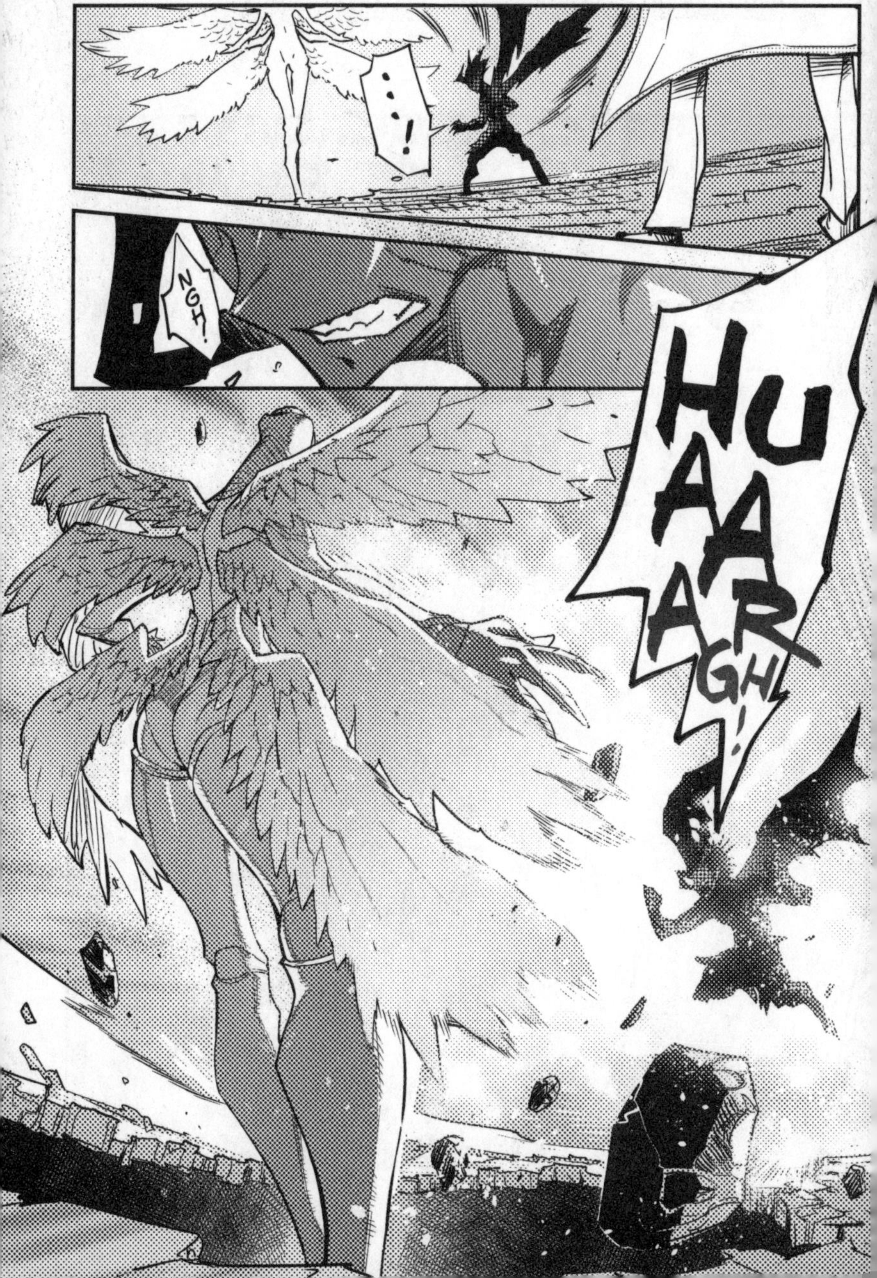

...!
NGH!
HUAAAARGH!

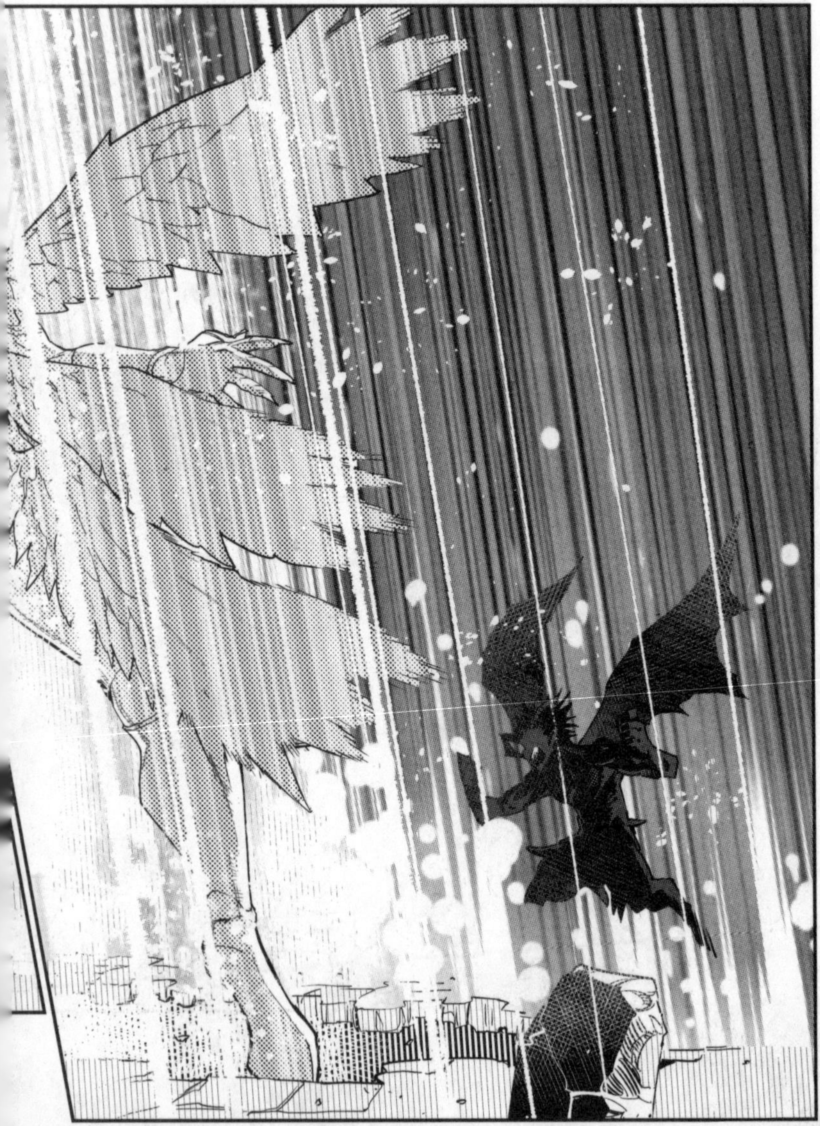

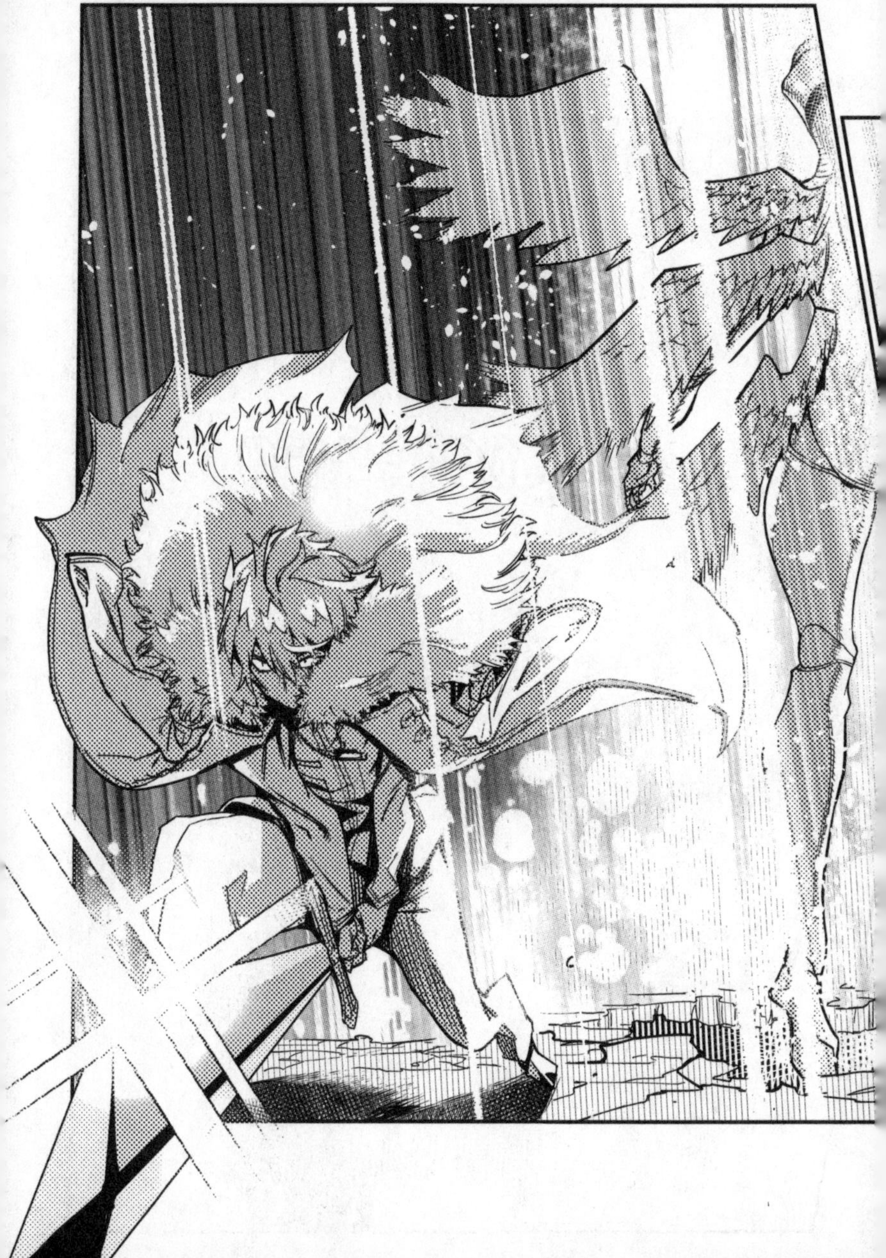

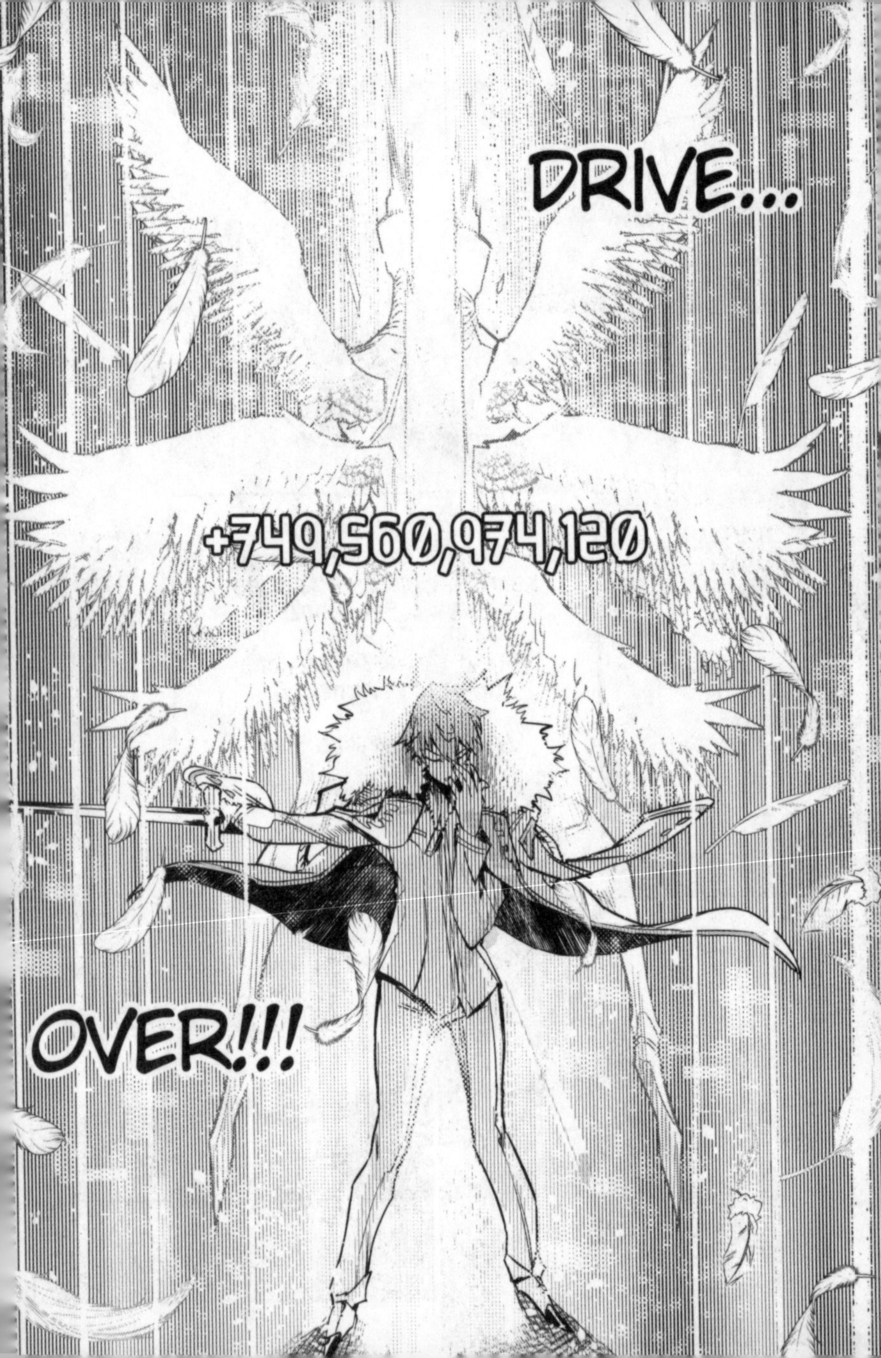
DRIVE...
+749,560,974,120
OVER!!!

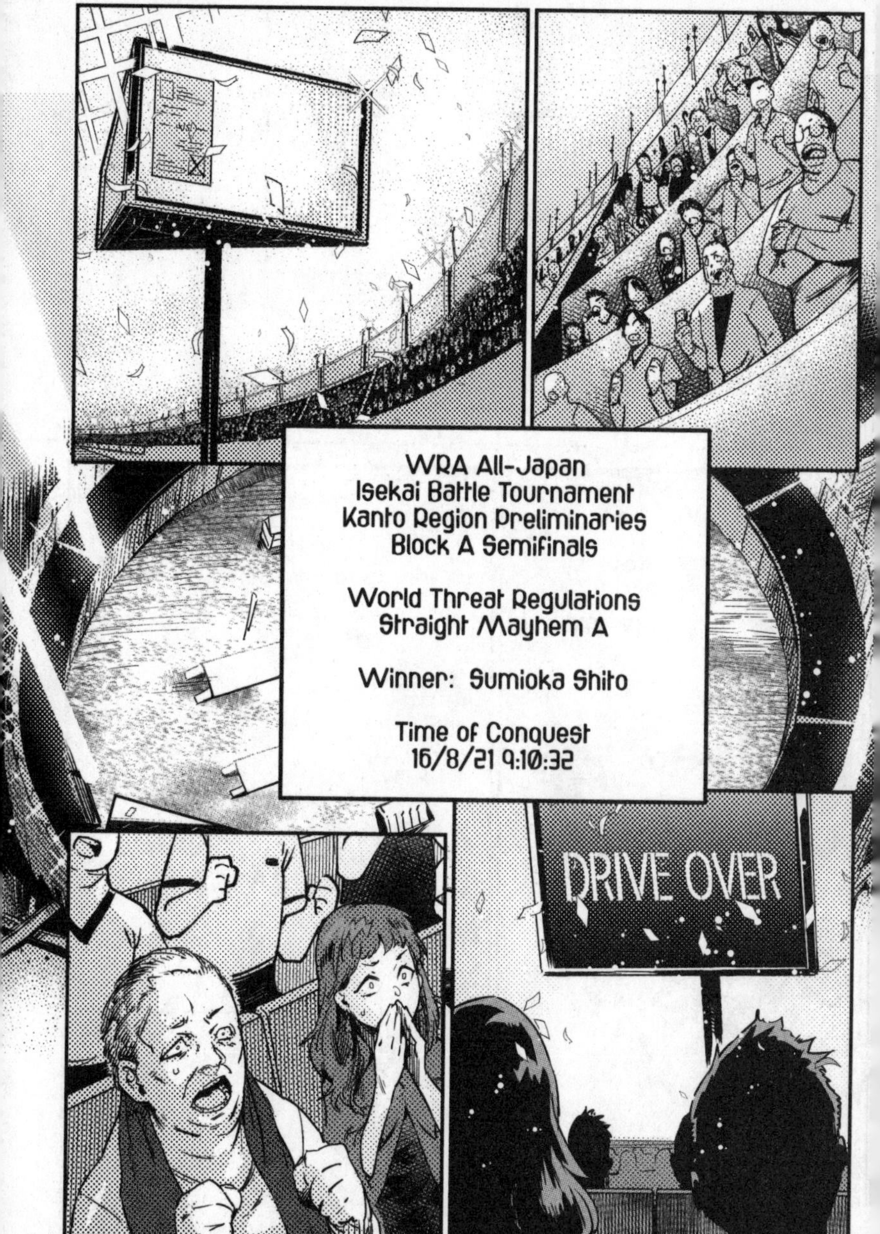
WRA All-Japan
Isekai Battle Tournament
Kanto Region Preliminaries
Block A Semifinals

World Threat Regulations
Straight Mayhem A

Winner: Sumioka Shito

Time of Conquest
16/8/21 9:10:32
DRIVE OVER

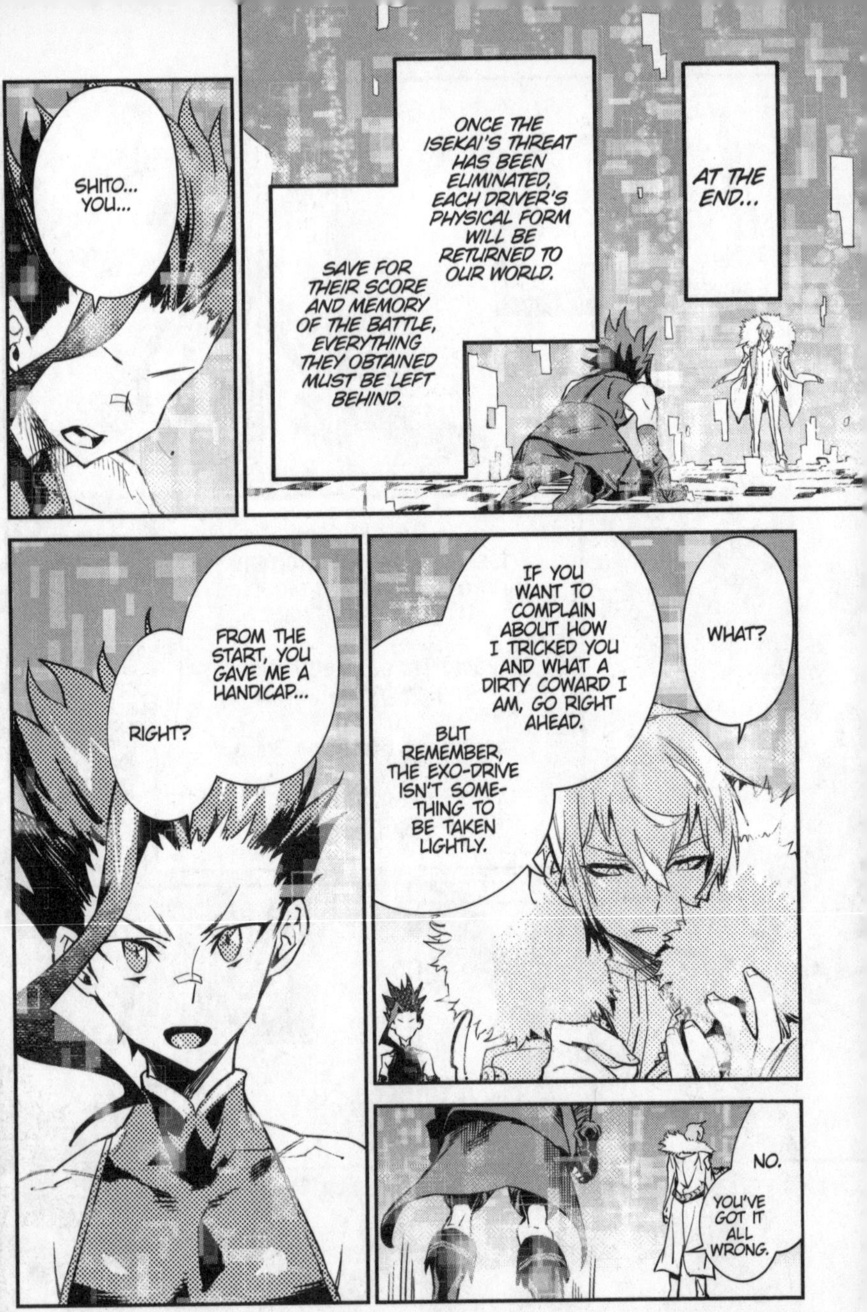
AT THE END...
ONCE THE ISEKAI'S THREAT HAS BEEN ELIMINATED, EACH DRIVER'S PHYSICAL FORM WILL BE RETURNED TO OUR WORLD.
SAVE FOR THEIR SCORE AND MEMORY OF THE BATTLE, EVERYTHING THEY OBTAINED MUST BE LEFT BEHIND.
SHITO... YOU...
WHAT?
IF YOU WANT TO COMPLAIN ABOUT HOW I TRICKED YOU AND WHAT A DIRTY COWARD I AM, GO RIGHT AHEAD.
BUT REMEMBER, THE EXO-DRIVE ISN'T SOME-THING TO BE TAKEN LIGHTLY.
NO.
YOU'VE GOT IT ALL WRONG.
FROM THE START, YOU GAVE ME A HANDICAP...
RIGHT?

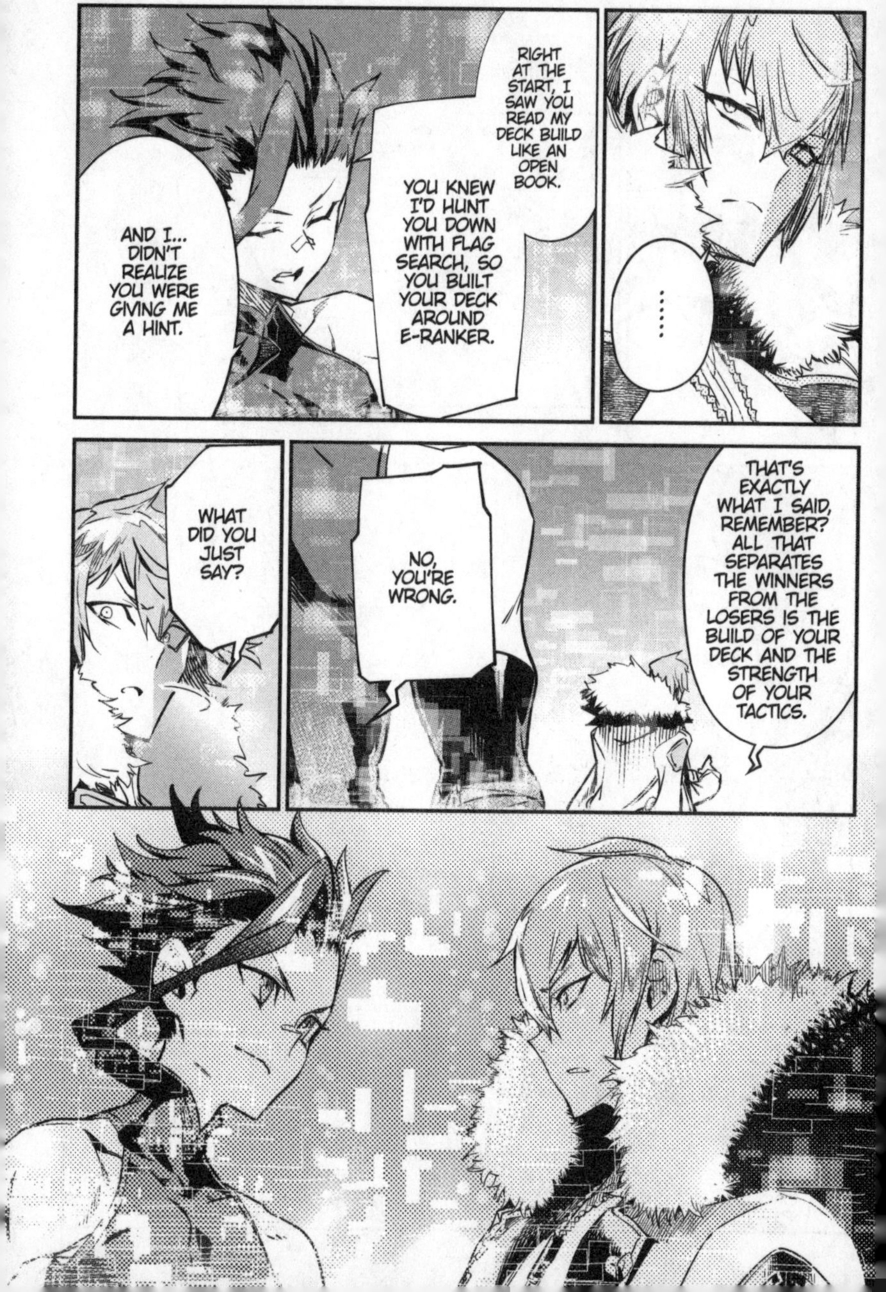
......
RIGHT AT THE START, I SAW YOU READ MY DECK BUILD LIKE AN OPEN BOOK.
YOU KNEW I'D HUNT YOU DOWN WITH FLAG SEARCH, SO YOU BUILT YOUR DECK AROUND E-RANKER.
AND I... DIDN'T REALIZE YOU WERE GIVING ME A HINT.
THAT'S EXACTLY WHAT I SAID, REMEMBER? ALL THAT SEPARATES THE WINNERS FROM THE LOSERS IS THE BUILD OF YOUR DECK AND THE STRENGTH OF YOUR TACTICS.
NO, YOU'RE WRONG.
WHAT DID YOU JUST SAY?

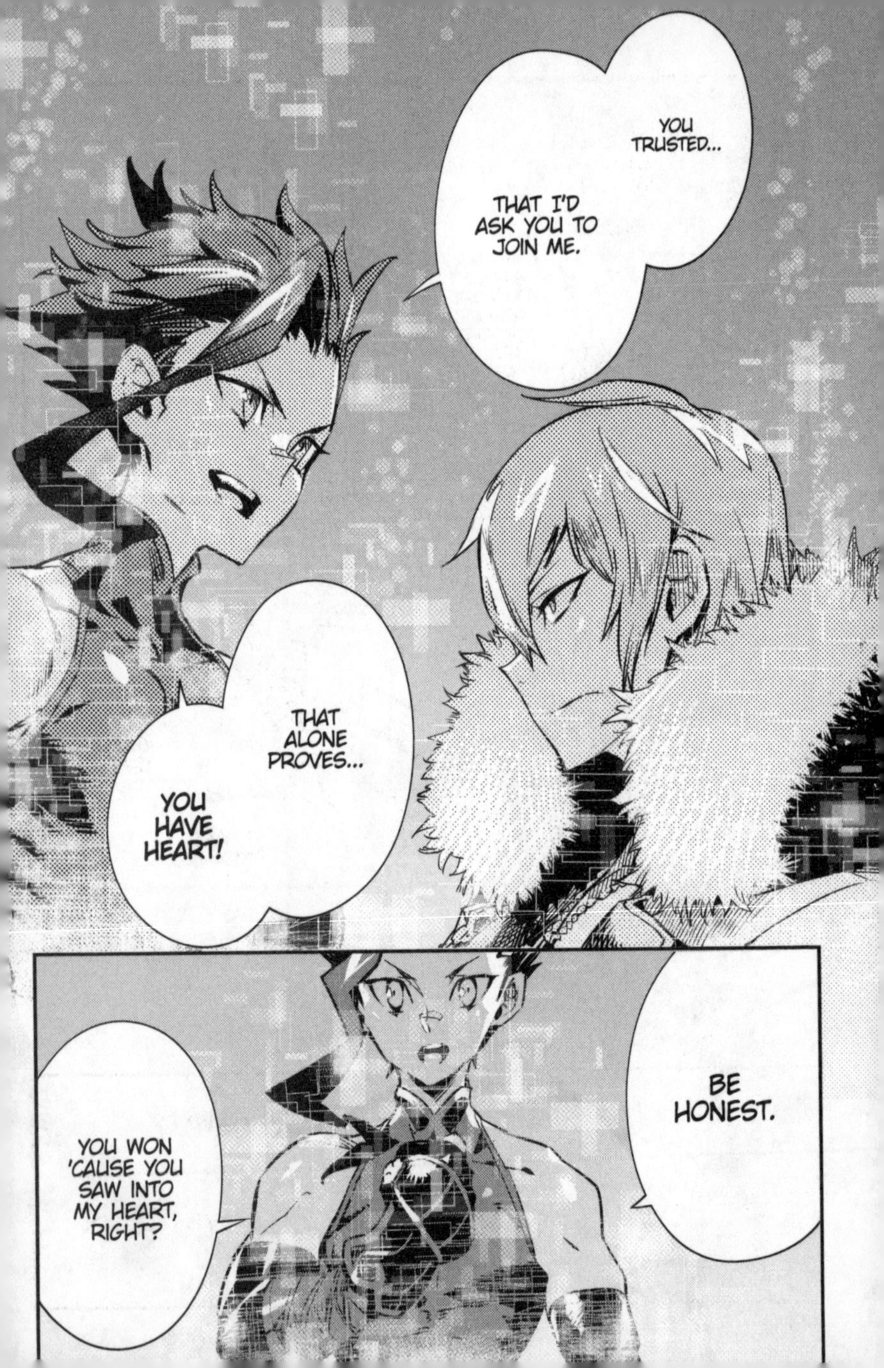
YOU TRUSTED...
THAT I'D ASK YOU TO JOIN ME.
THAT ALONE PROVES...
YOU HAVE HEART!
BE HONEST.
YOU WON 'CAUSE YOU SAW INTO MY HEART, RIGHT?

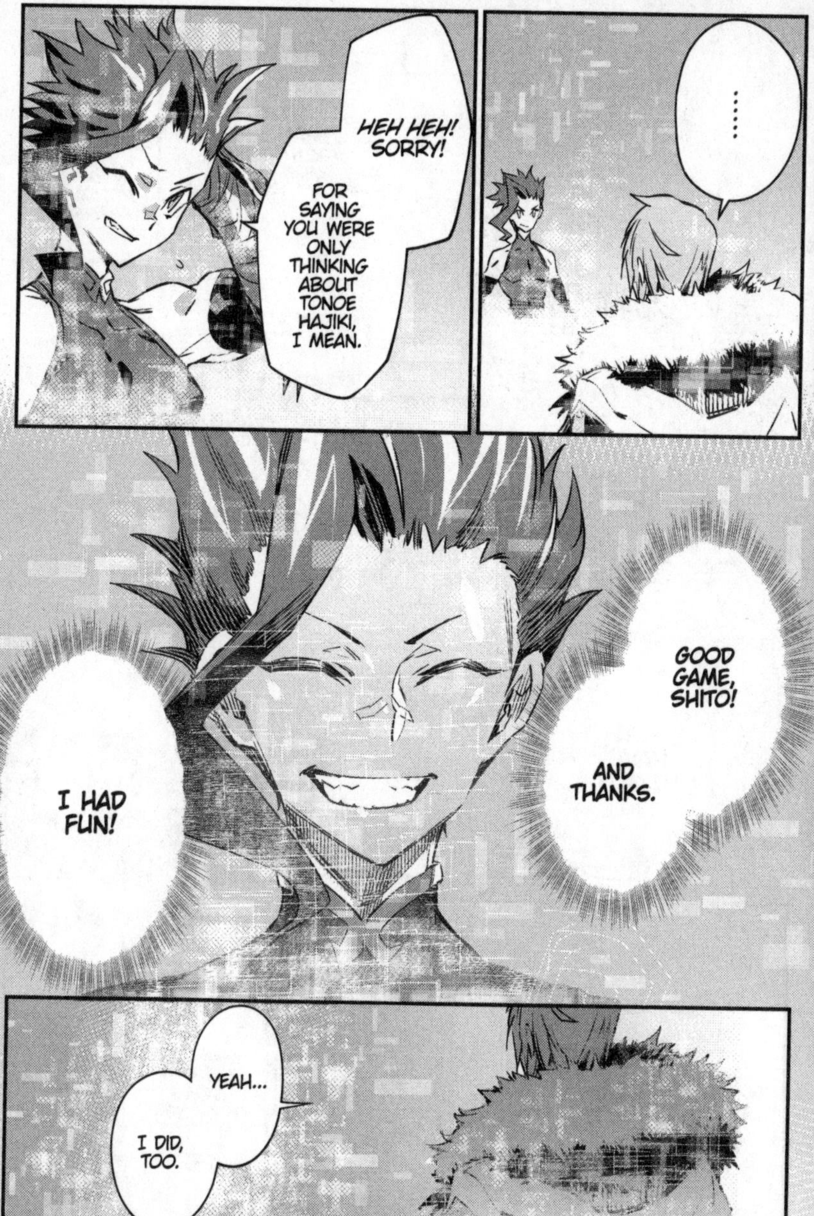
……
HEH HEH! SORRY!
FOR SAYING YOU WERE ONLY THINKING ABOUT TONOE HAJIKI, I MEAN.
GOOD GAME, SHITO!
AND THANKS.
I HAD FUN!
YEAH...
I DID, TOO.

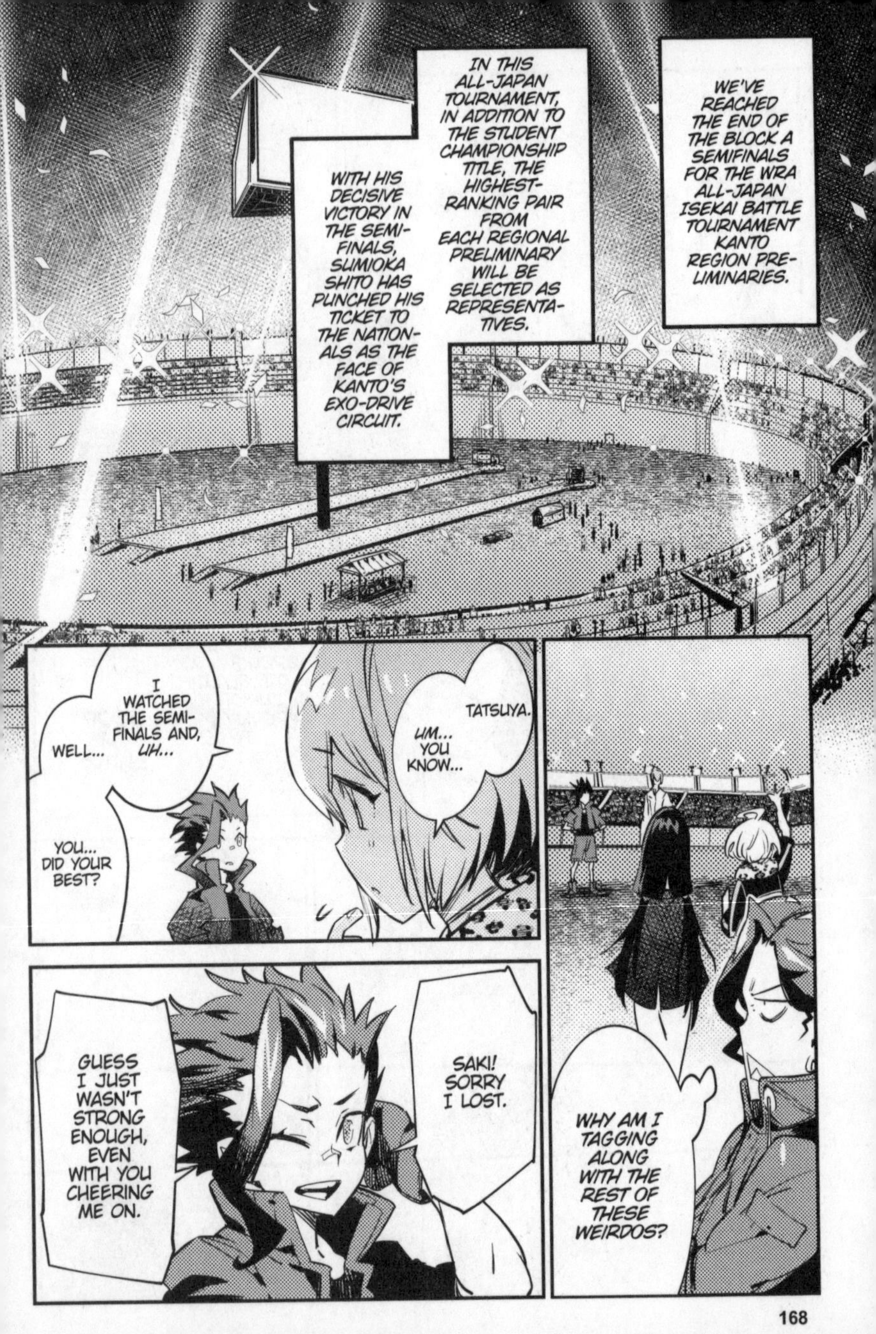
WE'VE REACHED THE END OF THE BLOCK A SEMIFINALS FOR THE WRA ALL-JAPAN ISEKAI BATTLE TOURNAMENT KANTO REGION PRE-LIMINARIES.
IN THIS ALL-JAPAN TOURNAMENT, IN ADDITION TO THE STUDENT CHAMPIONSHIP TITLE, THE HIGHEST-RANKING PAIR FROM EACH REGIONAL PRELIMINARY WILL BE SELECTED AS REPRESENTA-TIVES.
WITH HIS DECISIVE VICTORY IN THE SEMI-FINALS, SUMIOKA SHITO HAS PUNCHED HIS TICKET TO THE NATION-ALS AS THE FACE OF KANTO'S EXO-DRIVE CIRCUIT.
WHY AM I TAGGING ALONG WITH THE REST OF THESE WEIRDOS?
TATSUYA.
UM... YOU KNOW...
I WATCHED THE SEMI-FINALS AND, UH...
WELL...
YOU... DID YOUR BEST?
SAKI! SORRY I LOST.
GUESS I JUST WASN'T STRONG ENOUGH, EVEN WITH YOU CHEERING ME ON.

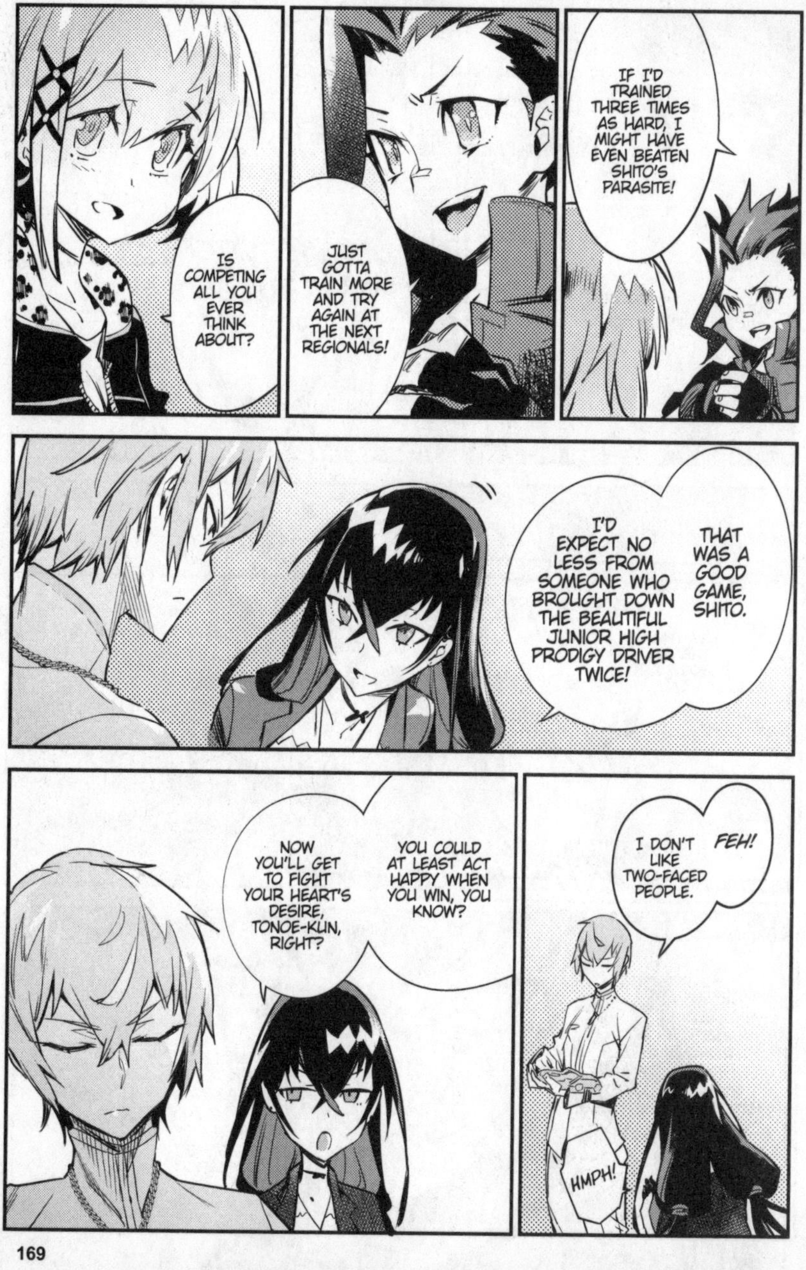
IF I'D TRAINED THREE TIMES AS HARD, I MIGHT HAVE EVEN BEATEN SHITO'S PARASITE!
JUST GOTTA TRAIN MORE AND TRY AGAIN AT THE NEXT REGIONALS!
IS COMPETING ALL YOU EVER THINK ABOUT?
THAT WAS A GOOD GAME, SHITO.
I'D EXPECT NO LESS FROM SOMEONE WHO BROUGHT DOWN THE BEAUTIFUL JUNIOR HIGH PRODIGY DRIVER TWICE!
FEH!
I DON'T LIKE TWO-FACED PEOPLE.
HMPH!
YOU COULD AT LEAST ACT HAPPY WHEN YOU WIN, YOU KNOW?
NOW YOU'LL GET TO FIGHT YOUR HEART'S DESIRE, TONOE-KUN, RIGHT?

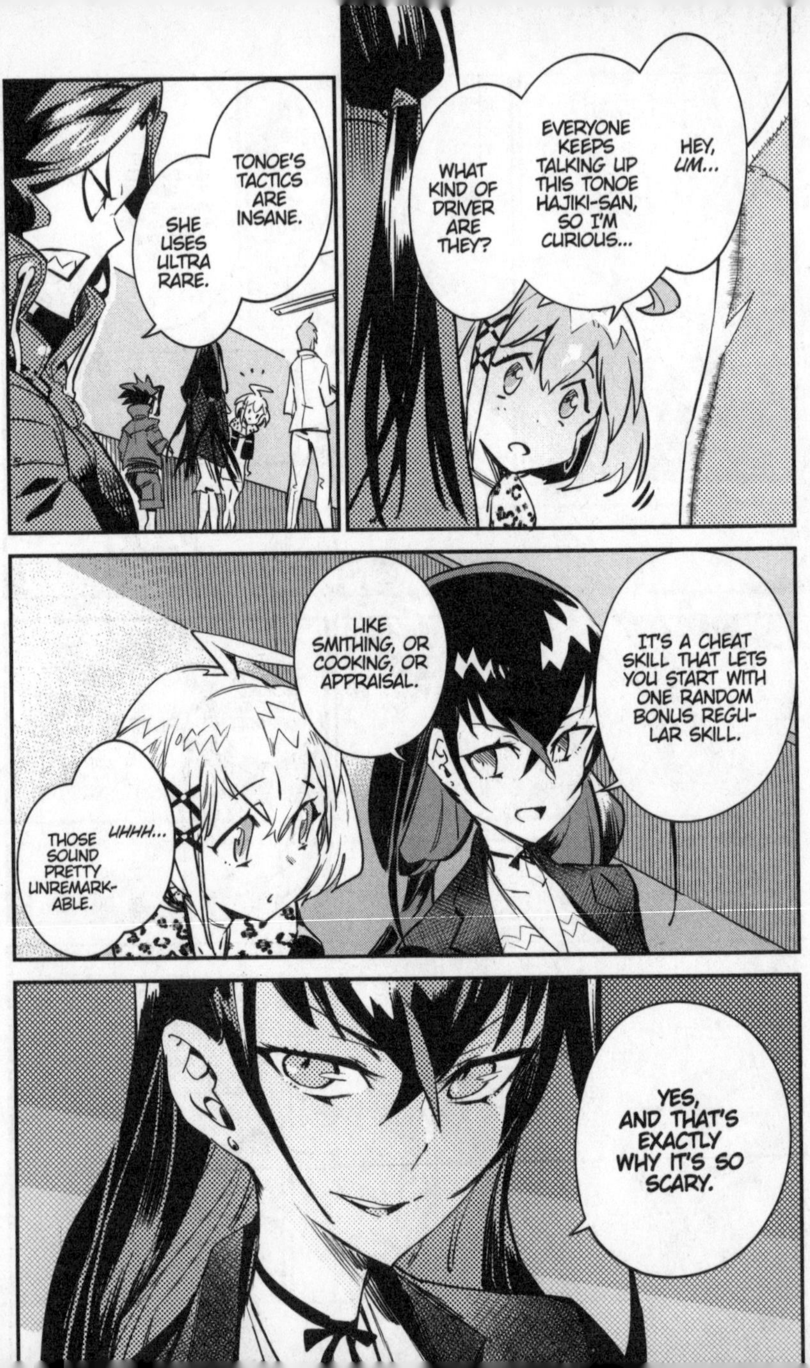
HEY, UM...
EVERYONE KEEPS TALKING UP THIS TONOE HAJIKI-SAN, SO I'M CURIOUS...
WHAT KIND OF DRIVER ARE THEY?
TONOE'S TACTICS ARE INSANE.
SHE USES ULTRA RARE.
IT'S A CHEAT SKILL THAT LETS YOU START WITH ONE RANDOM BONUS REGU-LAR SKILL.
LIKE SMITHING, OR COOKING, OR APPRAISAL.
UHHH...
THOSE SOUND PRETTY UNREMARK-ABLE.
YES, AND THAT'S EXACTLY WHY IT'S SO SCARY.

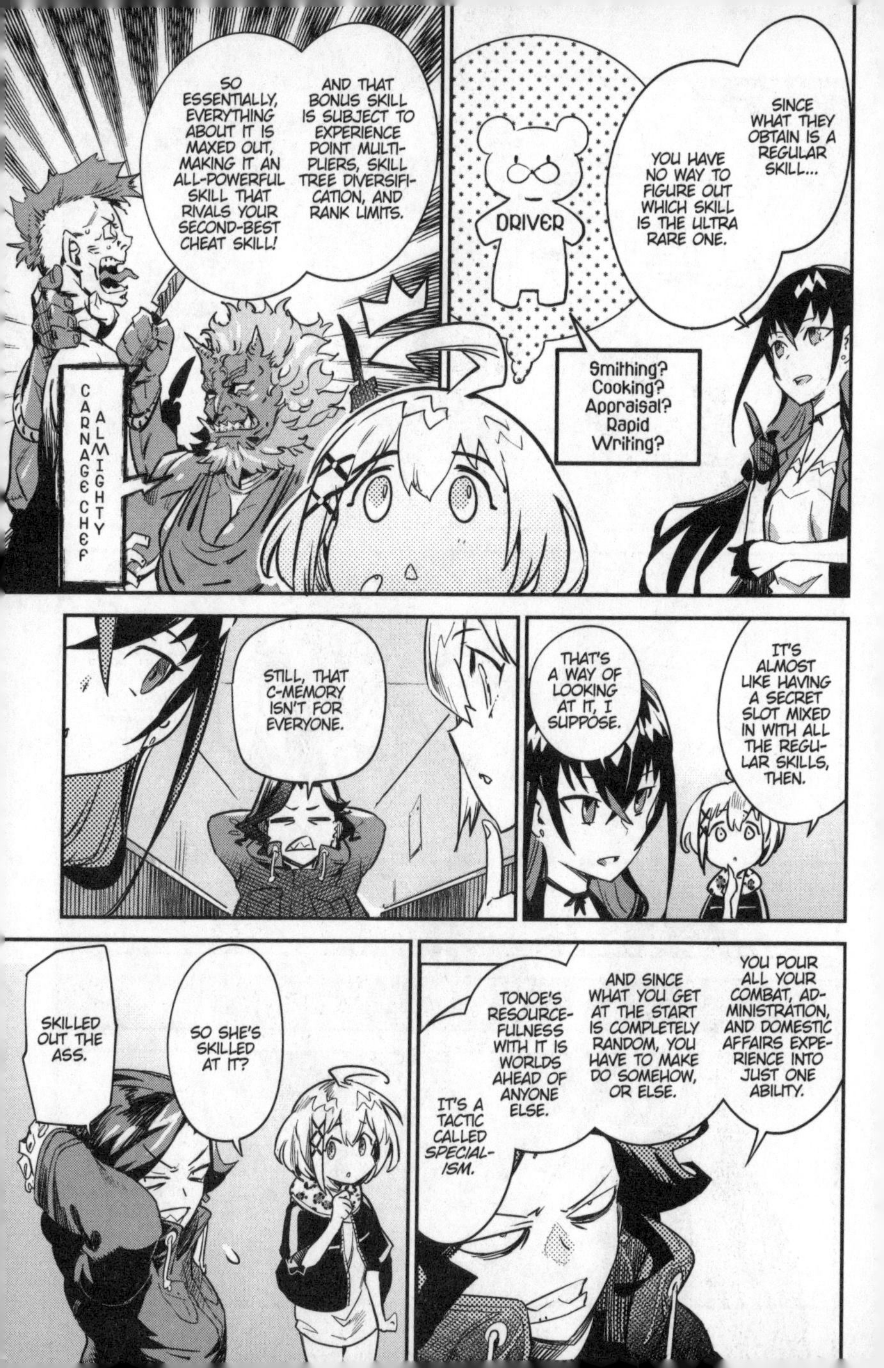
SINCE WHAT THEY OBTAIN IS A REGULAR SKILL...
YOU HAVE NO WAY TO FIGURE OUT WHICH SKILL IS THE ULTRA RARE ONE.
DRIVER
Smithing? Cooking? Appraisal? Rapid Writing?
AND THAT BONUS SKILL IS SUBJECT TO EXPERIENCE POINT MULTI-PLIERS, SKILL TREE DIVERSIFI-CATION, AND RANK LIMITS.
SO ESSENTIALLY, EVERYTHING ABOUT IT IS MAXED OUT, MAKING IT AN ALL-POWERFUL SKILL THAT RIVALS YOUR SECOND-BEST CHEAT SKILL!
ALMIGHTY CARNAGE CHEF
IT'S ALMOST LIKE HAVING A SECRET SLOT MIXED IN WITH ALL THE REGU-LAR SKILLS, THEN.
THAT'S A WAY OF LOOKING AT IT, I SUPPOSE.
STILL, THAT C-MEMORY ISN'T FOR EVERYONE.
YOU POUR ALL YOUR COMBAT, AD-MINISTRATION, AND DOMESTIC AFFAIRS EXPE-RIENCE INTO JUST ONE ABILITY.
AND SINCE WHAT YOU GET AT THE START IS COMPLETELY RANDOM, YOU HAVE TO MAKE DO SOMEHOW, OR ELSE.
TONOE'S RESOURCE-FULNESS WITH IT IS WORLDS AHEAD OF ANYONE ELSE.
IT'S A TACTIC CALLED SPECIAL-ISM.
SO SHE'S SKILLED AT IT?
SKILLED OUT THE ASS.

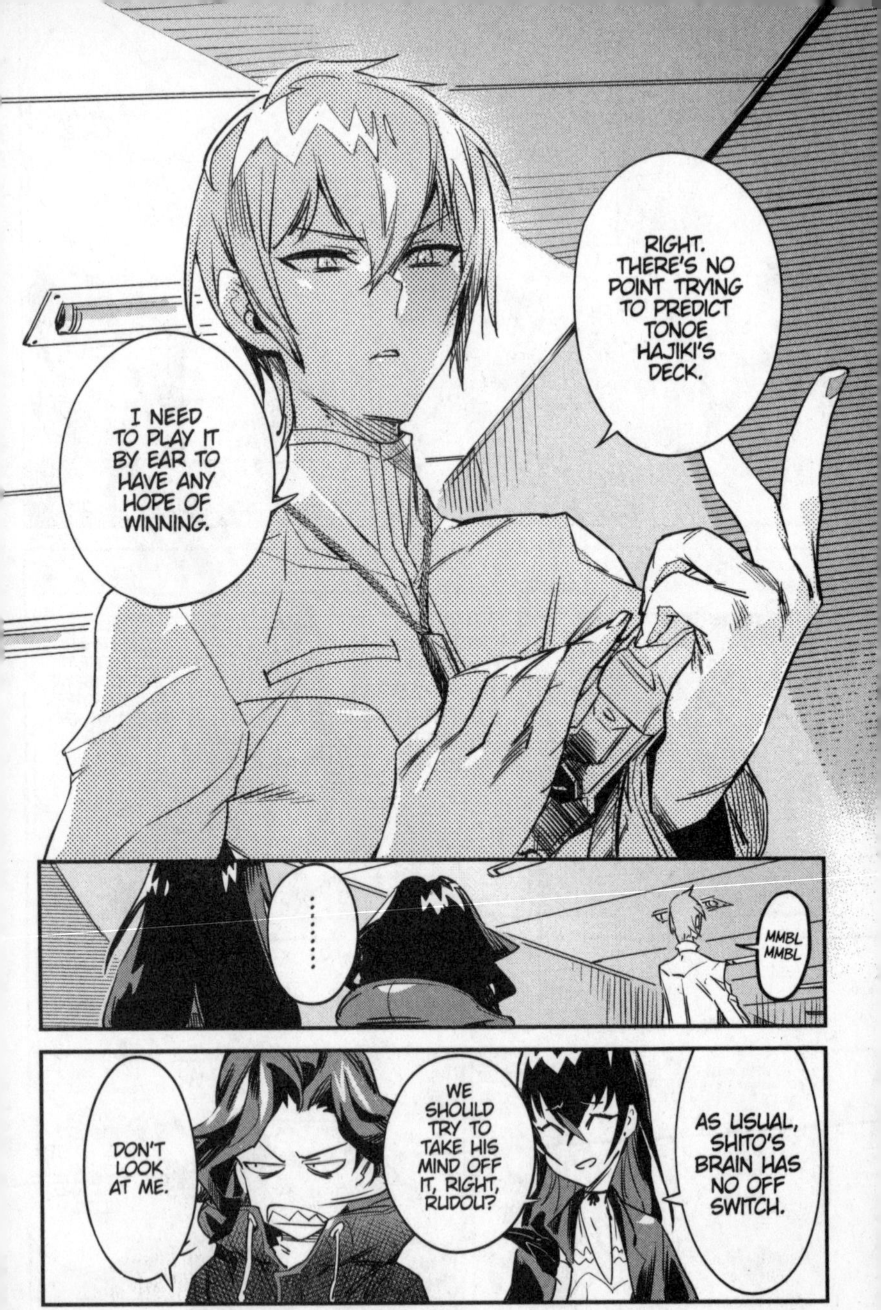
RIGHT. THERE'S NO POINT TRYING TO PREDICT TONOE HAJIKI'S DECK.
I NEED TO PLAY IT BY EAR TO HAVE ANY HOPE OF WINNING.
MMBL MMBL
......
AS USUAL, SHITO'S BRAIN HAS NO OFF SWITCH.
WE SHOULD TRY TO TAKE HIS MIND OFF IT, RIGHT, RUDOU?
DON'T LOOK AT ME.

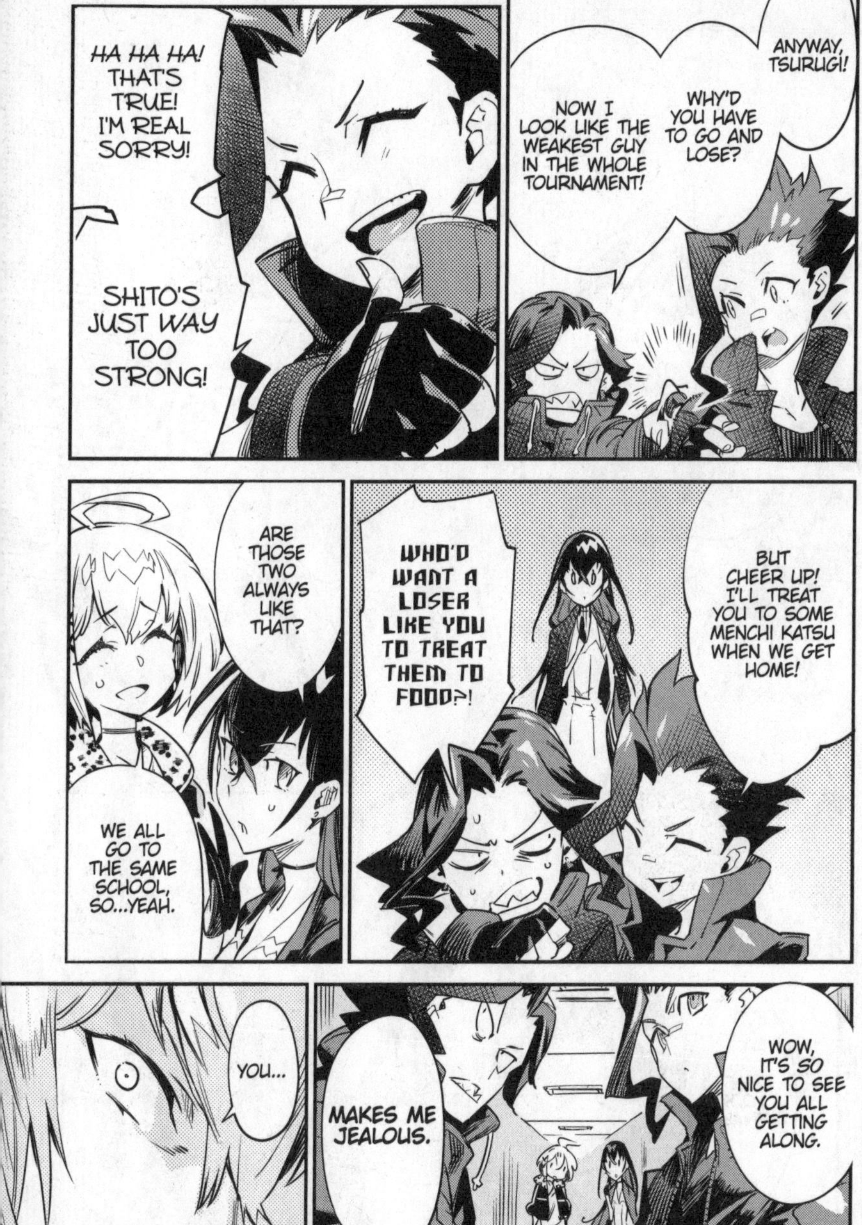
ANYWAY, TSURUGI!
WHY'D YOU HAVE TO GO AND LOSE?
NOW I LOOK LIKE THE WEAKEST GUY IN THE WHOLE TOURNAMENT!
HA HA HA! THAT'S TRUE! I'M REAL SORRY!
SHITO'S JUST WAY TOO STRONG!
BUT CHEER UP! I'LL TREAT YOU TO SOME MENCHI KATSU WHEN WE GET HOME!
WHO'D WANT A LOSER LIKE YOU TO TREAT THEM TO FOOD?!
ARE THOSE TWO ALWAYS LIKE THAT?
WE ALL GO TO THE SAME SCHOOL, SO...YEAH.
WOW, IT'S SO NICE TO SEE YOU ALL GETTING ALONG.
MAKES ME JEALOUS.
YOU...

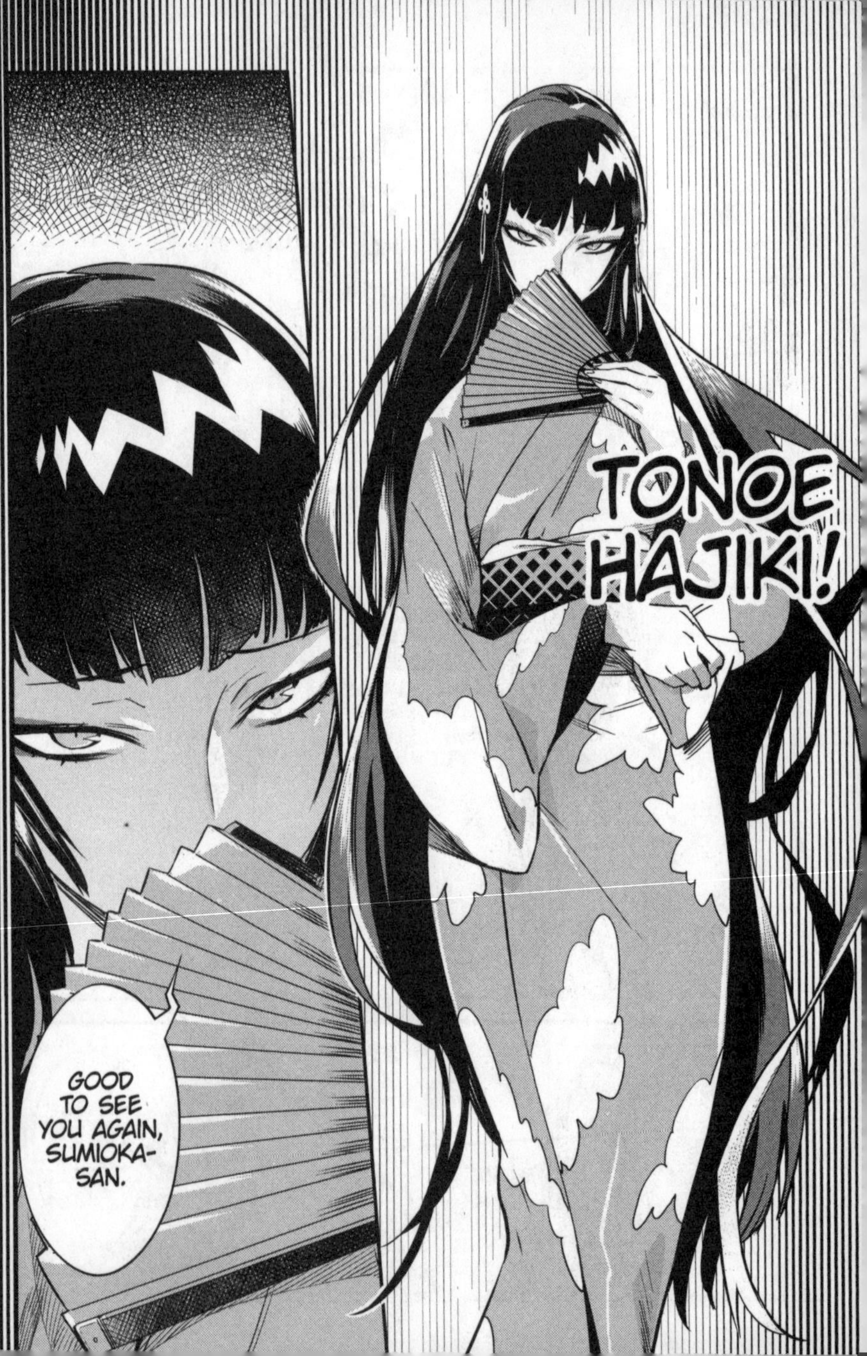
TONOE HAJIKI!
GOOD TO SEE YOU AGAIN, SUMIOKA-SAN.

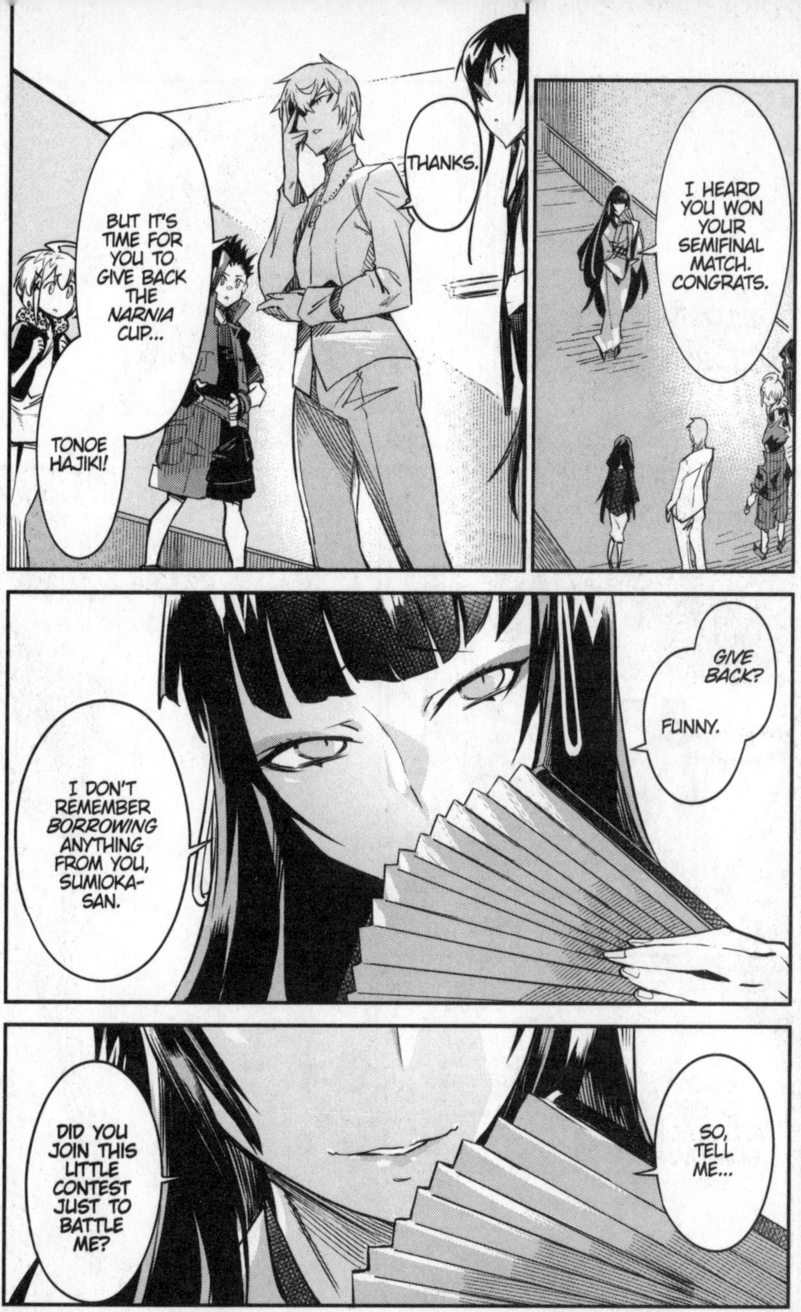
I HEARD YOU WON YOUR SEMIFINAL MATCH. CONGRATS.
THANKS.
BUT IT'S TIME FOR YOU TO GIVE BACK THE *NARNIA CUP*...
TONOE HAJIKI!
GIVE BACK?
FUNNY.
I DON'T REMEMBER *BORROWING* ANYTHING FROM YOU, SUMIOKA-SAN.
SO, TELL ME...
DID YOU JOIN THIS LITTLE CONTEST JUST TO BATTLE ME?

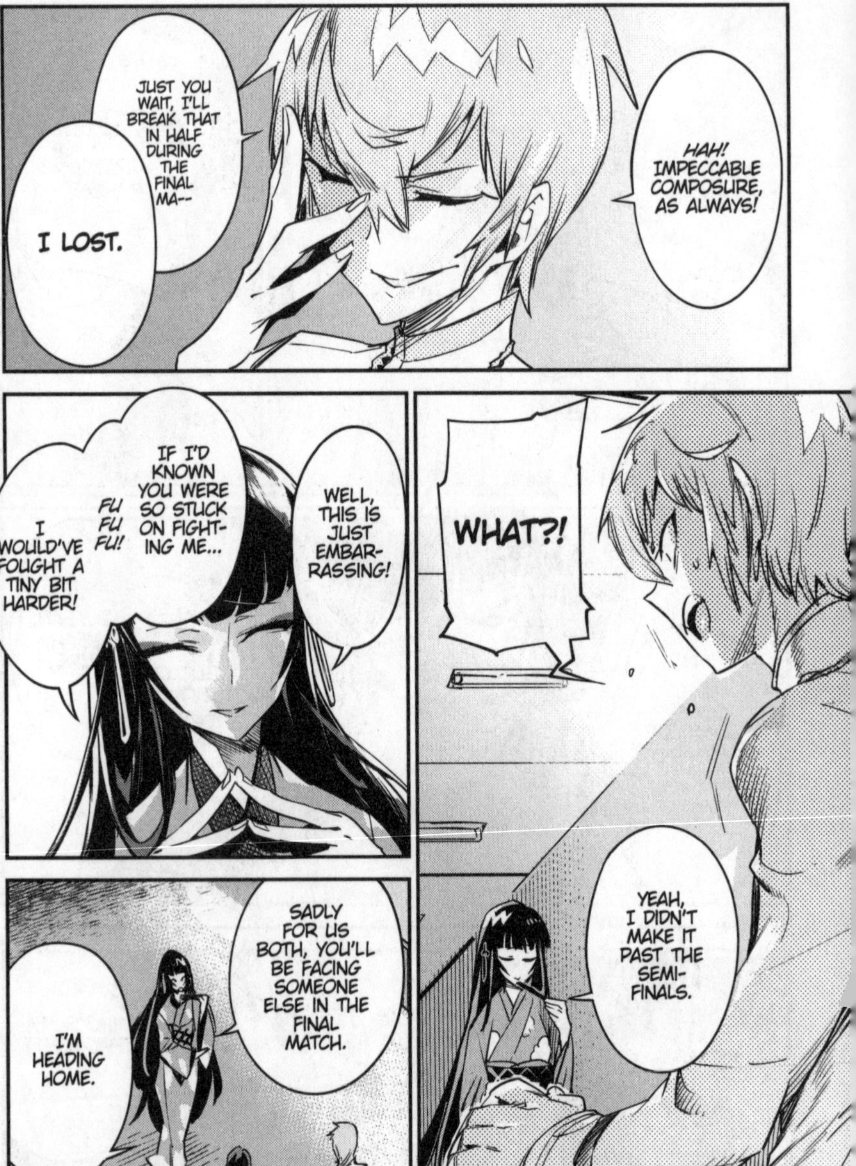
HAH! IMPECCABLE COMPOSURE, AS ALWAYS!
JUST YOU WAIT, I'LL BREAK THAT IN HALF DURING THE FINAL MA--
I LOST.
WHAT?!
YEAH, I DIDN'T MAKE IT PAST THE SEMI-FINALS.
WELL, THIS IS JUST EMBARRASSING!
IF I'D KNOWN YOU WERE SO STUCK ON FIGHTING ME...
FU FU FU!
I WOULD'VE FOUGHT A TINY BIT HARDER!
SADLY FOR US BOTH, YOU'LL BE FACING SOMEONE ELSE IN THE FINAL MATCH.
I'M HEADING HOME.

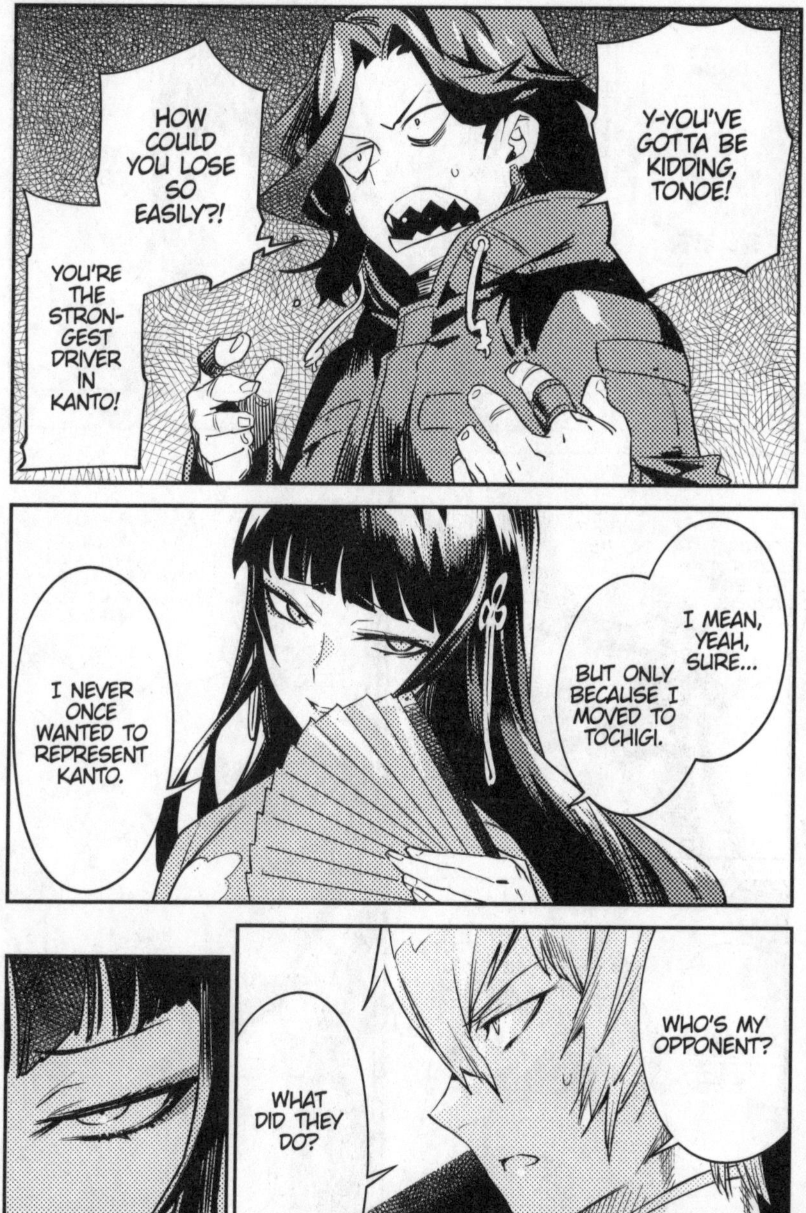
Y-YOU'VE GOTTA BE KIDDING, TONOE!
HOW COULD YOU LOSE SO EASILY?!
YOU'RE THE STRONG-GEST DRIVER IN KANTO!
I MEAN, YEAH, SURE...
BUT ONLY BECAUSE I MOVED TO TOCHIGI.
I NEVER ONCE WANTED TO REPRESENT KANTO.
WHO'S MY OPPONENT?
WHAT DID THEY DO?

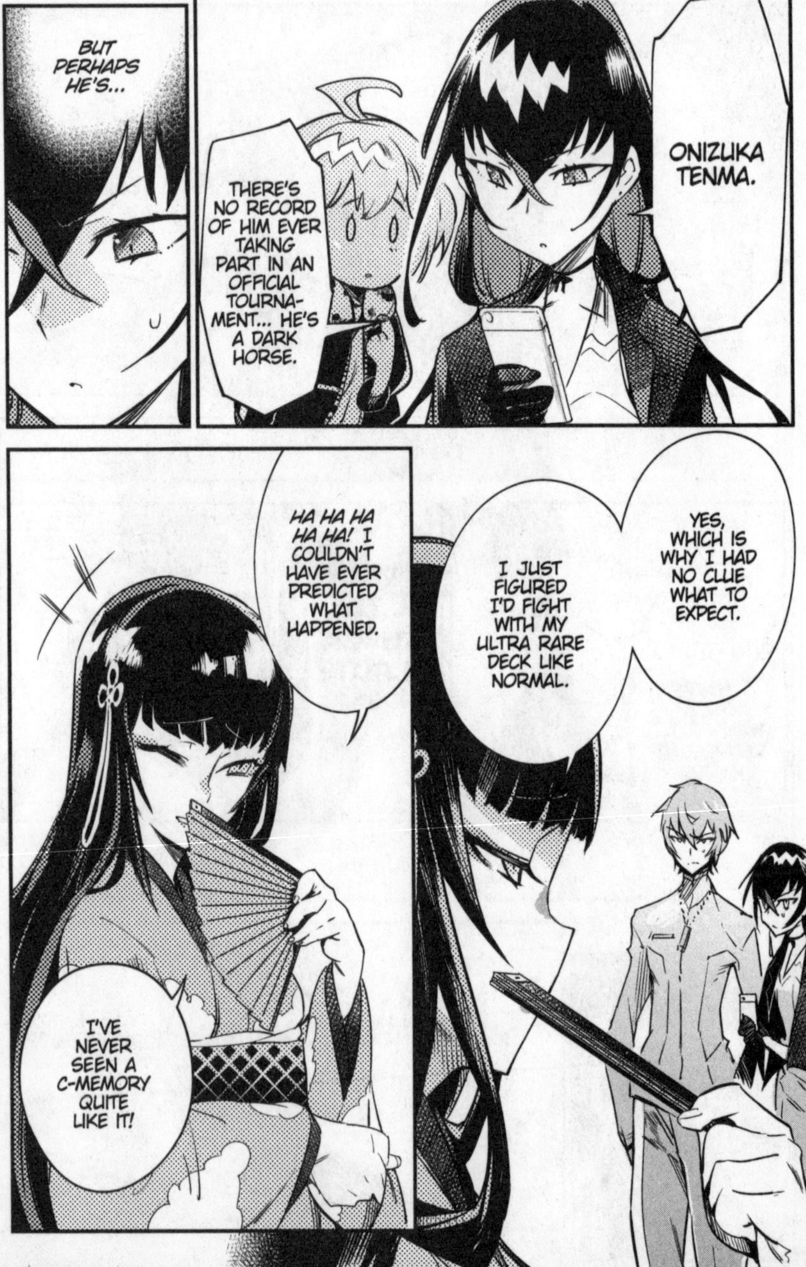
ONIZUKA TENMA.
THERE'S NO RECORD OF HIM EVER TAKING PART IN AN OFFICIAL TOURNAMENT... HE'S A DARK HORSE.
BUT PERHAPS HE'S...
YES, WHICH IS WHY I HAD NO CLUE WHAT TO EXPECT.
I JUST FIGURED I'D FIGHT WITH MY ULTRA RARE DECK LIKE NORMAL.
HA HA HA HA HA! I COULDN'T HAVE EVER PREDICTED WHAT HAPPENED.
I'VE NEVER SEEN A C-MEMORY QUITE LIKE IT!

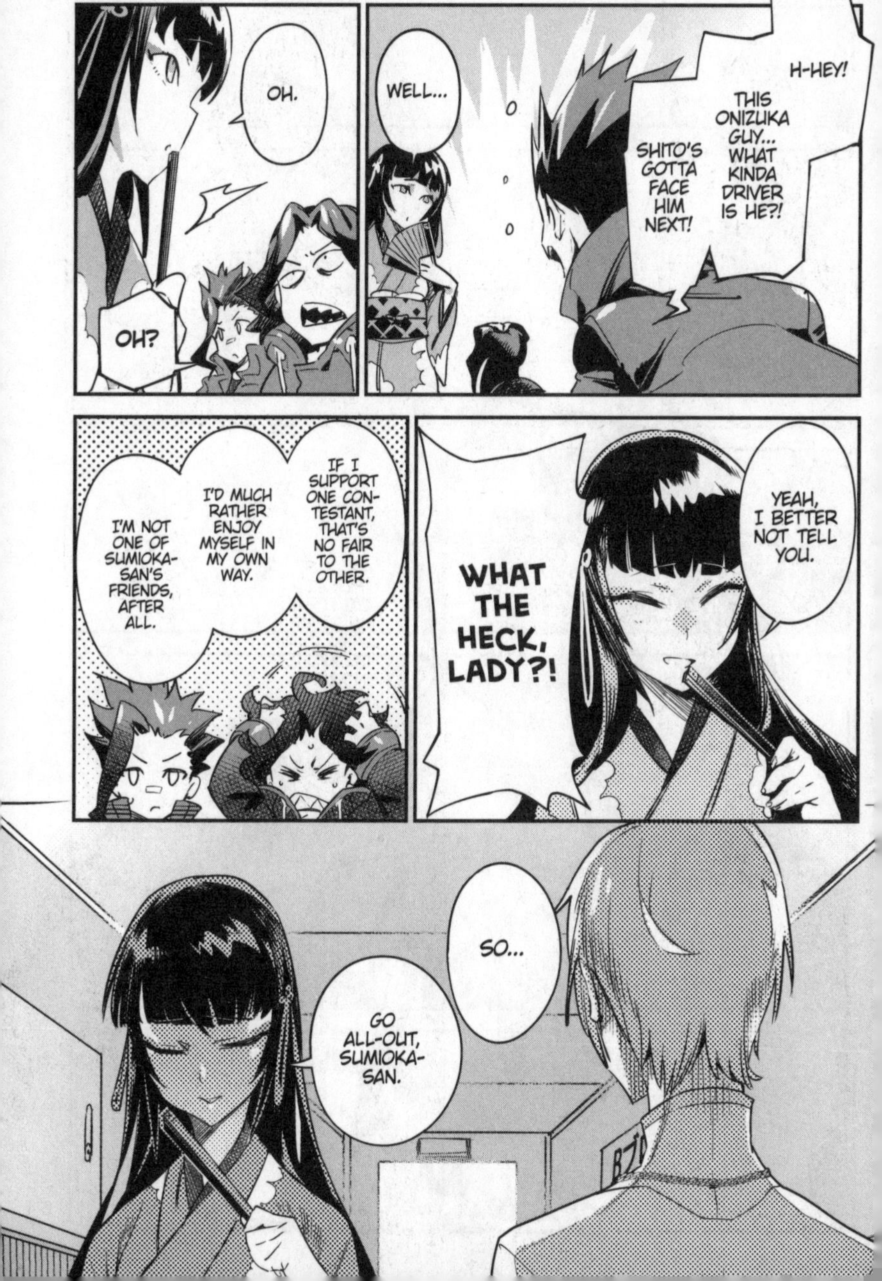
H-HEY!
THIS ONIZUKA GUY... WHAT KINDA DRIVER IS HE?!
SHITO'S GOTTA FACE HIM NEXT!
WELL...
OH.
OH?
YEAH, I BETTER NOT TELL YOU.
WHAT THE HECK, LADY?!
IF I SUPPORT ONE CONTESTANT, THAT'S NO FAIR TO THE OTHER.
I'D MUCH RATHER ENJOY MYSELF IN MY OWN WAY.
I'M NOT ONE OF SUMIOKA-SAN'S FRIENDS, AFTER ALL.
SO...
GO ALL-OUT, SUMIOKA-SAN.

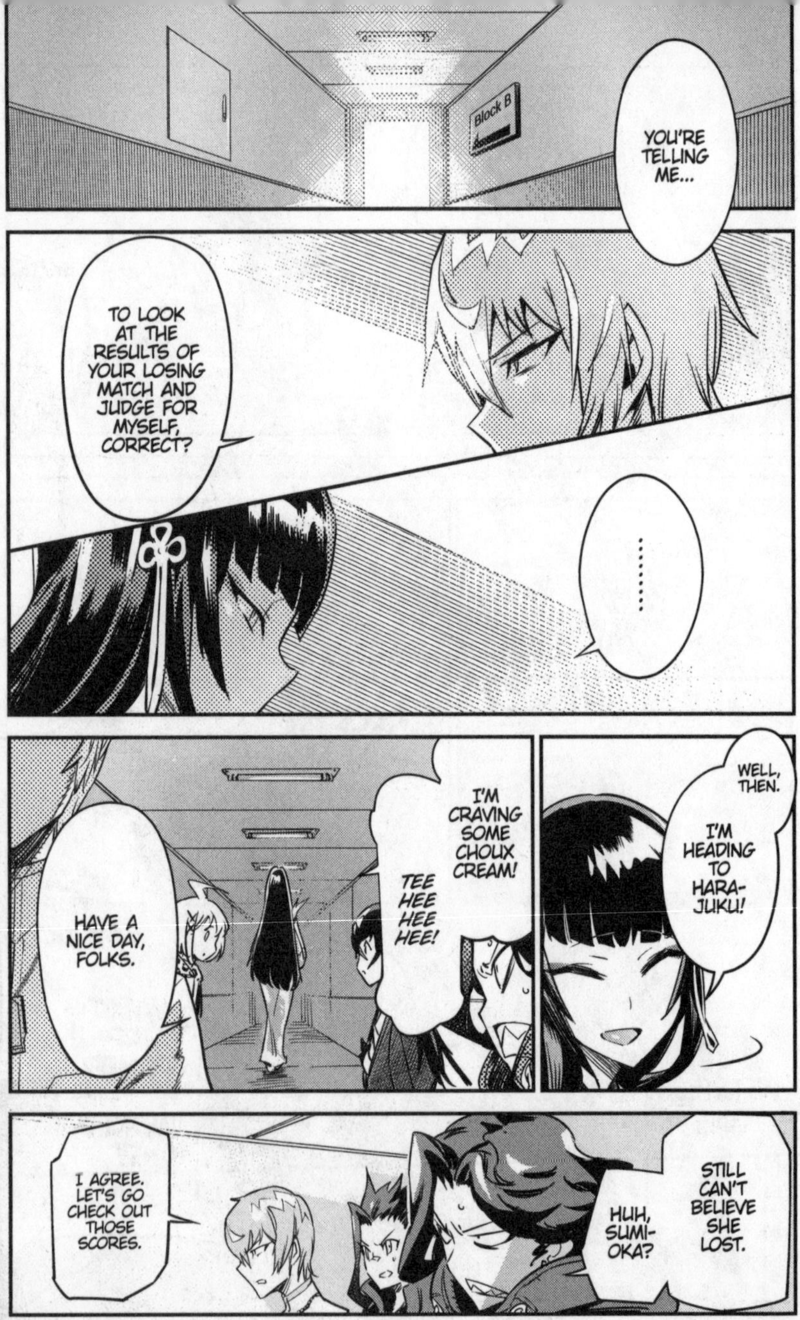
Block B
YOU'RE TELLING ME...
TO LOOK AT THE RESULTS OF YOUR LOSING MATCH AND JUDGE FOR MYSELF, CORRECT?
......
WELL, THEN.
I'M HEADING TO HARA-JUKU!
I'M CRAVING SOME CHOUX CREAM!
TEE HEE HEE HEE!
HAVE A NICE DAY, FOLKS.
STILL CAN'T BELIEVE SHE LOST.
HUH, SUMI-OKA?
I AGREE. LET'S GO CHECK OUT THOSE SCORES.

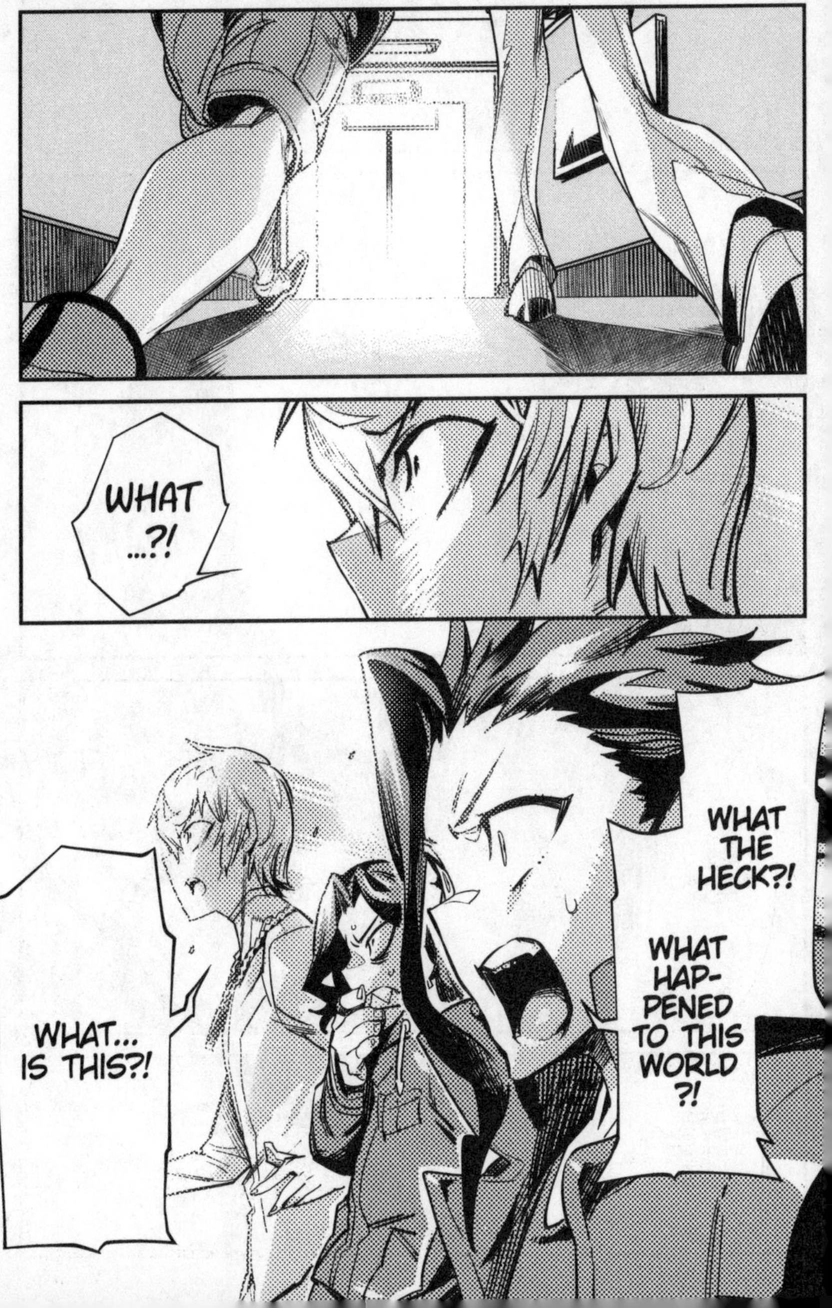
WHAT ...?!
WHAT THE HECK?!
WHAT HAP-PENED TO THIS WORLD ?!
WHAT... IS THIS?!

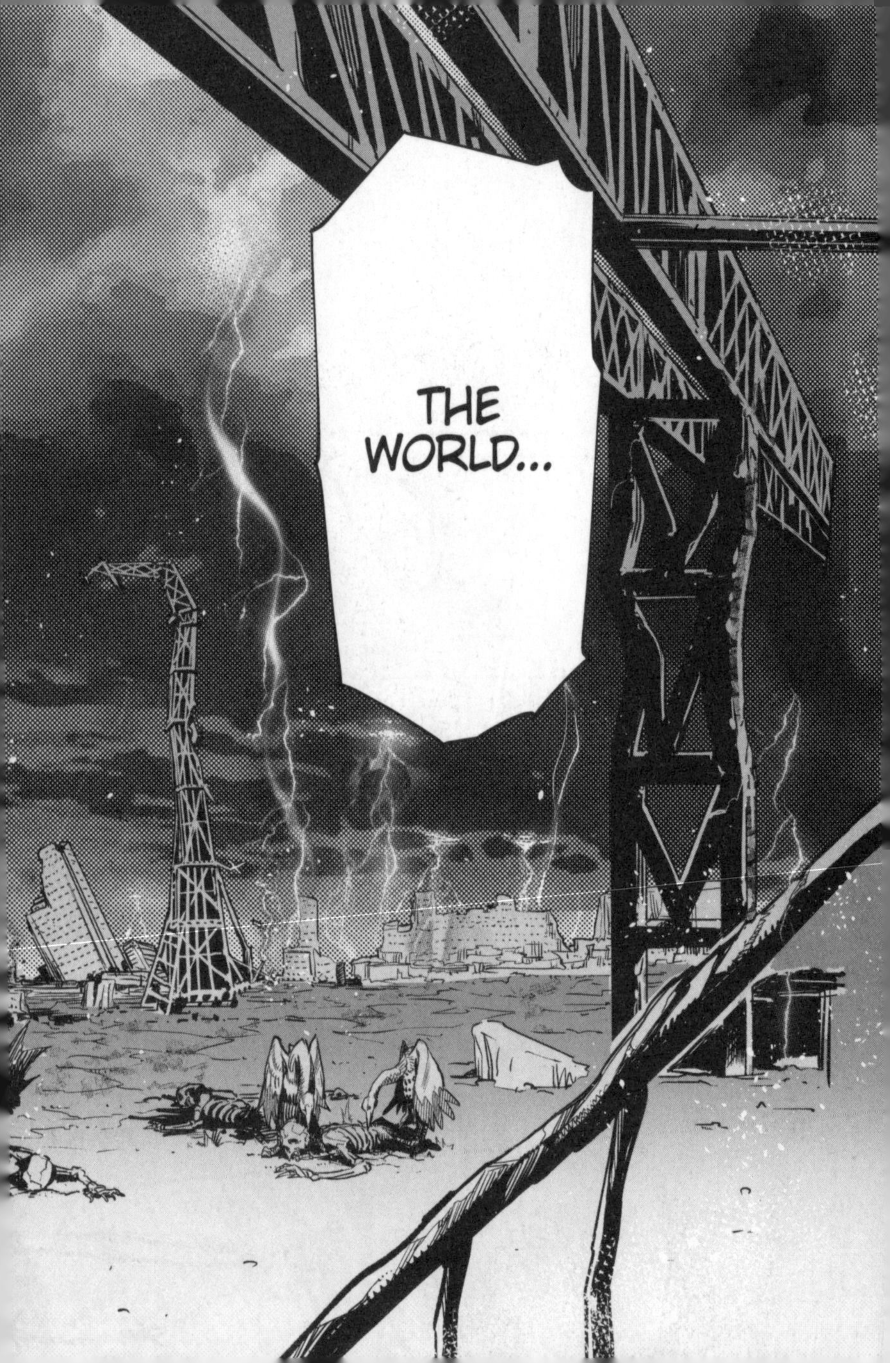
THE WORLD...

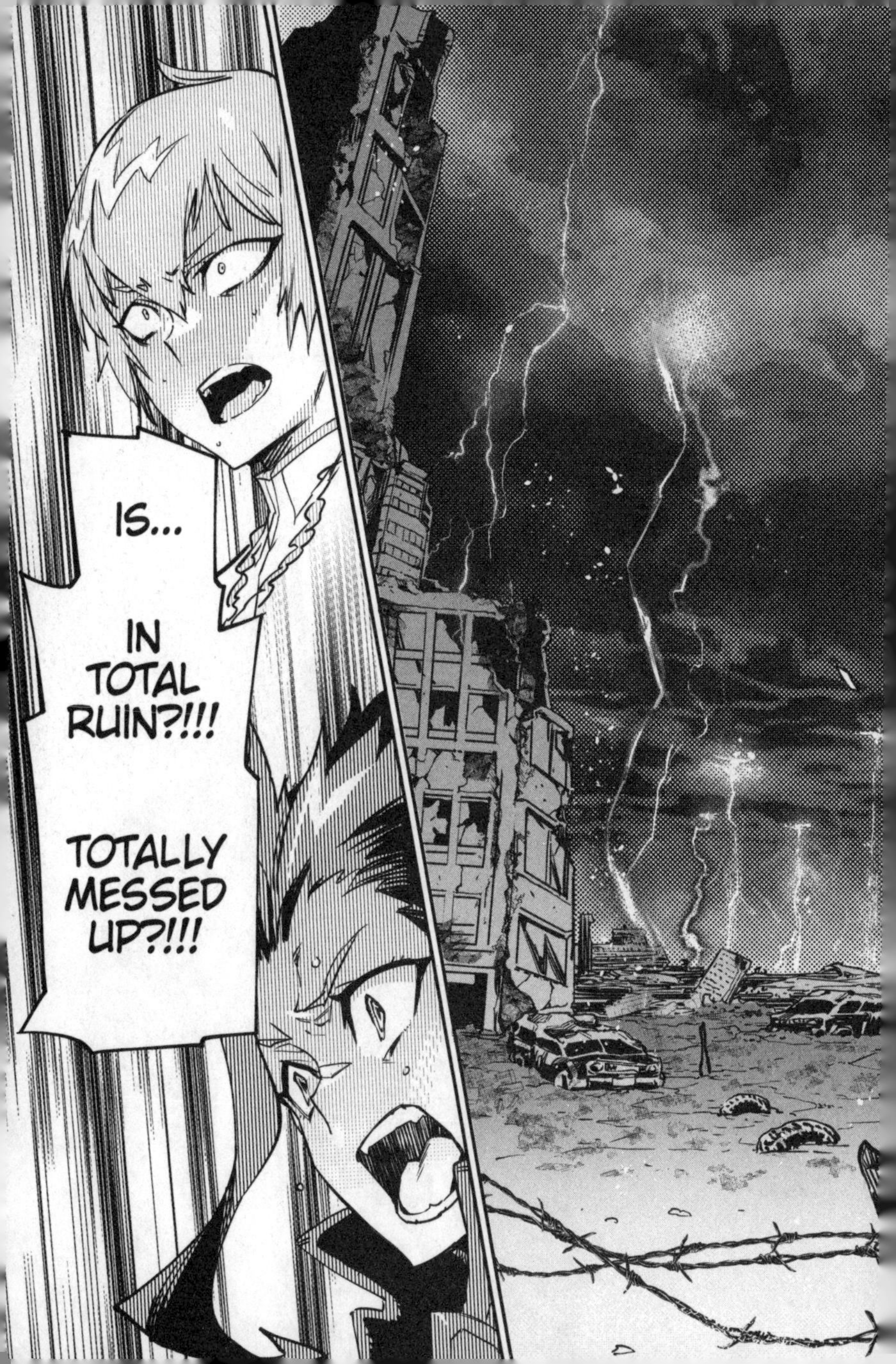
IS... IN TOTAL RUIN?!!! TOTALLY MESSED UP?!!!

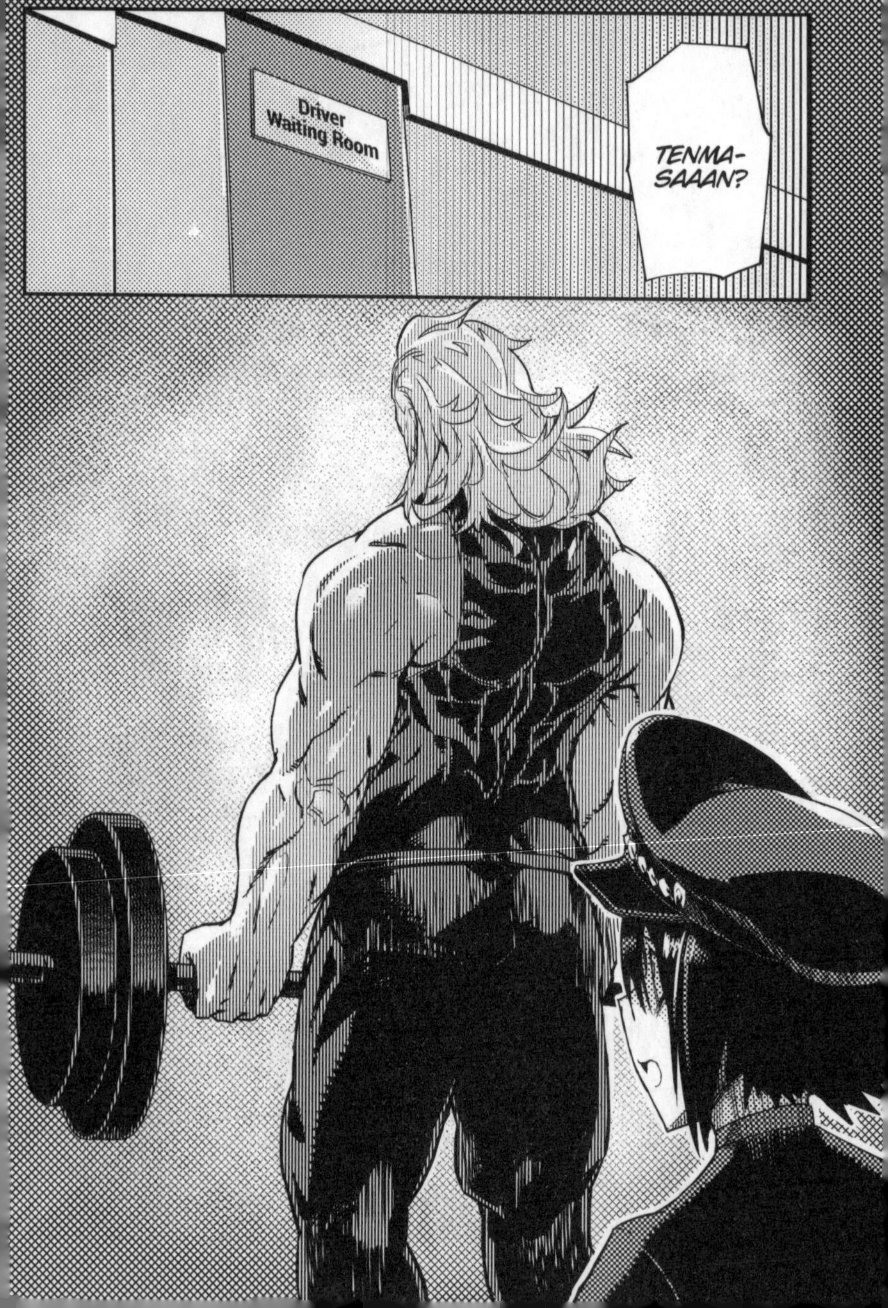
TENMA-SAAAN?
Driver Waiting Room

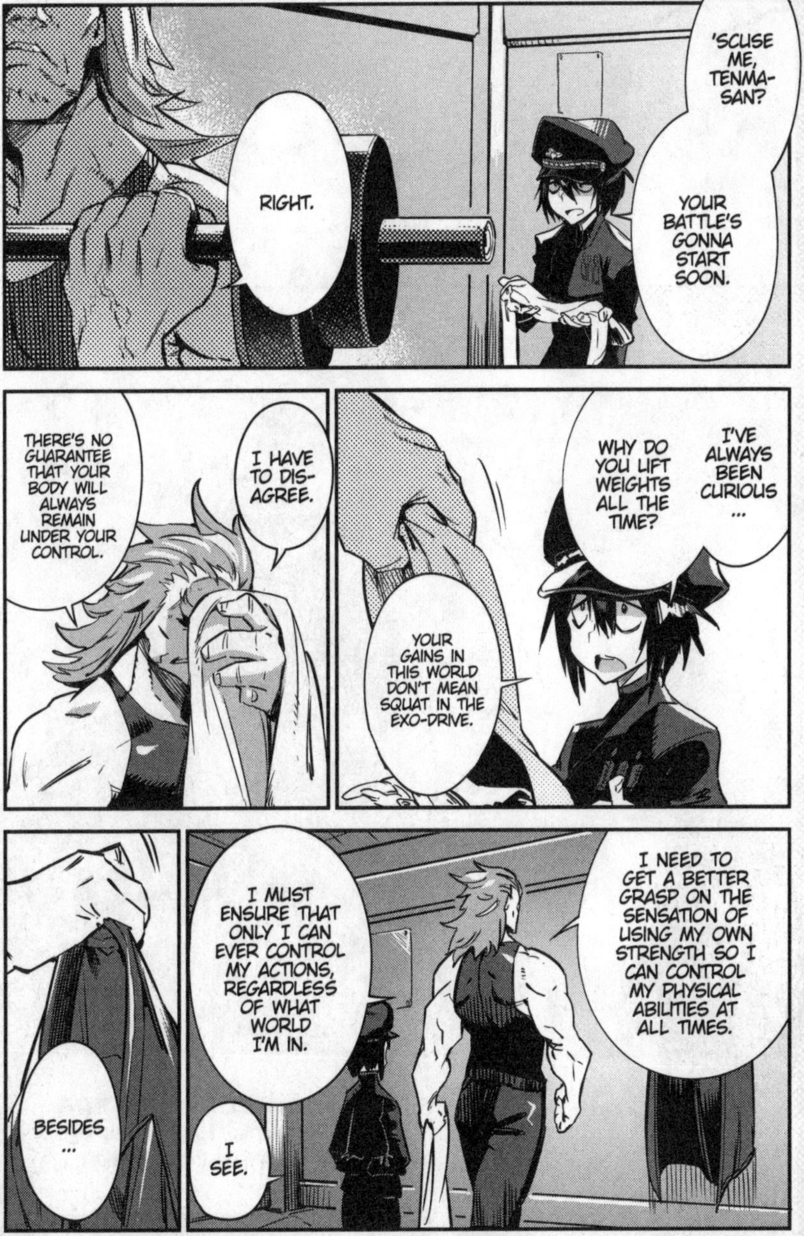
'SCUSE ME, TENMA-SAN?
YOUR BATTLE'S GONNA START SOON.
RIGHT.
I'VE ALWAYS BEEN CURIOUS ...
WHY DO YOU LIFT WEIGHTS ALL THE TIME?
YOUR GAINS IN THIS WORLD DON'T MEAN SQUAT IN THE EXO-DRIVE.
I HAVE TO DIS-AGREE.
THERE'S NO GUARANTEE THAT YOUR BODY WILL ALWAYS REMAIN UNDER YOUR CONTROL.
I NEED TO GET A BETTER GRASP ON THE SENSATION OF USING MY OWN STRENGTH SO I CAN CONTROL MY PHYSICAL ABILITIES AT ALL TIMES.
I MUST ENSURE THAT ONLY I CAN EVER CONTROL MY ACTIONS, REGARDLESS OF WHAT WORLD I'M IN.
I SEE.
BESIDES ...

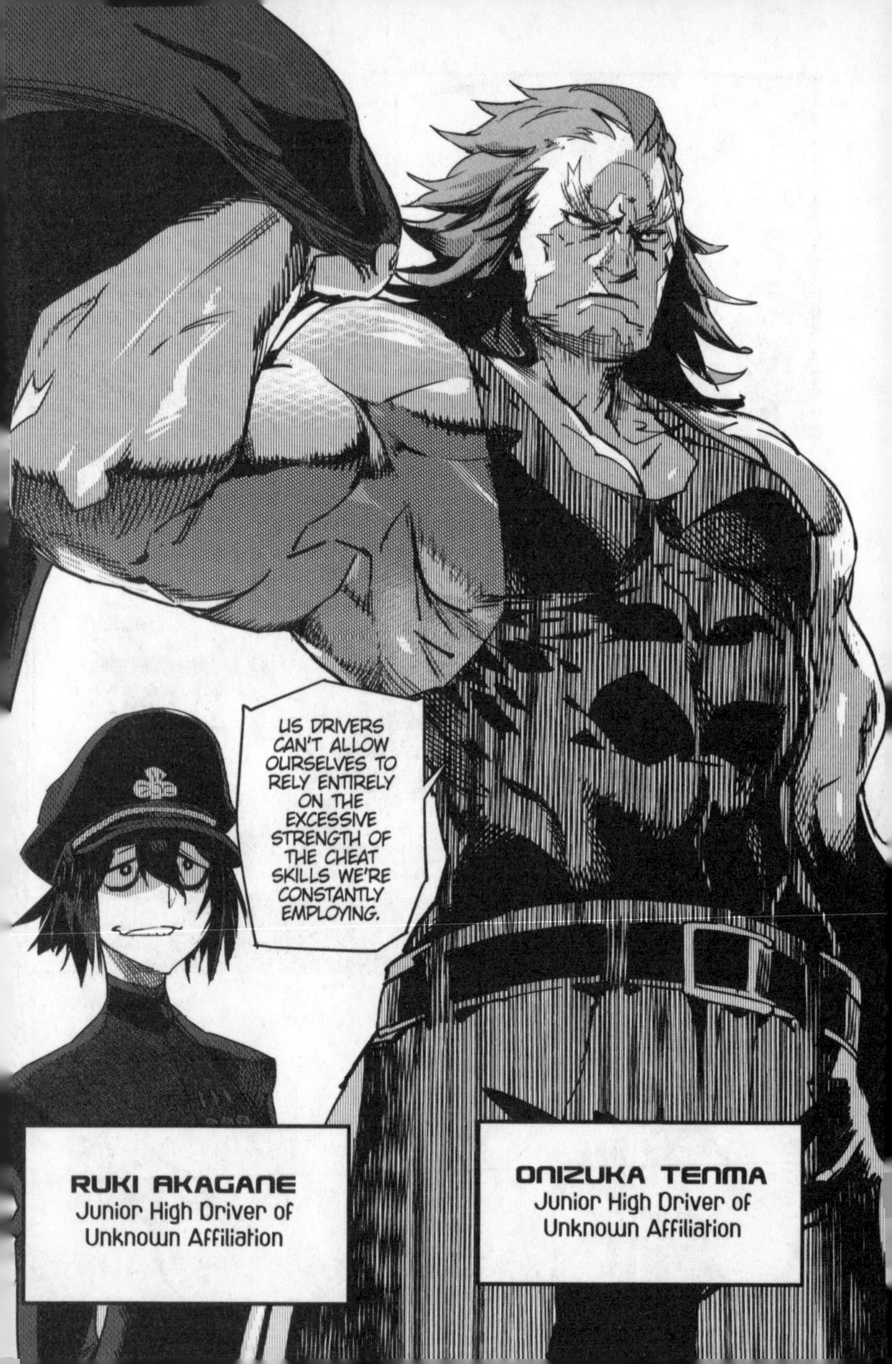
US DRIVERS CAN'T ALLOW OURSELVES TO RELY ENTIRELY ON THE EXCESSIVE STRENGTH OF THE CHEAT SKILLS WE'RE CONSTANTLY EMPLOYING.
ONIZUKA TENMA
Junior High Driver of Unknown Affiliation
RUKI AKAGANE
Junior High Driver of Unknown Affiliation

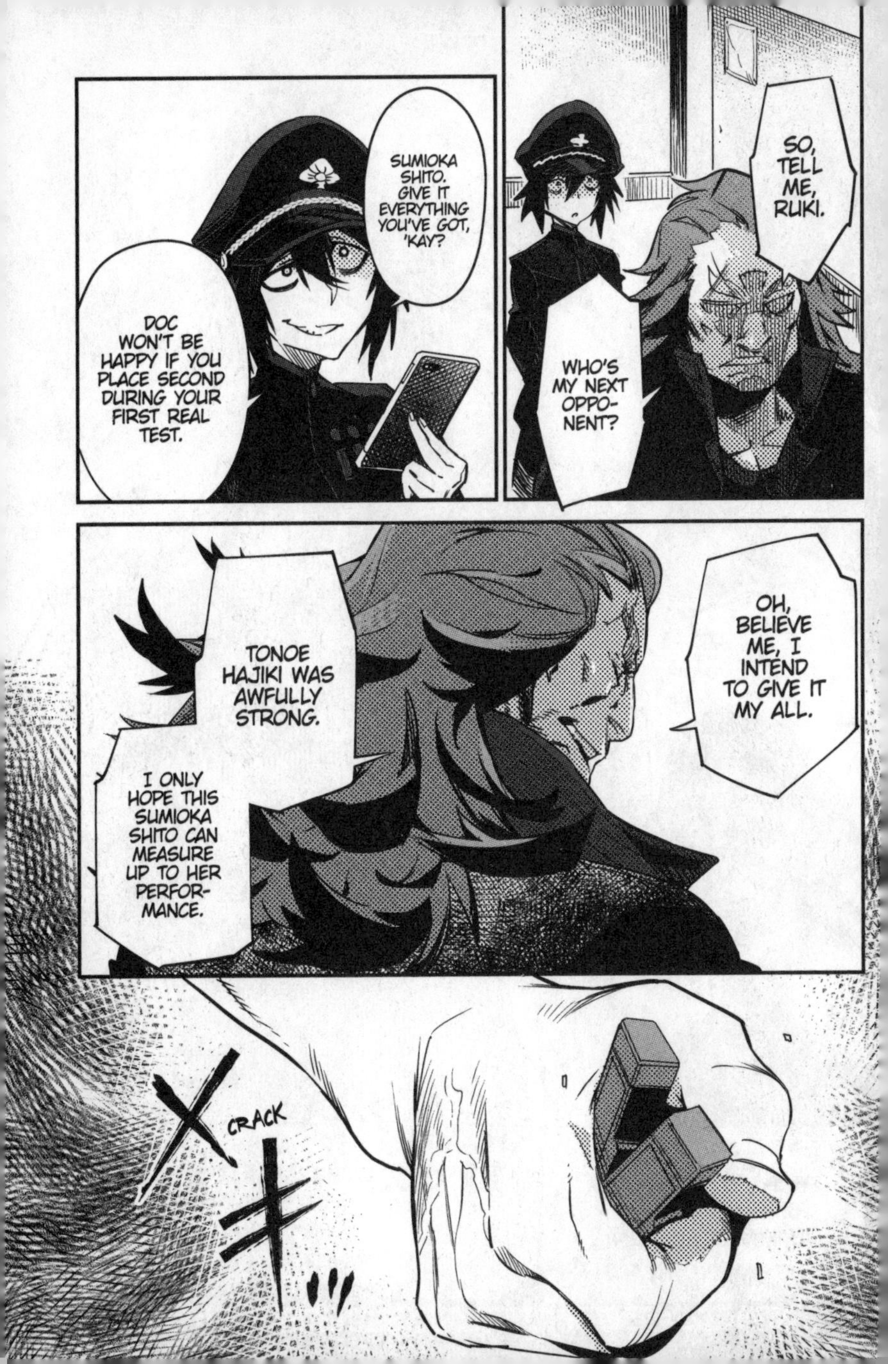
SO, TELL ME, RUKI.
WHO'S MY NEXT OPPO-NENT?
SUMIOKA SHITO. GIVE IT EVERYTHING YOU'VE GOT, 'KAY?
DOC WON'T BE HAPPY IF YOU PLACE SECOND DURING YOUR FIRST REAL TEST.
OH, BELIEVE ME, I INTEND TO GIVE IT MY ALL.
TONOE HAJIKI WAS AWFULLY STRONG.
I ONLY HOPE THIS SUMIOKA SHITO CAN MEASURE UP TO HER PERFOR-MANCE.
CRACK

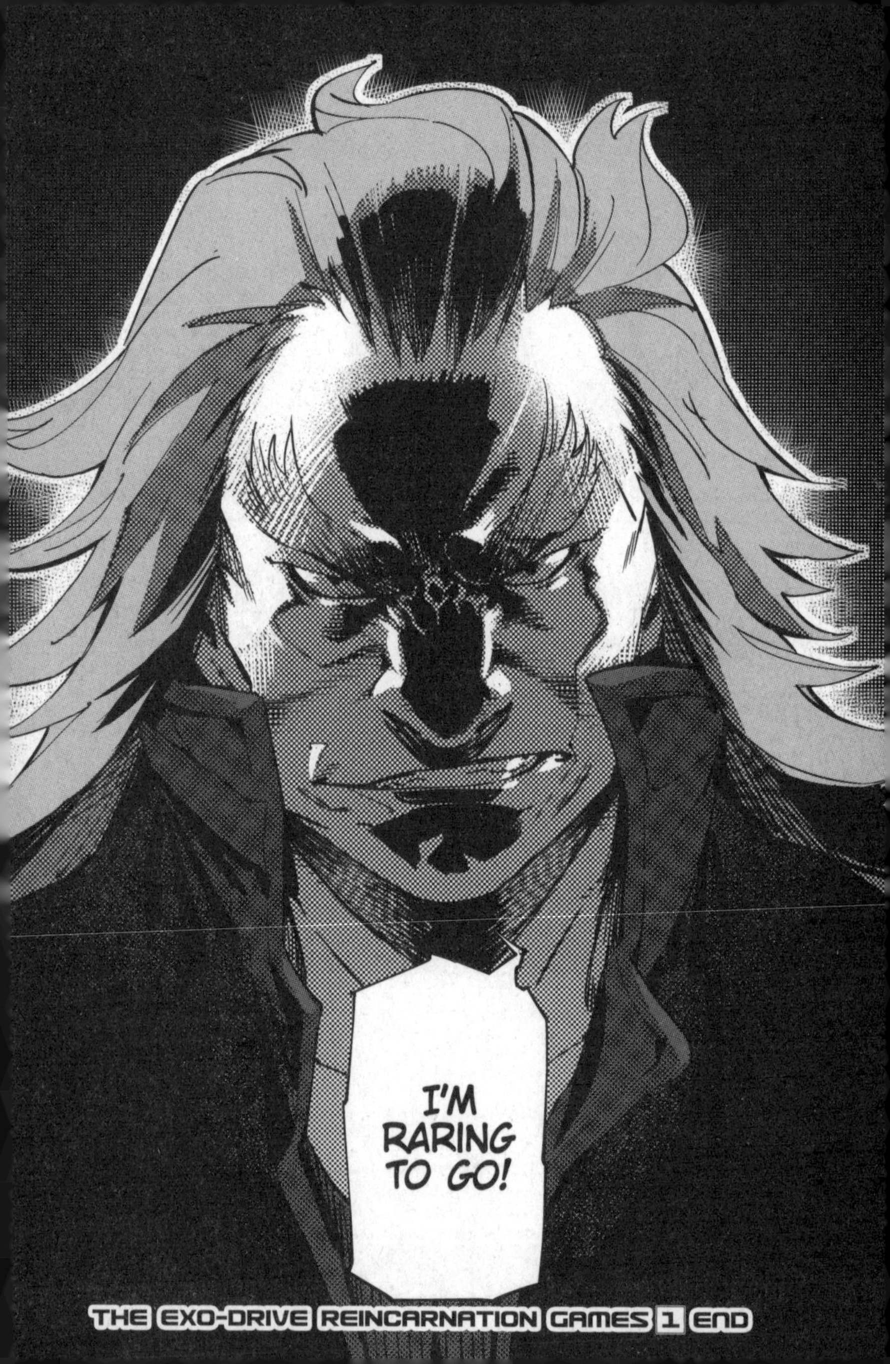
I'M RARING TO GO!
THE EXO-DRIVE REINCARNATION GAMES 1 END

INFORMATION BANK C-MEMORY ②

[HAREM MASTER]

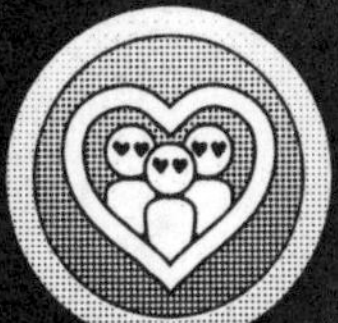

Allows the user to recruit an infinite number of other-world party members, called *retainers*, and prevents their loss. It is possible to keep a large number of retainers, depending on the user's negotiation or popularity skills in general, but this C-memory will automatically maintain their number regardless of whether the user possesses solid charisma or not. It cancels out any effects of estrangement, dissonance between retainers, or even ill effects caused by unfavorable events such as bereavement for as long as the user wishes. It can even safely maintain harems that include dangerous beings, such as draconic or demonic retainers. However, since this C-memory focuses on maintaining relationships, retainers' combat abilities will not increase. In a way, it can be said to be more suited for use with retainers who have a direct combat skill focus, rather than those with a domestic skill focus.

[SURPRISE]

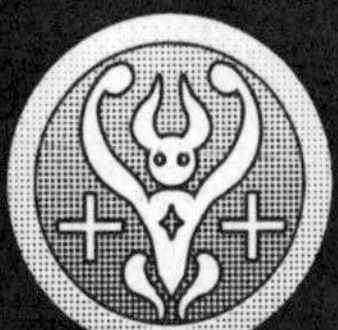

Changes the user's backstory. Skill ranks remain the same, but learned skills are reclassified as skills arbitrarily similar to the starting set. Many other ordinary C-memories can produce similar effects, but this C-memory is a cheat that can only be used once per reincarnation. Since, by nature, it's a big surprise attack, you can't bank on a big effect in cases where the changed skill's underlying level is low, so most Drivers only place it in their Secret Slot as an endgame finisher. As with Almighty, it is possible to acquire skills outside of your skill tree and acquired class, and you can immediately learn vastly superior skills that are outside the realms of your avatar's race. This C-memory is fittingly known as a finishing move, so it's worth assigning to a slot for Swift Hitter tactics.

[PARASITE]

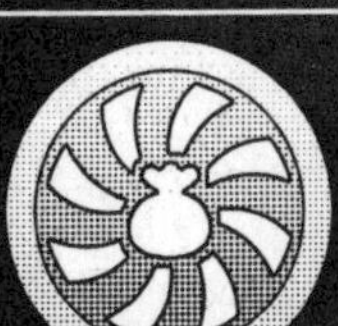

Automatically collects a proportional amount of experience points possessed by the people around the Driver. The ratio is minimal and experience points are only added to compliant skills in your own skill tree. The closer physically or emotionally, the higher the percentage taken, so actions such as forming relationships within a community of others whose skill trees are similar to one's own will increase how efficiently experience points are earned. The ability to multi-stack cheat skills such as Hyper-Growth, while unnecessary for pure upgrade efficiency, is a big strength of this C-memory, since it allows players to level skills automatically without sparing any personal resources to do so. Parasite is also compatible with Drive styles that focus on utilizing strong retainers to save the world.

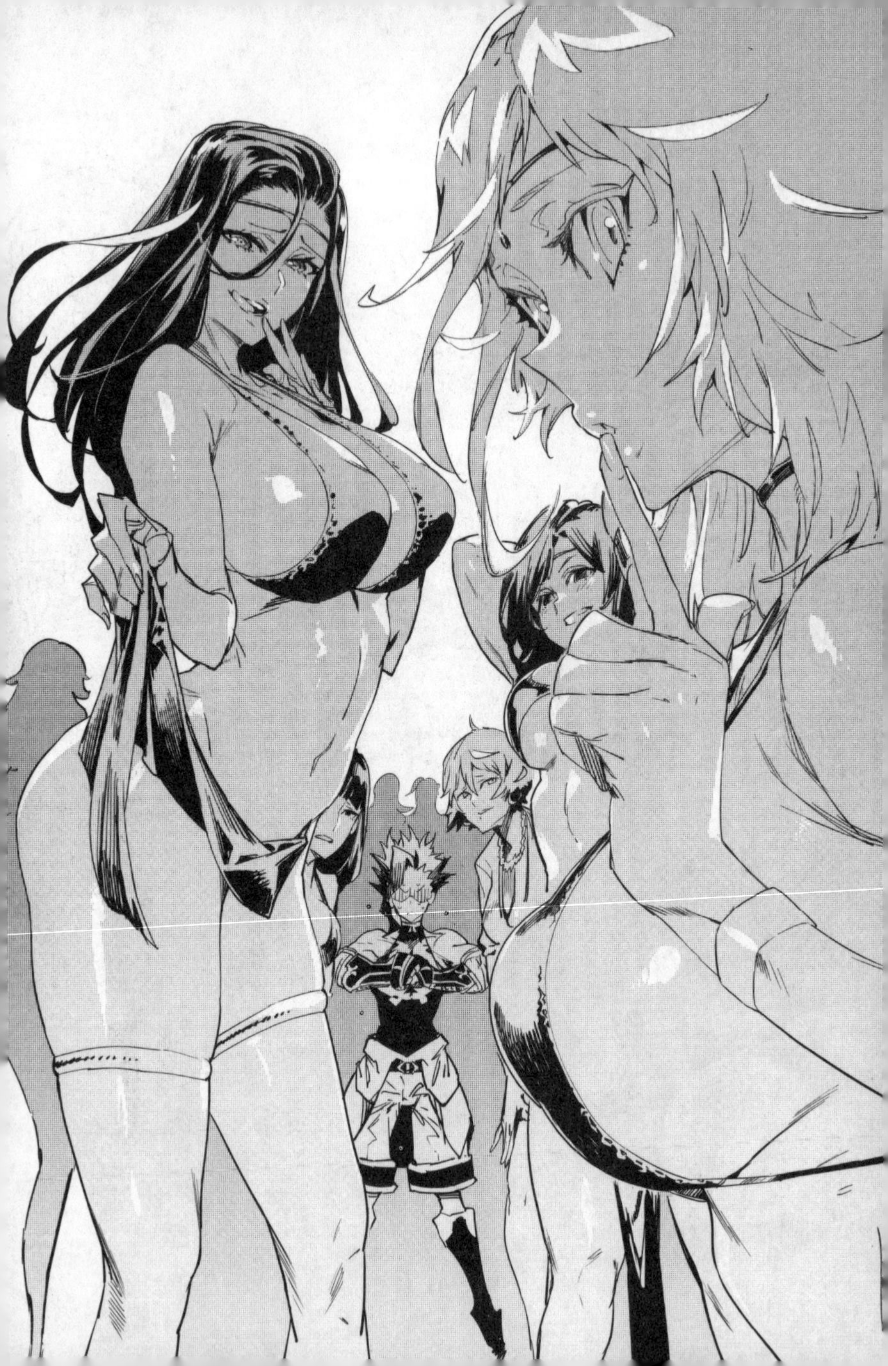